# Perennial Gardening Guide

## Fourth Edition

John M. Valleau

**Heritage Perennials**

## Acknowledgements

Photographs for this book come from a variety of sources. Most of these have been taken by Valleybrook photographers over the years including: John Schroeder, John Valleau, Greg Baxter, Mike Por, Geoff Lewis, Maureen Newman and Cameron Senum. All these images are © Valleybrook International Ventures Inc. Additional photographs were provided by Chicagoland Grows, Centerton Nursery, Dan Heims, Horticultural Printers, Steven Still, Rod Richards and Visions BV., Walter's Gardens, Yoder Brothers. All these images © their respective owners and are used with permission.

Photos on pp. 10, 12 © Theresa D'Monte 2000, 1999
Photo on p. 140 © Stuart McCall 1999
Photos on p. 139 (ML, MR) © Gera Dillon 2002

Garden photographs were taken in many places, including the superlative gardens at Heronswood Nursery in Washington State, Van Dusen Botanical Gardens in Vancouver, the Montreal Botanic Garden and many others in Canada, the USA and the UK. Gera Dillon's photographs were taken at the Toronto Music Garden.

Gardens in the UK include the Dorothy Clive Gardens, the Beth Chatto Gardens and Adrian and Alan Bloom's gardens at Bressingham, where credit for so many of the good things to have happened in the world of perennials is due.

Cover designed by Susan Minton Green, shot by Terry Guscott of Vancouver. Contents proofed and re-proofed by patient Valleybrook staffers including Les Szabo, Greg Baxter, Mike Por and others; even Doug, our accountant. Layout, production and final design by Edward Kehler.

The publishers acknowledge the appearance of Mocha the cat, enjoying his usual sleeping quarters in the *Stipa* planter.

Published in Canada by
Valleybrook International Ventures Inc.
Abbotsford, British Columbia
Fourth Edition, March 2003

National Library of Canada Cataloguing in Publication

Valleau, John M., 1962–
    Perennial gardening guide / John M. Valleau;
[edited by John D. Schroeder] – 4th ed.

    Includes index.
    ISBN 0-9699483-2-8

    1. Perennials  2. Perennials—Pictorial works.
I. Schroeder, John D. (John David), 1956–  II. Title.

SB434.V34 2003          635.9'32          C2003-910304-8

## Table of Contents

# Foreword

Paradise. That's what we want. Whether we have a grand country estate or a single container on a patio, when we garden we're hoping to bring a little touch of paradise into our lives. It all starts innocently enough, perhaps with spring bulbs, pansies and maybe some primroses.

Passion. That's what it is. Once we really get started on this plant thing, a funny thing happens. For some people a little may be enough, but for others, plants and gardening become a passion. You know you're developing plant passion when you start hanging out at garden centres waiting for the nursery delivery truck to arrive, hoping to find something new. You know that you are hopelessly ensnared once you start hiding from your spouse how much you paid for that new perennial you just had to have.

Pleasure. That's why we garden. And that's why perennials have become so incredibly popular everywhere. In late winter when buds begin to emerge throughout the garden, we feel the pleasure of seeing friends we haven't seen for a year or so. A flush of spring blooming alpines propels the garden to a riot of colour in May and June and finally the languorous days of summer invite us to enjoy the fruits of our work in our little slice of paradise.

So many choices exist that it's hard to know where to start. Actually, it's probably harder to know where to stop which is a good thing for perennial growers like ourselves! Sometimes we want a dramatic focal point, other times all we need is a little something to fill a corner for a while. We may be looking for a reliable classic that will last for years without fail, or wanting to try something new. Of course, once we've gardened for a while, we learn that not everything new is necessarily better.

Our purpose in publishing this book is to help gardeners in North America choose, identify, care for and learn more about perennials. Let us guide you as you explore this wonderful group of plants It's our opportunity to share our passion.

John Schroeder
Heritage Perennials

I'd like to dedicate this edition to:


My parents, Ethel and Jim Valleau, and my sister, Marilyn Bertsch,
who taught me about gardening from an early age.
They have given me a lifelong passion for plants, gardens and nature.

The late Warren Hartman,
who showed me that the concepts of design
could translate easily from one art form to another.

Alan,
who is just beginning to learn about gardening,
and teaching me to see it in a brand new way.

John and Kelly Schroeder,
who have provided the opportunity for my knowledge of perennials to continually grow,
and given me a marvellous forum to share it with others.


J.V.

## Introduction

It astonishes me how much the world has changed since the last edition of this book was published in 1998. At that time I was in the grips of a personal crisis, having lost my partner in the middle of completing revisions. I learned all about grieving firsthand, and, in the process, my garden – formerly "our" garden – was abandoned for a time. That time stretched on to a couple of years, and in retrospect it was a fascinating experience.

Mother Nature quickly grabs hold of an abandoned plot and begins to make it over in her own unique way. The weeds appeared, of course. A few coddled perennials did not survive the experience. But, by and large, things generally thrived. It's become rather interesting to rediscover plants that I had forgotten were there, given a second chance to prosper once the clumps of self-seeded native Goldenrod get cleared away. The realization that gardens are extremely transient creations has not been lost on me. I regret now that in the past I seldom made the effort to properly document special seasonal moments with photographs or jottings down in a garden journal. Ah well – live and learn.

Now the garden is being recreated: new partner, new ideas, shared frustrations and shared joys. One of my most astonishing and recent pleasures is to learn about gardening all over again, while trying to see it through the eyes of someone experiencing the mysteries for the very first time. How foreign and bizarre it must seem! You plant these strange shriveled-looking roots in the autumn and they actually *bloom* the following spring. These tiny specks of dust germinate and become 7-foot tall flowering tobacco plants. Then, they produce enough seed from one plant alone to fill every garden in our entire county. How marvellous Mother Nature truly is.

Whatever level of gardener you may be, truly one of the greatest pleasures comes not from nurturing your creation, but from sharing it with others. Gardeners are by and large a generous lot, and among my most favourite people in the world. They throw open the gates and invite you inside to explore. When you crow your delight over some prime and spectacular specimen, so often they send you away with a piece of your very own, or at least the promise of a "slip" when the time is right. The pleasure is as much theirs for the giving as yours for the receiving.

I've learned so much more about gardening over the past five years, yet it still feels like there is far more to learn than could ever possibly be packed into one lifetime. With such an enormous group of plants as perennials, it seems like new varieties appear more quickly than one person could ever possibly keep up with. I can only hope that this new edition of the *Perennial Gardening Guide* makes your learning experience a little bit easier, and a whole lot more interesting.

Even as this edition goes to print, a flurry of new plants is hitting the market while new gardening and design techniques are being created. Please keep in mind that our Heritage Perennials website (www.perennials.com) is a great place to check for the newest and latest ideas on perennial gardening. Through this book, the website and especially from answering your many e-mail questions, I hope to be able to offer my help as you continue on your personal perennial gardening journey.

John Valleau, February 2003

# About Botanical Names

To the beginning gardener, botanical names seem unwieldy and awkward, the common names so much simpler to learn and remember. It's a foreign language, of little use to any regular activity other than gardening. If you feel shy about pronouncing botanical names, don't feel alone. Even your long-lost knowledge of Latin from high school days is not really going to help when it comes to the "accepted" pronunciation of plant names. Believe me, I've heard names like *Heuchera* rolled off the tongue in so many variations, I've just picked the one for myself that feels most comfortable.

Why all the fuss about botanical names anyway? Well… one typical defence in their favour is that while many different plants might share one common name, the botanical names can only refer to one specific plant. Rose-of-Sharon is a common name for the shrubby *Hibiscus syriacus* but in certain parts of the country it is also used for a totally different plant, the yellow-flowered *Hypericum calycinum*. You can see that a gardener could easily purchase a totally different plant from what they had intended. The botanical name should help you to find exactly the plant you are after.

Another problem is that some perennials go under any number of different common names. Blue Cornflower, Perennials Bachelor's Button and Mountain Bluet are all names that refer to the same plant, *Centaurea montana*. For convenience, the index at the back of this book includes both botanical names and multiple common names for the plants listed, to help you navigate easily through these pages.

This book is used as a reference for the most up-to-date information by home gardeners, landscape designers, botanical gardens, college instructors, magazine writers and many other professionals in the industry. For this reason, we make every effort to try and keep up on the latest nomenclature information with each edition. The botanical names are used here as a way of organizing a large number of species into a format that helps you to find the right ones for your garden. If you as a home gardener are not particularly concerned about plant names, that is completely understandable! Learn them at your own pace and to whatever depth makes you feel comfortable. Or, if you prefer, don't use them at all.

Unfortunately, even botanical names are in a constant state of flux. Botanists and plant taxonomists are uncovering many secrets about the perennials in our gardens. New methods of DNA analysis in particular are slowly unlocking the clouded relationships between certain plants. I think we've only seen the tip of the iceberg so far as a huge revolution in plant nomenclature.

As a horticulturist, I find plant name changes to be both interesting as well as enormously frustrating. Nearly every week I'm checking and double-checking a name against one or more reference lists, these days often utilizing online resources.

Sometimes it's better to wait out the ongoing battles and discussions regarding new plant names. I've learned the hard way not to jump too quickly, thinking specifically about the "now it's *Chrysanthemum*, now it's *Dendranthema*, no – wait – now it's *Chrysanthemum* again" fiasco of a few years ago. In time these arguments are fought in ivory towers beyond my reach, and things settle out in a form the rest of us have no choice but to eventually go along with.

Below are the resources I use most regularly for settling plant nomenclature issues, particularly when writing this Guide. Sometimes they all disagree – then, I let out a loud expletive of disbelief and flip a coin.

***The Royal Horticultural Society Plant Finder*** (revised yearly) or their online version: (http://www.rhs.org.uk/rhsplantfinder/plantfinder.asp).

***Naamlijst van Vaste Planten*** (List of Name of Perennials), from the Boskoop Station for Applied Research for Nursery Stock, Netherlands. 2000 edition.

***Herbaceous Perennial Plants*** by Allan M. Armitage.

---

Within this book, plants are organized alphabetically by the most widely-accepted current botanical name. These appear in italic letters, something like **Leymus arenarius**, listed under Ornamental Grasses. Under this same listing a name within square brackets [**Elymus arenarius**] also occurs This indicates an out-of-date name or synonym for the same plant. We include this information because plants might appear under several different names at the nursery or in various reference publications on your bookshelf.

# Perennial Gardening Guide

# PEREN

"Perennial garden" can mean so many different things to different people. There are those of us who are passionate collectors, with an unexplainable urge to grow every plant within reach and to always attempt the impossible. Some people are first and foremost garden designers, intrigued by the colour, texture and form of plants. But by far the largest group are the vast majority who simply want a *nice* garden without having to dedicate every waking moment of their lives to creating and maintaining the garden of their dreams.

# NIALS

Let's talk about dreams for a moment. I have truly come to believe that – as perennial gardeners – North Americans are packing around a lot of excess baggage. The dream picture we carry around in our mind's eye (more often than not) is that of a lavish "English Border," overflowing with colour from spring to late fall in a seemingly endless display. We may demand a number of conflicting things from this vision: high performance/low maintenance, instant gratification/permanent results, big impact/minimal expenditure. You get the picture. Perhaps what really needs examining is the picture-perfect dream garden itself, when weighed against the limited time, money, resources (such as water), quirks of the site (maybe dry shade) and personal energy each of us has available to allocate to its creation and maintenance.

Once we open up the concept of the "English Border" to criticism, it is interesting what happens. Gardeners begin to realize that even if a huge English-style border were within the realm of possibility, more often than not it would look out of place within the confines of the modern suburban property. Few of us have the space available to dedicate to a border of sufficient size to provide impact all season long. After all, it was not uncommon for a Victorian perennial border to be over two hundred feet long and fifteen feet deep! The days of vast estates and cheap labour are most certainly long gone.

## Modern perennial gardens

What I see happening these days in gardens is tremendously exciting. Gardeners are pushing the limits with new and clever ways of using perennials. With greater frequency the "Perennial Border" is being banished in favour of the "Mixed Border", where there are *no* rules. Perennials can be freely combined with shrubs, trees, evergreens, bulbs, annuals, grasses, wildflowers, herbs and even vegetables to create a personal space that is one-of-a-kind. Mixed borders containing a selection of woody plants and evergreens can be particularly attractive all year round, something that the perennial-only garden often fails to be.

Looking through garden design books or magazines is a great way to open up the garden to new possibilities. Here is just a small sampling of what you might try as an alternative to the traditional perennial border concept:

- Transform boring foundation evergreen plantings into a more interesting mixed border.
- Tie a pond or water feature into the surrounding garden by planting perennials around its edges.
- Stop thinking of shady areas as being problem sites – plant a woodland garden filled with shade-loving plants such as Hosta, Astilbe, ferns and spring-flowering bulbs.
- Create a bog garden for moisture-loving perennials. It's as simple as

lining a hole with plastic, punching a few holes for drainage and filling it with a 50/50 mixture of soil and compost or peat.

- Make a rock garden that will allow you to grow many interesting alpine plants in a small area. What a great use for your kids' old sandbox!
- Replace the lawn on a steep slope with a selection of perennial groundcovers to create a rich tapestry effect.
- Soften the look of hardscaping elements, such as stone or concrete steps, paths, sidewalks, patios and walls with perennials.

- Consider using perennials in tubs, pots or window boxes, either with or without annuals.
- Use large perennial plants as specimens. Surround them with a low groundcover or even just plain old mulch to really set off their architectural form.
- Plant large numbers but fewer kinds of plants to reduce maintenance. Choose ones that have multi-season interest or a long season of bloom.
- Learn to rely on foliage to create interest in shady areas. There are very few long-blooming perennials for the shade.

- Use spring-flowering bulbs lavishly, especially all the little early-blooming kinds with names you can't pronounce. Don't buy ten, buy two hundred. These get better and better each year.
- Use an otherwise "dead" space (like along the side of your house) to create an intimate and special perennial garden – your personal "secret garden." Include a place to sit and enjoy your efforts.

## Perennial benefits

No matter what your garden situation, there are a number of perennials available that will adapt to the conditions you already have. There are

perennials for sun, shade, clay, sand, wet or dry soil, hot or cold climates, and everything in between.

Perennial flowers appear in every colour of the rainbow, as well as black, white and brown! No matter what colour scheme you can dream up, there will be a perennial available to match. Just as important, the range of form and texture among perennials is quite diverse. Low, spreading carpets, medium rounded bushes and tall spiky spires are all available from among the ranks. Texture ranges from fine and feathery to bold and glossy.

Perennials can provide you with a much broader selection of plant material to choose from when plan-

ning your landscape. Not using perennials in our gardens would be like not decorating the walls of a room. We would be ignoring the endless possibilities of colour, texture, and the changing seasons.

And perennials are a good investment. They not only provide you with many of the same benefits as annuals, they keep coming back! And they get bigger. Within a few years many varieties will need to be lifted and divided, and what an excellent opportunity that is to share or trade with friends and neighbours. One healthy, large clump of Summer Phlox can be divided into ten or more pieces, so you can easily see an increase in value right there in your own garden.

For people with a limited amount of time available to garden, some of the more rugged and carefree perennials will fit very nicely into a low-maintenance scheme. Careful selection is the key to this sort of approach, and the list of suitable candidates varies from region to region. It's an interesting observation that some of the more "instant" perennials are not the best long-term choices, while other types that take a few years to reach a mature size will often be with you for the long haul.

### Perennial misconceptions

One misconception about perennials is that they will somehow magically take care of themselves. In most cases this is not true. They will still need help both in getting established, and in staying healthy and vigorous.

This means regular watering, weeding, trimming back or pruning, dividing, transplanting, fertilizing, and sometimes dealing with pests or diseases. This might sound like a lot of work – and it is. But when compared to purchasing large numbers of annuals, or growing and maintaining a pristine lawn, it can actually amount to less time and money.

## Designing Your Garden

### An overwhelming choice

Modern gardeners are very fortunate to live in a time when the passion for perennial plants has reached a frenzy like never before. The selection is now overwhelming, to say the least. This is good in one sense, bringing diversity and greater possibilities into our lives, but it also makes the job of selecting

the *right* plant ever more difficult. For myself, it is a nearly constant exercise to keep up on the newest and latest introductions; hopefully in this book I will succeed in distilling some of the information into a format that becomes a quick and easy reference to help with your garden planning. In trying to achieve that goal I make every attempt to point out both the good and not-so-good features of a plant and to provide insight into how it should perform over a wide range of climates and zones.

### Gardens start with a plan

Look at the basic landscape that you already have, and try to determine what the good and bad elements are. Removing any diseased trees or shrubs might be a good place to start. Changing the line of a sidewalk or the shape of a planting might be all that is required. A basic book on landscaping will come in very handy at this point (I highly recommend any of the books written by British garden designer John Brookes).

Rather than look at your entire yard, try to focus in on just a few spots that could use some improvement. If you re-work a few areas each year, it won't take very long at all to see a remarkable difference in your whole garden.

### Thinking ahead

The hardest part about designing with perennials is planning for colour over an extended season. Although certain varieties will bloom for many weeks on end, most perennials bloom for three to four weeks at the most. If all the varieties in your garden begin blooming in early June, there won't likely be much colour left by September.

Check the blooming information under each plant listing, or check plant tags at your garden centre. This will help you to choose combinations that bloom at the same or different times, depending on the design you have in mind.

Ideally, a good selection of different perennials will give you colour somewhere in the garden from early April to late October. Learning which variety blooms at what time is part of the challenge of perennial gardening. One of the best ways to find out when plants are in bloom is to drop by your local garden centre throughout the year –

### BASIC TERMS

**ANNUALS** are plants that complete their life cycle within one year. Examples: marigolds, petunias, impatiens, zinnias.

**BIENNIALS** usually need two years to bloom, set seed and die. Sometimes they get mixed up and take one year or even three years to do this. Examples: sweet william, forget-me-not, foxglove, lupines, canterbury bells.

**PERENNIALS** generally live for several years, although some are longer-lived than others. This varies a lot, depending on your climate, soil conditions, insects or diseases, and the plant in question. *Herbaceous* is a word used to describe plants that do not develop woody stems. Most of our garden perennials therefore fall into the category of *herbaceous perennials*. This is to distinguish them from trees and shrubs.

## How to plant perennials

**1** Prepare soil, dig hole large enough to accomodate the root ball.

**2** Remove pot, break up the outside of the rootball if plant is root bound.

**3** Fill hole with water, place plant in hole and fill in around roots with soil.

**4** Continue filling with soil. Top of rootball must be at or slightly below soil surface.

Make sure the soil in the pot is moist. Planting a dry root ball makes it very difficult to provide sufficient water. Hold the pot upside-down and shake or tap to loosen the plant. If lots of roots are visible and all jumbled together, the plant may be rootbound. If so, use a sharp knife to slice up the bottom 2 cm (1") of roots and rough up the sides of the ball with your fingers.

With a spade or trowel, open up a hole deep enough to accommodate the root ball. Fill the hole with water, place the plant upright in the hole and fill in around the roots with soil. Pat the soil to thoroughly mix the soil and water. This helps to eliminate any air pockets around the roots and ensures sufficient moisture for growth. Be sure the root ball surface is at or just slightly below the garden soil surface. After planting, spread a mulch to a depth of 2–5 cm (1–2").

they're sure to have blooming perennials on display. You should also take a good look around your neighbourhood– try to take notes about when plants that appeal to you put on their best display. It is only one step further to begin combining different varieties together in clever ways that perhaps nobody ever thought of before!

## Marjorie's design trick

My friend Marjorie Mason Hogue told me of a clever way that she thought up to design for all-season interest without ever using graph paper or getting all complicated: simply stretch out your arms, and in an area of approximately that diameter, try to include a perennial that blooms in spring, one in summer and one in fall. For the finishing touch, include a fourth plant that primarily has good foliage interest. I think this is a simple and versatile way to include a variety of plants and achieve as close to year-round appeal as possible.

Let's look at an example: in an area with morning sun perhaps you have a nice big clump of old-fashioned pink Bleedingheart (*Dicentra spectabilis*). This flowers beautifully in late spring, then during the heat of summer it usually collapses and looks shabby. We need a plant that will fill the gap later in the season. One that comes to mind is White Fleeceflower (*Persicaria polymorpha*), which gets to a height of 3–4 feet and flowers non-stop from July to September. Now… something for autumn colour could be one of the many Toad Lily selections (*Tricyrtis*). Then, let's finish off the grouping with a clump or three of Barrenwort (*Epimedium*), which gives an airy but brief display of flowers in mid spring with handsome foliage that lasts all season long and most of the winter. We could go one step further and include a sprinkling of early spring flowering bulbs, such as Siberian Squills (*Scilla*), Snowdrops (*Galanthus*) and large purple Crocus. There you go – all-season colour in an instant, yet a variety of different plants that change over the course of the seasons.

Planting a combination of four plants together can easily lend itself to all sorts of interesting designs. Try to imagine combinations of herbs, perennials and annuals, for example; no need to just stick to perennials alone.

This little trick can easily be adapted to container gardening as well.

## It's never finished!

Because there is such a vast array of perennials to choose from, it would be difficult for anyone to become bored of growing them. For the addicted perennial gardener the possibilities become endless. Planning, arranging, planting, taking notes, rearranging again and again, these are the joys and challenges of perennial gardening. Indeed, most perennial fanatics would agree that the garden is never truly finished; there are always new ideas waiting to be tried. Those of you just recently bitten by the perennial-gardening bug – stand your ground, and tell your significant other to quit asking if it's done yet…

Beginning gardeners, please don't be scared off! One of the best things about perennial gardening is that it can be tailored to suit your needs, experience, and budget – there's no need to convert your entire lawn into an English-style border all at once. Start with your current landscaping as a base, and try to figure out a way to integrate perennials into what is already there. After all, you can always dig up the lawn next year.

## Planting your perennial garden

### Preparing your soil

Starting out with properly prepared soil will spare you future aggravation and hard work. Properly preparing your soil is the single most important step to having a healthy, successful perennial garden.

Most perennials grow best in a deep, rich, well-drained soil. Check the plant descriptions in this book or the plant tag for specific soil or site requirements.

Dry, sandy soils can be improved by adding plenty of organic matter, such as compost, moistened peat moss or composted manure. Dig the area to a depth of at least 20 cm (8″), preferably with a fork or spade.

Heavy clay soils need to be opened by adding plenty of organic matter, along with perlite, coarse sand or grit. A 12–15 cm (4–6″) layer of compost (or other organic matter) and 5 cm (2″) of grit will greatly improve clay soils for the long haul.

Few perennials do well in wet, poorly drained soils. Consider building raised beds or installing tile drainage if you have a soggy garden area. If you are not prepared to do this, choose perennials that do well under waterlogged conditions.

## Hardiness Zones

Use this table to help determine which plants are suitable for your winter conditions. Any plant with your zone number or lower should be suitable.

**If you are in doubt be sure to ask your local garden centre staff.**

| | Minimum Winter Temp. | |
| --- | --- | --- |
| Zone | °F | °C |
| 1 | Below -50 | Below -46 |
| 2 | -50 to -40 | -46 to -40 |
| 3 | -40 to -30 | -40 to -34 |
| 4 | -30 to -20 | -34 to -29 |
| 5 | -20 to -10 | -29 to -23 |
| 6 | -10 to 0 | -23 to -18 |
| 7 | 0 to 10 | -18 to -12 |
| 8 | 10 to 20 | -12 to -7 |
| 9 | 20 to 30 | -7 to -1 |
| 10 | 30 to 40 | -1 to 4 |

Use this information as a general guide for selecting suitable plants for your area. Many other factors affect overwintering of perennials. Some of these factors include: reliability and depth of snow cover, soil moisture levels, and site-specific micro-climates.

### Weeds

The planting area must be free of perennial weeds, especially spreading types like Canada Thistle, Bindweed and Couch or Quack Grass. Proper preparation before planting will save years of aggravation later on. If you are willing to use herbicides, ask your garden centre which products they recommend for controlling the specific weeds. Take fresh samples of the weeds with you for identification. Another option is to smother the weeds with black plastic or many layers of newspapers (weigh them down with bricks or rocks) for a period of three to four months.

Annual weeds or perennial weed seedlings are easily controlled by hand weeding, something that needs to be done about once a month for the first

season. In future years your plants will get larger and do a much better job of shading the soil below, reducing (but not eliminating) the chances of new weeds appearing from seeds.

### Selecting and planting new container-grown perennials

When buying perennials, look for fresh, healthy-looking plants that appear vigorous and ready to grow. Avoid overgrown, floppy or leggy-looking plants, or any that are small and struggling to stay alive. Certain perennials (especially those with daisy-type flowers) are so vigorous they are often root-bound in the pots; they usually overcome this quickly once planted in your garden.

Any plants that have live insects or foliage diseases should be avoided, since they might start even bigger problems on plants already in your garden. The odd bent leaf or broken stem is usually an indication of slight damage during shipping, and this will not generally cause any long term problems. Moss, liverwort or other weeds in the pot should be picked out and discarded before planting.

Although perennials may be held in their containers for up to three weeks or so, they should be planted as soon as possible to avoid having them accidentally dry out. The sooner you plant them, the faster they can become established in your garden.

If you must wait to plant them, perennials in pots will be happiest outside, so long as temperatures are above freezing. Regular watering may be necessary a couple of times a week during cool weather, and every day during warm spells. A lightly shaded location will help to keep your perennials evenly moist.

### When to Plant

**Mid to late spring** is the ideal time to plant container-grown perennials. They have a chance to get well established before the heat of summer arrives. Spring is also a good time to divide or transplant many types of perennials. Peonies, Iris and Oriental Poppies should not be divided in the spring, but can be planted from containers all season long. Perennials purchased in late winter or very early spring may need special handling, depending on where you live. Avoid putting perennials into the ground while there is still a good chance of hard night frosts.

**Summer planting** is very successful, so long as plants are not allowed to dry out. Watering is especially important when the weather is hot and dry. Transplanting or dividing perennials already established in your garden is not recommended during the summer, except for Bearded Iris and Oriental Poppies, which are best divided in July or August only.

**Fall planting** is highly recommended in most regions. Early-blooming varieties will put on a colourful display in spring if planted in the fall. Dividing or moving perennials in the fall is usually very successful. Winter frosts may "heave" summer or fall-planted perennials. Check them in late winter, and if any have popped out of the ground, gently press them back in place.

### Mulching

The benefits of organic mulches are many. They add humus-forming organic matter to the soil, improving its structure and eventually supplying food to your perennials. They cover the soil and smother many seeds, reducing the amount of weeding required. The biggest benefit with mulching is that it helps to keep the soil cool and moist during the summer months, thereby reducing watering needs and avoiding drought stress. Mulch should be no thicker than 5–8 cm (2–3") and should taper off to nothing as it approaches your perennial clumps. In other words, don't heap mulch all over the crowns of your perennials and risk smothering them to death.

Choose a mulch that is good value. This varies from region to region, and includes such things as shredded bark, cocoa beans, rice hulls, commercially bagged or municipal com-

post, composted steer manure, pine needles and many, many other products. Plain sphagnum peat moss is not a good mulch because it has a tendency to repel water and can blow all over the place.

A clever way to apply mulch around newly planted perennials is to turn the pots upside-down over the plants, spread your mulch, then remove the pots – it's quick and simple.

## Watering

Newly-planted perennials need to be watered immediately after planting and once a week or so for the first two weeks, unless the weather is rainy. Summer plantings may require more frequent watering, especially during periods of drought. During dry or hot weather be sure to watch for signs of wilting leaves, and supply water immediately if possible. If wilted plants do not perk up shortly after watering, it is usually a sign of serious overwatering and root rot.

## Fertilizing

Adding fertilizer while doing soil preparation is not a bad idea. If you choose slow-release organic products like bone or blood meal, this is an especially good time to get them down into the soil where the plant roots can make use of them. Granular fertilizers also can be applied as a top dressing and worked into the soil at the same time as you mix in compost and other soil amendments, before planting a new bed. See the fertilizing section in Spring Tasks below for advice on choosing a fertilizer.

# The perennial garden through the year

The specific plant listings in this *Perennial Gardening Guide* will help you to learn about any special things that need to be done for specific plants, such as staking, cutting back and controlling any diseases or pests. Many of these tasks are covered in detail on the Heritage Perennials web site: www.perennials.com.

## Spring tasks

For most of us, spring is the big cleanup time. In my garden, soggy-wet clay soil is often a hindrance to getting on with this job. Avoid walking in large borders when the soil is saturated in order to prevent compaction. It's also easy to snap off the new growth of perennials or bulbs that may still be hiding under the ground by tramping around too early. Laying down boards or walking on well-placed stepping-stones is one way to get around this problem.

If you have a large border, cutting back the dead tops of perennials may take more time than you anticipate. Hand pruners are good in most cases, but other tools can be put into action including hedge shears, electric hedge trimmers (great for big clumps of grasses) or even power string trimmers. I also find a pair of sharp scissors to be handy for cutting soft and flexible stems on things like Blue Fescue grass, or for removing dead tips of evergreen perennials. Here are some cutting-back tips:

- For perennials that have died back completely to the ground, remove the dead stems to just above the soil level. These can be chopped up and added to your compost heap unless the plants were diseased in the previous season.
- Late-summer and fall blooming daisies (such as Rudbeckia or Coreopsis) usually have dead flowering stems on top but green leaves at the base. Remove the dead stems only.
- Evergreen perennials (like Coral-bells and Lungwort) sometimes look worse for wear by spring. Remove any dead or damaged leaves to tidy up the appearance, but any healthy green leaves should be allowed to remain. Evergreen rock garden plants (such as Moss Phlox and Evergreen Candytuft) should *not* be cut back in the spring. This may kill them, or at the very least prevent them from flowering.
- Woody-stemmed perennials are usually cut back to a height of 15–30 cm (6–12″) in mid-spring. Doing this too early may lead to further dieback during sudden cold snaps. Examples include: Russian Sage (*Perovskia*), Butterfly Bush (*Buddleja*), Tree Mallow (*Lavatera*), Lavender (*Lavandula*) and Blue Spirea (*Caryopteris*).
- Barrenwort (*Epimedium*) and Lenten Rose (*Helleborus orientalis* hybrids) should both be cut back in late winter before any flower buds appear. This allows the flowers to be seen, rather than hidden among the old leaves. NOTE: Christmas Rose (*Helleborus niger*) and most other types of Hellebore should not be pruned.
- Cut back fall-flowering ornamental grasses before any new growth appears in spring. Otherwise the combination of old dead leaves and new growth is a cleaning nightmare.

spring feeding, and if you use a mulch of wood chips or bark it is a wise idea to fertilize your perennials every spring – when mulch begins to rot the bacteria responsible will rob the soil of available nitrogen.

There are boxes of fancy perennial food readily available in garden centers and these are fine if your garden is relatively small. For larger borders it's a much better deal to buy large bags of all-purpose vegetable garden fertilizer. Look for something with a higher middle number (e.g. 5-10-5, 10-15-10) to promote strong stems and lots of flowers. Do *not* be tempted to use lawn fertilizer on your perennials – it is too high in the first number, nitrogen. Also, don't ever use a "weed and feed" formulation on any part of your garden other than turf grass.

Apply fertilizer anytime from early to mid-spring. Whatever product you choose, follow the bag rate per square yard (or square meter) closely. I like to weigh or measure this amount into an empty plastic cup and mark a line that I can easily see, storing the cup right in the bag with any unused portions of the fertilizer. Sprinkle fertilizer *around* your perennials, not directly on top of the clumps, to avoid burning new growth. Then gently work it into the soil to a depth of approximately 5 cm (2″) using a claw hoe or metal garden rake. Slow-release products last well throughout the season and are my first choice. These are available as either inorganic or organic formulations.

**Mulching:** Spring is an excellent time to apply mulch to a perennial garden. If compost is used as a mulch, it not only acts as a reasonable source of nutrients but supplies plenty of organic soil-building matter and helps to suppress annual weeds at the same time. You can use your own compost, bagged compost or composted manure. Spread compost to a depth of 2–5 cm (1–2″), using it as a replacement for other fertilizer products.

If you have terrible problems with slugs, consider removing all of your old mulch in the spring, leaving the soil exposed to the sun for a few weeks; then replace with fresh mulch. This will help to eliminate overwintered slugs, snails and their eggs.

**Edging the beds:** This is a good time to freshen up those bed edges, unless you have already installed a permanent edging of some kind. When you do this, try to follow any invading grass roots and remove them entirely before they reach nearby clumps of perennials.

**Moving or dividing perennials:** Spring is an ideal time to move or divide the vast majority of perennials, particularly if you live in very cold regions (Zones 1–4). Even the early spring-bloomers can be moved, so long as it gets done before they flower. You might sacrifice a few blooms for the current season, but next year's display will be especially grand.

A few perennials are best divided or moved at other times of the year, or you risk seriously setting them back. These include: Peonies (mid-fall is best), true Lilies (mid to late fall), Oriental Poppies (August, while plants are dormant) and Bearded Iris (July through September).

Although some perennials are perfectly happy for years without being divided, others let you know it's time by dying out in the middle, creating a donut shaped clump.

**Staking:** Staking of very tall perennials needs to be done well before June winds and rain arrive to bash them down. Delphiniums and Peonies are the classic examples of perennials we wish we had staked! Special peony hoops are a good investment, or use those inexpensive tomato cages instead. Get the hoops out in the garden in late April so the new stems grow up through them. Delphiniums look best when each stem is staked individually, rather than using just one stake per plant. This allows for each stem to be tied in a more natural-looking way and at several points along the stake, as it lengthens and grows.

Plan to have a range of stakes on hand of various heights. I find bamboo lengths of three, four and six feet to be handy, and these are available in green or natural colour. Some gardeners make use of tree prunings to stake more rambling-type perennials, and these quickly disappear into the background as the plants cover them.

## Summer tasks

**Dead-heading:** In simple terms, dead-heading means to remove the spent or faded flowers regularly. In practical terms, few of us have time to do this chore constantly, so it becomes an occasional or weekly task.

Deadheading accomplishes two things: it spruces up the appearance of a plant

Spring is a good time to do a thorough weeding. Remove the entire root of spreading perennial weeds (the nasty types, like couch or quack grass, Canada Thistle, Sow Thistle) if at all possible, or wait until mid to late spring and spot-treat them carefully with a non-selective herbicide. Overwintered annual weeds are easy to pull in spring while the soil is moist. Germinating weeds should be removed with a hoe while still small.

**Fertilizing:** Some gardeners fertilize every spring, others not quite so often. Newly planted borders are usually good for a couple of years if the soil was well-prepared initially. Older gardens often are rejuvenated by a

instantly, allowing remaining flowers to be enjoyed without the visual competition of finished ones. It also prevents seed formation, often encouraging the plant to produce more flower buds as a result. This works especially well with daisy-type perennials as well as some others that bloom between early summer and fall (such as Summer Phlox and Blue Salvia). No amount of deadheading will encourage most spring-flowering perennials to repeat bloom, so don't waste your time on them.

**Cutting back:** The plain truth is this: most summer-blooming perennials look good from the time they come up in the spring until they are finished flowering. Beyond that point they take a sudden nosedive and look shabby for the remainder of the season. To encourage a round of fresh and attractive foliage, a hard cutting back is usually beneficial – particularly for late spring and early summer bloomers. The healthy new foliage also does a better job of storing energy in the roots for improved performance in future years and reduces the opportunity for fungal diseases to become established.

The classic example is Silver Mound Artemisia. Sometime in June you might notice tiny round silver balls appearing, which are the flowers. A few weeks later the whole plant collapses into a pile of black mush during the heat of summer. By cutting the whole plant back to 5 cm (2″) tall in mid June you can encourage fresh, new growth to appear that will remain attractive until fall frost. In case this

makes you nervous to do, just remember these are *perennials*, and if the result of summer pruning is less than successful, you get a chance next year to try something different.

Among the perennials most often in desperate need of a summer rejuvenative pruning: *Achillea, Aegopodium, Alchemilla, Anthemis, Aquilegia, Artemisia, Centaurea montana, Delphinium, Euphorbia polychroma, Geranium, Geum, Leucanthemum, Nepeta, Polemonium, Pulmonaria, Saponaria, Salvia, Tanacetum, Tradescantia, Veronica*.

How much to cut back depends on the growth habit of the plant in question. When in doubt, cut back no further than 15 cm (6″) to see what happens. With Cranesbill Geraniums and Delphiniums there is usually new foliage developing at the base around the time the taller stems begin to flop over or look ugly. This new foliage should be left alone, removing anything above it.

Spring-flowering bulbs should not be pruned back – they need to ripen their foliage to store energy in the bulb for the following season. True Lilies should not be cut back either, for the same reason. Peonies have handsome foliage through the summer and fall, so they don't need cutting back. Aside from these few plants, most spring and summer-blooming perennials can be safely cut back by at least half to two-thirds once flowering is finished.

Another group of plants that benefit from a less dramatic summer pruning are the popular spring-flowering rock garden plants, including Wall Cress (*Arabis*), Rock Cress (*Aubrieta*), Basket-of-Gold (*Aurinia*), Pinks (*Dianthus*), Moss Phlox (*Phlox subulata*) and Evergreen Candytuft (*Iberis*). In late spring, once the flowers are finished, plants should be pruned back by about half their height using hedge shears. Compact and bushy growth will result, and in warm, humid regions particularly, this simple pruning method can greatly improve summer survival.

**Pinching:** Everybody knows that fall garden mums need to be pinched in order to encourage that perfect cushion shape. Pinching simply means pruning the plant back once or twice to encourage more branching, and therefore a bushier habit. Plants that respond well to pinching usually flower in late summer or autumn; a good many of them having daisy-shaped flowers. Cutting the growth back by half anytime between mid May and late June will make for a bushier habit, reduced height, and usually more flowers (although often of a smaller size). A second pinching – cutting back half of the *new* growth – is sometimes done, especially for mums. Stop pinching before the middle of July, or flowering may be delayed until November! Here are some perennials that respond well: *Asters, Boltonia, Chelone, Chrysanthemum, Eupatorium, Helenium, Helianthus, Heliopsis, Leucanthemum, Lobelia, Monarda, Perovskia, Phlox, Physostegia, Rudbeckia, Sedum* (fall-blooming types), *Vernonia, Veronicastrum*.

**Watering:** More of us are experiencing water shortages or restrictions than ever before. The demand for drought-tolerant plants is steadily growing, and more gardeners are starting to plan their gardens in a way that makes better use of limited water resources. This is known as Xeriscaping – the basic concept being to group plants together that have similar water requirements, creating beautiful gardens with a reduced need for supplemental irrigation. There are plenty of books and online resources available on this topic.

Figuring out when to water is the first thing. Plants let us know when they are stressed by wilting. This is a sure sign that something needs to be

done, and soon! But wilting is a danger sign and best avoided. The best way to tell if watering is needed is to dig a small hole; the soil should feel moist and cool at a depth of about 10 cm (4″). If it feels dry and warm then it's time to water. Traditionally, early morning has been the time of day most often mentioned for applying water. It makes sense, since evaporation is lower, making better use of limited available water. Evening is not a bad second choice. The important thing is to apply water to a wilting plant immediately, if possible.

How much to water? Deep watering is the key, and experts recommend that 25 mm (1″) of water is sufficient. This is easiest to monitor with a shallow empty can set near the edge of the sprinkler – when it fills with 25 mm (1″) of water that section of the bed is done. Another way is to dig a hole to check if the moisture has penetrated to a depth of 12–15 cm (4–6″). A good rule-of-thumb is to water less often but more thoroughly.

I like hand-held wand sprayers for watering spots here and there in the garden, and most especially for containers. Oscillating sprinklers and impact-type sprinklers are good for watering beds, but these vary widely in their effectiveness. Investing in good-quality sprinklers is a good idea.

One dilemma with large borders is how to get water over the tops of medium to tall-sized perennials. A stepladder placed temporarily within the border works well, setting the sprinkler on top where nothing will block the spray pattern. You could also rig it up on the top of a fence. Some impact sprayers have extension tripods that raise their height as required.

## Autumn and pre-winter tasks

New gardeners in particular often panic when autumn draws to a close. It seems amazing and unbelievable that perennial plants can survive the rigours of winter, but in most cases they accomplish it with no additional help. My best advice is to relax! Here are a few tips:

- Don't be in a rush to cut everything back. Even in cold regions, September is simply too early. Late fall or early winter is ideal.
- Cut perennials back selectively, leaving any that might have good winter interest. Many ornamental grasses look spectacular when sur-

rounded by a blanket of snow. Some perennials have interesting seed heads (e.g. *Rudbeckia*, *Sedum*) and provide valuable food for wildlife.

- On the other hand, a goodly number of perennials have very little winter interest. Hostas and daylilies are two that collapse down to the ground in late fall. Cleaning the dead leaves away before the snow arrives will reduce your spring chores.
- If in doubt – leave a perennial alone for the first winter. In March you will have a much better sense of whether or not it had any redeeming features through the winter months. Since the tops are dead anyhow (in most cases), the plants themselves don't care one way or another.
- Some perennials are inclined to carry evergreen leaves through the winter, sometimes down towards the base of the plant – don't cut these off. Examples: Coral-bells, Shasta Daisies, low-growing Sedum, Lavender, many alpine or rock garden plants such as Dianthus.
- Woody perennials are a special group. Wait until mid-spring to cut these back, or they may suffer winter damage. Examples: Russian Sage (*Perovskia*), Butterfly Bush (*Buddleja*), Tree Mallow (*Lavatera*).
- Disease or insect-prone perennials should be cut back in late fall, which will reduce the chances of spores, bugs or eggs carrying over to the following year. Cut these back and clean up any fallen leaves: Hollyhocks (*Alcea*, Columbine (*Aquilegia*), *Crocosmia*, *Delphinium*, *Helenium*, *Heliopsis*, Daylily (*Hemerocallis*), Iris (Bearded types, but leave any green leaves alone), Beebalm (*Monarda*), Peonies, Summer Phlox (*Phlox paniculata*), Toad-lilies (*Tricyrtis*) and upright forms of Speedwell (*Veronica*).
- Fall mulching (laying a deep cover of straw or leaves over your perennials) is something that I have always found to be an utter waste of time and energy in most cases. If the plants you have selected are all rated hardy to your region or colder, there is little need to do this. However, if you are trying to "push

the limits" by growing slightly tender plants then a thick winter mulch might be beneficial. I also find a mulch can help bring these through the first winter, when planted after midsummer: Autumn-flowering ornamental grasses (if you live in Zones 4–6), Japanese Anemone (if you live in Zones 4–6).

## Winter tasks

Winter is a good time to read gardening books and catalogs and to plan what design changes you might want to make in the spring. A simple scrapbook is a great way to organize clippings, thoughts and ideas into one central spot. Consider adding photos of your garden taken at different times of the year. Remember to walk around your garden from time to time. No sense in planning for winter unless you actually get out there and enjoy it!

## ACAENA ☀☼
**(Sheepburr, New Zealand Burr)**
A unique and under-used group of low-growing groundcovers from the southern hemisphere, valued for their dense spreading carpets of evergreen foliage, and colourful burr-shaped seed heads which appear in mid to late summer. Although usually planted in rock gardens, they grow quickly and can sometimes smother out more choice alpines. Good cover plants in combination with early spring flowering bulbs. All are drought-tolerant once established and also tolerate poor soils.

**HT/SP** 5–10 cm (2–4") / 30–60 cm (1–2')
**SOIL** Average to dry, well-drained soil.
**BLOOM** June–August
**USES** ⏷⋏♦♠♣ Fast spreaders

***microphylla*** ZONE 3
**(Bronze-leaf New Zealand Burr)**
Good low carpeter. Unusual bronzy-green foliage and showy copper-red burrs. The toughest species, great between paving stones! Spreads quickly.

***saccaticupula* 'Blue Haze'** ZONE 6
Attractive powdery blue-green leaves, much larger than *A. microphylla*. Many stems of reddish-brown burrs in the fall. Superb in containers or for edging.

## ACANTHUS ☀☼
**(Bear's-Breeches)**
These bold specimen plants are very popular with landscape designers. When grown in borders or containers they form large leafy clumps with a tropical flair. Exotic upright spikes of light-pink flowers appear throughout the summer months. Choose a well-protected area or have a blanket handy as these can be damaged by late spring frosts. In colder regions, plant in tubs for easy overwin-

tering indoors. Where hardy, plants can spread to form a large patch – but not in a weedy or troublesome way.

**SP** 75–90 cm (30–36")
**SOIL** Well-drained soil. Dislikes winter wet
**BLOOM** July–August
**USES** ⋏♣ Dried Flower, Specimen, Borders

***hungaricus*** ZONE 5
**[*A. balcanus*]**
**(Hungarian Bear's-Breeches)**
Without a doubt the hardiest species, this has spiny leaves with a thistly appearance, olive-green in colour. Flower spikes are held well above the foliage and are superb for cutting, if you can bring yourself to do it. Clumps are medium in size and well suited to smaller gardens.

**HT** 90–120 cm (3–4')

***mollis*** ZONE 7
**(Common Bear's-Breeches)**
The most well-known and coveted species, with large, glossy and deeply-lobed leaves. Mauve-pink flowers, vigorous habit. Excellent cut flower. Although the roots may survive in cold-winter regions, plants may fail to bloom if the dormant underground flower buds are damaged by prolonged frosts. A deep winter mulch is recommended in Zones 6–7.

**HT** 90–150 cm (3–5')

## ACHILLEA ☀
**(Yarrow)**
The Yarrows are among the best perennials for hot and dry locations, providing good colour throughout the summer months, and even tolerating poor soils. All but the shortest varieties are superb for cutting, used fresh or dried. Some types are wanderers and need to be used carefully in the border – planting within a sunken, bottomless pot is one way to control them. A few kinds are clumping and well behaved. All are attractive to butterflies.

***filipendulina*** ZONE 2
**(Fern-leaf Yarrow)**
Non-spreading, mounding plants form an upright clump of ferny green leaves with large clusters of golden-yellow flowers on tall stems. Good for massing. Flowers are superb for drying. Very drought-tolerant. When grown in rich soils this usually needs to be staked. Several selections exist: 'Cloth of Gold' and 'Gold Plate' are both excellent.

**HT/SP** 90–150 cm (3–5') / 45–60 cm (18–24")
**SOIL** Average to dry well-drained soil. Heat tolerant.
**BLOOM** June–September
**USES** ⋏♣ Dried Flower, Borders

**× *lewisii* 'King Edward'** ZONE 3
**(Dwarf Yarrow)**
A compact, carpeting selection, similar to *A. tomentosa* in habit, but with flowers of a soft primrose-yellow shade. Foliage

is low and silvery-green in colour, slightly woolly in texture. Plants require excellent drainage and are best divided every 2–3 years to maintain vigour.

**HT/SP** 15–20 cm (6–8") / 20–30 cm (8–12")
**SOIL** Average to poor well-drained soil.
**BLOOM** May–July
**USES** △⋏♣ Edging, Rock Garden

***millefolium* Hybrids** ZONE 2
**(Common Yarrow)**
A catch-all group that includes a number of older selections as well as some outstanding newer hybrids that are offsprings of the commercial cut-flower trade. All selections sport good-sized clusters of flowers held above ferny olive-green foliage. Clumps are inclined to spread, which may be useful as a groundcover on slopes but is often troublesome in the perennial border without ruthless reduction of the clumps each spring. Growing inside a bottomless sunken tub is also an effective control.

Dead-head regularly or clip plants back hard after blooming to force a second flush of flowers. Remove faded flower heads to prevent seeds; resulting seedlings will not usually be true to colour. Very drought-tolerant.

**SP** 45–60 cm (18–24")
**SOIL** Average to dry, well-drained soil. Heat tolerant.
**BLOOM** June–September
**USES** ⋏♣ Dried Flower, Borders

**'Christel'** Gorgeous clear magenta-pink selection. Outstanding cutflower!
**HT** 45–70 cm (18–30")

**'Colorado'** A strain that produces a wide mixture of shades, from deepest red and wine through to pink, rose, salmon, apricot, creamy yellow and the occasional white. One of the best types for dried flowers.
**HT** 45–60 cm (18–24")

**'Heidi'** Clear dusky-pink flowers, fading to cream as they age. Compact form.
**HT** 45–60 cm (18–24")

**'Paprika'** Cherry-red flowers with a tiny golden eye, fading first to light pink and finally creamy yellow, often with all shades appearing at the same time.
**HT** 45–70 cm (18–30")

**'Red Beauty'** Deep crimson-red clusters. An old variety, but still the most reliable deep red.
**HT** 45–70 cm (18–30")

**Summer Pastels** A seed-grown mixture. Shades of red, wine, pink, salmon, lavender and cream. All-American Award winner.
**HT** 45–70 cm (18–30")

*Acanthus hungaricus*
*Acaena microphylla*
*Achillea millefolium* 'Paprika'
*Achillea millefolium* 'Summer Pastels'
*Achillea m.* 'Red Beauty'

'Terracotta' Gorgeous salmon-pink flowers that age to rusty terracotta orange.
HT  75–90 cm (30–36″)

'Walther Funcke' Brick-red flowers with a yellow eye. One of the best for cutting.
HT  75–90 cm (30–36″)

### 'Moonshine'  ZONE 3
An outstanding hybrid developed many years ago by Alan Bloom. Valued for its summer-long display of rich canary-yellow flowers, held in large clusters above silvery-grey leaves. Non-spreading habit. Combines well with ornamental grasses. Remove faded flowers for continual bloom. Still one of the best perennials of all time. Moderately drought-tolerant. Not always successful on the Prairies unless planted in a sheltered area. Evergreen in mild winter regions.
HT/SP  45–60 cm (18–24″) / 30–60 cm (1–2′)
SOIL  Average well-drained soil.
BLOOM June–October
USES  ✂✿▲♥❀ Dried Flower, Massing, Borders

### *ptarmica* 'Ballerina'  ZONE 1
(Double Yarrow, Sneezewort)
The airy sprays of fluffy white button flowers are closer in appearance to Baby's Breath than the other Yarrow kin. This compact selection performs better in gardens than some of the older, floppier forms. A steady spreader. Good for cutting, especially as a filler with roses. Also dries well.
HT/SP  30–45 cm (12–18″) / 45–60 cm (18–24″)
SOIL  Average to moist soil. Heat tolerant.
BLOOM June–July
USES  ✂✿♥❀ Dried Flower, Massing, Borders

### *sibirica* 'Love Parade'  ZONE 3
(Siberian Yarrow)
Quite new to gardens, this selection produces loose clusters of soft-pink flowers over a very attractive mound of deep-green saw-toothed foliage. Completely unlike any of the more common forms but equally superb for cutting. Deadhead regularly for continued blooming. Clumps will spread a little, but at a safe rate for including in the border.
HT/SP  45–60 cm (18–24″) / 45–60 cm (18–24″)
SOIL  Tolerates a wide range of soil conditions.
BLOOM June–September
USES  ✂✿▼♥❀ Borders

### *tomentosa*  ZONE 2
(Woolly Yarrow)
Carpet-forming, with short stems of bright-yellow flowers in late spring. An easy rock garden plant. Clip off the flowers after they fade. Must have good drainage. Divide plants every 2–3 years to maintain vigour. Very drought-tolerant.
HT/SP  15–20 cm (6–8″) / 20–30 cm (8–12″)
SOIL  Average to dry, well-drained soil.
BLOOM May–July
USES  △◭▲♥❀ Edging, Borders

## ACONITUM ☼◑
(Monkshood, Wolfsbane)
Tall, sturdy perennials, these often look their best in larger borders. Showy spikes of flowers appear during the summer or fall and are beautiful for cutting. They prefer a cool, moisture-retentive soil and generally perform best in regions with cool summer nights. **CAUTION: All species are toxic if eaten/harmful via skin; wear gloves when handling.**
SP  45–60 cm (18–24″)
SOIL  Cool, moist, well-drained soil.
USES  ✂ Borders

### × *cammarum* 'Bicolor'  ZONE 2
Good sturdy spikes of flowers in an intriguing, marbled combination of violet-blue and white. This soft tone blends well with golds and yellows of all shades.
HT  90–120 cm (3–4′)
BLOOM July–August

### *carmichaelii*  ZONE 2
(Azure Monkshood, Autumn Monkshood)
Incredible spikes of bright-blue hooded flowers, appearing in mid to late fall and lasting until hard frost. The species itself is shorter than the selection 'Arendsii'. Foliage is deeply cut and very glossy on the upper surface. Like so many other late-season bloomers, these look terrific all season long. Divide in the spring every 3–4 years. Superb for cutting!
HT  75–90 cm (30–36″)

'Arendsii' This taller selection towers over everything else in the fall border, bursting into saturated-blue bloom just when you might have given up on it ever opening. In mild autumn regions this can last into November. Tolerant of summer heat, so long as the soil remains moist.
HT  120–180 cm (4–6′)
BLOOM September–November

### Hybrids  ZONE 2
Several recent selections (and a few older ones) fit in here. Most of these are summer-bloomers, similar in habit and form to the common Blue Monkshood.
'Bressingham Spire' One of the best forms. Compact stems seldom require staking. Deep violet-blue flowers from midsummer through the fall.
HT  75–90 cm (30–36″)
BLOOM July–September

'Ivorine' Another neat, compact variety. Ivory-white flowers are on short, chubby spikes. The best of the white forms.
HT  60–90 cm (2–3′)
BLOOM June–August

'Pink Sensation' Quite new on the market, this promises to be the best of the pink forms to date. Plants have

deeply-cut leaves with good, strong stems of flowers in a soft lilac-pink.
HT  100–120 cm (39–48″)
BLOOM July–August

### *lamarckii*  ZONE 2
(Yellow Monkshood)
This species is a departure from the others listed, featuring soft creamy-yellow flowers. Just as easy to grow as the blue-flowered forms, blooming in summer.
HT  90–120 cm (3–4′)
BLOOM July–August

### *napellus*  ZONE 2
(Common Blue Monkshood)
The most familiar species, with tall stems of deep-blue helmet-shaped flowers. An old-fashioned favourite, flowering in summer. Seems happiest in regions with cool summers, like on the Prairies.
HT  120–150 cm (4–5′)
BLOOM July–August

'Carneum' (Pink Monkshood) A unique selection with pale rose-pink flowers. Similar in stature to the regular blue form, and a lovely contrast to it in the border. Flowers may fade to a ghostly white during hot weather.

## ACTAEA see CIMICIFUGA

## ADENOPHORA ☼◑
(Ladybells)
The Ladybells are seldom seen in gardens, or are perhaps mistaken for the more common Bellflowers, to which they are close cousins. Flowers are usually nodding bluebells, held on upright stems.

### *takedae*  ZONE 4
(Autumn Ladybells)
A nice addition to the fall garden, this forms a low mound of narrow green

*Achillea ptarmica* 'Ballerina'

*Achillea sibirica* 'Love Parade'

*Aconitum* 'Bressingham Spire'

leaves, bearing arching stems of lavender-blue bells that dangle gracefully. Combines beautifully with Toad-lilies (*Tricyrtis*), and they love similar moist, dappled shade positions. Dislikes being disturbed once established. Quite likely hardy to Zone 3 or colder.

HT/SP  30–45 cm (12–18″) / 30–45 cm (12–18″)
SOIL   Rich, moist, well-drained soil.
BLOOM  September–October
USES   ✂⚔△♜ Woodland, Borders

## AEGOPODIUM ☼•
### (Goat's foot, Snow-on-the-Mountain, Bishop's Weed, Goutweed)

*podagraria* 'Variegatum'     ZONE 1
(Variegated Goutweed)

Some consider Goutweed in the garden to be a good reason to move. I jump to its defense in certain situations where it may spread to its heart's content and never be criticized for a job well done! The familiar green and white variegated foliage is pleasant enough, particularly when used as a solid cover below trees and shrubs. Plants quickly form a solid patch, even in poor soil, but there is a distinct preference for sites that don't dry out overly much during summer droughts. Should this happen, simply mow the whole patch back to the ground and plants will quickly rejuvenate.

Consider using Goutweed in large tubs or other containers, where the spreading roots will not escape. Plants can be difficult to eradicate once established – but a non-selective herbicide containing glyphosate will give near-complete kill if applied when the leaves are only 10–15 cm (4–6″) tall. Clip off the flower stems, not only to improve the appearance, but also to prevent any seeds from forming. If you thought the

variegated selection was invasive, don't even consider leaving any green-leaved seedlings in your border!

HT/SP  30–60 cm (1–2′) / 60–90 cm (2–3′)
SOIL   Tolerates a wide range of soil conditions.
BLOOM  Flowers should be removed to prevent seeds from forming.
USES   ⚔♜☘ Invasive! Use carefully

## AGAPANTHUS ☼☀
### (African Lily, Lily-of-the-Nile)

Magnificent, exotic plants from South Africa, valued for their large flower heads. They make excellent container plants, especially in colder regions where the pots may be easily overwintered indoors. Don't be surprised if plants wintered indoors decide to burst into flower in early spring. Just stick them back outside for the summer, fertilize regularly and they could well bloom again in late summer. May be hardy in Zones 6–7 with sufficient winter protection. An excellent cut flower.

**Hybrids**     ZONE 8

The result of extensive breeding in England and New Zealand, resulting in many good selections with increased hardiness and deeper colours, in shades of blue through to white. Often sold simply by colour, or mixed as Headbourne Hybrids.

HT/SP  60–90 cm (2–3′) / 30–60 cm (1–2′)
SOIL   Well-drained soil.
BLOOM  July–September
USES   ✂⚔🦋 Borders, Massing

'Bressingham White' Large growing plant with pure-white flowers. A common white selection.

HT     80–90 cm (30–36″)

'Lilliput' With its dwarf, compact habit this is one of the best forms for containers. Bright-blue trumpet flowers.

HT     30–45 cm (12–18″)

'Streamline' A recent compact selection from New Zealand, featuring large heads of clear blue flowers.

HT     45–60 cm (18–24″)

## AGASTACHE ☼☀
### (Anise-hyssop, Licorice Mint)

All kinds of new forms of Anise-hyssop have hit the market lately, so it looks like this group of plants is finally gaining attention. Most types have pleasingly fragrant foliage, ranging from licorice to mysterious fruity fragrances, or even rootbeer! Showy spikes of flowers appear in high summer and are a magnet to butterflies and bees. Good for cutting.

**American Hybrids**     ZONE 6

A wonderful group of garden plants developed in recent years using several species native to the south-western US. Not surprisingly, these all hate having

wet feet in the winter and require perfect drainage. Because they perform so well the first year they make terrific flowering plants for pots and tubs, or could be included in the herb garden for their fragrance.

SP     30–60 cm (1–2′)
SOIL   Average well-drained soil. Avoid wet feet.
BLOOM  July–September
USES   ✂🦋🌿 Containers, Tubs, Borders, Herb gardens

'Apricot Sunrise' Clear apricot-orange flowers, grey-green fragrant foliage.

HT     60–75 cm (24–30″)

'Pink Panther' Bronzy-green foliage, long spikes of rose-pink flowers.

HT     75–120 cm (30–48″)

'Tutti-frutti' Spike of tubular lavender-pink flowers. Tall habit. Pinching regularly will make plants bushy and more compact. Foliage has a pleasant fruity scent.

HT     90–150 cm (3–5′)

'Blue Fortune'     ZONE 2

A recent hybrid selection from Holland, with a compact habit and terrific display of deep-violet flowers. Especially good in containers. Foliage has the typical licorice fragrance. Superb for cutting. The new selection 'Red Fortune' is of similar stature, with spikes of dusky plum-red flowers.

HT/SP  60–75 cm (24–30″) / 45–60 cm (18–24″)
SOIL   Average well-drained soil.
BLOOM  July–September
USES   ✂🦋🌿♜ Borders, Herb gardens

*foeniculum*     ZONE 2
(Giant Hyssop)

A beautiful North American wildflower, native to sunny prairies and meadows. Tall wands of pale violet to white flowers appear from midsummer through fall. The entire plant has a pleasant anise fragrance and can be used to make a soothing tea. Plants are not very long-lived but seedlings will appear in generous numbers. Flowers are edible in salads.

HT/SP  90–120 cm (3–4′) / 60–90 cm (2–3′)
SOIL   Average well-drained soil.
BLOOM  July–September
USES   ✂🦋🌿 Wildflower, Dried Flower, Borders, Herb gardens

**Other Hybrids**     ZONE 5

With dense spikes of flowers and a bushy habit, these hybrids may include our native *A. foeniculum*, *A. rugosa* and others in their parentage. These are good border plants, now in a wider range of colours and sizes than ever before.

SP     45–60 cm (18–24″)
SOIL   Average well-drained soil.
BLOOM  July–September
USES   ✂🦋🌿 Containers, Tubs, Borders, Herb gardens

*Aegopodium podagraria* 'Variegatum'

*Agapanthus* 'Lilliput'

*Agastache* 'Apricot Sunrise'

*Agastache* 'Blue Fortune'

**Honey Bee Series** Compact plants, with short, chunky spikes of violet-blue or white flowers over a long season.

HT      60–70 cm (24–28")

**Premium Series** Tall and bushy plants, with licorice-scented leaves. The series offers strains in several shades from an unusual champagne-blush through to carmine pink and violet-blue.

HT      90–120 cm (3–4')

### *rupestris*                    ZONE 5
### (Rootbeer Plant)

Silvery-grey foliage forms a bushy mound of medium height. Flower spikes are loose and open, salmon-orange in shade and appearing for months on end if deadheaded regularly. Truly a delightful plant, both attractive and unique for its rootbeer scented leaves. A southwest species, but somewhat tolerant of wet winter conditions with adequate drainage. Terrific in pots or tubs.

HT/SP   60–90 cm (2–3') / 60–90 cm (2–3')
SOIL    Average to dry, well-drained soil.
BLOOM June–October
USES    ✂❤➤♣♨ Wildflower, Borders,
        Herb gardens

## AJANIA ☼◐
## (Silver and Gold Chrysanthemum)

### *pacifica*                    ZONE 5
### [*Chrysanthemum pacificum*]

Bushy mounds of toothed green foliage, each leaf attractively edged with silver. Yellow button flowers will appear in very late fall if the season is long and warm, in some areas blooming into December. This begs to be used as edging but also makes a superb container plant. Many gardeners pass it by when shopping for perennials, but those who know and grow this plant absolutely adore it. **'Pink Ice'** is an interesting selection, the yellow button flowers are surrounded by a row of pale-pink petals.

HT/SP   30–60 cm (1–2') / 30–60 cm (1–2')
SOIL    Average well-drained soil.
BLOOM October–November
USES    ✂♣ Edging, Borders

## AJUGA ◐●
## (Carpet Bugle, Bugleweed)

Carpet Bugle is widely used as a groundcover for shady areas, but it really thrives best when free of competition from large, thirsty trees. Most types are fast-spreading but relatively easy to control, forming a low mat of rounded leaves. Showy spikes of flowers appear in late spring. There are a great number of varieties available.

### 'Mini Crisp Red'              ZONE 3
### ['Min Crispa Red']

(Sometimes incorrectly sold as 'Metallica Crispa') An unusual form, the deep burgundy-red leaves are crimped and crinkled like spinach. Growth is extremely slow compared to the other types. Can be used in a rockery with no fear of invasion. Short spikes of blue flowers.

HT/SP   5–10 cm (2–4") / 20–30 cm (8–12")
SOIL    Average to moist, well-drained soil.
BLOOM April–May
USES    ◭♏♣ Edging, Trough gardens

### *reptans*                     ZONE 3
### (Common Bugleweed)

Fast-spreading evergreen mats, usually with bright-blue flowers in spring. Among the many selections are some outstanding forms with unusual foliage colouring. The deep red types are especially dramatic when massed below green or gold-leaved shrubs. Often sold simply by the foliage colour, such as **Bronze Form**, **Green Form**, or **Mahogany Form**.

HT/SP   10–15 cm (4–6") / 30–45 cm (12–18")
SOIL    Average to moist, well-drained soil.
BLOOM April–May
USES    ♏♣ Edging

**'Arboretum Giant'** The best of the green-leaved selections, each leaf edged with a pencil-line of deep burgundy-purple. Large spikes of blue flowers in the spring. Good vigour.

**'Bronze Beauty'** A popular older bronze-leaved variety. Bright blue flowers.

**'Burgundy Glow'** Brightly-coloured leaves, variegated with scarlet, cream, and green. Bright blue flowers. Good fall colour. Remove any reverting shoots regularly. Not particularly vigorous.

**'Catlin's Giant'** (Giant Bugleweed) Unusually tall spikes of blue flowers, over huge bronzy leaves. Inclined to clump at first, later forming a solid patch. To get the largest leaves possible, divide plants each year in early spring. Excellent for edging!

HT      15–30 cm (6–12")

**'Palisander'** Medium-sized leaves in a rich bronzy-purple shade, blue flowers.

**'Purple Brocade'** Deep royal-purple leaves, near black in winter. Spikes of deep blue flowers.

### × *tenorii* Chocolate Chip    ZONE 2
### [A. × *tenorii* 'Valfredda']
### (Chocolate Chip Carpet Bugle)

Just when you thought Bugleweed was boring, along comes this new gem from Valfredda Nursery in Italy! Leaves are narrow and chocolate-brown, forming a low mat. Spikes of bright blue flowers appear in spring. Gorgeous as an edging or in containers.

HT/SP   10–15 cm (4–6") / 30–45 cm (12–18")
SOIL    Average to moist, well-drained soil.
BLOOM April–May
USES    ◭♏♣ Edging

## ALCEA ☼
## (Hollyhock)

### *rosea*                       ZONE 2

With their tall spikes of crepe-textured flowers, these have been grown in gardens for centuries. They look best at the back of a sunny border with medium-sized plants in front to hide the bare lower stems – bare because plants inevitably get infected with Hollyhock rust. Use a systemic fungicide to prevent this, (or just ignore it) and be sure to dispose of infected leaves, especially in the fall. Although more or less biennial, the plants will readily self-seed if allowed. Cutting plants back immediately after flowering may encourage them to return for another year. Hollyhocks are often said to attract hummingbirds, but it's likely that only red or pink forms will work for this.

HT/SP   150–210 cm (5–7') / 30–45 cm (12–18")
SOIL    Average well-drained soil.
BLOOM July–August
USES    ✂➤ Borders

**'Black Beauty'** A unique selection, featuring large single purple-black flowers with a maroon bee in the centre.

**Chater's Double** Large double ruffled blooms, as full and fluffy as the best kleenex flowers. Generally available in mixed colours or sometimes separately in shades of maroon, rose, pink, scarlet, white, and yellow. Seed saved from your own plants may not always come true to colour.

**'Nigra'** ['The Watchman'] Unique single maroon-black flowers.

**'Peaches 'n' Dreams'** Fluffy double flowers in a pleasing peachy-pink to apricot blend.

**Single Hybrids** [*A. ficifolia* hybrids] The single-flowered forms of Hollyhock

*Ajania pacifica* 'Gold & Silver'

*Ajuga* × *tenorii* Chocolate Chip

*Ajuga reptans* 'Palisander'

*Alcea ficifolia* Single Hybrids

have a certain grace and charm that is totally lacking in the double types. They are said to be more resistant to leaf rust, something I cannot vouch for in my own garden. Flowers will appear in the whole range of pastel shades.

**Summer Carnival** Similar to the Chater's types, in a pleasing mix of pastel shades. Plants are inclined to flower in their first season, if planted early. Somewhat more compact than other strains. This is similar to the older Powderpuff strain which is no longer available.

HT     120–150 cm (4–5')

## ALCHEMILLA ☼ ◐
### (Lady's Mantle)

Popular plants for edging, these form a mound of rounded leaves with billowing sprays of yellow-green flowers. Sometimes mass planted as a groundcover. They adapt well to many different garden conditions.

### *faeroensis* var. *pumila*    ZONE 4
### (Dwarf Lady's Mantle)

Fairly new to North America, this delightful dwarf form is well-suited to the rock or woodland garden. Leaves are round in shape with seven fingers or clefts, yellow-green in colour, with a velvety silver backing. Short sprays of chartreuse flowers appear in June.

HT/SP   7–10 cm (3–4") / 20–30 cm (8–12")
SOIL     Average to moist, well-drained soil.
BLOOM June–July
USES    ⛰〰🌱 Edging, Borders

### *mollis*    ZONE 2
### (Common Lady's Mantle)

Truly a garden classic, with its scalloped green leaves, covered in soft down. Both the sprays of chartreuse flowers and the foliage are good for cutting. Superb for

edging, and not very fussy as to soil or light conditions – this is almost a grow-anywhere plant! Although Lady's Mantle is said to self-seed readily, many gardeners (including myself) have not had problems. Seedlings would be easy enough to hoe out anyway.

HT/SP   30–45 cm (12–18") / 45–60 cm (18–24")
SOIL     Well-drained soil.
BLOOM June–August
USES    ⛰〰✂🌱 Edging, Borders

## ALLIUM ☼ ◐
### (Flowering Onion, Ornamental Onion)

A useful and under-used group of flowering perennials, offering a wide range of heights and colours for the sunny border. Flowers are arranged in a ball-shaped cluster, the taller varieties making excellent cut flowers. Some of the most popular types are usually planted as bulbs in the fall, but those listed here are fibrous-rooted. Most flowering onions will attract butterflies.

### *pyrenaicum*    ZONE 4
### [*A. angulosum*]
### (Lavender Onion, Mouse Garlic)

This forms a nice mound of bright green foliage, bearing lavender-pink pompon heads of flowers for several weeks in midsummer. Stems are a good height for cutting. Plants are best suited to the front of a sunny border. Likely hardy to Zones 2 and 3.

HT/SP   40–50 cm (16–20") / 25–30 cm (10–12")
SOIL     Average well-drained soil.
BLOOM July–August
USES    ✂🌱 Cutflower, Edging, Borders

### *schoenoprasum*    ZONE 2
### (Common Chives)

A familiar plant to most gardeners, but too often relegated to the herb garden or vegetable patch, rather than being included with other flowering perennials. The papery mauve-pink flowers are beautiful when combined with late tulips, and of course the leaves can be harvested at any time. Deadheading chives is a wise idea, since they often self seed all over the place. Chives are very drought tolerant.

HT/SP   25–30 cm (10–12") / 30–40 cm (12–16")
SOIL     Average well-drained soil.
BLOOM May–June
USES    ✂🌱 Borders, Herb gardens

**'Album' (White-flowered Chives)** Clean snow-white flowers, a most unusual form that is seldom seen. I was sent a few plants of this selection years ago by the Oxen Pond Botanical Garden in St. John's, Newfoundland. Their director, Dr. Bernard Jackson, was involved in a sort of "rescue mission" to preserve antique garden plants from his region. I didn't think the plant sounded too exciting, but when they flowered the next

spring in my garden I was astounded at how beautiful they were! Don't let this form go to seed, since most of the resulting plants will revert to the usual mauve shade.

**'Forescate' (Giant Chives)** A select variety with extra large rose-purple balls of flowers. Best to deadhead to prevent reverting seedlings from appearing.

### *senescens* var. *glaucum*    ZONE 3
### (Pink Curly Onion, Corkscrew Onion)

As much an interesting foliage perennial as a flowering one, this produces unique grey-green leaves that twist out from the base in a spiral arrangement. Small clusters of pink flowers appear in late summer, a welcome sight in the rock garden when little else is blooming. Great in containers or troughs.

HT/SP   15–20 cm (6–8") / 20–30 cm (8–12")
SOIL     Average well-drained soil.
BLOOM August–September
USES    ⛰🌱 Edging, Borders

### *tuberosum*    ZONE 2
### (Garlic Chives, Chinese Chives)

Most familiar as a resident of the kitchen garden or herb plot, Garlic Chives bursts into flower late in the season with many heads of snowy white flowers. The leaves are flat and grassy looking, strongly tasting and smelling of garlic but only when bruised or cut. Nearly any perennial garden design book you open raves about how wonderful this plant looks in the autumn border. They also warn you to remove the faded flowers to prevent seed from forming, since plants self-sow heavily. To be honest, I always forget to do this and every spring there are seedlings galore. Still – I wouldn't be without it.

HT/SP   30–60 cm (1–2') / 30–45 cm (12–18")
SOIL     Tolerates a wide range of soil conditions.
BLOOM August–October
USES    ✂🌱 Edging, Borders

## ALSTROEMERIA ☼ ◐
### (Peruvian Lily)

Most of us are familiar with Alstroemeria as a florist's cut flower, but there are several forms hardy enough for gardeners in Zones 6–9 to consider experimenting with. *A. aurea* and its forms such as 'Orange King' are the most common ones offered. Breeders have been busy trying to produce hardy dwarf selections, which should soon start to show up at nurseries.

**CAUTION: may cause skin allergy; wear gloves when handling.**

### *psittacina*    ZONE 7
### (Parrot Feather)

One of the most bizarre colour combinations occur in this plant. Each flower is brightly painted with wine-red and green, then marbled with maroon

*Alchemilla mollis*

*Alstroemeria psittacina* 'Variegata'

*Allium schoenoprasum* 'Forescate'

streaks. Plants creep, gradually forming a good-sized patch when grown in a rich, well-drained soil. Stems are tall, and excellent for cutting. Even more impressive is the form **'Variegata'**, with bright-green leaves edged in creamy white. Good success in Zones 5 and 6 would not be surprising, given reliable winter snowcover or a thick mulch in late fall.

HT/SP　70–90 cm (30–36") / 60–75 cm (24–30")
SOIL　Average well-drained soil.
BLOOM July–August
USES　✂❦ Cutflower, Borders

## ALTHAEA see ALCEA

## ALYSSUM ☼
(Madwort, Perennial Alyssum)
Popular plants for growing on walls or in sunny rock gardens. The species *A. saxatile* (Basket-of-Gold) is now listed under AURINIA.

### *montanum*　　ZONE 2
(Mountain Alyssum)
A low, spring-blooming species for the rock garden. Compact silvery mats are smothered by fragrant lemon-yellow flowers. Easy to please. Good for edging borders as well as in rock gardens or walls. Shear plants lightly after blooming to encourage a dense, bushy habit. Evergreen. Very drought tolerant.

HT/SP　10–15 cm (4–6") / 30–45 cm (12–18")
SOIL　Lean, well-drained soil.
BLOOM April–June
USES　▲▲❦ Edging, Walls

## AMSONIA ☼◐
(Blue Star Flower)
Little-known perennials that are mostly native to North America, and ideally suited to the border or wildflower meadow. Flowers are pale-blue stars. All are long-lived but take a few years to settle in and get to a mature size. Excellent choice for the low-maintenance garden. Deer resistant.

### *hubrichtii*　　ZONE 5
(Arkansas Blue Star)
Unique and special for its finely-feathered foliage, forming an upright bushy clump. Bright golden-yellow fall colour is truly outstanding. Silvery-blue flowers appear in early summer.

HT/SP　60–90 cm (2–3') / 75–90 cm (30–36")
SOIL　Average to moist, rich soil.
BLOOM May–July
USES　✂ Wildflower, Borders

### *tabernaemontana*　　ZONE 3
(Common Blue Star)
Bushy, nearly shrub-like in habit, this forms an arching clump of green willow-like leaves, bearing clusters of light-blue starry flowers in late spring and early summer. This plant grows on gardeners, once they discover how

long-lived and carefree it is. Foliage remains attractive well into late fall. Useful for cutting.

HT/SP　60–90 cm (2–3') / 75–90 cm (30–36")
SOIL　Average to moist, rich soil.
BLOOM May–July
USES　✂ Wildflower, Borders

## ANACYCLUS ☼
(Mount Atlas Daisy)
### *pyrethrum* var. *depressus*　　ZONE 4
This cute little alpine produces loads of little white daisy flowers, each petal brushed with red on the backside. Forms a low clump of ferny grey-green foliage. A good rock garden plant, blooms over a long season. Fairly drought-tolerant.

HT/SP　10–15 cm (4–6") / 20–30 cm (8–12")
SOIL　Well-drained soil. Dislikes winter wet.
BLOOM May–July
USES　▲▼❦ Walls, Slopes

## ANAPHALIS ☼
(Pearly Everlasting)
### *margaritacea*　　ZONE 2
A native wildflower over much of North America, and often gathered at the roadside for dried arrangements. Flowers are clusters of white buttons, contrasting nicely with the grey-green foliage. Makes a good border plant but needs some elbow room to spread. Plan to divide in the spring every 3–4 years. Prefers moist soil but tolerates a wide range of conditions. Attractive to butterflies.

HT/SP　30–90 cm (1–3') / 30–60 cm (1–2')
SOIL　Well-drained soil. Drought tolerant.
BLOOM July–September
USES　✂❦🦋 Meadows, Borders, Edging

## ANEMONE ☼◐
(Windflower)
Anemone is a large group of hardy perennials, many of easy garden culture. By far the most widely known are the fall-blooming Japanese Anemones, but there are also other species that flower in spring or summer. Some types are commonly planted as bulbs, purchased in the fall or spring.

　Recent work at the RHS Gardens in Wisley has made great strides in sorting out the muddled nomenclature of the Japanese Anemones. I have attempted to reflect some of their findings here.

### *hupehensis*　　ZONE 5
(Japanese Anemone)
These differ only slightly (from a gardener's perspective) from the hybrid forms listed below. Plants tend to be slightly more compact, flowering a week or two earlier. Otherwise, care and culture are the same.

HT/SP　60–90 cm (2–3') / 60–90 cm (2–3')
SOIL　Prefers a rich, moist soil.
BLOOM August–September
USES　✂❦❦ Massing, Borders

var. *japonica* A forerunner of the modern hybrids, with single and semi-double flowers in a range of pink shades through white. Grown from seed, and variable.
HT　70–75 cm (28–30")

**Prince Henry ['Prinz Heinrich']** Small, deep rose semi-double flowers. Compact habit.
HT　60–80 cm (24–30")

### × *hybrida*　　ZONE 5
(Hybrid Japanese Anemone)
These are outstanding plants for the late summer and fall garden. The branching stems of poppy-like flowers are superb for cutting. Blooms appear in single, semi-double or fully double forms, covering the spectrum of white through pink and rose shades. In time the plants will spread to form a solid patch, particularly when grown in a rich, moist soil. Good low-maintenance perennials. Mulch well for the first winter, especially if planted after mid summer.

HT/SP　60–120 cm (2–4') / 60–90 cm (2–3')
SOIL　Prefers a rich, moist soil.
BLOOM August–October
USES　✂❦❦ Massing, Borders

**'Alice'** Semi-double, light pink flowers. Compact.
HT　60–70 cm (24–28")

**'Andrea Atkinson'** Outstanding form with large, white single flowers. Mid-sized habit.
HT　75–90 cm (30–36")

**'Honorine Jobert'** Large, single white flowers, an excellent old historical variety. Very tall habit.
HT　90–120 cm (3–4')

Anemone × hybrida 'Honorine Jobert'

Anemone × hybrida 'Serenade'

Anemone × hybrida Queen Charlotte

Anemone × hybrida 'Whirlwind'

**'Margarete'** Semi-double deep-pink flowers. Mid-sized habit.

HT    75–90 cm (30–36")

**Queen Charlotte ['Königin Charlotte']** Large, semi-double bright pink blossoms. Mid-sized.

HT    80–90 cm (30–36")

**Rose Bowl ['Rosenschale']** Big single rose-pink flowers. Very tall.

HT    90–120 cm (3–4')

**'September Charm'** Distinctive single rose-pink flowers, darker on the backside of each petal. Mid-sized.

HT    60–90 cm (2–3')

**'Serenade'** Double, deep-pink flowers. Tall.

HT    90–100 cm (36–40")

**'Whirlwind'** Big semi-double white flowers. Tall.

HT    90–120 cm (3–4')

### *multifida*     ZONE 3
### (Cutleaf Anemone)

This is one of our North American wildflowers, found over a large chunk of the continent. Plants form a low clump of ferny green leaves, bearing a good display of small cup-shaped flowers in late spring, followed by fluffy seedheads during the summer. A nice addition to the rock garden or for edging, this will naturalize in wildflower meadow plantings, yet is also at home in the woodland garden. Easily divided in fall or early spring.

HT/SP    20–30 cm (8–12") / 30–45 cm (12–18")
SOIL    Average to moist, well-drained soil.
BLOOM May–June
USES    △✂❦ Borders, Rock garden

**'Major'** Charming buttery-yellow flowers, over silvery-green filigree leaves.

---

**Red form** This strain produces flowers ranging from soft-pink to deep rosy-magenta.

### *nemorosa*     ZONE 4
### (Wood Anemone)

Native throughout northern Europe, the Wood Anemone is a charming plant for the early spring garden. Clumps creep slowly to form a groundcover, studded with star-shaped flowers. There are scores of selections available to European gardeners, and a handful of them are beginning to appear here, ranging in shades from white through to pink, blue and violet. These combine beautifully with spring-flowering bulbs and wildflowers, particularly yellow narcissus. Once clumps get large they may be divided in early fall by digging and ripping apart into pieces. Becomes dormant during summer droughts.

HT/SP    15–30 cm (6–12") / 20–30 cm (8–12")
SOIL    Prefers a rich, moist soil and woodland conditions.
BLOOM March–April
USES    △✂ Massing, Woodland

### *pulsatilla* see PULSATILLA VULGARIS

### *sylvestris*     ZONE 2
### (Snowdrop Anemone)

Delicate nodding white flowers appear in late spring and intermittently throughout the summer, at least in cool-summer regions. Quickly spreads to form a dense patch, suitable for use as a groundcover. Good cover for spring bulbs.

HT/SP    30–45 cm (12–18") / 30–60 cm (1–2')
SOIL    Average to moist soil.
BLOOM May–June
USES    Ɱ✂ Massing, Borders

### *tomentosa* **'Robustissima'**   ZONE 3
### (Grapeleaf Anemone)

This is rather similar to a pink Japanese Anemone in effect, but even more vigorous and reliably hardy, even on the Prairies. Upright clumps of deep-green foliage remain attractive from spring to late fall. Light-pink single flowers are held on branching stalks well above the leaves. One of the showiest perennials for the late summer and fall garden. Plants will quickly spread to form a large patch.

HT/SP    90–120 cm (3–4') / 60–90 cm (2–3')
SOIL    Prefers a rich, moist soil.
BLOOM August–September
USES    Ɱ✂ Massing, Borders

## ANGELICA ☼◐
### (Angelica)

The traditional species grown is *A. archangelica*, usually relegated to the herb garden, but a stunning specimen plant for the border as well. Most of the garden Angelica are biennial or monocarpic — meaning they flower, set

---

seed, then die from exhaustion, usually in their second or third season. All prefer a rich, moist soil and a sunny to partly shaded site. Plants form a taproot and cannot be divided.

### *gigas*     ZONE 4
### (Red-flowered Angelica, Purple Parsnip)

A spectacular, bold-leafed specimen that forms a medium-sized clump of coarse green leaves. Large umbels of crimson-red flowers are held on tall stems for several weeks, starting in mid-summer. This always commands attention in the garden. Inclined to be biennial. Should be allowed to self-sow, seedlings are easily moved while small.

HT/SP    90–150 cm (3–5') / 60–90 cm (2–3')
SOIL    Prefers a rich, moist soil.
BLOOM July–September
USES    ✂❦ Borders, Tubs

### *pachycarpa*     ZONE 6
### (Shiny-leaved Angelica)

This is a bizarre and wonderful biennial species of Angelica from New Zealand, and quite new to North American gardens. In their first year plants will form a clump of large, glossy green leaves, a bit like a Cow Parsnip. The following summer an upright stem appears, bearing huge umbels of white flowers followed by big seed heads. A great textural plant.

HT/SP    90–120 cm (3–4') / 75–90 cm (30–36")
SOIL    Prefers a rich, moist soil.
BLOOM June–August
USES    ✂❦ Borders, Tubs

## ANTENNARIA ☼
### (Cat's-paw, Pussy-toes)

### *dioica* **'Rubra'**     ZONE 1
### (Pink Pussy-toes)

Forms a dense carpet of tiny, silver-grey leaves. Clusters of rosy-pink flowers appear briefly in late spring. An extremely drought-tolerant groundcover deserving of wider use. Trim flower stems off after blooming. Easily increased by ripping the patch apart into small pieces at almost any time. Native North American evergreen wildflower.

HT/SP    10–15 cm (4–6") / 25–30 cm (10–12")
SOIL    Well-drained soil. Withstands drought.
BLOOM May–June
USES    △Ɱ▲❦❧ Between paving stones

## ANTHEMIS ☼
### (Perennial Marguerite Daisy)

Hardy, showy members of the Daisy family. Best used as filler plants in hot sunny perennial borders. Although many are short-lived they will usually self-seed to form a patch. Excellent for cutting. Trim plants back hard after the first flush of flowers to encourage repeat blooming.

Anemone nemorosa

Angelica gigas

Antennaria dioica 'Rubra'

Anthemis tinctoria 'Sauce Hollandaise'

Gardeners often encounter other daisy-flowered plants commonly known as Marguerites. These are the Blue Marguerite (*Felicia amelloides*) and White or Pink Marguerite (*Argyranthemum*). Treat these types as annuals in most regions, unlike the perennial types listed below.

### *marschalliana*                    ZONE 4
### (Alpine Marguerite)
This species is an alpine or rock garden plant forming a mound of ferny silver-grey foliage. Showy bright-yellow daisies appear for several weeks beginning in early summer. Choose a site that is very well drained, particularly during the winter months or grow it in an alpine trough or gravel garden. Trim lightly after blooming and tidy clumps up a bit in the spring. Do not trim to less than 10 cm (4″) since this develops a woody base. Dislikes average border conditions.

HT/SP    15–20 cm (6–8″) / 20–30 cm (8–12″)
SOIL     Average to dry, well-drained soil. Dislikes
         winter wet.
BLOOM June–July
USES    Rock gardens, Edging

### *tinctoria*                        ZONE 2
### (Golden Marguerite Daisy)
Plants form a bushy mound of finely-cut, ferny green leaves. Lots of small yellow daisy flowers appear in early summer and these will continue for months, with regular deadheading. Divide selections every second year in the spring, to maintain vigour.

SP       30–45 cm (12–18″)
SOIL     Well-drained soil. Moderately drought-
         tolerant.
BLOOM June–August
USES    Borders, Meadows

**'Kelwayi'** Bright golden-yellow flowers with a mustard eye.
HT       60–90 cm (2–3′)

**'Sauce Hollandaise'** A lovely pale sulphur-yellow form, slightly more compact habit.
HT       50–70 cm (20–30″)

**'Wargrave Variety'** Soft primrose-yellow, a shade that blends with anything.
HT       60–65 cm (24–26″)

# AQUILEGIA ☼ ◐
## (Columbine)
Columbine are ever-popular old-fashioned perennials, available to gardeners now in a variety of sizes and colours. Both the flowers and ferny foliage are good for cutting. Although plants are short-lived (2–4 years is typical) they always self-seed freely and keep coming back. They also cross freely, so if you have more than one type to begin with, successive generations might be mon-

grels or amazing new gems, depending on your point of view.

Both the Columbine leaf miner (which tunnels inside the leaves) and sawfly (which devours the leaves completely) are now a problem over wide areas of the continent. In my own garden I fight with both, but basically I cut the leaves back at the first signs of damage in the spring and again in mid fall if necessary. Insecticides will also do the trick, but it often doesn't seem worth the bother. Cutting off all the leaves in the fall and cleaning up well around the plants is probably the best preventative approach.

### *alpina*                           ZONE 2
### (Alpine Columbine)
Glowing bright-blue flowers, fairly compact habit although not exactly dwarf, despite the name. Great towards the border edge.

HT/SP    45–60 cm (18–24″) / 25–30 cm (10–12″)
SOIL     Average to moist soil.
BLOOM May–June
USES    Borders, Woodland gardens

### *canadensis*                       ZONE 2
### (Wild Red Columbine)
Delicate, dangling brick-red flowers with yellow centres. Excellent in a woodland setting. A North American native wildflower.

HT/SP    60–90 cm (2–3′) / 30–60 cm (1–2′)
SOIL     Average to moist soil.
BLOOM May–June
USES    Borders, Woodland gardens

### *chrysantha*                       ZONE 2
### (Golden Columbine)
Large golden-yellow flowers with long spurs, long blooming season. Mildew-resistant. Reblooms reliably if deadheaded. A North American native wildflower.

HT/SP    75–90 cm (30–36″) / 30–45 cm (12–18″)
SOIL     Average to moist soil.
BLOOM May–June
USES    Borders, Woodland gardens

### *flabellata*                       ZONE 2
### (Japanese Fan Columbine)
A truly dwarf Columbine with large, waxy flowers, now in a range of pastel shades. Beautiful in rockeries. The especially handsome blue-green leaves are less prone to insect damage than other species.

HT/SP    15–20 cm (6–8″) / 15–20 cm (6–8″)
SOIL     Average to moist soil.
BLOOM May–June
USES    Walls, Edging

**'Alba'** Waxy white flowers.
**'Blue Angel'** A delightful combination of powder-blue and white.
**Cameo Series** This recent breeding breakthrough delivers a wider range of colours to this wonderful species. Flowers are in shades and bicolours in-

cluding white, blue, blush, pink and rose over a handsome mound of bluish leaves.

### **Hybrid Strains**                 ZONE 2
By far these are the most widely-grown Columbines, their large pastel flowers usually have long tails or spurs that create an effect like a flying bird. Plants are vigorous, the range of shades and bicolours truly amazing.

SP       30–45 cm (12–18″)
SOIL     Average to moist soil.
BLOOM May–June
USES    Borders, Woodland gardens

**'Crimson Star'** Bright crimson-red flowers with a white corolla, long spurs.
HT       60–75 cm (24–30″)

**'Dragonfly' hybrids** Full colour range in a mixture of blue, yellow, white, pink and red. Compact plants.
HT       45–60 cm (18–24″)

**'Irish Elegance'** A historical variety, recently reintroduced to commerce. Fluffy double white flowers have a pleated appearance, each petal tipped in shamrock green.
HT       45–60 cm (18–24″)

**McKana Group ['McKana's Giants']** Large, showy flowers in a wide mixture of pastel shades. Long spurs and widely flaring trumpets.
HT       75–90 cm (30–36″)

**Music Series** A newer hybrid strain, with a compact habit and grand display of large blooms. Flowers are usually bicoloured, including saturated shades of white, blue, pink, red, and gold.
HT       45–50 cm (18–20″)

### *viridiflora* **'Chocolate Soldier'**
                                       ZONE 2
### (Chocolate Soldier Columbine)
A novelty variety for those collectors out there. Maroon-brown flowers with

*Anthemis t. 'Wargrave Variety'*

*Aquilegia alpina*

*Aquilegia 'Irish Elegance'*

*Aquilegia f. 'Blue Angel'*

*Aquilegia v. 'William Guiness'*

contrasting green sepals, and a sweet fragrance.

HT/SP 45–60 cm (18–24") / 25–30 cm (10–12")
SOIL Average to moist soil.
BLOOM May–June
USES ✂ ➤ ♈ Borders, Woodland gardens

### *vulgaris*      ZONE 2
### (Granny's Bonnet)

This enormous group includes all of the old cottage-garden forms with small, frilly rounded flowers in a range of colours. These lack the long spurs that are featured in the Hybrid strains listed above. Especially nice are the dark maroon, blue and violet shades that always seem to appear over the years. These self-seed quite nicely.

SP 25–30 cm (10–12")
SOIL Average to moist soil.
BLOOM May–June
USES ✂ ➤ ♈ Borders, Woodland gardens

**'Barlow' mixture** A blend of all the stunning new double 'Barlow' strains, including white, rose, pink, blue, and black.

HT 60–70 cm (24–28")

**'Christa Barlow'** Pleated double flowers in a rich violet-blue.

HT 60–70 cm (24–28")

**var. *flore-pleno*** Mixture of double forms, usually including rose, pink, blue, purple, maroon and white. Eventually singles will also appear among the seedlings.

HT 50–60 cm (20–24")

**'Leprechaun Gold'** Boldly variegated foliage, the leaves streaked and blotched with chartreuse yellow and green, later fading to all-green. Deep-purple flowers.

HT 60–75 cm (24–30")

**'Lime Frost'** Leaves are dappled with green and yellow, flowers appearing in shades of blue, violet, pink and white.

HT 45–60 cm (18–24")

**'Nora Barlow'** Nearly spherical, fully-double quilled flowers in a unique combination of red, pink, and green. Totally unlike any other variety; looks like a miniature dahlia!

HT 60–70 cm (24–28")

**'Ruby Port'** A gorgeous deep ruby-red shade of Granny's Bonnet.

HT 60–70 cm (24–28")

**'William Guinness'** Small, single flowers in a striking purple-black shade.

HT 45–60 cm (18–24")

**Woodside Strain** The original variegated strain, with green and yellow marbled foliage. Woodside made the rounds among rock garden hounds for years before the rest of us learned about it. Flowers are in shades of white, red, blue and purple.

HT 45–60 cm (18–24")

## ARABIS ☀
### (Wall Cress, Rock Cress)

Popular spring-flowering perennials, often seen cascading over rock gardens and walls. Plants form a dense carpet of leaves, smothered with flowers for several weeks. All are evergreen. Reportedly attracts butterflies.

### *alpina* subsp. *caucasica*    ZONE 3
### [*A. caucasica*]
### (White Wall Cress)

The old-fashioned type, so widely planted in rockeries. Shear plants back lightly immediately after blooming to maintain a compact habit. Several selections are widely available. Fairly drought-tolerant.

HT/SP 15–20 cm (6–8") / 30–60 cm (1–2')
SOIL Average to dry, well-drained soil.
BLOOM April–June
USES △⋀➤♈✿ Walls, Slopes, Edging

**'Rosea'** Shades of soft to dark pink, a refreshing change from the more usual white forms.

**Snow Ball ['Schneeball']** Compact, mounded pure white strain.

**Snowcap ['Schneehaube']** Very similar to Snow Ball, forming a cushion of sweetly-fragrant white flowers.

**'Variegata'** Olive-green leaves are strongly edged with creamy-white. Looks attractive throughout the year. White flowers. Remove any plain green shoots before they take over. Needs excellent drainage.

### *blepharophylla*      ZONE 5
### (Fringed Rock Cress)

Unlike the mounding types, this species has a low, tufted habit forming a rosette. Flowers range in shade from

pink to magenta. Native to California, this is a short-lived species but will sometimes self seed. Needs excellent drainage. Fairly drought-tolerant.

HT/SP 15–20 cm (6–8") / 15–20 cm (6–8")
SOIL Well-drained soil.
BLOOM April–June
USES △⋀➤♈✿ Walls, Slopes

**'Red Sensation'** Slightly closer to a true red. Loads of flowers.

**Spring Charm ['Frülingszauber']** Bright magenta-pink flowers, fragrant.

### *ferdinandi-coburgi*    ZONE 3
### (Alpine Wall Cress)

A very low alpine species, slowly forms a low mat of leaves with short stems of small white flowers in spring. Mostly the variegated selections are seen in gardens. An excellent and easy alpine! Fairly drought-tolerant.

HT/SP 5–10 cm (2–4") / 15–20 cm (6–8")
SOIL Well-drained soil.
BLOOM April–June
USES △⋀➤♈✿ Walls, Slopes

**'Old Gold'** A stunning yellow-and-green variegated form, especially bright in spring.

**'Variegata'** [*A. procurrens* 'Variegata'] Reliable white and green variegation, with hints of pink during the colder months.

### × *sturii*      ZONE 3
### (Creeping Wall Cress)

Makes a very tight low mat of glossy-green leaves, bearing short stems of white flowers. One of the best varieties available. Especially useful as a groundcover for smaller areas. Fairly drought-tolerant.

HT/SP 5–10 cm (2–4") / 25–30 cm (10–12")
SOIL Average to dry, well-drained soil.
BLOOM April–June
USES △⋀➤♈✿ Walls, Slopes

## ARENARIA ☀
### (Sandwort)

The Sandworts are not well-known plants yet, but some of them make choice groundcovers for between paving stones, as well as fine rockery plants. They are cousins to the better-known *Dianthus*.

### *balearica*      ZONE 4
### (Corsican Sandwort)

Flat and mosslike in habit, with miniscule olive-green leaves and short stems of tiny white flowers. This appreciates the shelter of a partly-shaded rock garden and gritty soil that doesn't dry out too much.

HT/SP 2–5 cm (1–2") / 30–45 cm (12–18")
SOIL Average to moist, well-drained soil.
BLOOM May–June
USES △⋀➤♈ Rock Garden, Troughs

*Aquilegia v.* Barlow mixture

*Arabis caucasica* 'Snowball'

*Arabis ferd.* 'Variegata'

*Aquilegia vulgaris* 'Leprechaun Gold'

*Arabis alp. caucasica* 'Rosea'

*montana* ZONE 2
(Mountain Sandwort)

A very classy little alpine, like a refined *Cerastium* without the scary spreading tendencies. Large white flowers cover a compact green mat of leaves in the spring. Appreciates good drainage.

HT/SP 5–10 cm (2–4") / 25–30 cm (10–12")
SOIL Average to dry, well-drained soil.
BLOOM May–June
USES ⬛△▲▼ Walls, Slopes

*procera* subsp. *glabra* ZONE 3
(Siberian Sandwort)

This species is very hardy, forming a low cushion of green pine-needle type leaves, and bearing small starry white flowers in late spring and early summer. Good in the rock garden, also nice in trough gardens and mixed containers, and low enough to use between flagstones.

HT/SP 5–10 cm (2–4") / 20–30 cm (8–12")
SOIL Average to dry, well-drained soil.
BLOOM May–July
USES ⬛△▲▼ Walls, Slopes

# ARMERIA ☀
(Thrift, Sea Pink)

Thrifts form showy ball-shaped clusters of flowers complemented by narrow grassy foliage. Shorter varieties have long been used to edge perennial beds and in the rockery. Flowers eventually fade into papery everlastings. Taller forms have good fresh cut flower potential.

Joystick Series ZONE 3
(Drumstick Thrift)

A taller border strain, features large balls of flowers in shades of magenta-red, pink, salmon or white. Superb for cutting, fresh or dried.

HT/SP 40–50 cm (16–20") / 30–45 cm (12–18")
SOIL Average to moist, well-drained soil.
BLOOM May–July
USES ✂▲ Dried Flowers, Borders

*juniperifolia* ZONE 2
(Spanish Thrift)

A true alpine species. Forms a very dense tuft or bun of needle-like green leaves. Soft-pink flowers are held just above the leaves. Best planted in a scree or trough garden where it can easily be seen and admired. High cute factor.

HT/SP 5–10 cm (2–4") / 10–15 cm (4–6")
SOIL Needs very well-drained soil, scree.
BLOOM April–June
USES △▲ Walls, Troughs

*maritima* ZONE 2
(Common Thrift)

These are easy and rewarding rock garden plants. Flowers are showy over a long period, particularly if dead headed once in a while. Low grassy tufts of evergreen leaves. Tolerant of seaside conditions and also of road salt. Very drought-tolerant.

HT/SP 10–15 cm (4–6") / 15–30 cm (6–12")
SOIL Average to dry, well-drained soil.
BLOOM April–June
USES △▲▼ Walls, Edging

'Alba' (White Thrift) Pure white pompon flowers, slightly later to flower than the pink forms.

Dusseldorf Pride ['Düsseldorfer Stolz'] Long considered the best pink form, with rosy-magenta heads. Remove faded flowers for continuous blooms.

'Nifty Thrifty' (Variegated Thrift) Pink pompon heads set over a tuft of green-and-white striped leaves. A unique new introduction.

'Vesuvius' (Black-leaved Thrift) Unique form with smoky-purple grassy leaves, really setting off the bright-pink flower heads. Very similar to the variety 'Rubra'.

# ARTEMISIA ☀◐
(Wormwood, Artemisia)

These are highly valued for their silvery-grey foliage, which can be most effective in the landscape. A surprisingly wide range of heights and textures are displayed among the various types, making them suitable for many different purposes. With a couple of exceptions they are all drought and heat tolerant, preferring a well-drained site. The flowers are insignificant unless otherwise noted.

'Huntingdon' ZONE 5
(Huntingdon Artemisia)

A near-shrubby hybrid. Similar foliage to 'Powis Castle' but easily twice the size, forming a loose upright bush of silvery-grey. Grows fabulously well in the Pacific Northwest and likely over a much wider area. Cut back to 15 cm (6") in mid spring to encourage fresh growth – cutting back too early can lead to plant death. Very drought-tolerant.

HT/SP 90–120 cm (3–4') / 90–120 cm (3–4')
SOIL Average to dry, well-drained soil.
USES ✂▼ Specimen, Borders

*lactiflora* ZONE 3
(White Mugwort)

Outstanding for its showy plumes of creamy-white flowers in late summer, which always remind me a bit of Astilbe. Highly recommended as a cut flower! An excellent background plant for a late season display. Definitely prefers a moist site.

HT/SP 120–150 cm (4–5') / 75–90 cm (30–36")
BLOOM August–October
USES ✂▼ Dried flower, Borders, Specimen

Guizhou Group ['Guizho'] Even better than the species, with red-brown stems and ferny black-green leaves that are pleasantly musk-scented. The showy sprays of creamy-white flowers are a lovely contrast.

*ludoviciana* ZONE 2
(Silver Sage)

A species native to the plains of North America. The foliage is exceptionally effective, the leaves entire rather than ferny, and strongly silver-grey in colour. Plants are bushy and upright, spreading at the roots to form a patch or large clump, and doing so rather quickly in lighter soils. Good heat tolerance, generally remaining attractive throughout the season. The species itself is seldom available but there are several excellent selections, all useful for cutting fresh or drying. Some gardeners find the plant collapses in July when the tiny flowers appear. Don't be afraid to run for the shears and chop these back to about 8 cm (3") if this happens. Extremely drought-tolerant.

SP 60–75 cm (24–30")
SOIL Average to dry, well-drained soil.
BLOOM July–August
USES ✂△▼ Massing, Borders

'Silver King' [*A. ludoviciana* subsp. *mexicana* var. *albula*] Intensely grey leaves and stems, followed by a mist of fine-textured silver-white flowers that give a cloud-like effect. A vigorous selection hardy to Zone 2. Don't say I didn't warn you that it spreads.

HT 75–90 cm (30–36")

'Valerie Finnis' Like a compact version of 'Silver King', with very wide silvery leaves, and a less invasive habit. Some say this is the best grey foliage plant available.

HT 45–60 cm (18–24")

*pontica* ZONE 2
(Roman Wormwood)

A vigorous ground-covering species, with grey-green filigree leaves. Very feathery in appearance. Good choice

Arenaria montana

Armeria maritima Dusseldorf Pride

Artemisia l. Guizho group

Artemisia s. 'Silver Brocade'

Artemisia ludoviciana 'Valerie Finnis'

for containers. Can be fairly invasive, particularly in lighter soils, so site carefully. Very drought-tolerant and useful in difficult situations.

**HT/SP** 25–30 cm (10–12") / 30–60 cm (1–2')
**SOIL** Average to dry, well-drained soil.
**USES** ⋈✿❦☘ Borders, Massing

### 'Powis Castle'          ZONE 6
Like 'Huntingdon', this makes a bushy, upright clump of feathery, silver-grey leaves. An excellent non-invasive variety for the border, sometimes clipped to form a low hedge. Plants should be cut back to 15 cm (6") in mid-spring to encourage fresh bushy growth – cutting back too early can lead to plant death. Non-flowering. This selection is proving to be hardier than we first expected, so long as it has excellent drainage through the winter. Very drought-tolerant.

**HT/SP** 60–70 cm (24–28") / 60–70 cm (24–28")
**SOIL** Well-drained soil.
**USES** ✿❦☘ Massing, Borders

### schmidtiana 'Nana'          ZONE 1
(Silver Mound)
Perhaps the most popular grey-leaved perennial of all time. The feathery leaves form a beautiful compact dome. Valuable as a rock garden plant, accent, or edging. Plants should be ruthlessly clipped back hard to 5 cm (2") when they begin to flower (mid to late June), otherwise they will melt out, get floppy and generally look like the dog slept on them. Fresh new growth will appear in about two weeks. Very drought-tolerant.

**HT/SP** 25–30 cm (10–12") / 30–60 cm (1–2')
**SOIL** Average to dry, well-drained soil.
**USES** △⋈✿❦☘ Edging, Borders, Massing

### 'Silver Frost'          ZONE 4
(Silver Frost Artemisia)
This is a bit of a mystery plant, making the rounds for years as a selection of

*A. ludoviciana*, which it is not. Plants form a semi-shrubby mound of very narrow, feathery silver-grey leaves. Spreads a little to form a small patch in time. Excellent drought and heat tolerance. Trim back hard in spring.

**HT/SP** 45–60 cm (18–24") / 30–45 cm (12–18")
**SOIL** Average to dry, well-drained soil.
**USES** ✂✿❦☘ Specimen, Borders

### stelleriana 'Silver Brocade'  ZONE 2
[*A. stelleriana* 'Boughton Silver']
(Silver Brocade Artemisia)
A low, compact selection, fairly similar in appearance to Dusty Miller, with scalloped silvery-white foliage. Excellent for edging, groundcover, pots and hanging baskets. Trim plants back in early spring and again in midsummer to encourage fresh growth. Introduced by the University of British Columbia Botanical Garden about the same time it was introduced in England under the name **'Boughton Silver'**, which is now considered correct.

**HT/SP** 15–30 cm (6–12") / 60–75 cm (24–30")
**USES** △⋈✿❦☘ Massing, Edging

### vulgaris 'Variegata'          ZONE 3
(Variegated Mugwort)
A handsome variegated form of the herb Mugwort. This forms an upright, bushy clump that fits in well towards the middle to back of a sunny border. Leaves are medium green, brightly splashed with creamy-white. Flowers are insignificant. One of the best uses for this selection is in tubs or containers with other perennials, so the foliage can be enjoyed from up close. For best effect, cut back hard in late June to rejuvenate the plant with new growth. Plants should not be allowed to set seed, trim off flowers heads as they appear to prevent green-leaved seedlings from appearing all over your garden.

**HT/SP** 75–120 cm (30–48") / 75–90 cm (30–36")
**USES** ✂✿ Borders

**Oriental Limelight ['Janlim']** This new selection is supposed to be even more heavily variegated. Foliage is splashed and marbled with creamy yellow, some leaves completely lack any green at all. Do not allow plants to flower. Rated hardy to Zone 5 but quite possibly fine in Zones 3–4.

**HT** 90–120 cm (3–4')

## ARUM ❅•
(Arum)

### italicum          ZONE 5
(Italian Arum)
A unique and wonderful plant for the woodland garden. Big, exotic arrowhead shaped leaves make an appearance in the fall, remaining throughout the winter only to disappear by late spring. Creamy-white flowers push out

of the ground in May, followed by clusters of bright orange berries in the summer. A plant for all seasons! Appreciates some shelter from winter winds. The leaves of this species may be green or marbled with creamy white. **'Marmoratum'** has especially outstanding white marbling. **CAUTION: toxic if eaten/skin and eye irritant; wear gloves when handling.**

**HT/SP** 20–30 cm (8–12") / 20–30 cm (8–12")
**SOIL** Rich, moist woodland soil.
**BLOOM** May–June
**USES** △▲✂✿ Woodland borders

## ARUNCUS ☼❅
(Goat's Beard)
Moisture-loving plants, well suited to waterside or woodland plantings. All have creamy-white plumes of flowers in summer, and attractive lacy foliage, somewhat resembling Astilbes. Full sun is tolerated in cool-summer regions, so long as the plants get plenty of moisture.

### aethusifolius          ZONE 2
(Dwarf Goat's Beard)
The miniature form of the genus. Produces a delicate mound of crispy green leaves, with short forked spikelets of creamy-white flowers. Good rock garden plant.

**HT/SP** 20–30 cm (8–12") / 20–30 cm (8–12")
**SOIL** Prefers a rich, moist soil.
**BLOOM** June–July
**USES** △✿ Woodland borders

### dioicus          ZONE 2
(Giant Goat's Beard)
A rather monstrous border plant, spectacular in flower with its enormous creamy plumes the size of your head. Elegant lacy leaves form a very dense and bushy clump. This plant demands space. Inclined to sulk in hot summer areas unless planted at the waterside or in peaty, moist soil. Cut plants back in summer if they look untidy.

**HT/SP** 120–180 cm (4–6') / 90–150 cm (3–5')
**SOIL** Rich, moist soil.
**BLOOM** June–July
**USES** ✂ Dried Flower, Waterside, Borders

**'Kneiffii' (Cutleaf Goat's beard)** Leaves are finely cut, resembling a green Japanese Maple, which set off the creamy-white flowers. A more reasonable size for the smaller garden. Looks beautiful beside a tiny pool. Can be increased by division only.

**HT/SP** 75–90 cm (30–36") / 75–90 cm (30–36")

## ASARUM ❅•
(Wild Ginger)
The Wild Gingers are among the classiest-looking perennials for those gardeners lucky enough to have a moist, shady site. The most common types in gardens are the European Wild Ginger and the native Canadian Wild

Artemisia vulgaris 'Variegata'

Artemisia schmidtiana 'Nana'

Aruncus aethusifolius

Asarum canadense

Ginger (*A. canadense*). Also, a number of superb forms from China are becoming available now, some from collector's nurseries and a few in more abundant supply. These Chinese types, such as *A. maximum*, *A. splendens* and *A. delavayi* are mostly evergreen, and best suited to gardens in the southeastern US or Pacific Northwest. None of the Wild Gingers are particularly easy for growers to produce in pots, which explains why they can be difficult to obtain. Once planted they usually adapt readily in the garden.

### *europaeum*     ZONE 2
### (European Wild Ginger)
The most readily available species, and a low edging variety for shady borders. Foliage is rounded, dark green and brightly polished, forming a low mound. Brownish flowers are hidden underneath the leaves. This is a texture plant, contrasting beautifully against lacy ferns or the dark-leaved forms of Coral Bells. Will slowly form a first-class ground-cover for a small area and will even self-seed if you are very lucky! Established clumps are best divided in early fall or spring. Evergreen in Zones 8–9.

**HT/SP** 10–15 cm (4–6") / 15–20 cm (6–8")
**SOIL** Moist, rich woodland soil.
**BLOOM** May–June
**USES** ⬛〰️🌲 Woodland border, Edging

## ASCLEPIAS ☀️
## (Milkweed)
Not all the members of this genus are weedy, and a few are excellent summer-blooming perennials for the sunny border. Flowers are extremely attractive to butterflies but the foliage is critically important to the larval (caterpillar) stages of several butterfly species. This includes the Monarch, which depend solely on Milkweed leaves as a food source. The species in cultivation are mostly native North American wildflowers.

### *incarnata*     ZONE 3
### (Swamp Milkweed)
Only in recent years has the Swamp Milkweed started to be used to any extent in gardens. If the name doesn't put you off (and it shouldn't), the result is a big, bold-leaved clump of powdery-green leaves. Bears clusters of showy vanilla-scented flowers followed by the usual milkweed seedpods. Another magnet to butterflies, and superb as a cutflower. Sear the ends of the cut stems over a flame to stop the milky sap from flowing.

**HT/SP** 90–120 cm (3–4') / 60–75 cm (24–30")
**SOIL** Average to moist soil.
**BLOOM** July–September
**USES** ✂️🦋 Borders, Meadows

'Cinderella' Big clusters of dusty rose-pink flowers.
'Ice Ballet' Clusters of clean white flowers.
'Soulmate' One of the showiest forms. Clusters of deep rose-pink bracts hold tiny individual white flowers. These almost look like a pink *Achillea* but for the typical milkweed foliage.

### *tuberosa*     ZONE 4
### (Butterfly Weed)
Native to eastern North America where the clusters of bright-orange flowers appear along sandy roadsides in midsummer. Modern seed strains often include red and yellow forms as well. Plants prefer a well-drained sandy or gravelly site. Flowers are good for cutting, the immature seed pods are cut and dried for floral arranging. Removing faded flowers will encourage continual blooming. Butterfly milkweed comes up very late in the spring. Drought-tolerant.

**HT/SP** 60–90 cm (2–3') / 45–60 cm (18–24")
**SOIL** Well-drained sandy soil.
**BLOOM** July–August
**USES** ✂️🦋🌲 Borders, Meadows

## ASTER ☀️
## (Aster, Michaelmas Daisy)
These are reliable, showy plants mostly for a late summer and fall display. They have a wide range of flower colours and plant heights to choose from. The different varieties all have similar daisy-style flowers, and plenty of them! The modern types are mostly descended from common roadside species, selected over the years for improved form, colour and disease resistance. Often the parentage of specific hybrids is lost or unknown, so reference books commonly disagree on what to call them.

In general, taller cultivars should be staked by midsummer to prevent flopping. Pinching or pruning plants back by half (before July 1st) will encourage dense, compact growth and more flowers. Plants will grow best in a rich moist soil – too dry a location will invariably lead to problems with unsightly powdery mildew on the leaves. If mildew is a consistent problem each season, a preventative fungicide applied every two weeks starting in late May should help. Early frosts may damage the flowers in Zones 2–4, but in years with a mild fall the display is so wonderful that it's usually worth chancing. All cultivars are excellent for cutting.

### *alpinus*     ZONE 2
### (Alpine Aster)
Unlike their taller fall-flowering cousins, these low-growing plants put on a bright display of single golden-eyed daisies in late spring. Ideal for the

border front or rock garden. These are not long-lived but often will self-seed if conditions are to their liking. Drought tolerant.

**HT/SP** 20–25 cm (8–10") / 20–30 cm (8–12")
**SOIL** Average to dry, well-drained soil.
**BLOOM** May–June
**USES** ⬛✂️🌲 Walls, Edging

'Albus' White petals, cheery yellow eye.
**Dark Beauty ['Dunkle Schöne']** Rich violet-blue.
**Fairyland ['Märchenland']** A mixture of double and single flowered forms, ranging from white through pink to soft and deep violet blue.
'Goliath' Large flowers with soft-blue petals.
'Happy End' Rose-pink flowers, compact.

### *amellus* Violet Queen     ZONE 4
### [*amellus* 'Veilchenkönigin']
### (Italian Aster)
From Europe comes this summer and fall bloomer, producing sprays of large violet-purple daisies, each with a yellow eye.

**HT/SP** 45–60 cm (18–24") / 30–45 cm (12–18")
**SOIL** Average to moist well-drained soil.
**BLOOM** July–October
**USES** ✂️🦋 Borders

### 'Anja's Choice'     ZONE 4
A brand new hybrid, selected in Holland by famed perennial garden designer Piet Oudolf and named after his wife Anja. Plants are medium in height, forming a bushy mound of tiny green leaves and just loaded with masses of starry blush-pink flowers. Superb for cutting. Good mildew resistance.

**HT/SP** 60–90 cm (2–3') / 60-75 cm (2')
**SOIL** Average to moist, rich soil.
**BLOOM** September–October
**USES** ✂️🦋 Borders, Meadow gardens

*Aster alpinus* Dark Beauty

*Aster alpinus* 'Happy End'

*Aster alpinus* 'Goliath'

*Aster amellus* Violet Queen

### *divaricatus*   ZONE 4
### (White Wood Aster)

A wild North American species, widely grown in Europe. Medium-size starry white flowers are held on branching purple-black stems. Plants are shade-tolerant, especially attractive grouped among shrubs where they can spread as a low maintenance groundcover. Responds to pinching but this is seldom needed. Amazingly tolerant of dry soil conditions and competing tree roots.

**HT/SP**   45–90 cm (18–36") / 45–60 cm (18–24")
**SOIL**   Average to dry well-drained soil.
**BLOOM** August–October
**USES**   ✂ ⋒ ☕ 🦋 ⚘ Borders, Woodland gardens

### *ericoides*   ZONE 3
### (Heath Aster)

Another of our native roadside Asters, widely grown in European gardens and as a commercial cutflower. Plants have a bushy, mounded habit, with tiny leaves and clouds of small yellow-eyed daisies. Flowers are always in nice soft blending shades. Great as a filler plant in the fall garden and for cutting. Quite mildew resistant and tolerant of drier sites.

**HT/SP**   75–90 cm (30–36") / 60–75 cm (24–30")
**SOIL**   Average to moist well-drained soil. Tolerates dry soils.
**BLOOM** August–October
**USES**   ✂ 🦋 Borders, Meadow gardens

**Earlking ['Erlkönig']** Copious sprays of soft-blue flowers. Tall vase-shaped habit, but not usually floppy.

**HT**   90–120 cm (3–4')

**'Pink Cloud'** Soft pastel-pink flowers, mid-sized habit. RHS Award of Garden Merit winner.

**HT**   75–90 cm (30–36")

### × *frikartii*   ZONE 5
### (Frikart's Aster)

A hybrid group of Asters with a habit of blooming non-stop from summer through fall. Mildew resistant. Planting before midsummer is recommended in cold-winter regions. Inclined to be a little temperamental, but good drainage in winter is the key!

**SP**   60–90 cm (2–3')
**SOIL**   Average well-drained soil.
**BLOOM** July–October
**USES**   ✂ 🦋 ⚘ Borders, Meadow gardens

**'Flora's Delight'** Lovely lilac-mauve single flowers with a yellow eye. Compact habit and less inclined to flop than the better-know selection 'Mönch.'

**HT**   30–45 cm (12–18")

**'Mönch'** Lavender-blue flowers, a strong bloomer over a very long season. An excellent taller variety. Responds well to pinching in May or June.

**HT**   60–75 cm (24–30")

### *laevis* 'Bluebird'   ZONE 4
### (Smooth Aster)

A recent American introduction of a species native over much of the continent. Features strong upright red stems loaded with single violet-blue daisies in late summer. Good mildew resistance and tolerant of most soils. Should not need staking if grown in full sun.

**HT/SP**   90–120 cm (3–4') / 45–60 cm (18–24")
**SOIL**   Average to moist well-drained soil.
**BLOOM** August–October
**USES**   ✂ 🦋 Borders, Meadow gardens

### *lateriflorus*   ZONE 4
### (Calico Aster)

This species is seldom seen in gardens in its natural form, but a few superb selections have been made in recent years. Plants are tolerant of a wide range of soil conditions and have good tolerance to mildew. Leaves are tiny, the flowers also small but in abundance.

**SOIL**   Average to moist well-drained soil.
**BLOOM** August–October
**USES**   ✂ 🦋 ⚘ Borders, Meadow gardens

**'Lady in Black'** A good, tall arching habit that features leaves in a rich smoky-black shade. Flowers are white to very pale lilac, contrasting in a lovely way against the foliage.

**HT/SP**   90–100 cm (36–40") / 60–75 cm (24–30")

**'Prince'** Better suited to smaller spaces. This variety is similar in foliage and flower colour to 'Lady in Black' but with a much more compact habit. Stunning as a foreground to orange Crocosmia!

**HT/SP**   50–60 cm (20–24") / 45–60 cm (18–24")

### *novae-angliae*   ZONE 2
### (New England Aster, Michaelmas Daisy)

Some of the best cutting types are in this group. The taller growing cultivars form large clumps of upright branching stems that will require staking (or multiple pinchings), and are best used behind other plants as the lower leaves may wither early. Tolerant of wet soils. Watch for mildew.

**SP**   45–60 cm (18–24")
**SOIL**   Prefers a rich, moist soil.
**BLOOM** August–October
**USES**   ✂ 🦋 Wildflower, Borders, Meadow gardens

**Alma Pötschke ('Andenken an Alma Pötschke')** Warm, glowing salmon-pink. One of the best tall asters but Alma MUST be staked or ruthlessly pinched to prevent flopping.

**HT**   90–120 cm (3–4')

**'Hella Lacy'** Selected by noted plantsman Allen Lacy, and named for his wife Hella. Probably the best of the tall blue forms, with loads of big, single lavender-blue flowers. Very good for cutting.

**HT**   120–150 cm (4–5')

**'Pink Winner'** Medium rose-pink blooms, mid-sized habit. Pinching is recommended.

**HT**   75–90 cm (30–36")

**'Purple Dome'** Carefree, compact habit. Masses of deep-purple flowers. A superb introduction from the Mt. Cuba Centre in Delaware.

**HT**   40–45 cm (16–18")

**September Ruby ['Septemberrubin']** Deep ruby red. Very tall and needs to be staked. Not terribly mildew resistant.

**HT**   100–120 cm (39–48")

### *novi-belgii* Hybrids   ZONE 3
### (New York Aster, Michaelmas Daisy)

This species is a common sight along roadsides in the eastern part of the continent, and is extremely variable. In addition, it has been used to create a large number of hybrids that vary considerably in their height, habit and resistance to powdery mildew. Many of the dwarf types listed here are often included in the hybrid group **Aster × dumosus** but the truth of the matter is their exact parentage is seldom known with any amount of certainty.

Regardless of height, all these perform best in rich, evenly moist soils, with a sunny exposure and good air circulation. Given these conditions, unsightly powdery mildew infections will be far less likely to occur. Divide every year or two in the spring to maintain health and vigour. Fertilize every spring. Taller selections may be pinched to reduce their height if desired.

**SP**   30–45 cm (12–18")
**SOIL**   Rich, moist soil.
**BLOOM** August–October
**USES**   ✂ 🦋 ⚘ Wildflower, Borders, Meadow gardens

Aster lateriflorus 'Prince'

Aster novi-belgii 'Blue Lagoon'

Aster divaricatus

Aster × frikartii 'Mönch'

Aster novi-belgii 'Porzellan'

**'Alert'** Deep crimson red, very compact habit.

HT    25–30 cm (10–12″)

**'Audrey'** Single lilac-blue flowers. Compact.

HT    25–30 cm (10–12″)

**'Blue Lagoon'** Rich violet-blue flowers, mid-sized habit.

HT    40–60 cm (16–24″)

**'Diana'** Good mid-sized variety. Single soft-pink flowers.

HT    45–60 cm (18–24″)

**'Lady in Blue'** Semi-double bright lavender-blue flowers. Compact.

HT    25–30 cm (10–12″)

**'Little Pink Beauty'** Semi-double flowers in a bright pink shade.

HT    30–40 cm (12–16″)

**'Porzellan'** Shining pale-lavender blossoms, a very unusual and refreshing shade. Mid-sized.

HT    50–60 cm (20–24″)

**'Professor Anton Kippenberg'** Clear and bright blue, semi-double flowers. A longtime favourite.

HT    30–40 cm (12–16″)

**'Royal Ruby'** Deep red, semi-double. Mid-sized habit.

HT    45–50 cm (18–20″)

**'White Opal'** White flowers with a yellow eye. Compact.

HT    30–40 cm (12–16″)

***pringlei* 'Monte Cassino'**    ZONE 4
**(Florist's Aster)**
Widely grown in Europe and imported year-round for use by commercial florists. Only recently introduced to gardens however, but proving to be one of the best border forms in existence. The sturdy, upright clumps of tiny green leaves have a delicate texture all season long, developing nice bronzy tones in late fall. Masses of small starry white flowers go on blooming for several weeks, well into late fall. Seems tolerant of average to moist conditions.

HT/SP    75–120 cm (30–48″) / 60-75 cm (2′)
SOIL    Average to moist, rich soil.
BLOOM September–November
USES    ✂🦋 Borders, Meadow gardens

***sedifolius* 'Nanus'**    ZONE 2
**(Rhone Aster)**
Clouds of narrow-petalled starry violet-blue flowers, each with a charming yellow centre. Has a delicate billowing appearance in the border and, I think, especially handsome foliage. Always a reliable bloomer on the Prairies. Mildew resistant. In my own garden this contrasts smashingly well against *Heuchera* 'Palace Purple'.

HT/SP    45–60 cm (18–24″) / 45–60 cm (18–24″)
SOIL    Average to moist soil.
BLOOM August–October
USES    ✂🦋♀ Borders, Meadow gardens

# ASTILBE ☼●
**(Astilbe, False Spirea)**
Long considered to be the Queen of Flowers for shady areas, their fluffy plumes are a familiar sight in the summer garden. With the many new varieties available there is a much wider selection of flower and leaf colour, plant form, and bloom time than ever before. Their blooming season can easily be extended by choosing varieties with different flowering times. In Zones 5–6 the seasons roughly fall into **Early** (June), **Mid-season** (July), and **Late** (August).

All cultivars share the same need for a rich moist soil free of tree root competition, and a partly shaded location. The taller types in particular are heavy feeders; they should be lifted and divided every two to three years (in fall or spring), also fertilized in early spring and again after blooming. Remove faded flowers spikes and any tired-looking leaves throughout the season. Astilbes will also tolerate full sun in cool summer regions. Some gardeners enjoy leaving the dried seedheads for winter interest.

**× *arendsii* Hybrids**    ZONE 3
**(Garden Astilbe)**
Large and showy flower spikes appear over upright mounds of elegant, lacy foliage. Complex breeding has resulted in many modern varieties, offering flowers in a complete range from clear white to cream, rose, peach, pink, red and magenta.

SP    45–60 cm (18–24″)
SOIL    Moist, rich, well-prepared soil. These dislike dry shade.
BLOOM June–August
USES    ✂♀ Borders, Woodland gardens

**'Amethyst'** Violet-rose tending towards magenta, erect habit. Green foliage. Early/Mid-season.

HT    75–80 cm (30–32″)

**'Bressingham Beauty'** Rich pink, long lasting spikes over green foliage. Early/Mid-season.

HT    90–100 cm (36–40″)

**'Catherine Deneuve' ['Federsee']** Feathery rose-pink plumes, lacy green leaves. Early/Mid-season.

HT    60–75 cm (24–30″)

**'Darwin's Dream'** New compact selection with dense dark-pink plumes. Highly rated. Early/Mid-season.

HT    40–50 cm (16–20″)

**Diamond ['Diamant']** Mid-sized selection with pure white plumes that are long and somewhat diamond shaped. Mid-season.

HT    75–80 cm (30–32″)

**'Fanal'** Bronzy-red foliage in spring, later becoming green. Narrow spikes of deep maroon-red. Extremely popular selection. Early/Mid-season.

HT    50–60 cm (20–24″)

**'Flamingo'** Forms a tall mound of glossy-green leaves, with big arching plumes of deep flamingo pink. Early/Mid-season.

HT    70–75 cm (28–30″)

**Glow ['Glut']** Long and narrow dark scarlet-red spikes with a rosy cast. Foliage is bronze in spring. Late.

HT    70–80 cm (28–32″)

**'Peaches and Cream'** Pale pink to creamy-white flowers appear simultaneously over bushy green leaves. Mid-season. Possibly an *A. japonica* hybrid.

HT    60–75 cm (24–30″)

**'Showstar' mixture** A seed strain that produces a range of flower shades, including white, cream, pink and red. Good compact habit. Early/Mid-season but variable.

HT    30–45 cm (12–18″)

**'Snowdrift'** Clear snow-white flowers. Fine-textured green foliage. Early/Mid-season.

HT    50–60 cm (20–24″)

***chinensis***    ZONE 3
**(Chinese Astilbe)**
These have very dense, lacy foliage. Plants will spread somewhat to form a patch, the shorter varieties in particular are excellent for massing as a groundcover. Because they bloom after most of the Garden Astilbes, the *A. chinensis*

Aster novi-belgii 'Royal Ruby'

Aster novi-belgii 'Lady in Blue'

Astilbe × arendsii 'Amethyst'

Astilbe × arendsii Diamond

Astilbe × arendsii 'Bressingham Beauty'

selections are useful for extending the season into late summer.

**SP** 30–45 cm (12–18")
**SOIL** Average to moist well-drained soil.
**BLOOM** July–September
**USES** ⬚△🌢✂🏺

**'Finale'** Pale mauve-pink flowers, held just above the compact mound of leaves. Late.

**HT** 35–40 cm (14–16")

**'Intermezzo'** Salmon pink flowers, upright habit. Late.

**HT** 50–60 cm (20–24")

**var. _pumila_ (Dwarf Chinese Astilbe)** Makes a low, spreading patch, the best type of Astilbe for general groundcover purposes. Rose-purple flowers in short spikes. Will tolerate a fair bit of sun or dry shade. Undemanding. Late.

**HT** 25–30 cm (10–12")

**Purple Candles ['Purpurkerze']** A tall form with narrow spears of bright magenta-purple flowers. Late.

**HT** 90–105 cm (36–42")

**'Superba'** [_A. chinensis_ var. _taquetii_ **'Superba'**] Very tall spikes of lavender-magenta flowers held in a long, narrow spike. Late.

**HT** 90–120 cm (3–4')

**'Veronica Klose'** Deep rosy-purple plumes, elegant lacy leaves. Late.

**HT** 40–45 cm (16–18")

**'Vision in Pink'** A nice soft-pink companion to 'Visions'. Unusual bluish-green leaves. Midseason/Late.

**HT** 40–45 cm (16–18")

**'Visions'** Glowing bright mauve-pink plumes, elegant dark-green to bronzy leaves. Midseason.

**HT** 40–45 cm (16–18")

### × _crispa_ 'Perkeo'    ZONE 4
### (Dwarf Astilbe)

Unusual dark-green and crispy foliage. Short branching spikes of deep-pink flowers, appearing midseason/late. Good compact habit for edging or a shady rock garden.

**HT/SP** 15–20 cm (6–8") / 20–30 cm (8–12")
**SOIL** Moist to average well-drained soil.
**BLOOM** July–August
**USES** △🏺 Woodland garden, Edging

### _japonica_ Hybrids    ZONE 3
### (Japanese Astilbe)

Quite similar to the _A._ × _arendsii_ Hybrids, this group for the most part has big pyramidal-shaped plumes and vibrant colouration. Blooms towards the middle of summer. Good vigour and growth habit make these an excellent choice.

**SP** 60–75 cm (24–30")
**SOIL** Moist, rich, well-prepared soil.
**BLOOM** June–July
**USES** ✂🏺 Borders, Woodland gardens

**'Peach Blossom** [× _rosea_ **'Peach Blossom']** Delicate shell-pink plumes over glossy green foliage. Early/Midseason.

**HT** 50–60 cm (20–24")

**'Red Sentinel'** Very full scarlet-red plumes, held on red stems over a bushy mound of green leaves. Early/Midseason.

**HT** 55–60 cm (22–24")

**'Washington'** Bushy green mound with full and sumptuous white plumes. Early/Midseason.

**HT** 55–60 cm (22–24")

### _simplicifolia_ Hybrids    ZONE 3
### (Star Astilbe)

Another distinct group of hybrid Astilbe, developed in recent years mainly by British and German breeders. Most of these have a compact habit, the foliage is generally crispy or finely-textured and rich in colour. Well suited to mass plantings, providing colour in late summer when it is so often lacking in shade gardens.

**SP** 30–45 cm (12–18")
**SOIL** Moist, rich well-drained soil.
**BLOOM** July–August
**USES** △🌢✂🏺 Edging, Woodland gardens

**'Aphrodite'** Beautiful bright cherry to rose-red panicles. Somewhat coarse foliage. Midseason.

**HT** 30–45 cm (12–18")

**'Darwin's Snow Sprite'** Open and elegant white plumes. Very compact. Late.

**HT** 25–30 cm (10–12")

**'Hennie Graafland'** Like a taller, more vigorous version of 'Sprite'. Delicate arching sprays of soft shell-pink flowers. Midseason/Late.

**HT** 40–45 cm (16–18")

**'Pink Lightning'** Crisped bronzy-purple leaves contrast beautifully against pale-pink plumes. An exciting breakthrough in low edging types. Midseason.

**HT** 35–40 cm (14–16")

**'Sprite'** The first of this group of hybrids to become widely known when it was selected as _Perennial Plant of the Year_ in 1994. Spikes of delicate shell-pink flowers are held just above bronzy-green leaves. Dense and compact. Late.

**HT** 20–30 cm (8–12")

**'White Wings'** A new dwarf hybrid, forming fluffy plumes of white flowers that age to very soft pink. Mid-season.

**HT** 25–30 cm (10–12")

### _thunbergii_ Hybrids    ZONE 3
### (Tall Japanese Astilbe)

These later blooming hybrids differ from the _A._ × _arendsii_ hybrids in their typical large, weeping panicles of bloom. These are tall, and if surrounded by a low groundcover they can supply a superb specimen effect.

**SP** 75–90 cm (30–36")
**SOIL** Moist, rich, well-prepared soil.
**BLOOM** July–August
**USES** ✂🏺 Borders, Woodland gardens

**'Moerheim's Glory'** The tallest of the bunch. Long, drooping plumes of soft-pink flowers. Late.

**HT** 150–180 cm (5–6')

**Ostrich Plume ['Straussenfeder']** Luscious arching plumes of rich dusty rose. Really magnificent when full grown. Mid-season/Late.

**HT** 90–100 cm (36–40")

**'Professor van der Wielen'** Huge drooping plumes of white flowers. Large mounding habit. Mid-season/Late.

**HT** 80–90 cm (30–36")

**'Red Charm'** Cascading plumes of bright cherry-red, green foliage. Mid-season/Late.

**HT** 80–90 cm (30–36")

## ASTILBOIDES ☼ ◑
### (Rodgersia)

### _tabularis_    ZONE 3
[_Rodgersia tabularis_]
### (Shieldleaf Rodgersia)

A bold-leaved perennial for the woodland or bog garden. Produces very large, round umbrella-like leaves that look like something right out of Dr. Seuss. Big plumes of creamy flowers resemble _Astilbe_, appearing in early summer. Will tolerate full sun if given a rich, constantly moist soil.

**HT/SP** 90–120 cm (3–4') / 75–90 cm (30–36")
**SOIL** Rich, moist soil.
**BLOOM** June–July
**USES** ✂🏺 Dried Flower, Borders, Waterside

Astilbe japonica 'Red Sentinel'

Astilbe chinensis var. taquetii 'Superba'

Astilbe simplicifolia 'Aphrodite'

Astilbe chinensis 'Visions'

Astilboides tabularis

## ASTRANTIA ☼◑
### (Masterwort)

Adored by floral designers for their unique umbels of starry flowers, these are a bit like a refined Queen-Anne's-Lace in effect. Terrific "filler" plants for the border, their button flowers softening the effect of more bold-flowered companions. Dead-heading is recommended to avoid self-seeding. Flower heads are also great for drying.

### *carniolica* 'Rubra'          ZONE 4
### (Dwarf Red Masterwort)

A compact selection for the front of the border. This has rich maroon-red flowers, surrounded by green bracts, and lacy green foliage. Some authorities consider this to be a selection of *Astrantia major*.

HT/SP  30–45 cm (12–18") / 30–45 cm (12–18")
SOIL  Prefers a rich, moist soil.
BLOOM June–August
USES  ✄ ▼ Borders, Woodland

### *major*          ZONE 3
### (Great Masterwort)

A variable species, offering good-sized umbels of greenish-white flowers with a distinctive showy collar or bract that ranges in colour from white through green to deep blood-red. Loose clumps of dark-green compound leaves. Likes to self-seed if given half a chance, but not to the point you wish you had never planted it. Blooms over a long season when deadheaded regularly.

HT/SP  60–90 cm (2–3') / 45–60 cm (18–24")
SOIL  Prefers a moist, rich soil.
BLOOM June–August
USES  ✄ ▼ Borders, Woodland

'Claret' Seedlings from the popular selection 'Ruby Wedding.'Although these vary, the best forms are much like the parent,with a compact habit, rich red flowers and near-black stems.Some pink to rose-flowered plants may also appear.

HT  55–60 cm (22–24")

'Hadspen Blood' Dark blood-red bracts, possibly the darkest form that is readily available.

HT  70–75 cm (28–30")

'Lars' Good dark-red flowered selection with an especially long blooming-season.

HT  60–70 cm (24–28")

'Rubra' A variable strain producing forms with flower bracts in various shades of red through pink.

'Ruby Wedding' Rich ruby-red blooms, and a reliable repeat display in the autumn.

HT  60–70 cm (24–28")

'Sunningdale Variegated' One of the most sought-after collector's plants of the decade. The mound of brightly splashed green and creamy-white

foliage is the main attraction here, with a bonus display of ivory to soft-pink flowers. Foliage turns green by summer.

HT  60–70 cm (24–28")

### *maxima*          ZONE 4
### (Large Masterwort)

This species is quite distinct, with large rose-pink or white flowers that are surrounded by sharp pinkish-green bracts. Individual flowers look a bit like a *Scabiosa*. Plants spread underground somewhat, forming a patch. Considered by some to be the most beautiful species.

HT/SP  50–70 cm (20–30") / 45–60 cm (18–24")
SOIL  Prefers a moist, rich soil.
BLOOM June–August
USES  ✄ ▼ Borders, Woodland

## AUBRIETA ☼◑
### (Rock Cress)

### *deltoidea* Hybrids          ZONE 4

This extremely popular rock garden plant is smothered with brightly-coloured flowers in spring. The grey-green carpet of leaves will cascade over sunny banks or walls. Seed-grown colour forms will show some variation; buy plants in flower if you require a specific shade. Shear plants back lightly after blooming to keep them compact.

HT/SP  10–15 cm (4–6") / 30–60 cm (1–2')
SOIL  Average to moist, well-drained soil.
BLOOM April–June
USES  ◮ ⋀ ▼▲ Walls, Slopes

'Argenteovariegata' Leaves are strongly variegated with creamy-white and green; lovely as a backdrop to the rich purple flowers. Be sure to remove any all-green sections should they appear. Occasionally the foliage will mutate to creamy-yellow and green. Regardless, the plants are absolutely stunning in bloom.

'Doctor Mules' An especially good deep violet-purple form. May rebloom in fall in cool-summer regions.

'Royal Blue' Various shades of blue through violet.

'Royal Red' Red to rose flowers.

'Royal Violet' Rich shades of deep blue to purple.

'Whitewell Gem' Velvety purple to violet.

## AURINIA ☼
### (Perennial Alyssum)

Formerly included under the genus *Alyssum*, these popular spring alpines have been given a name of their own.

### *saxatilis*          ZONE 3
### [*Alyssum saxatile*]
### (Basket-of-Gold)

A springtime favourite, forming fairly large mounds of good silvery-grey foliage with contrasting yellow flowers.

Especially nice on slopes or walls. Fairly drought-tolerant.

HT/SP  20–30 cm (8–12") / 30–60 cm (1–2')
SOIL  Average to dry, well-drained soil.
BLOOM April–June
USES  ◮ ⋀ ▲ ▼ Edging, Walls

'Citrina' Like 'Compacta' but in a pale lemon-yellow shade, an easier colour to design with.

'Compacta' Profuse, bright canary-yellow flowers. The most popular variety.

Gold Ball ['Goldkugel'] A more compact habit, smothered with golden-yellow flowers.

HT  10–15 cm (4–6")

## AZORELLA ☼◑
### (Bolax)

### *trifurcata* 'Nana'          ZONE 6
### [*Bolax glebaria* 'Nana']
### (Cushion Bolax)

This bizarre plant looks soft and feathery in appearance but actually has a hard, brittle texture. Plants slowly creep to form a bun or cushion, at home in the rock garden or in paving cracks. Tiny yellow flowers appear in summer but these are hardly noticeable. Requires excellent drainage – consider growing with a mulch of pea-gravel. Performs especially well in alpine troughs or scree gardens. Evergreen.

HT/SP  2–4 cm (1–2") / 15–20 cm (6–8")
SOIL  Average to dry soil, best in gravel.
BLOOM June–July
USES  ◮ ⋀ ▲ ▼ Pathways, Edging, Walls

## BAPTISIA ☼
### (False Indigo, Wild Indigo)

Cousins to the Lupines, with similar spikes of pea-like flowers in late spring or early summer. These are sturdy wildflowers native to the Prairies of North America. Easy to grow in average sunny

Aubrieta 'Doctor Mules'

Aurinia saxatilis 'Compacta'

Azorella trifurcata 'Nana'

Astrantia major 'Hadspen Blood'

Astrantia m. 'Sunningdale Variegated'

border conditions, the plants are long-lived but resent being disturbed once established. Consider these as a substitute if you have not succeeded in growing Lupines. *Baptisia* are one of those perennials that might take a few seasons to settle in and reach maturity, but once established they can thrive for many years with a minimal amount of maintenance. Attractive to butterflies.

### *alba*                                ZONE 4
### [*B. pendula*]
### (White False Indigo)
A little-known yet beautiful species, the white spikes of flowers are held on charcoal-grey stems against bluish green foliage. Medium-sized habit. Very tolerant of summer heat and humidity, and a wide range of soil conditions. Great for cutting.

HT/SP  75–90 cm (30–36″) / 75–90 cm (30–36″)
SOIL     Average to moist well-drained soil.
BLOOM May–June
USES    ✂❮🦋🌿 Wildflower, Borders, Meadows

### *australis*                          ZONE 2
### (Blue False Indigo)
Tapering spikes of deep-blue flowers, followed by attractive curly black seed pods, sometimes used for dried arrangements. Olive-green foliage forms a dense bushy mound and remains attractive well into the winter. Moderately drought-tolerant.

HT/SP  90–120 cm (3–4′) / 90 cm (3′)
SOIL     Average well-drained soil.
BLOOM May–June
USES    ✂🌱🦋🌿 Wildflower, Borders, Meadows

### 'Purple Smoke'                    ZONE 4
An outstanding hybrid selection introduced a few years back by the North Carolina Botanical Garden. Plants form bushy mounds of grey-green leaves,

bearing bicoloured flowers of smoky violet-blue and purple, held on black stems. This should become more widely available over the next few years and is well worth hunting down.

HT/SP  100–135 cm (39–54″) / 75–90 cm (30–36″)
SOIL     Average to moist well-drained soil.
BLOOM May–June
USES    ✂🌱🦋🌿 Wildflower, Borders, Meadows

## BELLIS ☼◐
## (English Daisy)

### *perennis*                          ZONE 3
Widely used for bedding with spring-blooming bulbs, English Daisies are an old-fashioned favourite. Usually treated as a biennial or short-lived perennial, they sometimes self-seed. These perform best in coastal climates or regions with cooler summers. Great for spring containers.

SP       15–20 cm (6–8″)
SOIL     Average well-drained soil. Dislikes hot weather.
BLOOM April–June
USES    ✂❮🌱🌿 Massing, Edging

**'Habanera' Series** A fairly recent development, with double rows of petals surrounding a yellow eye. Shades include the usual pink, rose, red or white, but the most interesting is **'Habanera White with Red Tips'**, the quilled white petals painted bright red on the ends.
**'Monstrosa' Series** Flowers are double and extra large, in shades of white, pink or red, with distinctive quilled or rolled petals.
**'Pomponette'** Smaller button-type flowers in profusion. Compact habit. Shades include pink, red and white.

HT       10–15 cm (4–6″)

**'Tasso' Series** A recent improvement on the 'Pomponette' types. Series includes white, deep rose, pink, red and the stunning **'Strawberries and Cream'** with bicoloured pink and white flowers.

## BERGENIA ☼◐
## (Bergenia, Pig-squeak)
I have often observed that gardeners either really like, or really despise Bergenia – there seems to be no middle ground. Perhaps bold foliage is a turn-off to some, while others embrace this texture and use it to good advantage. These are terrific for mass plantings and for edging beds in either shade or sun. Many fine introductions have recently become available. Moderately drought tolerant.

SP       45–60 cm (18–24″)
SOIL     Average to moist soil, but these tolerate a wide range of conditions.
BLOOM April–June
USES    ✂🌱🌱▲🌿 Massing, Edging, Borders

### *ciliata*                            ZONE 5
### (Fringed Bergenia)
Much less commonly seen, this species is unique in having leaves covered on both sides with soft, downy hairs. Habit is deciduous. Short spikes of soft-pink flowers appear in spring. Not yet tested over a wide region, so may be hardier than we list.

HT       30–40 cm (12–16″)

### *cordifolia*                         ZONE 2
### (Heartleaf Bergenia)
Reliably evergreen in most climates, the large glossy green leaves take on rich bronzy-red tones throughout the fall and winter months. Clusters of nodding magenta-pink flowers rise above in early spring, and both these and the leaves are valuable for cutting. Tolerant of a wide range of soils and conditions, including dry shade.

HT       30–45 cm (12–18″)

### Hybrids                              ZONE 2
Fairly wide variations in flower colour and plant heights are the result of European breeders at work. Parks and gardens in Germany and Holland make especially good use of these durable plants.
**'Baby Doll'** Baby-pink flowers, reliable bloomer.

HT       25–30 cm (10–12″)

**'Bressingham Ruby'** Winter colour is deep burnished maroon and can be truly astounding. Typical magenta-pink flowers. Green foliage in summer.

HT       30–35 cm (10–12″)

**'Bressingham White'** Robust growth, snowy white flowers that age quickly to pale pink. Early-blooming.

HT       30–40 cm (12–16″)

**'Eroica'** Vivid magenta-purple flowers are held way above the clump of wavy green leaves. Stunning beet-red winter colour.

HT       30–45 cm (12–18″)

## BLETILLA ◐
## (Hardy Orchid)

### *striata*                            ZONE 5
### (Chinese Ground Orchid)
Arching sprays of magenta-pink flowers rise over slender, pleated leaves. This easy-to-grow deciduous orchid is a treasure for the shady rock garden. Also reported to tolerate sunny locations with regular moisture. May be overwintered indoors in pots in colder regions. The white-flowered form **'Alba'** is equally as beautiful.

HT/SP  20–30 cm (8–12″) / 20–30 cm (8–12″)
SOIL     Prefers a cool, woodland soil.
BLOOM May–June
USES    ▲❮✂ Woodland gardens

*Bellis perennis* 'Pomponette'

*Bergenia* 'Eroica'

*Baptisia australis*

*Bergenia* 'Bressingham Ruby'

# BOLTONIA ☼ ❀
(Boltonia)

## *asteroides*  ZONE 4
(Bolton's Aster)

These are similar in effect to a tall fall-blooming *Aster* or Michaelmas Daisy. Billowing clouds of small daisies appear in late summer and fall. Foliage remains disease free. Nice background plant for borders, growing especially big and tall in moist, rich soils. Good for cutting. North American wildflower. The selections below are more commonly grown than the species itself.

HT/SP 90–150 cm (3–5') / 75–90 cm (30–36")
SOIL Average to moist, well-drained soil.
BLOOM August–October
USES ✂ 🦋 Borders, Meadows

**'Pink Beauty'** Pale pink flowers and a somewhat lax habit that can be either intriguingly billowing, or messy-looking – depending on your point of view. May be pinched early in the season to promote bushiness, staked a little later or simply allowed to flop about. Found by Edith Edelman in North Carolina.

HT 120–150 cm (4–5')

**'Snowbank'** Masses of white daisies, good bushy habit that usually does not require staking. A completely under-rated plant that deserves more consideration for late season gardens.

# BRUNNERA ❀•
(Bugloss)

## *macrophylla*  ZONE 2
(Siberian Bugloss)

Low clumps of heart-shaped leaves produce upright stems of sky-blue Forget-me-not flowers for many weeks in the spring. Lovely woodland plant for moist, shady sites. A true perennial. The straight old species is a terrific plant, but the fancy-leaved forms are a real knockout and highly treasured by those who know and grow them.

HT/SP 30–45 cm (12–18") / 30–45 cm (12–18")
SOIL Prefers a rich moist soil.
BLOOM April–May
USES ⛰M❀✂☂ Massing, Woodland gardens

**'Dawson's White'** This form just recently arrived from England. Plants appear identical to 'Variegata', with green leaves edged in clear white. Said to be more sun tolerant without the bad leaf-scorch that plagues 'Variegata'. Some authorities say the two plants are actually identical while others maintain there is a difference in performance.

**'Hadspen Cream'** Leaves are heavily variegated with a wide creamy-white margin, at first glance very similar to 'Variegata'. Once the spring weather warms up, the margins take on more of an ivory then soft-yellow shade. Overall, this is just as handsome as 'Variegata' but with better

vigour. Flowers are the typical sky blue. Best with protection from direct sun, particularly in the afternoon.

**'Jack Frost'** A totally new look, with frosted silver leaves that are veined in chalky mint-green, almost like a fancy *Heuchera*. A magnificent backdrop to the sky-blue flowers. Quite sun tolerant in moist soils.

**'Langtrees'** Green leaves with subtle aluminum spots arranged in a V-shaped pattern. Blue flowers.

**'Variegata'** The original variegated form, with absolutely stunning leaves boldly edged in clear white. The sky-blue flowers are a wonderful contrast. This needs full shade or the leaves will scorch, particularly in warm summer regions. When your clump becomes large enough to divide be sure to keep the root pieces large or else some might revert to the plain green form.

# BUDDLEJA ☼
[Buddleia]
(Butterfly Bush)

These are actually shrubs, attaining a large size in mild winter areas. In colder regions the woody stems often die back severely, regrowing again from the base and flowering on new wood in late summer. Many gardeners just treat *Buddleja* like a perennial, cutting them back to 15–30 cm (6–12") each spring. By pruning them this way the flowers are produced on shorter stems where they can be easily seen at eye level, and associate nicely with other perennials in the fall border. The long wands of flowers are fragrant and attract butterflies and hummingbirds like crazy!

## *davidii*  ZONE 5

This species has given rise to numerous selections and hybrids, some of them naturally compact and well suited to border use. There is an excellent range of colours to choose from. Great for cutting. Moderately drought-tolerant.

SP 90–120 cm (3–4')
SOIL Average well-drained soil.
BLOOM July–October
USES ✂🦋🐦☘ Borders

**'Black Knight'** The deepest midnight-blue flowers. Tall.

HT 120–240 cm (4–8')

**'Dartmoor'** Unusual for its branching flower spikes, in a lovely soft lilac-purple shade.

HT 120–240 cm (4–8')

**'Harlequin'** Gorgeous leaves, variegated creamy-yellow and green, with magenta-red flowers. Fairly compact. Seems to be a little less hardy. Be sure to remove any all-green shoots when

they appear. A sport from 'Royal Red', and not terrifically stable.

HT 90–120 cm (3–4')

**Masquerade ['Notbud']** Recently arrived from England, this is an improved variegated type, the foliage heavily splashed with creamy-white and green. Wands of reddish-magenta flowers. Not as inclined to revert as 'Harlequin'.

HT 150–240 cm (5–8')

**Nanho Blue ['Mongo']** Naturally compact. Silvery-grey foliage, bright-blue flowers.

HT 90–120 cm (3–4')

**'Potter's Purple'** Quite new, and likely to become the most popular purple form. Long wands of deep violet-purple flowers on a tall plant.

HT 150–210 cm (5–7')

**'Royal Red'** Fairly compact habit, rich magenta-red flower spikes.

HT 120–150 cm (4–5')

**'Summer Beauty'** Terrific newer selection. Very large wands of deep-pink flowers.

HT 120–240 cm (4–8')

**'White Profusion'** Long tapering spikes of bright white, tall habit.

HT 120–240 cm (4–8')

## Hybrids  ZONE 5

Various hybrids with *B. davidii* and other parents occasionally occur and are listed here. Needs and plant care do not differ from the others.

**'Lochinch'** Stunning silvery-grey foliage, setting off a display of lavender-blue flowers, each with a tiny orange eye. Outstanding!

HT 120–240 cm (4–8')

*Boltonia a.* 'Pink Beauty'
*Buddleja davidii* 'Black Knight'
*Buddleja* 'Pink Delight'
*Brunnera m.* 'Langtrees'
*Brunnera m.* 'Hadspen Cream'
*Brunnera macrophylla* 'Jack Frost'

**'Pink Delight'** Good clear pink flowers in long spikes, tall habit.

HT     120–240 cm (4–8')

**× weyeriana**     ZONE 6
**(Yellow Butterfly Bush)**
These hybrids introduced yellow into the Butterfly Bushes, a shade that is otherwise lacking. Generally they are not quite as hardy.
**'Honeycomb'** Probably the best of the yellow forms to date, with extra-long spikes of creamy-yellow flowers with grey-green leaves. Excellent heat tolerance. Rated hardy to Zone 5.

HT     180–240 cm (6–8')

**'Sungold'** Long the standard in yellow types. Fragrant butter-yellow blooms and olive-green leaves.

HT     120–180 cm (4–6')

# CALAMINTHA ☼ ◐
**(Calamint)**
Competely unknown to most gardeners until fairly recently, these distant cousins to the Mints are well-behaved plants, lacking the invasive, spreading roots of their kin. Flowers are in short spikes, held above a low mound of fragrant foliage, full of nectar that will attract butterflies and bees.

**grandiflora 'Variegata'**     ZONE 4
**(Variegated Calamint)**
Stunning foliage is the feature here, the leaves splashed with soft green and creamy white. Short spikes of rose-pink flowers are attractive as a contrast. This plant spreads underground to form a small patch, but not in a troublesome or invasive manner. Nice accent for containers, or as a frontal plant in a border. Trimming the plants back hard after flowering will rejuvenate the leaves and keep clumps neat and tidy all

season long. Remove any all-green sections that might appear.

HT/SP     30–45 cm (12–18") / 45–60 cm (18–24")
SOIL     Average to moist, well-drained soil.
BLOOM June–July
USES     ✂◀ 🦋🪴 Containers, Edging

**nepeta subsp. nepeta**     ZONE 4
**[C. nepetoides]**
**(Dwarf Calamint)**
A superb choice for edging pathways, where the minty-fragrant foliage might be brushed on passing, releasing its scent. Tiny pale-lilac flowers are produced abundantly on upright stalks over an extremely long season. Nice frontal plant for the summer and fall border. Clumps are not at all invasive, although some gardeners report self-seeding and others not. It's been no problem in my own garden, and I would not be without this plant!

HT/SP     20–30 cm (8–12") / 30–45 cm (12–18")
SOIL     Average to moist, well-drained soil.
BLOOM July–October
USES     ✂ᴧ⋀⋅🦋🪴🥀 Massing, Edging

# CALTHA ☼ ◐
**(Marsh Marigold)**

**palustris**     ZONE 2
**(Common Marsh Marigold)**
Marsh Marigolds are native wildflowers over most of the northern hemisphere, and much loved for their showy single buttercup flowers that grace streamsides and other wet places in early spring. They grow best in a rich moist soil that never dries out, but will adapt to moist border conditions. Performs well as a pond plant. There are a couple of selections that are sometimes available. **CAUTION: all parts of this plant are considered poisonous.**

HT/SP     15–30 cm (6–12") / 20–30 cm (8–12")
SOIL     Rich, constantly moist to wet soil.
BLOOM March–May
USES     ✂◀△🪴 Waterside, Moist areas

**'Alba'** (White Marsh Marigold) Compact mound, pure white flowers. A delightful variation.
**'Plena'** (Double Marsh Marigold) Perfectly double golden buttercups.

# CAMPANULA ☼ ◐
**(Bellflower)**
One of the most popular groups of perennials, ranging in height from low creeping alpines to tall stately specimens for the back of a border. Their bell-shaped flowers seem to have a universal appeal, usually blue in colour, but sometimes ranging to lavender, violet, rose or white. The taller varieties are excellent for cutting. Most prefer a sunny exposure, although many are tolerant of partial shade.

**'Birch Hybrid'**     ZONE 4
**(Dwarf Bellflower)**
An outstanding variety, the trailing stems are smothered with nodding purple-blue flowers. Choice rock garden plant, blooming all summer long if deadheaded regularly. Not invasive.

HT/SP     10–15 cm (4–6") / 20–30 cm (8–12")
SOIL     Average to moist, well-drained soil.
BLOOM June–September
USES     ⋀⋀⋅🪴 Walls, Slopes

**carpatica**     ZONE 2
**(Carpathian Bellflower)**
Plants form compact rounded clumps bearing large, upturned cup-shaped flowers in various shades, blooming over a long period. Excellent for edging, they are also happy growing among rocks. Fairly drought tolerant. Deadheading regularly is the key to keeping these in bloom.

HT/SP     15–30 cm (6–12") / 20–30 cm (8–12")
SOIL     Average to moist well-drained soil.
BLOOM June–September
USES     ⋀△🪴🥀 Edging, Borders

**'Clips' Series ['Chips' Series]** The standard selections, available in different shades including medium blue ('Blaue Clips'), dark violet-blue ('Deep Blue Clips') and white ('Weisse Clips').
**'Pearl' Series** Just recently developed, with a more uniform habit than the 'Clips' types, and larger blooms. Available in blue or white.

**cochleariifolia**     ZONE 2
**[C. pusilla]**
**(Fairy Thimble)**
Forms a low creeping mat with an abundant display of little nodding soft-blue bells in summer. Very easy alpine plant, attractive growing in cracks and crevices or between patio stones. Divide clumps every two years in spring, to maintain vigour. Dislikes heavy clay.

HT/SP     5–10 cm (2–4") / 15–20 cm (6–8")
SOIL     Well-drained soil.
BLOOM June–July
USES     ⋀⋀⋅🪴 Walls, Troughs

**'Elizabeth Oliver'** Double mauve-blue flowers, like tiny little roses.

**garganica 'Dickson's Gold'**     ZONE 4
**(Italian Bellflower)**
An exciting, unique selection with bright golden-chartreuse leaves and loose clusters of lavender-blue flowers. Good rock garden specimen, appreciates protection from hot sun and regular moisture. Nearly evergreen.

HT/SP     10–15 cm (4–6") / 15–30 cm (6–12")
SOIL     Average to moist, well-drained soil.
BLOOM June–August
USES     ⋀🪴 Troughs, Edging

**glomerata**     ZONE 2
**(Clustered Bellflower)**
The most "un-bellflower-like" of any listed here, this species is popular for its lavish display of rich violet-purple

Caltha palustris

Calamintha grandiflora 'Variegata'

Campanula cochleariifolia

flowers, held in large clusters during early summer. Good choice for a lightly shaded border. Clumps should be divided frequently in order to keep them from wandering too far from their intended spot. Often benefits from a good hard pruning back as soon as the flowers have faded. These combine beautifully with any of the mounding forms of Cranesbill Geraniums, especially soft-pink or white ones.

SOIL    Average to moist well-drained soil.
BLOOM June–July
USES    ✂ Borders, Woodland, Meadows

**var. *acaulis* (Dwarf Clustered Bell-flower)** A nice dwarf form, useful for edging. Flowers are a typical rich violet-purple, but the heads are slightly smaller. Tempting for the rock garden, but the spreading nature might cause regrets later.

HT/SP   15–25 cm (6–10") / 30–60 cm (1–2')

**'Purple Pixie'** Mid-sized in habit, with great big clusters of glowing violet-purple flowers. Not floppy, yet the stems are a good length for cutting.

HT/SP   30–40 cm (12–16") / 45–60 cm (18–24")

**'Superba'** Rich violet-purple clusters, the best selection for cut-flower use but sometimes floppy. Plants usually need a hard trim back after blooming to tidy them up.

HT/SP   60–75 cm (24–30") / 60–70 cm (24–28")

### *incurva*     ZONE 6
### (Grecian Bellflower)
An alpine species from the Mediterranean, most at home in a rock garden or scree. Plants form a rosette of olive-green leaves, with upright stems of large light lavender-blue bells. Usually acts as a biennial, so plants should be allowed to set seed for future generations. Seedlings may be moved while small.

HT/SP   15–30 cm (6–12") / 15–20 cm (6–8")
SOIL    Very well-drained soil. Best in a rock garden.
BLOOM May–June
USES    ◢△▼ Rock Garden, Edging

### 'Kent Belle'     ZONE 4
Catching on quickly with gardeners, this terrific British introduction produces arching stems of dangling dark violet-purple bells. In rich, moist soil this selection may need to be staked but the height seems to vary from climate to climate. If spikes are cut back to the main foliage clump after blooming the result is a summer-long display. Great for cutting!

HT/SP   70–120 cm (30–48") /
45–60 cm (18–24")
SOIL    Average to moist well-drained soil.
BLOOM June–August
USES    ✂▼ Borders

### *lactiflora*     ZONE 4
### (Milky Bellflower)
Generally this is a tall plant for a mid or back-of-the-border position, but a few compact varieties also exist. Their large clusters of starry flowers bloom for many weeks. Best in part shade.

SP      30–60 cm (1–2')
SOIL    Prefers a cool, moist soil.
BLOOM June–August
USES    ✂ Borders, Woodland

**'Blue Cross'** A tall-growing selection with clusters of soft china-blue flowers that bloom for several weeks. Excellent for cutting. Terrific with shrub roses.

HT      90–120 cm (3–4')

### *medium*     ZONE 2
### (Canterbury Bells, Cup-and-Saucer)
Old-fashioned cottage-garden plants, valued for their showy display in early summer. Huge bell-shaped flowers are held on upright spikes, in shades of rose, pink, blue and lilac through white. Usually sold in mixed colours, but occasionally in separate tones. The regular single-flowered form is charming, but the double form **'Calycanthema'** has bizarre cup-and-saucer style flowers that are most intriguing. Superb for cutting. Biennial, sometimes self-seeding.

HT/SP   60–90 cm (2–3') / 30 cm (1')
SOIL    Average to moist, well-drained soil.
BLOOM June–July
USES    ✂ Bedding, Massing

### 'Mystery'     ZONE 6
### [*Michauxia* 'Mystery']
### (Mystery Bellflower)
Just recently introduced, this selection looks unlike any typical bellflower, bearing soft-pink flowers with narrow spidery petals in a star configuration. Leaves first form a low rosette, producing tall upright stems in early summer. Should make a good cut flower.

HT/SP   65–80 cm (24–30") / 30–45 cm (12–18")
SOIL    Average to moist, well-drained soil.
BLOOM June–July
USES    ✂▼ Borders

### *persicifolia*     ZONE 2
### (Peachleaf Bellflower)
Flowers are large lavender-blue bells, arranged on strong stems that are excellent for cutting. Blooms continue to open over a long period. A real old-fashioned cottage garden perennial. Often self-seeds but not in a troublesome way. Still one of the easiest and most rewarding perennials.

HT/SP   60–90 cm (2–3') / 30–45 cm (12–18")
SOIL    Average well-drained soil.
BLOOM June–August
USES    ✂▼ Borders

**'Alba'** Charming old-fashioned white form. Especially nice when grown together with the standard blue.

**'Chettle Charm'** Palest porcelain-blue flowers, rimmed with darker violet-blue. Outstanding in those popular pastel border schemes!

HT      75–90 cm (30–36")

**'Moerheimii' (Double Peachleaf Bell-flower)** An old historical selection, producing frilly double white flowers. Must be increased by divisions.

### *portenschlagiana*     ZONE 3
### (Dalmatian Bellflower)
Probably the best type for groundcover use. Plants quickly form a spreading patch of small green leaves, bearing soft-blue starry flowers in loose sprays. Dead-heading will help the show continue for weeks. Keep this away from delicate alpines that might be smothered.

HT/SP   20–30 cm (8–12") / 60–90 cm (2–3')
SOIL    Average to moist, well-drained soil.
BLOOM June–August
USES    ✂◢△▼ Walls, Slopes

**'Resholdt's Variety'** Flowers are a deep lavender-blue tone.

### *poscharskyana*     ZONE 2
### (Serbian Bellflower)
Also a trailing rockery plant, smothered with starry lavender-blue flowers. Spreads at a steady pace, though not as quickly as the Dalmatian Bellflower. Useful as a groundcover but also worth trying in containers. Grows well in part shade. Several good forms of this exist.

HT/SP   10–15 cm (4–6") / 45–60 cm (18–24")
SOIL    Average to moist, well-drained soil.
BLOOM May–July
USES    ◢△▼ Walls, Slopes

**'Blue Waterfall'** Just newly introduced, this form boasts a grand display of deeper violet-blue flowers, often repeating in late summer or fall. Shows good promise for mixed containers or tubs.

Campanula lactiflora 'Blue Cross'

Campanula punctata 'Cherry Bells'

Campanula p. 'Blue Waterfall'

**'E.H. Frost'** Flowers are porcelain-white with a pale-blue eye, overtop of light green foliage. Long-blooming habit. This one is my own personal favourite of any of the trailing Bellflowers.

### *punctata*          ZONE 3
### (Spotted Bellflower)
This species and *C. takesimana* are quite similar, forming a spreading clump of soft-green leaves and bearing upright stems with big, chunky dangling bells that are a delight. The invasive habit can be a bit troublesome in the border. I recommend dividing plants every second spring to reduce the clumps. Also worth trying in containers to help control the spreading. Nice for cutting.
HT/SP    45–60 cm (18–24") / 60–75 cm (24–30")
SOIL     Average to moist, well-drained soil.
BLOOM June–August
USES     ✂🌱 Borders

**'Cherry Bells'** Great big, deep rose pink bells.
**'Pink Chimes'** A newer dwarf selection, featuring large cherry-pink bells. More reliable repeat-bloomer, especially with deadheading. This shows great promise for containers and tubs especially.
HT       30–40 cm (12–16")

**'Wedding Bells'** Unusual double flowers in a hose-in-hose arrangement (one flower inside another). Petals are clear white on the outside, heavily spotted with deep red on the inside.
HT       45–60 cm (18–24")

### *rotundifolia* 'Olympica'          ZONE 2
### (Bluebells of Scotland)
A delightful native North American wild flower. Wiry stems hold airy sprays of nodding lavender-blue flowers. Performs best in cool-summer regions. Terrific cut flower. If grown in a rich border this one is always inclined to flop unless given some support.
HT/SP    25–30 cm (10–12") / 20–30 cm (8–12")
SOIL     Average to lean, well-drained soil.
BLOOM June–September
USES     △△✂🌱 Borders, Meadows

**'Samantha'**          ZONE 5
A new dwarf hybrid, with a compact and non-spreading habit. Plants form a low mat of deep green foliage, bearing short sprays of fragrant mauve-blue flowers in early summer. Remove faded flowers to encourage repeat blooming. Could well prove to be hardier than listed here.
HT/SP    10–15 cm (4–6") / 25–40 cm (10–16")
SOIL     Average to moist, well-drained soil.
BLOOM June–July
USES     △△🌱 Rock Garden, Edging

**'Sarastro'**          ZONE 4
**(Hybrid Bellflower)**
Terrific new compact selection, in every respect like a dwarf version of 'Kent Belle'. This produces upright stems of rich dark-purple bells, blooms over a long season when regularly deadheaded. Shows good promise in containers and near the border front.
HT/SP    45–60 cm (18–24") / 45–60 cm (18–24")
SOIL     Average to moist, well-drained soil.
BLOOM June–August
USES     ✂🌱 Borders

### *takesimana*          ZONE 4
### (Korean Bellflower)
Plants form medium-tall spreading clumps, with arching stems of large dangling bells. Flowers are pale lilac with dark maroon spots on the inside. Tolerant of dry shade. Plan to divide and reduce clumps every 2–3 years in spring, so they are easier to control.
HT/SP    45–70 cm (18–30") / 60–75 cm (24–30")
SOIL     Average well-drained soil.
BLOOM June–August
USES     ✂🌱 Borders, Woodland garden

**'Elizabeth'** An outstanding British introduction featuring large drooping raspberry-pink bells.

### *trachelium* 'Bernice'          ZONE 4
### (Nettle-leaved Bellflower)
A hose-in-hose double-flowered selection from England, for the woodland or border. Wide-open bells of bright purple, held on arching stems. Dislikes summer drought.
HT/SP    60–75 cm (24–30") / 45–60 cm (18–24")
SOIL     Average to moist, well-drained soil.
BLOOM July–August
USES     ✂🌱 Borders

## CARDIOCRINUM ☼
### (Giant Himalayan Lily)

### *giganteum*          ZONE 7
This monstrous plant is truly a sight to behold in summer, when the enormous, fragrant white lily flowers appear on stems that can grow more than 10′ tall. Leaves are large and heart-shaped, held mostly at the base. Requires semi-shaded and moist woodland conditions to thrive. Bulbs take several years to reach blooming size, then flower and die, leaving smaller side bulbs in their place. A plant this impressive needs the care and attention of an experienced gardener, who can rise to the challenge. Performs best in maritime areas with a cool summer climate, such as the Pacific Northwest. Terrific for cutting, but who would ever dare to? Watch for slugs.
HT/SP    250–400 cm (8–13') / 90–100 cm (36–40")
SOIL     Requires rich, moist woodland soil.
BLOOM June–July
USES     ✂ Woodland

**var. *yunnanense*** Leaves are flushed with bronzy-maroon, and flower stems are purple. Some say this is even more spectacular.

## CARLINA ☼
### (Friendly-thistle)

### *acaulis* subsp. *simplex* bronze
### form          ZONE 3
This is not a thistle to be afraid of, but a rather well-behaved, clumping perennial. Plants form a low clump of bronzy-green, prickly thistle leaves. Bears huge heads of silvery-white flowers with a rusty-brown centre. A very unusual cutflower, which can be used fresh or dried. Performs well in hot, sunny sites, even with poor soil. Combines beautifully with other drought-tolerant plants, such as Blue Fescue, Yucca, creeping Sedums, Artemisia or Lavender. Unique in containers. It really is a friendly thistle!
HT/SP    30–45 cm (12–18") / 30–40 cm (12–16")
SOIL     Average to dry, well-drained soil.
BLOOM June–July
USES     ✂🌱🎋 Dry gardens

## CARYOPTERIS ☼
### (Bluebeard, Blue Spirea)

### × *clandonensis*          ZONE 5
### (Blue Mist Shrub)
Although actually a woody shrub these are usually cut back each spring to around 15 cm (6") and treated more like a perennial. Blooms appear in the autumn on new wood. Upright stems hold clusters of fragrant blue flowers from late summer on. This colour is welcome in the fall border as a contrast to the many yellow and gold daisies blooming at the end of the season. Planting before midsummer is recommended. Fairly drought-tolerant, also noted to be a butterfly magnet.
HT/SP    60–90 cm (2–3') / 60–90 cm (2–3')
SOIL     Average well-drained soil.
BLOOM August–October
USES     ✂🦋🌱🎋 Borders, Massing

*Cardiocrinum giganteum*

*Campanula* 'Kent Belle'

*Campanula glomerata* 'Purple Pixie'

**'Dark Night'** One of the darkest forms, rich deep-purple flowers over greenish foliage.

**'First Choice'** A recent introduction from England, with luscious, dark purple-blue flowers.

**'Longwood Blue'** Sky-blue flowers, silver-grey leaves. Floriferous.

HT 90–100 cm (36–40")

**'Pershore'** New European form featuring bright-blue flowers over silvery-grey leaves.

**'Worcester Gold'** Bright-blue flowers contrast well against golden-green foliage, which holds a lot of interest in the garden throughout the season.

# CATANANCHE ☼
(Cupid's Dart)

### *caerulea*     ZONE 4
Papery lavender-blue flowers with a maroon eye. Plant forms a neat, slender clump of grey-green leaves. Moderately drought-tolerant. Short-lived, but will usually re-seed itself freely. Excellent for cutting, fresh or dried.

HT/SP 45–70 cm (18–30") / 25–30 cm (10–12")
SOIL    Average to dry, well-drained soil. Dislikes winter wet.
BLOOM June–August
USES   ✂✿ Borders, Dry gardens.

# CENTAUREA ☼
(Perennial Cornflower)

Sturdy, handsome perennials for planting in the border. Brightly coloured thistle-shaped blooms are long-lasting cut flowers. All types benefit from a hard shearing back after blooming. Reliable and long-lived, although some types have a tendency to self seed a little too freely.

### *bella*     ZONE 5
(Beautiful Cornflower)
The new kid on the block, this Cornflower is a great choice for rock gardens or edging. Plants form a mound or low mat of divided grey-green leaves. Flowers are soft lilac-pink, reblooming well if deadheaded regularly.

HT/SP 20–25 cm (8–10") / 25–30 cm (10–12")
SOIL    Average well-drained soil.
BLOOM June–August
USES   ▲✿ Rock Garden, Edging

### *dealbata*     ZONE 3
(Persian Cornflower)
Rosy-purple flowers appear in early summer. Foliage is grey-green and handsomely lobed.

HT/SP 45–75 cm (18–30") / 45–60 cm (18–24")
SOIL    Average well-drained soil.
BLOOM June–July
USES   ✂ Borders

### *hypoleuca* 'John Coutts'     ZONE 3
An especially attractive form with finely-lobed greyish foliage and masses of clear magenta-pink flowers over a long

season. This will usually rebloom in the fall if dead-headed. Excellent for massing in the border.

HT/SP 50–60 cm (20–24") / 45–60 cm (18–24")
SOIL    Average well-drained soil.
BLOOM June–September
USES   ✂✿ Borders, Massing

### *macrocephala*     ZONE 2
(Globe Centaurea)
Showy golden-yellow thistle flowers are held on stiffly upright stems. Superb for cutting, fresh or dried. Foliage is a bit coarse, and best used at the back of a border. I once saw a nursery attempt to make this plant more desirable by selling it under the amusing name "Lemon Fluff".

HT/SP 90–120 cm (3–4') / 60–80 cm (24–30")
SOIL    Average well-drained soil.
BLOOM July–September
USES   ✂ Borders, Dried flowers.

### *montana*     ZONE 2
(Perennial Bachelor's Button, Mountain Bluet)
Cornflower-blue blossoms are an old-fashioned favourite. A nice filler plant towards the front of a border. Will usually rebloom in the fall if cut back in midsummer. Very drought-tolerant. Inclined to self-seed prolifically, this actually has the potential to become weedy in the Pacific Northwest and possibly other regions. To prevent this, cut back hard after flowering.

HT/SP 30–60 cm (1–2') / 30–60 cm (1–2')
SOIL    Tolerates a wide range of soil conditions.
BLOOM May–July
USES   ✂✿ Borders

**'Gold Bullion' (Gold-leaved Cornflower)** An intriguing new selection, forming a bushy mound of chartreuse-yellow leaves with contrasting heads of sapphire-blue flowers. Remove any sections of the plant that revert to green. Divide every 2–3 years.

# CENTRANTHUS ☼
(Red Valerian)

### *ruber*     ZONE 4
(Red Valerian, Jupiter's Beard)
An old-fashioned cut flower, out of fashion for many years but now once again being enjoyed by gardeners who appreciate plants that are easy and fool-proof. Large rounded clusters of fragrant rosy-red flowers appear for many weeks, beginning in early summer. Plants are upright and bushy. Sometimes short-lived, but will self-seed. Moderately drought-tolerant. Does especially well in high lime soils. A favourite of butterflies. Soft-pink and white forms may also begin to appear in the garden.

HT/SP 30–90 cm (1–3') / 30–45 cm (12–18")
SOIL    Average to dry well-drained soil.
BLOOM June–September
USES   ✂🦋✿ Borders, Slopes, Walls

# CERASTIUM ☼
(Snow-in-Summer)

### *alpinum* var. *lanatum*     ZONE 2
(Woolly Snow-in-Summer)
Quite different from the common Snow-in-Summer, this makes a very small cushion of fuzzy olive-green leaves that beg to be touched. Short stems of tiny white star flowers appear in early summer. Best in a scree garden or alpine trough. Divide every 2–3 years to maintain vigour. Likes growing in gravel. Evergreen.

HT/SP 5–8 cm (2–3") / 15–30 cm (6–12")
SOIL    Average to dry, well-drained soil. Dislikes winter wet.
BLOOM May–June
USES   ▲▼✿ Rock garden, Troughs

### *tomentosum*     ZONE 1
(Snow-in-Summer)
In a carefully chosen location this can always be depended upon to form a vigorous, spreading mat of bright silvery-grey leaves, smothered with white flowers in early summer. Spreads quickly, so is best used as a ground-cover in difficult places like dry, sunny slopes. Not recommended for rock gardens! Very drought-tolerant. Shear plants back after blooming to keep them dense and compact. Evergreen.

HT/SP 15–20 cm (6–8") / 60–75 cm (24–30")
SOIL    Average to dry, well-drained soil.
BLOOM May–June
USES   ∿▲▼✿ Slopes, Walls

*Caryopteris* × 'Worcester Gold'

*Catananche caerulea*

*Centaurea bella*

*Cerastium alpinum* var. *lanatum*

## CERATOSTIGMA ☼◑
**(Blue Leadwort, Plumbago)**

***plumbaginoides***                    ZONE 5

An unusual low-growing perennial, valuable for late summer and fall display. Flowers are brilliant blue, the foliage turning from green to maroon-red in late fall. Nice as a ground cover or at the front of the border. Needs a winter mulch in colder areas. Planting before midsummer is strongly recommended. Makes an interesting and colourful underplanting to either Colchicums or Magic Lilies (*Lycoris*).

**HT/SP**  20–30 cm (8–12") / 45–60 cm (18–24")
**SOIL**    Average well-drained soil. Dislikes winter wet.
**BLOOM** August–October
**USES**   ◬❦❦❦ Massing, Edging, Borders

## CHAMAEMELUM ☼◑
**(Chamomile, Camomile)**

***nobile***                            ZONE 4
[*Anthemis nobilis*]
**(Creeping Chamomile, Roman Chamomile)**

Sometimes used as a herb, this is delightful when grown as an ornamental edging or groundcover for hot, dry sunny sites. Plants form a low, evergreen mat of ferny leaves, bearing small white daisy flowers in early summer. Flowers can be dried and used for tea. The foliage is pleasantly fragrant. An excellent choice for a lawn substitute but plants should be mowed or clipped back hard after blooming to maintain a compact habit. Easily divided in spring or early fall by digging up and ripping apart into smaller pieces. Evergreen in mild winter regions.

**HT/SP**  10–15 cm (4–6") / 25–30 cm (10–12")
**SOIL**    Average to dry, well-drained soil.
**BLOOM** June–July
**USES**   ◬❦❦❦❦❦ Edging, Lawn substitute

**'Flore Pleno' (Double-flowered Chamomile)** An antique variety with fluffy double white flowers that hardly even look like daisies. Same foliage and growing habit as the species.

## CHEIRANTHUS see ERYSIMUM

## CHELONE ☼◑
**(Turtlehead)**

Turtleheads are native to eastern North America, where they delight in finding moist spots along streams and ponds. Plants are late to emerge in spring but form an attractive clump of dark-green leaves, finally rising upright and blooming towards late summer. Valuable for cutting, these adapt readily to average border conditions. Attractive to butterflies.

**SP**     60–75 cm (24–30")
**SOIL**    Average, moist or wet soil.
**BLOOM** August–October
**USES**   ✂❦❦ Borders, Waterside

***lyonii* 'Hot Lips'**                 ZONE 3
**(Pink Turtlehead)**

Quite similar to *C. obliqua* in habit and form, this selection has shiny green leaves that begin the season with a bronzed appearance. Produces rosy-pink spikes of flowers.

**HT**     60–90 cm (2–3')

***obliqua***                           ZONE 3
**(Pink Turtlehead)**

Stiff spikes of rose-pink flowers, blooming over a long period in late summer and fall. This is one of those plants that does not attract much attention until it blooms, then suddenly everybody wants to know what it is. Long-lived and reliable.

**HT**     60–90 cm (2–3')

**'Alba' (White Turtlehead)** A beautiful white-flowered selection, especially nice in combination with the pink forms. Some authorities consider this to actually be *Chelone glabra*.

## CHIASTOPHYLLUM ◑
**(Cotyledon)**

***oppositifolium***                    ZONE 5
[*Cotyledon simplicifolia*]
Finally rescued from the ranks of obscurity, this is a charming little woodland succulent, with dangling chains of bright-yellow flowers over succulent green leaves. Looks very much like a *Sedum*. Will cascade nicely over rocks and walls. An unusual and easy alpine plant for a shaded rock garden. Does well in containers. Evergreen.

**HT/SP**  15–20 cm (6–8") / 25–30 cm (10–12")
**SOIL**    Well-drained soil. Dislikes hot sun.
**BLOOM** May–July
**USES**   ◬❦❦ Edging, Walls

**'Jim's Pride' (Variegated Cotyledon)** Just beginning to make the rounds now, this delightful form has leaves that are edged in creamy yellow, with the usual bright-yellow flowers.

## CHRYSANTHEMUM ☼◑
**(Mum, Daisy, Chrysanthemum)**

A few years ago the genus *Chrysanthemum* was split up into several new genera – including the familiar Garden Mums, which briefly became *Dendranthema* before being restored back to their old, familiar and pronounceable name. For convenience, we have included cross-references here for those species that have been affected by name changes. **CAUTION: may cause skin allergy. Wear gloves when handling.**

***coccineum* see TANACETUM coccineum**

**Hybrids**                             ZONE 5
[*Chrysanthemum* × *morifolium*, *Dendranthema* × *grandiflorum*]
**(Garden Mum, Fall Chrysanthemum, Korean Mum)**

Fall-blooming Mums have been enormously popular for years, and each season there are always new introductions that broaden the already wide scope of colours and flower shapes. Modern Mum breeding is aimed primarily at creating plants that look good in the pots when you purchase them. In other words, the goal is to produce a plant that responds well to commercial production, with much less consideration given to hardiness and performance for future years. Many gardeners attempt to overwinter the big, husky plants they purchase in the autumn, which leads to mixed results more often than not. Plants that survive the experience need to be pinched regularly the following summer or the result is a tall, leggy-looking thing that bears little resemblance to the dense, dome-shaped cushion of blooms that the gardener hoped to end the season with.

   Pinching is quite simple; start when summer truly arrives – early June or so – and simply take hedge shears and trim the whole plant back to about 10 cm (4"). A second pinching about 3 or 4 weeks later, this time trimming the whole plant back to 15–18 cm (6–7") will result in loads of blooms and a dense, bushy habit. In most regions, stop pinching in early July or flowering might be delayed until too late, resulting in damage by fall frosts. Mums are also heavy feeders, and a regular dose

*Cerastium tomentosum*

*Chiastophyllum oppositifolium 'Jim's Pride'*

*Chamaemelum nobile 'Flore Pleno'*

*Chelone obliqua*

of 5-10-5 (or a similar formulation highest in the middle number) will make a huge difference. Watch for signs of spider mites and aphids, controlling as soon as you notice them. If all of this sounds like a big hassle, do what I do and just buy new ones each fall, then throw them out! Mums are usually very reasonable in price and give you weeks of bloom.

Unlike the typical modern garden mums, those listed below are vigorous older varieties that have stood the test of time. Plants spread to form a clump, and should be divided in the spring every year or two to maintain vigour. Pinch as for regular garden mums, one to three times between spring and mid-July. In addition, look for some of the older selections by Agriculture Canada known as the Morden Series or a similar range from the University of Minnesota known as the Minn Series. Both of these series have proven to be more reliable in short summer regions.

SP　　45–60 cm (18–24")
SOIL　　Average to rich, well-drained soil.
BLOOM September–November
USES　 ✂❦🦋 Borders

**'Mei-kyo'** Small deep-rose double pompon flowers with a yellow centre. Late blooming.
HT　　60 cm (2')

**'Sheffield'** ['Hillside Pink'] Soft-pink single daisy flowers with a yellow eye.
HT　　60–70 cm (24–28")

*nipponicum* see
NIPPONANTHEMUM
*pacificum* see AJANIA
*parthenium* see TANACETUM
parthenium

× *rubellum* **Hybrids**　　ZONE 3
[*Dendranthema zawadskii*]
Large, fragrant single daisies are held in loose sprays. Plants form a densely branching clump. Easy and reliable border selections, blooming several weeks ahead of fall Mums. Plants will be more compact if pinched back by half in early June. Very few selections from this hybrid group are still in existence.
HT/SP　60–75 cm (24–30") / 60–90 cm (2–3')
SOIL　　Average well-drained soil.
BLOOM July–September
USES　 ✂❦🦋 Borders

**'Clara Curtis'** Large, deep-pink single flowers with a yellow eye.
**'Mary Stoker'** Golden-apricot flowers, fading to peach. A warm tone that blends well with most other colours.

× *superbum* see
LEUCANTHEMUM

*weyrichii*　　　　　　ZONE 3
[*Dendranthema weyrichii*]
**(Dwarf Chrysanthemum)**
A low, creeping species, in effect like a dwarf garden mum. Flowers are large yellow-centred single daisies. These usually bloom in early fall.
HT/SP　25–30 cm (10–12") / 45–60 cm (18–24")
SOIL　　Well-drained soil
BLOOM September–October
USES　 ◮❦<❦🦋 Edging, Massing

**'White Bomb'** Creamy-white flowers, fading to pale pink. Excellent vigour.
**'Pink Bomb'** is similar, but a darker rosy-pink shade.

# CHRYSOGONUM ☼ •
**(Golden Star)**

*virginianum*　　　　　ZONE 5
This is a useful little groundcover, tolerating shady locations and spreading to form a low patch of green foliage, studded with yellow star-shaped flowers for many weeks. A native North American wildflower. Appreciates a site sheltered from winds, and an evenly moist soil. Evergreen in mild winter regions.
HT/SP　15–20 cm (6–8") / 30–45 cm (12–18")
SOIL　　Moist, well-drained soil.
BLOOM May-July
USES　 ◮ᐱᴡ▲❦ Borders, Woodland gardens

# CIMICIFUGA ☼ ◐
**(Bugbane)**

The good news is that many interesting and unusual forms of Bugbane are now readily available here in North America, thanks to the modern wonders of tissue culture. The bad news – more name changes seem very likely, as botanists appear to be settling on moving these all into the closely-related genus *Actaea*. For now, we are listing them here under the old name while the debate continues to run its course.

Bugbanes form handsome, lacy clumps of foliage similar to *Astilbe*, but flowers are held on tall stems in a bottle-brush spike. Good for late summer and fall interest. All types prefer a rich, moist humus-rich soil and a woodland setting. Bugbane will take a few years to settle in and reach a mature size. Avoid disturbing established clumps.
SP　　60–75 cm (24–30")
SOIL　　Likes a rich, moist soil. Dislikes greedy tree roots.
BLOOM August–October
USES　 ✂<❦ Woodland, Borders

*racemosa*　　　　　　ZONE 3
[*Actaea racemosa*]
**(Black Snakeroot, American Bugbane)**
Tall spikes of ivory-white flowers in mid to late summer. Fruit capsules remain attractive into early winter. A wildflower,

native to damp forests of eastern North America.
HT　　120–150 cm (4–5')

*simplex*　　　　　　ZONE 3
[*Actaea simplex, C. ramosa*]
**(Branched Bugbane, Kamchatka Bugbane)**
The species itself is not often seen in gardens, but several excellent selections are now available, with either green or purple to black foliage. Native to China and neighbouring Russia, these prefer damp woodland conditions. This species and its selections bloom a little later than our own native types, generally in September and October. Most have delightfully fragrant flowers. These are proving to be exceedingly hardy, even on the Canadian Prairies.
HT　　150–180 cm (5–6')

**Atropurpurea Group (Purple-leaved Bugbane)** The first dark-leaved type available, this is generally grown from seed and quite variable in it's depth of foliage colour. Select out the darkest ones, or enjoy a range of shades. Largely surpassed now by superior selections.
**'Brunette' (Black-leaved Bugbane)** An early colour breakthrough and still a wonderful selection. Foliage is deep bronzy-purple, the flowers pale-pink and exceedingly fragrant. 'Brunette' seems to colour best with morning sun, or even all-day sun in cool regions when given plenty of moisture.
**'Hillside Black Beauty' (Black-leaved Bugbane)** Just when we all thought 'Brunette' was the ultimate in black, along came this even darker-leaved selection. Planted side-by-side, this clone wins the prize hands down and makes poor old 'Brunette' look like cafe au lait! This difference is especially significant in

*Cimicifuga simplex* 'Hillside Black Beauty'

*Chrysanthemum* 'Mei-kyo'

*Cimicifuga simplex* 'Brunette'

hot climates. Flowers are pale pink and also fragrant. Superb in mixed container plantings.

**'White Pearl'** [*Actaea matsumurae* **'White Pearl'**] Tall bottlebrush spikes of creamy-white flowers are held above light green, lacy leaves. A nice background plant for the fall border, and excellent for cutting. Some people consider this selection to have an unpleasant fragrance. Although hardy in many colder regions, the flowers appear so late they are often damaged by early frosts.

HT      90–120 cm (3–4')

## CLEMATIS ☼☀
### (Clematis)

Although the flashy, large-flowered hybrid types are great favourites, the smaller flowering species listed here are valuable garden plants as well, deserving of wider use. Some of these are woody climbing vines. Others are sprawling perennials that die back to the ground each year, leaning on the nearest shrub or stake in the border for support.

### *heracleifolia*     ZONE 3
### (Blue Bush Clematis)

Not a climbing type, but more of a vigorous bush that benefits from a small teepee or perhaps a peony ring to hold it upright. The fragrant flowers are the colour of blue hyacinths, appearing in late summer. Cut the tops back to 10 cm (4") in early spring. Several named selections exist, including 'Davidiana', 'Wyevale', 'Alan Bloom' and others. Any of them are excellent and usually long lived. Clumps may be divided in early spring.

*Clematis heracleifolia*      *Clematis tangutica*

*Clematis recta* 'Purpurea'

HT/SP   90 cm (3') / 60–90 cm (2–3')
SOIL      Prefers a rich, moist soil.
BLOOM August–September
USES     ✄ Borders

### *integrifolia*     ZONE 2
### (Solitary Clematis)

Another non-climbing species, best in a sunny border where it will form a sprawling clump. Nodding, urn-shaped flowers are in shades of rich indigo blue through to soft blue or even pink, followed by fluffy seed heads. Plant this where it can sprawl up or over a shrub, or plan on staking it. Cut back to the ground in late fall or early spring.

HT/SP   60–90 cm (2–3') / 60–75 cm (24–30")
SOIL      Prefers a rich, moist soil.
BLOOM June–August
USES     ✄ Borders

**'Olgae'** Sweetly fragrant flowers in a soft blue shade.

**'Rosea'** Shades of old-rose and dusty pink. Superb as a companion to the more usual blue forms.

### × *jouiniana* **'Mrs Robert Brydon'**     ZONE 4
### (Pillar Clematis)

Another herbaceous type, dying back nearly to the ground each winter. Extremely vigorous upright habit, with clouds of the palest blue starry flowers in late summer. Needs to be tied to a tall stake, fence or trellis, or allowed to scramble through a shrub or obelisk. Might even be interesting as a sort of billowing groundcover. Cut back to about 15 cm (6") in early spring. Combines well with climbing roses.

HT/SP   150–200 cm (5–7') / 60–90 cm (2–3')
SOIL      Prefers a rich, moist soil.
BLOOM July–September
USES     ✄☗⋔ Borders

### **'Prairie Traveler's Joy'**     ZONE 1

A very hardy climbing hybrid developed by the late Dr. Frank Skinner in northern Manitoba. Sprays of starry white flowers bloom from midsummer, followed by fluffy seed heads. Vigorous to the point of being aggressive. Mow or prune back hard every two to three years. Use as either a hardy vine or pin the stems down for a sprawling groundcover. Very drought-tolerant.

HT/SP   30–500 cm (12–198") / 90 cm (3')
SOIL      Tolerates a wide range of soil conditions.
BLOOM July–September
USES     ⋔☗✄ Climbing vine

### *recta* **'Purpurea'**     ZONE 2
### (Ground Clematis)

Another herbaceous species, this requires some support to be at its best, though it is not really a climbing vine. In spring the plant bursts out of the ground with a display of rich maroon-purple leaves and stems, followed by fragrant little white star flowers in early summer. Foliage colour usually fades to green

just after bloom time. Silvery seed heads are attractive in fall. Plants should be cut back to ground level in late fall or early spring. I love to combine this plant with hardy shrub roses. Very long lived. For an especially dark form, keep your eyes open for the variety **'Lime Close'**.

HT/SP   90–120 cm (3–4') / 60–90 cm (2–3')
SOIL      Prefers a rich, moist soil.
BLOOM June–July
USES     ✄ Borders

### *tangutica*     ZONE 2
### (Golden Clematis)

Bright yellow bell-shaped flowers appear through the summer and fall, followed by large feathery puffs. Excellent groundcover for difficult areas with poor soil, or trained as a climbing vine. May be pruned back hard in early spring, since plants flower on new wood.

HT/SP   30–400 cm (1–13') / 75–90 cm (30–36")
SOIL      Tolerates a wide range of soil conditions.
BLOOM July–September
USES     ⋔☗ Climbing vine

**'Radar Love'** This seed strain produces a long succession of nodding yellow bells, followed by silvery seed heads. There may be a slight difference from the straight species, but I have yet to see them side by side.

## CONVALLARIA ☀•
### (Lily-of-the-Valley)

### *majalis*     ZONE 1
### (Common Lily-of-the-Valley)

An old-fashioned cut-flower, the fragrant, white bell-shaped flowers appear for several weeks in the spring. A sturdy groundcover for difficult shady sites, even under trees. Unfortunately, in regions with hot summers these often look a little bedraggled by August unless given regular watering. New plantings may sit for a several years before the plants begin to spread vigorously underground. **CAUTION: toxic if eaten.**

HT/SP   10–15 cm (4–6") / 30–60 cm (1–2')
SOIL      Average to moist soil.
BLOOM April–May
USES     ⋔✄ Woodland gardens

**var. *rosea* (Pink Lily-of-the-Valley)** A very old form with small pale-pink flowers. Rare and difficult to find.

## CONVOLVULUS ☼
### (Morning Glory)

### *sabatius*     ZONE 7
### [*C. mauritanicus*]
### (Ground Morning Glory)

This species is well-behaved and not to be feared, unlike some of its weedy cousins (Bindweed, for example). Plants form a low trailing bush, bearing a summer-long succession of trumpet-shaped flowers in a soft violet-blue shade. Ideally suited to the Pacific Northwest climate. Needs very good drainage in winter so a raised bed or rock garden is advised. Prune stems back to 15 cm (6″) in early spring. Evergreen.

**HT/SP** 15–30 cm (6–12″) / 60–75 cm (24–30″)
**SOIL** Requires excellent drainage.
**BLOOM** June–September
**USES** ⛰️〰️🦋⚘🌸 Rock Gardens

# COREOPSIS ☼
## (Tickseed)

Bright yellow daisy-like flowers characterize this popular group of plants. Most bloom constantly from midsummer to frost, particularly when fading flowers are removed. Good for cutting. The original species are all native North American wildflowers.

### *auriculata* 'Nana'   ZONE 4
### (Maysville Daisy)

A long-lived dwarf variety, ideal for edging or in the rock garden. Plants give a showy display of single orange-yellow flowers in late spring over a low carpet of rounded leaves. Will repeat bloom if deadheaded.

**HT/SP** 15–25 cm (6–10″) / 25–30 cm (10–12″)
**SOIL** Average to moist well-drained soil.
**BLOOM** May–July
**USES** ⛰️✂🦋⚘ Edging, Borders

### *grandiflora* and hybrids   ZONE 4

Many selections abound, all with good-sized golden-yellow flowers, blooming for several weeks in the summer or for much longer if faded flowers are removed weekly. Both single and double-flowered forms exist, in a range of heights. Hybrids between this species and *C. lanceolata* have produced some of these modern selections, however the parentage is often tangled or unknown. These all have a tendency to bloom themselves to death. Removing the flower stems starting in early September will encourage plants to form overwintering leaves rather than going to seed and wearing themselves out. Taller varieties make outstanding cut flowers.

**SP** 30–60 cm (1–2′)
**SOIL** Prefers a rich, moist soil.
**BLOOM** June–September
**USES** ✂🦋⚘ Borders, Massing

**Baby Sun ['Sonnenkind']** Single golden-yellow flowers.

**HT** 30–50 cm (12–20″)

**'Brown Eyes'** Single golden daisies with a charming mahogany-brown centre. Compact habit.

**HT** 25–30 cm (10–12″)

**'Domino'** Brown-eyed golden flowers. Similar to 'Brown Eyes' but slightly taller.

**HT** 30–40 cm (12–16″)

**'Early Sunrise'** A semi-double seed strain with a compact habit and long flowering season. An All America Award winner. Superb at the front of the border.

**HT** 45–60 cm (18–24″)

**Flying Saucers ['Walcoreop']** The best of this group in terms of long-blooming and minimal maintenance. Sterile golden-yellow flowers continue to appear for months on end. Nice compact form. Tolerates summer heat and humidity well. A superb container plant.

**HT** 30–40 cm (12–16″)

**'Goldfink'** Miniature single flowers on a truly dwarf plant. Does not come true from seed.

**HT** 20–25 cm (8–10″)

**'Sterntaler'** Single golden flowers with a circle of mahogany-brown in the middle. Medium habit.

**HT** 40–45 cm (16–18″)

**'Sunburst'** Fluffy double and semi-double flowers. Inclined to be floppy in rich soils, so plan on a support of some kind. The best of the bunch for cutting.

**HT** 75–90 cm (30–36″)

**'Tequila Sunrise'** Unusual green and creamy-white variegated foliage, taking on pink tones during the colder months. Single golden flowers. This appears to lack vigour and may not prove to be quite as hardy as other forms. Remove any all-green shoots.

**HT** 30–40 cm (12–16″)

### *rosea*   ZONE 4
### (Pink-flowered Coreopsis)

The true species itself is seldom seen in gardens. Plants form a low mound of ferny green leaves, studded with very pale pink flowers that fade to white in the heat of summer, but bloom for weeks on end. The selections listed below are an enormous improvement, with larger blooms of a richer colour. All are charming plants for edging or massing but with a vigorous, spreading habit that means they must be watched and contained if they begin to wander. If flowering stops during summer heat just shear the outside of the plants lightly to encourage more buds to form. All prefer an evenly moist soil.

**SP** 45–60 cm (18–24″)
**SOIL** Average to moist soil.
**BLOOM** June–September
**USES** ✂〰️🦋⚘ Massing, Borders

**'American Dream'** This was the first selection to hit the market a number of years ago, and was sold simply as *Coreopsis rosea*. Confusion with a white form already being sold in Europe led to this new cultivar name being created. Plants produce small rose-pink daisies with a tiny yellow eye, blooming most of the summer.

**HT** 20–40 cm (8–16″)

**'Limerock Ruby'** (Red-flowered Coreopsis) Instinct tells me that this brand-new selection is going to knock *Coreopsis* 'Moonbeam' off of its pedestal. Flowers are an amazing saturated ruby-red shade with a contrasting tiny yellow eye. The slightly taller habit makes it especially useful for containers. The look reminds me a bit of Chocolate Cosmos, without any of the hassles of wintering indoors. One of the best new perennial plant discoveries in years!

**HT** 45–60 cm (18–24″)

**'Sweet Dreams'** Also new to the scene, this form produces quite large blooms in a delightful combination of creamy-white with a red eye, ageing to soft raspberry-pink. If grown in too rich a soil this has a tendency to get floppy by midsummer, but a quick chop with the shears makes plants more compact and bushy.

**HT** 30–60 cm (1–2′)

### *verticillata*   ZONE 4
### (Thread-leaved Coreopsis)

This species has produced some of the best garden perennials available. Plants form an airy dome of narrow threadlike leaves, covered with starry flowers for many weeks. Especially effective when mass planted as a groundcover. Excellent for combining with ornamental grasses. Generally long-lived and care-free. Very drought-tolerant.

**SP** 30–45 cm (12–18″)
**SOIL** Tolerates a wide range of soil conditions.
**BLOOM** June–September
**USES** ✂〰️⚘🦋🌸 Massing, Borders

**'Golden Gain'** A good free-flowering British selection. Golden-yellow flowers, nice bushy habit.

**HT** 50–60 cm (20–24″)

**'Golden Shower' ['Grandiflora']** Large golden-yellow flowers. Vigorous, with an upright habit. Can get floppy if grown in too rich a soil.

**HT** 60–75 cm (24–30″)

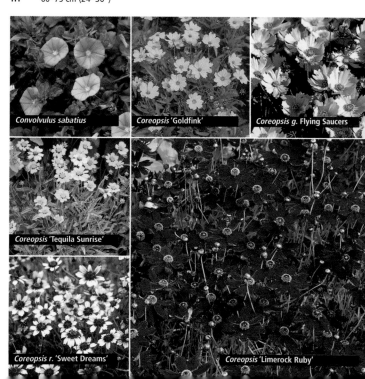

*Convolvulus sabatius*

*Coreopsis* 'Goldfink'

*Coreopsis g.* Flying Saucers

*Coreopsis* 'Tequila Sunrise'

*Coreopsis r.* 'Sweet Dreams'

*Coreopsis* 'Limerock Ruby'

**'Moonbeam' (Moonbeam Coreopsis)**
Unusual pale yellow flowers. Deservedly popular, and perhaps one of the all-time best perennials, blending particularly well with pastel colour schemes. Not always long-lived, however, and very late to make an appearance in spring. Division every 2–3 years in spring will help greatly to retain plant vigour. 1992 *Perennial Plant of the Year.* There is good evidence to suggest that 'Moonbeam' is in fact a complex hybrid. I can hardly wait to try combining 'Moonbeam' together with the new *Coreopsis rosea* 'Limerock Ruby'.

**HT**     30–45 cm (12–18″)

**'Zagreb'** An especially bushy form. Bright chrome-yellow flowers, similar to 'Golden Shower'. One of the best types for the border front.

**HT**     30–45 cm (12–18″)

## CORONILLA ☼
### (Crown Vetch)

***varia***         ZONE 3
Widely used by municipalities as a groundcover on roadsides and other difficult sunny sites. Valued for its ability to fix nitrogen from the air, thereby improving the soil. Rose-pink clover-like flowers bloom all summer. This is very aggressive and unsuitable for most garden situations. Plant this in the ditch. Extremely drought-tolerant once established.

**HT/SP**   30–60 cm (1–2′) / 60–90 cm (2–3′)
**SOIL**     Very tolerant of poor soils.
**BLOOM** June–August
**USES**   Roadsides, Slopes

## CORYDALIS ☼
### (Fumitory)
Related to the familiar Bleedingheart, these have similar ferny foliage, and upright stems of delicate locket-shaped or tubular flowers. They appreciate a cool, moisture-retentive yet well-drained soil, perhaps at the edge of a woodland.

***elata***         ZONE 5
### (Blue Corydalis)
Those of us who garden in warm-summer regions and have struggled with the *C. flexuosa* selections should do much better with this heat-tolerant species. Clusters of cobalt-blue flowers are every bit as charming as 'Blue Panda', but the foliage remains healthy through summer. The habit is slightly more upright.

**HT/SP**   30–45 cm (12–16″) / 30–45 cm (12–18″)
**SOIL**     Prefers a moist, well-drained soil.
**BLOOM** May–July
**USES**   Edging, Woodland Gardens

***flexuosa***         ZONE 5
### (Blue Corydalis)
Lacy blue-green foliage with arching stems of the most incredible sky-blue, fragrant flowers over a long season. A recent arrival from China, and worth a try in any partly shaded rockery. Flowering is intermittent from spring to fall, although plants have a tendency to go summer-dormant in regions with hot and humid weather. Evergreen in mild-winter areas. Since the introduction of 'Blue Panda' about ten years ago, several new selections have appeared. A thick organic mulch is recommended, to conserve moisture and also to help prevent frost heaving in the winter. Clumps are easily divided in early spring.

**HT/SP**   20–40 cm (8–16″) / 25–30 cm (10–12″)
**SOIL**     Rich, moist well-drained soil.
**BLOOM** May–October
**USES**   Edging, Woodland Gardens

**'Blackberry Wine'** An especially interesting new selection, bearing clusters of fragrant plum-violet flowers over a mound of powdery blue-green leaves. Better evergreen habit than most others.
**'Blue Panda'** Clear, true sky-blue, that elusive Himalayan Blue Poppy colour! This selection was the first to hit the market in a big way, creating an instant demand that even tissue culture cloning could not keep up with.
**'China Blue'** A good, vigorous habit, with flowers of a soft smoky-blue shade.
**'Golden Panda'** Foliage begins green in early spring, becoming chartreuse-yellow at about the same time the dusty-blue flowers appear. A stunning combination.

**'Père David'** Electric-blue flowers are featured here, over a spreading mound of fresh green foliage. Slightly more upright than some of the other forms. Good vigour.
**'Purple Leaf'** Well-named for its bronzy-purple leaves, which really set off the clusters of violet-blue flowers in a unique and special way. Said to have better vigour than most other selections, bulking up into good-sized clumps in time.

***lutea***         ZONE 3
### (Golden Corydalis)
A charming little plant for a rock wall or slope, with pretty golden-yellow locket-shaped flowers for months! The fresh green leaves make a low ferny mound. In a partly shaded site this will happily self-seed all over the place. Seedlings are easily moved (or removed) while small. In my own garden this plant literally has flowers from April through December. I love the way the seedlings appear in the most unlikely places, like between the cracks of patio blocks.

**HT/SP**   20–40 cm (8–16″) / 25–30 cm (10–12″)
**SOIL**     Prefers a moist, well-drained soil.
**BLOOM** May–September
**USES**   Walls, Borders

## COSMOS ☼
### (Cosmos)

***atrosanguineus***         ZONE 8
### (Chocolate Cosmos)
All the rage a few years back, the dark maroon-red flowers are delightfully chocolate-scented on warm days. Great for cutting, as all Cosmos are. Plants form a tuberous root which can be lifted and stored indoors like a Dahlia, so it can be fairly easily grown even in cold-winter regions. Easier still, grow this in a large pot and just bring it into the basement for the winter. Chocolate Cosmos are notoriously slow to begin growing in the spring, so don't discard plants before the middle of June. If you crave this colour but want a hardy no-fuss plant instead, try the new *Coreopsis rosea* 'Limerock Ruby'.

**HT/SP**   45–75 cm (18–30″) / 25–30 cm (10–12″)
**SOIL**     Needs good drainage, especially in winter.
**BLOOM** June–September
**USES**   Borders, Rock Gardens

## COTULA see LEPTINELLA

## COTYLEDON see CHIASTOPHYLLUM

## CRAMBE ☼
### (Seakale)

***cordifolia***         ZONE 4
### (Giant Seakale, Colewort)
A most bizarre and unusual plant, something like a Baby's Breath crossed

*Coreopsis verticillata* 'Moonbeam'

*Coreopsis verticillata* 'Zagreb'

*Corydalis elata*

*Cosmos atrosanguineus*

with a cabbage! Huge green leaves are deeply lobed and form a large mound. Clouds of tiny white star-shaped flowers are held above on tall stalks in early summer. An interesting specimen plant for the larger border. Very long-lived. Flea Beetles can be troublesome, causing the leaves to look like somebody took a holepunch to them. Use an insecticidal dust, just as you would with cabbage.

| | |
|---|---|
| **HT/SP** | 120–180 cm (4–6′) / 90–120 cm (3–4′) |
| **SOIL** | Average well-drained soil. |
| **BLOOM** | June–July |
| **USES** | ✂ Specimen, Borders |

### *maritima*     ZONE 4
### (Blue Seakale)

Although this species forms loose, branching sprays of off-white flowers, it really is grown more for the fantastic powdery-blue foliage. Leaves are large and cabbage-like, forming an undulating clump. Especially good in dry xeriscape situations. Like the Giant Seakale, Flea Beetles sometimes attack the leaves.

| | |
|---|---|
| **HT/SP** | 60–90 cm (2–3′) / 60–75 cm (24–30″) |
| **SOIL** | Well-drained soil. |
| **BLOOM** | June–July |
| **USES** | Specimen, Dry borders |

## CROCOSMIA ☼
### (Montbretia)

These have become popular both in gardens and as a cut flower. British efforts at breeding have greatly increased the selection of heights and flower colours and generally improved hardiness. Upright clumps of sword-shaped leaves produce arching stems of brilliant nodding funnel flowers from midsummer on, the effect a bit like some kind of exotic gladiola.

In Zones 1–4 the fleshy roots may be overwintered indoors like Canna lilies, and this is well worth the effort. Divide plants every 2–3 years for best blooming. A deep winter mulch is recommended in Zones 5–7, or wherever snowcover is unreliable.

### Hybrids     ZONE 5

Although our zoning may seem optimistic, there are gardeners in Zones 5 and 6 that have succeeded with Crocosmia. Reliable snowcover and/or a deep mulch of leaves in winter appears to be the key to success in these regions. In addition, planting before the end of June would be well advised. It's also easy to grow these in pots and just stick them down in the basement for the winter. As with Gladioli, both thrips and spider mites can be problematic.

| | |
|---|---|
| **SP** | 30–60 cm (1–2′) |
| **SOIL** | Average well-drained soil. |
| **BLOOM** | July–September |
| **USES** | ✂ Borders, Massing |

**'Emberglow'** Very large flowers in a burnt scarlet-red shade.

| | |
|---|---|
| **HT** | 60–75 cm (24–30″) |

**Jenny Bloom ['Blacro']** Large blossoms in a cheery bright-yellow shade. Vigorous habit.

| | |
|---|---|
| **HT** | 70–80 cm (28–32″) |

**'Lucifer'** Brilliant flame-red flower. The most famous of the older Alan Bloom hybrids, and the variety that is always readily available.

| | |
|---|---|
| **HT** | 90–120 cm (3–4′) |

**'Mars'** Flowers are bicoloured, bright scarlet with a contrasting yellow eye.

| | |
|---|---|
| **HT** | 80–90 cm (30–36″) |

**'Norwich Canary'** Bright canary-yellow flowers and a compact habit.

| | |
|---|---|
| **HT** | 60–75 cm (24–30″) |

**'Queen Alexandra'** A big, tall selection, featuring bright orange flowers with a dark maroon-red eyezone.

| | |
|---|---|
| **HT** | 90–120 cm (3–4′) |

**'Severn Sunrise'** Orange-red flowers with a cheery yellow eye.

| | |
|---|---|
| **HT** | 75–90 cm (30–36″) |

**'Solfatare'** One of the most unique and sought-after forms. Foliage is an unusual bronzy-copper shade, with spikes of soft apricot-orange blooms. Distinctly less hardy and not particularly vigorous. Zone 7.

| | |
|---|---|
| **HT** | 50–60 cm (20–24″) |

**'Star of the East'** Soft apricot-yellow blooms with peachy tips and a cream throat. Fairly tall.

| | |
|---|---|
| **HT** | 80–90 cm (30–36″) |

**'Venus'** One of the most compact selection, the flowers are a soft peachy-yellow shade that will delight even haters of orange.

| | |
|---|---|
| **HT** | 45–60 cm (18–24″) |

## CRYPTOTAENIA ☼
### (Mitsuba, Japanese Parsley)

### *japonica atropurpurea*     ZONE 4
### (Purple-leaved Mitsuba)

An interesting foliage plant that is attractive as well as edible! Related to parsley, the leaves are divided and somewhat ferny in texture, in a beautiful shade of bronzy-purple. Add this to your list of 'black' leaved plants. Umbels of pale pink flowers appear in summer. An excellent companion to gold-leaved Hostas. Inclined to self-sow prolifically, something that will drive neat and tidy gardeners crazy – the rest of us enjoy leaving some of the seedlings when they appear. Plants should be cut back after blooming to encourage fresh new growth. Use leaves like regular parsley.

| | |
|---|---|
| **HT/SP** | 40–60 cm (16–24″) / 25–30 cm (10–12″) |
| **SOIL** | Prefers a rich, moist soil. |
| **BLOOM** | June–July |
| **USES** | ✂ Borders |

## CYCLAMEN ☼
### (Hardy Cyclamen)

### *hederifolium*     ZONE 5
### [*C. neopolitanum*]
### (Fall Cyclamen)

Suited to a shady rockery or woodland area, these form low clumps of ivy-shaped green leaves with intricate grey and bronzy markings. The little pink or white rocket-shaped flowers appear in early fall, followed by the leaves. Clumps remain evergreen for the winter, going dormant during the heat of summer. Large corms develop underground. They resent overhead watering in the summer, so are best paired up with plants that are fairly drought tolerant. Excellent under trees and shrubs. For those gardeners lucky enough to have just the right conditions these will sometimes self-seed.

| | |
|---|---|
| **HT/SP** | 10–15 cm (4–6″) / 15–20 cm (6–8″) |
| **SOIL** | Very well-drained soil. |
| **BLOOM** | September–December |
| **USES** | Woodland gardens |

## CYNARA ☼
### (Cardoon)

### *cardunculus*     ZONE 7

Gardeners with a dramatic design style sooner or later learn about this fantastic foliage plant. Even those of us in cold winter regions cannot be without this, and in a single season it forms a huge mound of jagged thistle-like leaves of intense silvery-white. In warm regions (or where hardy) big heads of mauve thistles form in late summer, looking very much like giant artichokes – no surprise, since the plants are

*Crambe cordifolia*

*Crocosmia* 'Severn Sunrise'

*Crocosmia* × 'Solfatare'

*Cyclamen hederifolium*

closely related. It makes a smashingly good specimen for the sunny border, especially fine in large containers. No other foliage perennial attracts as much attention, even if you have to grow this as an annual. I've had it occasionally winter in Zone 6 but it comes through sort of half alive and new plants grow much better.

**HT/SP** 90–180 cm (3–6′) / 75–90 cm (30–36″)
**SOIL** Average well-drained soil.
**BLOOM** August–October
**USES** ✂🌷 Specimen

## DARMERA ☼ ◐
### (Mayapple, Umbrella Plant)

### *peltata*     ZONE 3
### [*Peltiphyllum peltatum*]

An interesting waterside plant, with large rounded rhubarb-like leaves that form a wide clump. Bizarre clusters of pink flowers appear before the leaves in early spring. In effect it is like a small *Gunnera* but far hardier. This is a wild-flower native to southern Oregon but despite this it has proven to be successful over a wide range of climates.

**HT/SP** 90–120 cm (3–4′) / 90–120 cm (3–4′)
**SOIL** Rich, constantly moist soil.
**BLOOM** April–May
**USES** Waterside, Specimen

## DELOSPERMA ☼
### (Hardy Ice plant)

Spreading, succulent plants similar in effect to *Sedum*. Flowers are single stars, studding the evergreen mat of leaves. These require very good drainage, especially in wet winter regions. Best on a slope or gravelly rock garden. Drought-tolerant.

### *cooperi*     ZONE 6
### (Purple Ice Plant)

Mats of cylindrical olive-green leaves bear magenta-purple daisy-like flowers all summer long. Intolerant of wet soil, and usually treated as an annual in the eastern part of the continent. Foliage develops good red fall and winter colour. Much used as a groundcover in the south-western U.S. Very drought-tolerant.

**HT/SP** 5–10 cm (2–4″) / 30–60 cm (1–2′)
**SOIL** Very well-drained soil.
**BLOOM** June–September.
**USES** ⬔ ⋔ ▲🌷❄ Slopes

### *floribundum* 'Starburst'     ZONE 4
### (Starburst Ice Plant)

With more of a clumping habit, this plant produces a summer-long display of bright lavender-pink flowers with a creamy-yellow eye. Selected at the Denver Botanical Gardens, and a Plant Select winner for 1998. Best as a border edging or rock garden plant.

**HT/SP** 5–10 cm (2–4″) / 25–30 cm (10–12″)
**SOIL** Average to dry well-drained soil.
**BLOOM** June–September.
**USES** ⬔ ⋔ ▲🌷❄ Rock Gardens

### *nubigenum*     ZONE 3
### (Yellow Ice Plant)

Forms a low weed-proof mat of light-green foliage, turning bronze-red in cold weather. Flowers are bright yellow, mostly appearing in late spring or early summer. Reliably hardy, and much more tolerant of wet soils and extended cold than other species. Worth considering as a lawn substitute. Very drought-tolerant.

**HT/SP** 5–10 cm (2–4″) / 30–60 cm (1–2′)
**SOIL** Average to very well-drained soil.
**BLOOM** May–June.
**USES** ⬔ ⋔ ▲🌷❄ Slopes

### *sutherlandii*     ZONE 7
### (Purple Ice Plant)

Similar in effect to *D. cooperi*, this produces a display of white-centred magenta-pink to purple flowers in late spring and early summer.

**HT/SP** 7–10 cm (3–4″) / 25–30 cm (10–12″)
**SOIL** Very well-drained soil.
**BLOOM** June–September.
**USES** ⬔ ⋔ ▲🌷❄ Slopes

## DELPHINIUM ☼
### (Delphinium, Larkspur)

One of the classic garden perennials, so important to the traditional English-style herbaceous summer border. We are all familiar with the taller types, the Pacific Giants, with their stately spires of colour. However, the smaller-flowered larkspur-style varieties are also excellent border plants – so useful for cutting – and often succeeding in hot, humid climates where the taller forms do not.

All Delphiniums prefer a rich, moist but well-drained soil and full sun. Taller types are especially heavy feeders and so

they should be fertilized regularly. Removing faded flowers will encourage repeat blooming; cut taller varieties back to 20 cm (8″) or so after flowering, shorter types need only to be dead-headed. Staking of the tall types beginning in May will help to prevent damage by strong winds at flowering time.

Gardeners in regions with hot, humid summers really struggle to grow Delphiniums well; this is normal. Plants are susceptible to powdery mildew and a number of other diseases that can kill them quickly in warm weather. Here are a few more tips worth considering:

- plan to divide your healthy plants every second spring and to discard any sickly ones;
- or, discard old plants and purchase new ones every 2–3 years;
- when dividing, move plants to a new location, if possible. This will help you to stay ahead of soil-borne diseases;
- choose a site that gets good air circulation, away from a wall or fence;
- use a preventative fungicidal spray to control powdery mildew;
- control aphids and other insects that may spread disease.

**CAUTION: All species are harmful if eaten.**

### Belladonna Group     ZONE 2

Larkspur-style flowers are held in loosely-branching spikes, rather than in a single main one. These come in various shades of soft blue, all are excellent for cutting. Remove faded flower spikes where they join the main stem, to encourage a round of repeat bloom.

**HT/SP** 90–120 cm (3–4′) / 45–60 cm (18–24″)
**SOIL** Rich, average to moist soil.
**BLOOM** June–August.
**USES** ✂ Borders

### 'Centurion Sky Blue'     ZONE 2

A recent winner of the European Fleuroselect Award, this disease-resistant strain forms tall spikes of double flowers in a gorgeous satiny sky-blue shade. Stems will need to be staked in May.

**HT/SP** 120–150 cm (4–5′) / 45–60 cm (18–24″)
**SOIL** Rich, average to moist soil.
**BLOOM** June–July.
**USES** ✂🌷 Borders

### Connecticut Yankees Group   ZONE 2

Also with larkspur-type flowers on compact, bushy plants that usually require minimal staking. These are more suited to a smaller garden, with an extended season of bloom. Flowers are in mixed shades of white, blue, lavender and purple. Deadhead as for the Belladonna types, by removing faded spikes back to the main stem.

*Darmera peltata*

*Delphinium* 'King Arthur'

*Cynara cardunculus*

*Delosperma nubigenum*

**HT/SP** 60–75 cm (24–30″) / 45–60 cm (18–24″)
**SOIL** Rich, average to moist soil.
**BLOOM** July–September
**USES** ✄ Borders

### *grandiflorum* ZONE 2
### [*D. chinense*]
### (Dwarf Delphinium, Chinese Delphinium)

These are totally unlike the taller spiky types, forming dwarf bushy mounds that are covered with large brilliant satiny flowers all summer and fall. Excellent for edging or massing. Although short-lived, these put on such a spectacular show that they are worth using even as a bedding annual. Sometimes self-seeds, particularly in cool-summer regions.

**SP** 25–30 cm (10–12″)
**SOIL** Average to moist well-drained soil.
**BLOOM** June–September.
**USES** ✄ Borders, Edging

**Banner Series** A recent introduction, forming bushy mounds with single flowers in shades from soft to deep blue. One of the best for mixed container plantings.

**HT** 25–30 cm (10–12″)

**Blue Elf** [**'Blauer Zwerg'**] Sprays of single gentian-blue flowers.

**HT** 30–40 cm (12–16″)

**'Blue Mirror'** Slightly taller, with amazing electric-blue flowers.

**HT** 30–45 cm (12–18″)

### Pacific Giant Hybrids ZONE 2
With their tall colourful spikes of double flowers, these can be the backbone for the early summer border. Flowers often have a contrasting centre, known as a bee. Plan to renew plantings every three years, otherwise the plants will get woody and begin to decline in quality. Fall flowering is usually reliable if plants are trimmed back after the summer flush is over. Many seed strains have been developed in a wide range of colours, although the plants that result are somewhat variable.

**HT/SP** 120–180 cm (4–6′) / 45–60 cm (18–24″)
**SOIL** Rich, average to moist soil.
**BLOOM** June–July, repeating in fall.
**USES** ✄ Borders

**'Astolat'** Lavender pink, with a darker bee.
**'Black Knight'** Deep midnight violet, the darkest.
**'Blue Bird'** Clear medium blue, contrasting white bee.
**'Blue Fountains'** A more compact, windproof strain in a good range of colours, including blue, lavender, rose and white.

**HT** 75–90 cm (30–36″)

**'Blue Jay'** Medium blue, with a darker bee.
**'Cameliard'** Lavender blue shades.

**'Clear Springs'** Similar to 'Blue Fountains', this strain gives a mixture of shades on plants with a sturdy, compact habit. Flowers are in a wide range of pastel shades, all with a contrasting white bee in the middle.

**HT** 75–80 cm (30–32″)

**'Galahad'** Pure white.
**'Guinevere'** Lavender-pink with white bee.
**'King Arthur'** Royal violet with a white bee.
**'Summer Skies'** Soft powdery blue, white bee.

### Stand-up Series ZONE 2
This dwarf type is a recent breeding breakthrough, producing the large Pacific Giant type spikes on a truly compact plant. Flowers are in a mixture of light and dark-blue shades. Shows much promise as a container plant. Deadhead by cutting spent spikes down to about 15 cm (6″).

**HT/SP** 45–60 cm (18–24″) / 30–45 cm (12–18″)
**SOIL** Rich, average to moist soil.
**BLOOM** June–July
**USES** ✄ Borders

## DENDRANTHEMA see CHRYSANTHEMUM

## DIANTHUS ☼
## [Pinks, Carnations]

This is a large and diverse group of plants, including many forms of Pinks as well as Carnations and Sweet William. Many are low growing and therefore well-suited to rock gardens or for edging. The name "Pinks" is not derived from the flower colour, but rather from the fringed petal edges, which look like somebody took a pair of pinking shears to them when their mother wasn't watching. Nearly all types are sweetly fragrant and attractive to butterflies. All produce edible flowers but be sure to remove the bitter green calyx.

Divide all but the tightly-cushioned alpine types every two years to keep plants vigorous and young. Most are evergreen. Cushion-forming *Dianthus* will benefit from a bit of clean-up after flowering, by removing flower stems and giving a light trim to the foliage with sharp scissors or shears.

### *alpinus* ZONE 3
### (Alpine Pinks)
Very dwarf rock-garden type. Grassy clumps of green leaves and large, single hot-pink flowers. Appreciates a little afternoon shade.

**HT/SP** 5–10 cm (2–4″) / 15–30 cm (6–12″)
**SOIL** Well-drained soil. Prefers a gravel scree.
**BLOOM** May–June.
**USES** Scree, Troughs

### *barbatus* ZONE 2
### (Sweet William)
A classic cottage garden plant. Large showy clusters of flowers, blooming all summer if dead-headed regularly. A biennial or short-lived perennial, Sweet William will usually self-seed freely. Taller types make excellent cut flowers. There are several mixed seed strains available in both single and double-flowering forms, with varying heights and in colours ranging from shades of red, pink, and salmon, through to white.

**HT/SP** 15–60 cm (6–24″) / 20–30 cm (8–12″)
**SOIL** Average well-drained soil.
**BLOOM** May–August.
**USES** Edging, Borders

**'Diadem'** Good cutting strain. Heads of bright crimson-red flowers, each with a contrasting white eye.

**HT** 50–60 cm (20–24″)

**'Newport Pink'** Large heads of deep salmon pink.

**HT** 50–60 cm (20–24″)

**'Nigrescens'** A unique and antique strain. Plants have bronzy-green leaves and bear heads of flowers that range in tone from maroon-red to velvety black.

**HT** 50–60 cm (20–24″)

### *caryophyllus* ZONE 4
### (Hardy Carnation)
Ever popular as cut-flowers, the garden strains of Carnations are as close as one can get to the greenhouse-grown florist's types. These are not long-lived and benefit from yearly division to keep the plants thriving. A thick mulch will help to bring them through cold winters. Their large, fragrant double flowers appear throughout the summer in a good range of shades, including pink, red, white, and soft yellow.

*Delphinium* 'Black Knight'

*Delphinium* 'Cameliard'

*Delphinium grandiflorum* Blue Elf

*Delphinium* 'Blue Jay'

Flowers reliably as an annual in cold-winter regions. The **'Grenadin'** strains are most commonly available.

HT/SP  40–50 cm (16–20″) / 25–30 cm (10–12″)
SOIL  Well-drained soil. Dislikes hot summers.
BLOOM June–September
USES  ✂✿🦋 Borders

### *deltoides*                    ZONE 2
### (Maiden Pinks)

Low, spreading mats of foliage are smothered by small single flowers in summer. Good edging or rock garden plants, although not long-lived without regular division every 2–3 years. Will often self-seed. Several colour strains are available.

HT/SP  15–20 cm (6–8″) / 30–45 cm (12–18″)
SOIL  Average well-drained soil.
BLOOM June–August
USES  △⋀▲✿🦋🌿 Edging, Borders

**'Albus'** Bright-green foliage, white flowers.

**'Arctic Fire'** Fringed white flowers with a charming red eye over fresh green foliage.

**'Brilliant'** Dark green to bronzy leaves with cherry-red flowers.

**Flashing Light ['Leuchtfunk']** Deep ruby-red flowers over bronzy-brown leaves.

**'Shrimp'** A refreshing variation, with salmon to shrimp-pink flowers and green leaves.

**'Vampire'** One of the darkest, with blood-red flowers on top of a low green carpet.

**'Zing Rose'** Deep rose-red flowers on a bushy green mound with a fairly upright habit. A reliable repeat bloomer and one of the best selections for containers. Likely a hybrid.

**'Zing Salmon'** A recent addition to the Zing series, with a repeat-flowering habit

just like 'Zing Rose' Blooms are in antique salmon tones. A designer colour.

### *gratianopolitanus* **'Tiny Rubies'**
ZONE 2
### (Cheddar Pinks)

The true species is seldom seen in gardens but has been an important parent to the many hybrid forms. 'Tiny Rubies' is a low-growing selection best suited to the rock garden or trough garden. Hundreds of small, double rose-pink flowers burst out from the tight mound of olive-green leaves in late spring. They are extremely fragrant. Outstanding in a sunny rock wall or between flagstones.

HT/SP  5–10 cm (2–4″) / 20–30 cm (8–12″)
SOIL  Average well-drained soil.
BLOOM May–July
USES  ✂△▲✿🦋🌿 Edging, Walls, Borders

### Hybrid Pinks                ZONE 2
### [D. × *allwoodii* hybrids]
### (Border Pinks, Cheddar Pinks, Modern Pinks)

This is sort of a catch-all group that includes a wide number of garden hybrids covering the whole range of colours from white through pink, red and near-purple. Plants vary quite a bit in habit but most have sweetly-scented flowers resembling small carnations with single, double or semi-double petals. Foliage tends to be blue-green to silvery-grey in colour, forming a low grassy-looking evergreen mound. Superb for edging a sunny border, in the rock garden and also in containers. Vegetative propagation is usually the only way these forms will come true, so either take cuttings or make divisions. Shear off the flower stems after blooming, to prevent plants from seeding into themselves. Good drought tolerance.

SP  20–30 cm (8–12″)
SOIL  Average well-drained soil, prefers alkaline conditions.
BLOOM May–July
USES  ✂△▲✿🦋🌿 Edging, Walls, Borders

**'Bath's Pink'** An American selection, with fringed soft-pink flowers appearing in great numbers. Tolerates hot, humid summers better than any other variety. Forms a vigorous mound of grey-green leaves. Sturdy enough for a border edging.

HT  20–30 cm (8–12″)

**'Blue Hills'** Silvery-blue foliage, single rose-pink flowers. This is a stunning selection best suited to the rock garden.

HT  10–15 cm (4–6″)

**'Cherry Moon'** Unusual for its foliage, which is a delightful smoky grey-plum shade. Good-sized flowers are bright pink with a contrasting cherry-red eye. This selection should be grown in lean

soil to prevent plants from getting open and floppy.

HT  10–15 cm (4–6″)

**'Dottie'** Fringed single flowers are white with a crimson eye over a compact grey-green foliage clump. Especially reliable for repeat blooming in the fall. I rate this as one of the best all-purpose Dianthus for edging borders and in the rock garden.

HT  15–25 cm (6–10″)

**'Frosty Fire'** Produces deep ruby-red fringed flowers above a dense hummock of silvery-blue leaves. An outstanding Canadian selection, but sadly lacking in vigour. Best grown in an alpine scree or trough.

HT  10–15 cm (4–6″)

**'Gold Dust'** This taller selection has the most amazing flowers, the single deep-red petals seem to be dappled with actual metallic gold flakes. Grow this one in lean soil to prevent a loose and open habit. Trim after blooming to maintain a tight foliage mound. Best as a border edging.

HT  20–30 cm (8–12″)

**'Little Boy Blue'** Nice display of single white flowers with a red eye. The foliage is intensely steel-blue but a little lax in habit unless grown in a rock garden or poor soil. Be sure to shear lightly after blooming.

HT  15–20 cm (6–8″)

**'Mountain Mist'** Exceptionally blue foliage, loads of single dusty-rose flowers. Good heat tolerance. The taller habit makes this one among the best for border edging.

HT  20–30 cm (8–12″)

**'Painted Beauty'** A taller variety. Branching stems of lavender-rose flowers with burgundy streaks. Also good as a border edging.

HT  20–30 cm (8–12″)

**'Royal Midget'** Semi-double deep pink flowers, on a very tight hummock of blue-green leaves. Best in the rock garden or scree.

HT  10–15 cm (4–6″)

**'Spotty'** Bluish leaves, unusual cerise-red flowers with white spots. Among the most popular selections.

HT  15–20 cm (6–8″)

**'Spring Beauty'** [D. *plumarius* 'Spring Beauty'] A variable seed strain, producing sweetly-fragrant fringed flowers in a range of lovely shades including pink, rose, salmon and white. Sturdy tufts of blue-grey leaves and a tallish habit make this well-suited to the border edge.

HT  25–30 cm (10–12″)

Dianthus barbatus

Dianthus deltoides 'Albus'

Dianthus 'Blue Hills'

Dianthus c. 'Grenadin' yellow

Dianthus 'Cherry Moon'

Dianthus 'Tiny Rubies'

**'Whatfield Magenta'** Tight hummock of silvery-blue leaves, bearing hot magenta-pink flowers with a rose throat. Alpine or scree type.
HT     10–15 cm (4–6")

**'Whatfield Mini'** Shell-pink single flowers, nice tight mound of grey-green leaves. Best in the rock garden or scree.
HT     10–15 cm (4–6")

### 'Velvet and Lace'                ZONE 5
### (China Pinks)
China Pinks are a hybrid group commonly grown as bedding annuals, but plants often survive for a couple of years in regions with mild winters or reliable snowcover. This delightful selection produces small double maroon-purple carnation-type flowers with lacy or fringed white petal edges. Stems are a nice height for cutting. Deadhead regularly for continual summer bloom. Best to divide every two years in spring, or treat as a biennial.
HT/SP   25–30 cm (10–12") / 20–30 cm (8–12")
SOIL    Average well-drained soil.
BLOOM June–September
USES    ✂❦❦ Borders

## DIASCIA ☼◔
### (Twinspur)
Until recently these were not well-known plants here in North America, but that has all changed. Gardeners in all different climates have discovered how well Twinspur performs in containers and hanging baskets, where they produce their chubby spikes of flowers all summer long in shades of pink, rose, lavender or white. These are hardy and reliable in areas like the Pacific Northwest so long as plants have good drainage through the wet winters. Plan to renew plantings every 2–3 years by dividing clumps in early spring.

### Selections and Hybrids    ZONE 7
Vigorous growers, all of these form low spreading clumps of fresh green leaves, with clusters of bright flowers all summer long. Removing faded flowers regularly is a good idea, to encourage lots of new buds to form. Terrific for weaving through the front of a border. There are now over twenty selections available, with more being released each year.
HT/SP   15–20 cm (6–8") / 45–60 cm (18–24")
SOIL    Well-drained soil. Dislikes winter wet.
BLOOM May–October
USES    △❦ Edging, Baskets, Borders

*barberae* **'Blackthorn Apricot'** A gorgeous shade of pale apricot pink. Very unusual!
**Coral Belle ['Hecbel']** Deep coral-pink flowers, compact habit.

## DICENTRA ◔☼●
### (Bleedingheart)
Bleedinghearts are much-loved shade garden plants, although most will also tolerate full sun if provided with adequate moisture. The various types all have the same classic heart-shaped flowers. Divide dwarf varieties every three years to maintain vigour. All are excellent for cutting.

### *eximia*                    ZONE 3
### (Fringed Bleedingheart)
Native to eastern North America. Flowers are light pink, held in clusters over a low clump of ferny leaves. Similar to the hybrid Fernleaf types but more delicate in effect. A nice little woodlander, it prefers bright shade. May go summer dormant during drought or hot weather. Even more charming is the selection **'Alba'**, with light-green foliage and ghostly white flowers.
HT/SP   25–30 cm (10–12") / 30–45 cm (12–18")
SOIL    Rich, moist well-drained soil.
BLOOM May–July
USES    △❦✂ Massing, Woodland garden

### *formosa* Hybrids            ZONE 2
### (Fern-leaved Bleedingheart)
These are vigorous dwarf fern-leaved selections, excellent in a wide range of shade or part-shade situations. Foliage makes a lacy mounding clump with flowers held just above on arching stems. Long-blooming.
HT/SP   25–30 cm (10–12") / 30–45 cm (12–18")
SOIL    Well-drained soil.
BLOOM May–August
USES    △❦✂❦ Borders, Massing

**'Adrian Bloom'** Blue-green leaves with deep ruby-red flowers. An outstanding British introduction.
**'Aurora'** Probably the best of the white forms, with excellent vigour. Plants form a sturdy clump of powdery grey-green leaves and clusters of snow-white blooms.
**'Bacchanal'** Lacy grey-green leaves, with clusters of dark purplish-red blooms. Plants spread to form a small patch. Highly regarded.
**'King of Hearts'** Quite new to the scene, this selection gives a heavy display of bright rose-red flowers over a long season. Foliage makes a healthy mound of powdery-green leaves. Compact habit.
HT     20–25 cm (8–10")

**'Langtrees' ['Pearl Drops']** Powdery blue-grey leaves and delicate ivory-white flowers with a pink flush.
**'Luxuriant'** Cherry-pink flowers bloom continually above clumps of ferny blue-green leaves. An older selection, but still excellent.

### *spectabilis*                ZONE 2
### (Old-fashioned Bleedingheart)
An old favourite from everyone's childhood, with the familiar drooping chains of pink hearts over a large, bushy mound of powdery-green leaves. These often become dormant by late summer, especially in hot climates, so be sure to plant something in front that will get big later in the season. Sometimes the leaves can be rejuvenated by cutting plants back to 15 cm (6") as soon as flowering is over.
HT/SP   70–90 cm (30–36") / 70–90 cm (30–36")
SOIL    Rich, moist well-drained soil.
BLOOM May–June
USES    ✂❦❦ Borders, Woodland gardens

**'Alba'** Perhaps even more charming than the familiar pink form, this white selection is a refreshing change at the very least. The two look magnificent when planted together. Foliage is more of a light green shade.
**'Gold Heart'** Bright butter-yellow foliage and pink flowers might sound like a horrid combination, but the effect in the shade garden is really rather amazing. So far this selection has presented cultural problems to the nursery grower, but seems to be just fine once planted in the garden. Protect from hot afternoon sun. Expect this to go summer dormant.

## DICTAMNUS ☼
### (Gas Plant)

### *albus*                    ZONE 2
### [*D. fraxinella* 'Albiflorus']
Truly a superb plant for the sunny border, where it will form a large green clump with airy spikes of white flowers in the early summer. The old tale about the flowers giving off a flammable gas is true; I've tried lighting it on fire several

*Dianthus* 'Gold Dust'

*Dicentra formosa* 'Aurora'

*Dicentra spectabilis* 'Gold Heart'

times, and on a hot day – when the air is still, it works. But, does it ever stink! Spectacular once established in the garden, these always look rather pathetic for the first year or two until they take hold, so be patient. Very long-lived. Plants resent being disturbed once established, but plenty of seedlings will appear, which are easily moved while still small. **CAUTION: Skin irritant with sunlight;** avoid direct contact with the foliage, especially on warm sunny days.

**HT/SP**  60–90 cm (2–3') / 60 cm (2')
**SOIL**  Average well-drained soil.
**BLOOM** June–July
**USES**  ✂ 🦋 Borders

**var. purpureus** This form has soft mauve-pink flowers with darker veins, and is even more worthwhile seeking out.

## DIGITALIS ☼ ◐
**(Foxglove)**

With their showy spikes of large, dangling tubular flowers, Foxgloves are a classic sight in the early summer border. They grow best in a woodland setting but adapt well to border conditions. Dead-heading is worth trying, to encourage more buds to form. Most will self-seed if conditions are to their liking. **CAUTION: All types are toxic if eaten.**

**grandiflora**                    ZONE 2
[**D. ambigua**]
**(Yellow Foxglove)**

Subtler in effect than the tall Common Foxglove, this species is a carefree and reliable perennial, which really deserves more consideration. Plants are compact and wind-proof, bearing chubby spikes of pale butter-yellow flowers that are spatter painted with mahogany-brown on the inside. Excellent for cutting.

Deadheading or trimming back the plants after blooming will encourage a repeat round of flowers in early fall. This is near the top of my list of "Sadly Neglected Perennials".

**HT/SP**  60–90 cm (2–3') / 30–45 cm (12–18")
**SOIL**  Moist, well-drained soil.
**BLOOM** June–August
**USES**  ✂ Borders, Woodland gardens

**'Carillon'** An especially compact form, ideal for the front of a border and especially in mixed containers. Flowers are the usual creamy yellow.

**HT**          30–40 cm (12–16")

**ferruginea**                    ZONE 4
**(Rusty Foxglove)**

Nothing at all like the blousy Common Foxglove, this species forms very tall but narrow spikes that are packed full of small bell-shaped blooms in a ruddy honey-brown shade. Despite this, I find it a charming addition to the perennial or woodland garden, with an architectural effect similar to a *Verbascum*. The stalks are nice for cutting. Biennial.

**HT/SP**  120–180 cm (4–6') / 45–60 cm (18–24")
**SOIL**  Moist, well-drained soil.
**BLOOM** June–July
**USES**  ✂ Borders, Woodland gardens

**Yellow Herald ['Gelber Herold']** Tall spikes of soft primrose-yellow or cream flowers, a colour that is easier to appreciate.

**HT**          120–150 cm (4–5')

**× mertonensis**                ZONE 4
**(Pink Foxglove, Strawberry Foxglove)**

This is a terrific hybrid strain featuring spikes of large deep-pink flowers. Plants form a big, velvety rosette of foliage, attractive even when not blooming. These act as short-lived perennials, so plan to replant every 2–3 years, or divide every couple of years (in spring) to maintain vigour.

**HT/SP**  90–120 cm (3–4') / 45–60 cm (18–24")
**SOIL**  Moist, well-drained soil.
**BLOOM** June–July
**USES**  ✂ Borders, Woodland gardens

**purpurea**                     ZONE 4
**(Common Foxglove)**

Very showy in bloom, with the biggest individual flowers of the genus. These require an evenly moist soil yet must have good drainage through the winter months or the fleshy rosettes may succumb to rotting. Biennial, but usually self-seeding. Various seed strains are available; in the garden these will often revert back to magenta-purple after several years of self-seeding, so plan to get fresh plants every few years.

**SP**          30–45 cm (12–18")
**SOIL**  Moist, well-drained soil.
**BLOOM** May–July
**USES**  ✂ Borders, Woodland gardens

**'Albiflora' ['Alba']** Ghostly white flowers in a one-sided spike like the wild species. Plants will seed true if no other foxgloves are in the vicinity. Excellent for naturalizing in a woodland.

**HT**          90–120 cm (3–4')

**'Apricot Beauty' ['Sutton's Apricot']** Unusual soft apricot-pink flowers.

**HT**          100–120 cm (39–48")

**Excelsior Hybrids** Mixed shades of white, rose, pink, and lavender, most often with contrasting spots. Very large flowers, absolutely amazing when well grown.

**HT**          120–150 cm (4–5')

**Foxy Hybrids** A bright mix of many colours on sturdy, compact plants. Sometimes treated as a bedding annual since plants will often flower in their first year.

**HT**          75–90 cm (30–36")

**'Pam's Choice'** Very special and unique, producing spikes of huge white bells that are heavily spotted with maroon-purple on the inside.

**HT**          90–120 cm (3–4')

**'Pink Champagne'** Soft-pink bells are spotted inside with creamy white. Mid-sized habit.

**HT**          75–90 cm (30–36")

**'Primrose Carousel'** Creamy-yellow bells with inside spotting of rich maroon purple. Mid-sized habit.

**HT**          70–75 cm (28–30")

**'Silver Fox'** Spikes of soft-pink bells, ivory on the inside with charming darker speckles. Foliage is silvery-green and felty to the touch. Compact habit.

**HT**          75–90 cm (30–36")

## DODECATHEON ☼ ◐
**(Shooting Star)**

**meadia**                       ZONE 2

A native North American wildflower. Delicate umbels of flowers rise up from a flat rosette of leaves. Flowers are rose-pink with a yellow band and cyclamen-shaped – the petals reflex backwards like the fire from a rocket's tail. Plants usually go dormant by midsummer, so mark the area well to avoid digging these out! Nice companions to various *Primula*. Suited to the moist border, they are worth trying in a bog garden. Other species are sometimes offered, but all are quite similar in effect and culture.

**HT/SP**  30 cm (1') / 15 cm (6")
**SOIL**  Likes a rich, moist soil.
**BLOOM** May–June
**USES**  △ ✂ Bog gardens

Dictamnus albus var. purpureus

Digitalis × mertonensis

Digitalis purpurea 'Primrose Carousel'

# DORONICUM ☼☼
(Leopard's Bane)

*orientale*                                    ZONE 2
[*D. caucasicum*]
These large, perky yellow daisies bloom in mid-spring, combining so nicely with tulips, blue Forget-me-nots or any of the creeping *Phlox stolonifera* selections. Plants often go summer-dormant in warmer regions but seem to return year after year. Great for cutting. Tolerant of woodland conditions.

SP     25–30 cm (10–12″)
SOIL   Average to moist, well-drained soil.
BLOOM  April–June
USES   ✂☙ Borders, Woodland gardens.

'Goldcut' Especially large heads of clear yellow, was first developed as a commercial cut flower.

HT     50–60 cm (20–24″)

'Little Leo' A new compact strain, with semi-double yellow daisies. Better suited to a rock garden situation, or for edging the spring border.

HT     25–30 cm (10–12″)

'Magnificum' The standard strain, with good-sized canary-yellow flowers on a bushy plant. Stems are ideal for cutting.

HT     45–60 cm (18–24″)

# DRABA ☼☼
(Draba, Whitlow Grass)

*sibirica*                                     ZONE 2
Draba are true alpines, and among the first of the early spring rock garden plants to burst into bloom. This species forms a low, evergreen mat of tiny green leaves, bearing short stems of mustard-yellow flowers as soon as the snow is gone. Well suited to growing in troughs or between flagstones in any sunny area.

HT/SP  5–10 cm (2–4″) / 20–30 cm (8–12″)
SOIL   Average to dry, well-drained soil.
BLOOM  March–April
USES   ◭☙▲ Rock gardens, Troughs

# ECHINACEA ☼
(Coneflower)

Similar to Rudbeckia, and highly valued for their large brightly-coloured daisies. Each flower has a prominent central cone, the petals often drooping down attractively. These make a rich display in the border and are also excellent for cutting. The seed-heads provide winter food for finches and other birds and are useful for dried arrangements. Plants bloom over a long season, standing up well to summer heat and humidity. A simple trick is to remove faded flowers weekly – this will easily double the blooming season. A favourite of butterflies. Native North American wildflowers.

The world of Coneflowers is about to be turned on it's ear. Watch for a series of plants from the Chicago Botanic Garden and breeder Jim Ault become available over the next few years, with colours never before seen in coneflowers.

*pallida*                                      ZONE 4
(Pale Purple Coneflower)
There is nothing quite like the "natural" form of a flower, lacking the improvements and general meddling of the hybridizer. This species gets the trophy for "droopiest Coneflower", the nubbly brown centres are surrounded by seriously lax petals in a soft pastel mauve shade. Plants have a more loose and open habit than the garden forms of Purple Coneflower, but respond well to deadheading. The roots of this species are harvested for medicinal teas and other herbal products.

HT/SP  80–120 cm (30–48″) / 45–60 cm (18–24″)
SOIL   Tolerates a wide range of soil conditions.
BLOOM  July–October
USES   ✂☙🦋 Borders, Meadows

*paradoxa*                                     ZONE 3
(Yellow Coneflower)
Native to the Ozark mountains of Arkansas and Missouri, this species is a departure from the others with its large drooping heads of bright yellow petals surrounding a brownish cone. Plants form a taproot that makes them quite drought tolerant but rather difficult to divide. Deadhead to promote continued blooming.

HT/SP  60–90 cm (2–3′) / 45–60 cm (18–24″)
SOIL   Average to dry, well-drained soil.
BLOOM  July–September
USES   ✂🦋 Borders, Meadows

*purpurea*                                     ZONE 3
(Purple Coneflower)
The most common garden species, it forms bushy, upright clumps of mauve-purple flowers with a contrasting orange-brown cone, the petals drooping gracefully. Recent breeding work is bringing a host of interesting selections to the marketplace, so this is a group of plants that still holds plenty of promise. Tolerates partial shade, although plants may then require staking to prevent flopping over. Very drought-tolerant. Easily divided in early spring, and seedlings will usually appear in quantity.

HT/SP  75–120 cm (30–48″) / 45–60 cm (18–24″)
SOIL   Tolerates a wide range of soil conditions.
BLOOM  July–October
USES   ✂☙🦋 Borders, Meadows

'Kim's Knee High' This recent arrival shows great promise of staying around for many years to come. This is the first truly dwarf Coneflower to appear, providing us gardeners with a myriad of new uses to dream up. Its bushy and

free-blooming habit make this perfect for using in mixed containers or at the border front.

HT     45–60 cm (18–24″)

'Kim's Mophead' An even more compact selection. Flowers have somewhat drooping white petals surrounding an orange-green cone.

HT     30–60 cm (1–2′)

'Magnus' An improved strain with a good, bushy habit. Flower petals are reddish-purple and stick straight out, rather than drooping downwards. Selected as *Perennial Plant of the Year* in 1998.

HT     75–100 cm (30–40″)

'Razzmatazz' A brand new and amazing selection of this popular perennial. Flowers are fully double with a central pom-pom of rose pink, surrounded by a circle of magenta-purple daisy petals. Flowers well from midsummer through fall, particularly when regularly deadheaded.

HT     80–90 cm (30–36″)

Ruby Star ['Rubinstern'] A recent colour improvement on 'Magnus', offering flat petals in a deeper magenta-red shade.

HT     90–100 cm (36–40″)

'White Swan' (White Coneflower)
Tremendously underused, this selection produces snow-white petals that droop around a central greenish-brown cone. Plant habit is fairly compact and bushy. Gorgeous when combined with any of the purple forms, but also valuable on its own as a reliable and long-blooming summer daisy. For some reason this strain does not self-seed around the garden, so plan to divide clumps every 3–4 years in the spring. Other white

*Echinacea purpurea* 'Kim's Knee High'

*Echinacea* (future colours)

*Echinacea purpurea* 'Razzmatazz'

strains commonly offered ('White Lustre', 'Alba', 'Amado', 'Cygnet') are virtually identical.

**HT**    75–90 cm (30–36")

## ECHINOPS ☼
### (Globe Thistle)

It's funny how a simple word like "thistle" can doom a plant forever to the fringes of the gardening world. Thistles make us think of weeds, of nasty, prickly plants that take over and are uncontrollable, that will make us regret ever allowing them into the garden. Believe me, the Globe Thistles are a friendly bunch, not to be feared in the least. They deserve to be appreciated as an outstanding cut flower, for fresh or dried use. Most will tolerate hot sites with reasonably good soil. They respond fairly well to deadheading, and are attractive to butterflies.

### *ritro*      ZONE 2
### (Blue Globe Thistle)

Globular, metallic-blue flowers are excellent for cutting, fresh or dried. Tall, thistly-looking plants are dramatic at the back of the border. Not invasive. May require staking in rich soils.

**HT/SP**   90–120 cm (3–4') / 60–75 cm (24–30")
**SOIL**     Average to moist well-drained soil.
**BLOOM** June–September
**USES**    ✂ ❦ 🦋 Borders, Specimen

**'Vietch's Blue'** Smaller flower heads in a lighter silvery steel-blue shade with a reliable repeat-blooming habit. Slightly more compact. Sometimes grown as a commercial cut flower.

**HT**    90–100 cm (36–40")

### *sphaerocephalus* 'Arctic Glow'   ZONE 2
### (White Globe Thistle)

This new selection stands out in a genus full of copycats and look-alikes. Plants form a mound of prickly-looking grey-green leaves, bearing ball-shaped heads of silvery-white flowers held on contrasting red stems. Slightly more compact and bushy habit than most.

**HT/SP**   80–90 cm (30–36") / 75–90 cm (30–36")
**SOIL**     Average to moist, well-drained soil.
**BLOOM** June–August
**USES**    ✂ 🦋 Borders, Specimen

## EPIMEDIUM ☽●
### (Bishop's Hat, Barrenwort)

Barrenworts are well-respected and stalwart performers for the shade garden, including those difficult dry areas under thirsty trees. Modern plant explorers have recently been bringing back formerly unknown species and selections from the mountains of China. Although some of these new plants will prove to be tremendously exciting, be prepared to wait – slow propagation by division ensures it will be a while before any of the new ones become available to the general gardening public. In the meantime, these older selections are still worthwhile and virtually carefree.

### Species and Hybrids    ZONE 4

Valued for their distinctive and dense semi-evergreen foliage, the leaves often become bronzy during the colder months. Superb as a slow-spreading groundcover for shady areas. Short sprays of starry flowers appear in spring, looking something like tiny Columbines. Varieties are either clumping or slowly-spreading in habit, so choose according to the site requirements. Trimming off all of the foliage in late winter is a clever and timely trick to get more punch out of the flower display. Very drought-tolerant once established. Many gardeners in Zones 2 and 3 are successfully growing Barrenwort.

**HT/SP**   20–30 cm (8–12") / 30–45 cm (12–18")
**SOIL**     Prefer a rich, moist woodland soil but will adapt to a wide range of conditions.
**BLOOM** April–May
**USES**    ✂ ▲ ▲ ♣ 🦋 Woodland garden, Borders

**×** *cantabrigiense* Strange orange-brown blooms, splashed with red. Dark green foliage. Clumping habit. Evergreen.
**×** *grandiflorum* Lilac Fairy ['Lilafee'] Very compact selection but vigorous. Leaves tinged purple at first, flowers are deep violet-purple. Deciduous.

**HT**    20–25 cm (8–10")

**×** *perralchicum* 'Frohnleiten' Compact variety. Bright yellow flowers, bronzy marbled foliage. Spreading habit. Evergreen.
**×** *rubrum* Smallish cherry-red flowers, but showy. Spreading habit. Deciduous.
**×** *versicolor* 'Sulphureum' Light prim-rose-yellow flowers. Clumping habit. Deciduous.

**×** *warleyense* Orange Queen ['Orangekönigin'] Evergreen. Pale-orange flowers. Clumping habit. Often difficult to find.
**×** *youngianum* 'Niveum' Pure-white flowers. Clumping habit. Deciduous.
**×** *youngianum* 'Roseum' Lilac-rose flowers. Clumping habit. Deciduous.

## EREMURUS ☼
### (Foxtail Lily, Desert Candle)

These tall spires of lily-like flowers are a spectacular sight. Since the foliage dies back at flowering time, it's a good idea to plant something of medium height at the base. Try these in a sunny, very well-drained location. Protect from late-spring frosts. Sometimes the fleshy, starfish-shaped roots can be found for sale with all the other bulbs in the fall.

### × *isabellinus*      ZONE 5
### (Hybrid Foxtail Lily)

These are the type most often seen in pictures and instantly coveted. Flowers are produced on tall stems in a wide range of soft pastel shades, including pink, white, yellow, salmon and coppery orange. Excellent drainage is a must. Some gardeners plant these right in gravel, allowing the fleshy roots to reach down into fertile soil below.

**HT/SP**   120–240 cm (4–8') / 45–60 cm (18–24")
**SOIL**     Very well-drained soil.
**BLOOM** June–July
**USES**    ✂ Borders

### *stenophyllus*      ZONE 5
### (Yellow Foxtail Lily)

A more reasonable height for the smaller garden. Flowers open dark yellow, fading to an attractive burnt orange, usually with multiple stems. Also good for cutting. Plants are long-lived and easier than the taller species.

**HT/SP**   90–150 cm (3–5') / 45–60 cm (18–24")
**SOIL**     Very well-drained soil.
**BLOOM** June–July
**USES**    ✂ Borders

## ERIGERON ☼
### (Fleabane Daisy)

The Fleabanes are finally starting to gain some degree of popularity for the sunny summer border, where their small but brightly-coloured daisy flowers are a welcome addition. Plants are usually carefree, the taller selections are great for cutting and attractive to butterflies. These remind me of the fall-blooming Asters, in effect.

### Hybrids      ZONE 2

Among these hybrids are a number of valuable early-summer bloomers that are at home towards the border front. Stems are great for cutting and last well. Divide clumps every 2–3 years to maintain vigour. Inclined to be floppy if planted in too rich a soil, so grow these

*Echinops ritro* 'Vietch's Blue'

*Echinops sphaerocephalus* 'Arctic Glow'

*Epimedium warleyense*

*Epimedium × perralchicum* 'Frohnleiten'

*Epimedium × 'Sulphureum'*

lean or plan to provide support. Shear plants back after blooming to rejuvenate the leaves and hopefully encourage a second flush of bloom in the fall.

HT/SP  50–60 cm (20–24") / 30–60 cm (1–2')
SOIL  Average well-drained soil.
BLOOM June–July
USES  ✄ 🐝 Borders

**Azure Fairy ['Azurfee']** Semi-double flowers of soft lavender-mauve.
**'Blue Beauty'** Double flowers of bright lavender-blue. Slightly taller than most.
**Pink Jewel ['Rosa Juwel']** Bright-pink to rose flowers. Compact habit.
**'Prosperity'** Large single lavender-blue flowers. We accidentally planted this next to Lady's Mantle, and it was a smashing combination.

### *karvinskianus* 'Profusion' ZONE 8
### (Profusion Fleabane Daisy)

Almost constantly in flower, this plant is one of the very best "fillers" for any sunny area, from border to rock garden or containers. Plants form a low mound of ferny greyish leaves, bearing tiny white daisies that age to soft pink. Well worth growing even where plants are not winter hardy. Self-sown seedlings will appear in large numbers but these are easily removed while small. Even tolerates growing in gravel, which is where I am planning to get it started on my back terrace. Drought tolerant.

HT/SP  15–20 cm (6–8") / 15–20 cm (6–8")
SOIL  Average to dry, well drained soil.
BLOOM June–October
USES  △🌱 🦋 Edging

# ERODIUM ☼
## (Heronsbill)

Closely related to the hardy *Geraniums*, these are long-flowering plants for the alpine garden or trough. Plants seem to resent wet winters, and are not always reliably hardy, but they are worth a little extra effort to grow. In cold-winter regions the tender forms are well worth trying as annuals for their near-constant flower display.

### *glandulosum* ZONE 4
### [*E. petraeum glandulosum*]
### (Fragrant Heronsbill)

A tough little species that seems to be reliably hardy over a wide area, especially if grown in a well-drained rock garden. Makes a slowly-spreading mat of olive-green ferny foliage with small orchid-like flowers – pale lavender with wine-purple markings. Blooms for most of the season.

HT/SP  10–20 cm (4–8") / 30–45 cm (12–18")
SOIL  Well-drained gravelly soil.
BLOOM May–September
USES  △🌱 Walls, Edging

### × *variabile* ZONE 7
### (Dwarf Heronsbill)

Looks like a miniature hardy *Geranium*, with a show of dainty flowers all season long. Forms a cute little clump. Excellent in a pot, indoors or out.

HT/SP  5–10 cm (2–4") / 15–30 cm (6–12")
SOIL  Well-drained gravelly soil.
BLOOM May–September
USES  △🌱🌺 Troughs, Edging

**'Album'** White flowers with a tiny pink stripe.
**'Bishop's Form'** Bright lipstick-pink flowers, very cheery.

# ERYNGIUM ☼
## (Sea Holly)

The more usual types produce open umbels of prickly steel-blue flowers, which are a favourite for cutting and drying. Tolerant of hot, dry sites and high salt soils. Attractive in the border and generally well-behaved.

### *alpinum* 'Blue Star' ZONE 3
### (Alpine Sea Holly)

Not an alpine in the dwarf sense, this species produces very large prickly-looking heads of rich metallic blue flowers held on even darker blue stems. One of the best border types, with a clumping and non-invasive habit. Great for cutting.

HT/SP  70–80 cm (28–32") / 30–45 cm (12–18")
SOIL  Average to dry, well-drained soil.
BLOOM June–August
USES  ✄🌺🌿 Dried Flower, Borders

### *giganteum* ZONE 3
### (Miss Willmott's Ghost)

Unique among Sea Hollies, this species has very large silvery-grey flower bracts, and is superb for drying. Plants generally behave as a self-seeding biennial. British plantswoman Ellen Willmott, it is said, used to secretly scatter seeds of this whenever she went visiting other people's gardens. It has proven itself to be hardy in cold regions like the Canadian Prairies.

HT/SP  75–90 cm (30–36") / 30–45 cm (12–18")
SOIL  Average to dry, well-drained soil.
BLOOM June–August
USES  ✄🌺🌿 Dried Flower, Specimen, Borders

### *planum* ZONE 2
### (Blue Sea Holly)

One of the hardiest species, a reliable and long-lived plant for the border. Umbels of small steel-blue flowers are fine for drying. Will spread underground to form a small patch. Some gardeners consider it to be invasive, particularly on light soils.

HT/SP  75–100 cm (30–40") / 45–60 cm (18–24")
SOIL  Average to dry, well-drained soil.
BLOOM June–August
USES  ✄ 🦋 🌿 Dried Flower, Borders

**Blue Cap ['Blaukappe']** A more compact selection, first developed as a commercial cutflower. Good strong blue colour.
HT  60–75 cm (24–30")

### 'Sapphire Blue' ZONE 4
### ['Jos Eijking']

The steely heads of this selection are among the largest available. Long prickly-looking blue bracts surround a bristly central cone. Stems are strong and excellent for cutting, fresh or dried. The showiest of the Sea Hollies listed here.

HT/SP  60–75 cm (24–30") / 45–60 cm (18–24")
SOIL  Average to dry, well-drained soil.
BLOOM June–August
USES  ✄🌺🌿🌿 Containers, Borders

### *variifolium* ZONE 4
### (Marble-leaf Sea Holly)

The lower leaves of this species are particularly interesting, forming a low, leathery green rosette marbled with white veins. Branching heads of whitish flowers are surrounded by spiny blue bracts. Foliage remains evergreen in mild winter regions. Superb in a rock garden or raised bed.

HT/SP  40–50 cm (16–20") / 30–45 cm (12–18")
SOIL  Average to dry, well-drained soil.
BLOOM July–August
USES  ✄△🌺🌿▲🌿 Containers, Rock Gardens

### *yuccifolium* ZONE 4
### (Rattlesnake Master)

A species native to North America, and quite different from the other Sea Hollies listed. Leathery leaves are arranged at the base like a yucca plant, with tall stems of creamy-green golf-ball shaped flowers. Very unusual for cutting.

*Erigeron* Pink Jewel

*Erodium* × *variabile* 'Bishop's Form'

*Eryngium* 'Sapphire Blue'

*Erigeron* 'Prosperity'

HT/SP  90–120 cm (3–4') / 30–60 cm (1–2')
SOIL  Average to dry, well-drained soil.
BLOOM July–September
USES  ✂🦋🌿 Dried Flower, Specimen, Borders

## ERYSIMUM ☀
## [Cheiranthus]
## (Wallflower)

Best known are the spring-blooming bi-ennial Wallflowers, often used for massing with bulbs. These include both the Siberian Wallflower (*E.* × *allionii* and Common or English Wallflower (*E. cheiri*), both easily started by sowing seeds directly in the home garden. All types have sweetly-fragrant flowers that are attractive to butterflies. Drought tolerant.

### × *allionii*                    ZONE 3
### [*Cheiranthus* × *allionii*]
### (Siberian Wallflower)

Often mass-planted with tulips, these late-spring bloomers will cleverly dis-guise any unsightly shriveling bulb foliage. Usually treated as a biennial, these will freely self-seed in a favorable location, especially in well-drained gravelly soils. The loose spikes of flowers are typically bright yellow or orange, and spicy-fragrant. Sow these directly in the garden for best results.

HT/SP  30–60 cm (1–2') / 15–20 cm (6–8")
SOIL  Well-drained soil.
BLOOM May–July
USES  ✂🦋🌿 Bedding, Naturalizing

### 'Bowles' Mauve'                ZONE 6
### (Shrubby Wallflower)

An upright plant that remains evergreen in milder regions. Handsome grey-green leaves nicely set off the profuse clusters of mauve flowers. Blooms over a long season, sometimes all winter on the West Coast. Plants develop a woody

base and should be sheared back to around 15 cm (6") in midsummer to promote fall flowering. In colder regions this performs well as an annual container plant. Tolerates climates with hot, humid summers.

HT/SP  60–75 cm (24–30") / 45–60 cm (18–24")
SOIL  Well-drained soil.
BLOOM May–October
USES  ✂🦋🌿 Specimen, Borders

### 'John Codrington'              ZONE 6

Another shrubby selection, with a bushy and compact habit. Dark green leaves set off clusters of bicoloured pale-yellow and brownish-purple flowers, which from any distance have more of a soft-apricot appearance. Shear back to (15 cm) 6" in midsummer where hardy. Begs to be combined with maroon-foliaged neighbours.

HT/SP  20–25 cm (8–10") / 25–30 cm (10–12")
SOIL  Well-drained soil.
BLOOM April–July
USES  △❄✂🦋🌿 Rock Garden

## EUPATORIUM ☀◐
## (Boneset)

With increasing frequency these hardy, reliable plants are showing up in peren-nial gardens from coast to coast. They can provide welcome colour and struc-ture to late summer and fall schemes. Most are selections of native North American wildflowers.

### *cannabinum* 'Flore Pleno'     ZONE 2
### [*E. cannabinum* 'Plenum']
### (Double Hemp Agrimony)

Produces loose heads of double mauve-pink flowers. Used in Europe as a long-lasting commercial cut-flower. The coarse, bright-green fragrant foliage is amazingly hemp-like, which is always fun when you can trick garden visitors for a moment or two. This is a thirsty plant, so give it a moist location. Bene-fits from a hard clipping back after blooming.

HT/SP  90–120 cm (3–4') / 60–75 cm (24–30")
SOIL  Rich, moist to wet soil.
BLOOM July–August
USES  ✂🦋 Borders

### *purpureum*                    ZONE 3
### [*E. maculatum*]
### (Joe-Pye Weed)

Often described as an architectural plant, these form very large clumps, with big umbrella-like heads of flowers in late summer and fall. Foliage is bold and green, arranged in whorls around the hollow green stems. As specimen plants in the sunny garden, any of the big Joe-Pye Weeds will attract attention – and I mean in a *good* way! Adored by butterflies.

HT/SP  210–300 cm (7–10') / 90–120 cm (3–4')
SOIL  Rich, moist to wet soil.
BLOOM August–October
USES  ✂🦋 Specimen, Borders

### 'Bartered Bride' An interesting and welcome departure from the usual purple forms, this variety features huge clusters of off-white flowers. Equally attractive to butterflies, and a terrific cut flower.

HT  180–240 cm (6–8')

### subsp. *maculatum* 'Atropurpureum' [*E. maculatum*] The classic form, with purple-spotted stems and huge rose-purple flower heads. Often sold incor-rectly as *E. purpureum*, the solid stems (not hollow) are a distinguishing feature of this group.

HT  210–300 cm (7–10')

### subsp. *maculatum* 'Gateway' More compact in habit, with especially dark wine-red stems and big clusters of dusky-purple flowers.

HT  150–180 cm (5–6')

### *rugosum*                       ZONE 5
### (Boneset, White Snakeroot)

Quite unlike the taller purple Joe-Pye Weeds, this is a species of medium texture that forms a fairly large bushy mound. The clusters of pure white flowers look very much like annual Ageratum. This is an easy border peren-nial, and the flowers are excellent for cutting. Tolerates dry shade.

HT/SP  90–120 cm (3–4') / 75–90 cm (30–36")
SOIL  Moist to average well-drained soil.
BLOOM August–September.
USES  ✂🦋🌿 Borders

### 'Chocolate' (Chocolate Boneset) A vast improvement on the species, with ex-ceptionally dark bronze-purple foliage, later becoming dark green at flowering time. Blooms a little bit later. This rates as one of the all-time best purple foliage plants.

## EUPHORBIA ☀◐
## (Spurge)

This huge group of plants includes the well-known Christmas Poinsettia. These all have colourful leaf bracts surround-ing the true (but insignificant) flowers. **CAUTION: all are toxic if eaten/skin and eye irritant; wear gloves when handling.**

### *amygdaloides*                  ZONE 5
### (Wood Spurge)

Upright stems support clusters of greenish-yellow flowers in late spring, produced on the previous year's growth. Plants are somewhat woody and should be pruned back in spring. Recommended as a ground-cover for partial shade, especially among trees or shrubs. Evergreen in mild-winter regions. Prune lightly after blooming. Depending on the selection, they may self-seed. Superb companions to late tulips. Drought tolerant.

Erysimum allionii

Erysimum 'Bowles' Mauve'

Eupatorium rugosum 'Chocolate'

Eupatorium purpureum 'Atropurpureum'

**SOIL** Average well-drained soil.
**BLOOM** April–June
**USES** ✂⋔⋀≋ Massing, Shady borders

**'Purpurea' ['Rubra'] (Purple Wood Spurge)** Beautiful mounding purple foliage, a gorgeous contrast to the clusters of chartreuse flowers. Tends to self sow, but seedlings are easily removed while small.
**HT/SP** 30–45 cm (12–18″) / 30–45 cm (12–18″)

**var. *robbiae* [*E. robbiae*] (Leatherleaf Spurge)** Large lime-green flower heads, leathery dark-green foliage. Highly recommended as a spreading groundcover for dry shady sites. Can become invasive in the border. Not quite as hardy as 'Purpurea'.
**HT/SP** 30–60 cm (1–2′) / 60–75 cm (24–30″)

### *characias*     ZONE 7
### (Evergeen Spurge)
Several selections from this spectacular plant have recently become available here in North America, and all of them are terrific specimens for mild-winter regions, especially in the Pacific Northwest. The species itself forms a bushy, upright mound of leathery blue-green leaves that remain evergreen. Huge clusters of flowers open in very early spring, chartreuse-yellow with a brownish eye. Unsurpassed as a unique, bold sculptural plant that may be used as a specimen or massed towards the back of the border or among shrubs. Can also be grown in a cool greenhouse. Flowering stems should be cut back hard to 15 cm (6″) after blooming, leaving the non-flowering stems alone.
**HT/SP** 90–150 cm (3–5′) / 80–90 cm (30–36″)
**SOIL** Average well-drained soil.
**BLOOM** February–May
**USES** ⋀✂≋ Specimen, Borders

**'Black Pearl'** Bizarre heads of green flowers, each blossom with a black eyeball centre. Compact habit.
**HT/SP** 60–70 cm (24–28″) / 60–70 cm (24–28″)

**'Burrow Silver'** Beautiful grey-green leaves are strongly edged in creamy yellow. Loose heads of whitish flowers, each with a golden eye. Slow growing and not terribly vigorous, which makes it well-suited to smaller gardens. Compact habit.
**HT** 60–70 cm (24–28″)

**'Forescate'** The most compact form, like a miniature version of subsp. *wulfenii*. Big heads of chartreuse-yellow flowers.
**HT/SP** 40–60 cm (16–24″) / 45–60 cm (18–24″)

**'Humpty Dumpty'** Mid-sized in habit, the greenish flowers have an especially bright red eye.
**HT/SP** 60–70 cm (24–28″) / 60–70 cm (24–28″)

**'Portuguese Velvet'** One of the most unique forms, forming a good-sized mound of velvety blue-grey leaves. Flower clusters are an interesting bronzy-gold shade.
**HT** 80–90 cm (30–36″)

**subsp. *wulfenii* [*E. wulfenii*]** Slightly broader heads of solid chartreuse-yellow flowers, lacking the brownish eye. Stems are coral, contrasting nicely with the powdery blue-grey leaves. This is the most commonly grown form.
**HT** 90–120 cm (3–4′)

### *dulcis* 'Chameleon'    ZONE 4
### (Chameleon Spurge)
Handsome burgundy-purple foliage, with a low mounding habit. Flower clusters are greenish-yellow with a purplish flush. Leaves become maroon in the fall, with fiery highlights. Best in semi-shade. Plants will be much more tidy in the garden if cut back hard right after flowering. A prodigious self-seeder, cutting the plants back in summer will also help to prevent this from becoming a weed. Contrasts beautifully with silver foliaged plants.
**HT/SP** 30–45 cm (12–18″) / 45–60 cm (18–24″)
**SOIL** Average well-drained soil.
**BLOOM** May–June
**USES** ✂≋ Edging, Specimen

### Excalibur     ZONE 6
### ['Froeup']
This is a brand new hybrid Spurge from England, selected for its outstanding early spring red foliage colour. Plants form a bushy, upright mound of grey-green leaves, bearing clusters of chartreuse-yellow flowers in mid to late summer. In the fall, both the leaves and stems turn purplish-red, lasting right through until late spring. Evergreen in mild winter regions. A wonderful specimen plant, both in the garden as well as in tubs or mixed containers. Foliage may be tidied up in early spring before the brightly coloured new growth appears. Not yet widely tested, this may turn out to be hardy in Zones 4 or 5.
**HT/SP** 70–80 cm (28–32″) / 75–80 cm (30–32″)
**SOIL** Average well-drained soil.
**BLOOM** July–August
**USES** ✂≋⋀ Borders, Specimen

### *griffithii* 'Fireglow'    ZONE 4
### (Griffith's Spurge)
This makes a large shrub-like mound of olive-green leaves. Heads of flame-orange flower bracts are showy over a long period, held atop coral-red stems. A superb plant, deserving of much wider use where hardy. Fall foliage is often a good red. Best in lean soil, otherwise the plants can get floppy towards late summer. We previously rated this as hardy to Zone 2, but it was seemingly optimistic.

**HT/SP** 60–90 cm (2–3′) / 60–75 cm (24–30″)
**SOIL** Average well-drained soil.
**BLOOM** May–August
**USES** ✂≋ Borders, Massing

### × *martinii*     ZONE 7
### (Martin's Spurge)
This hybrid Spurge has quickly gained popularity in mild-winter regions. Plants form an evergreen clump of leathery grey-green foliage. Both the stems and new growth are flushed with burgundy. Heads of lime-green flowers are an attractive feature from late spring through early summer. Plants will spread to form a small patch. Excellent in containers lending a special Mediterranean effect. Seems to prefer a sunny, well-drained site. Certainly worth a try in Zone 6.
**HT/SP** 45–60 cm (18–24″) / 45–60 cm (18–24″)
**SOIL** Average to dry, well-drained soil.
**BLOOM** May–July
**USES** ✂⋔≋⋀≋ Massing, Groundcover

**'Red Martin'** An especially dense and compact selection. Both the stems and new growth tips are beautifully flushed with red. Flowers are the usual chartreuse yellow.
**HT/SP** 30–45 cm (12–18″) / 30–45 cm (12–18″)

### *myrsinites*     ZONE 5
### (Donkey-tail Spurge)
A succulent, evergreen species with leathery steel-blue leaves arranged around the stems. This trails and flops in all directions, the ends of the stems producing clusters of sulphur-yellow flowers in spring. A unique rockery or wall plant. Plants will self-seed freely. Very heat and drought-tolerant. The sap of this species can be extremely irritating to the skin, so wear gloves when weeding around it. A knock-out when combined with *Veronica peduncularis* 'Georgia

*Euphorbia* × *martinii*

*Euphorbia* Excalibur

*Euphorbia a.* var. *robbiae*

*Euphorbia c.* 'Portuguese Velvet'

*Euphorbia amygdaloides* 'Purpurea'

Blue'. Some gardeners in Zones 3 and 4 are reporting success with this.

**HT/SP** 15–20 cm (6–8") / 30–45 cm (12–18")
**SOIL** Average to very dry soil.
**BLOOM** April–June
**USES** ⬥▽▼▲🌿 Edging, Walls

### *palustris* 'Walenburg's Glorie' ZONE 5
### (Marsh Spurge)

A seldom-seen selection that is perfect for the waterside or other moist sunny places. Plants form a tall, narrow clump of fresh green, willowy-looking leaves, bearing clusters of chrome-yellow flowers in late spring through early summer. Fall foliage colour is bright buttery yellow. Stems are excellent for cutting.

**HT/SP** 90–100 cm (36–40") / 60–75 cm (24–30")
**SOIL** Prefers a rich, moist to wet soil.
**BLOOM** May–July
**USES** ✂ Borders, Waterside

### *polychroma* ZONE 2
### [*E. epithymoides*]
### (Cushion Spurge, Chrome Spurge)

Forms a perfect dome of light-green leaves, covered by bright, chrome-yellow flower bracts in late spring. An unusual cut-flower. Foliage sometimes turns red in fall. Extremely drought-tolerant. Probably the best Spurge for colder regions. Trim plants back to 10 cm (4") after blooming.

**HT/SP** 30–45 cm (12–18") / 45–60 cm (18–24")
**SOIL** Average well-drained soil.
**BLOOM** May–June
**USES** ⬥▽✂▼🌿 Borders, Massing

### Redwing ZONE 7
### ['Charum']

Another new British hybrid, with amazing red foliage colour during the colder months, contrasting against a smothering early-spring display of bright lime-yellow flower clusters. Summer colour is dark green. Prune

*Euphorbia polychroma*

*Filipendula rubra* 'Venusta'

lightly in late spring after flowering is finished, to maintain a compact, bushy habit. May prove hardy to Zone 6.

**HT/SP** 45–50 cm (18–20") / 45–60 cm (18–24")
**SOIL** Average to moist, well-drained soil.
**BLOOM** March–May
**USES** ✂▼▲ Borders

## FARFUGIUM ☼
## (Leopard Plant)

### *japonicum* ZONE 8
### [*Ligularia tussilaginea*]

These make rather interesting and sturdy foliage plants, at their best in containers. This allows them to be easily wintered indoors, where they put up with "living room" conditions better than most inside/outside plants. The foliage is leathery, glossy and rounded, forming a sturdy evergreen mound that seems to resist most pests. Short spikes of yellow daisy flowers may appear in the autumn, something the plants usually fail to do in cool summer regions. The plain green species is not grown nearly as often as the more interesting forms listed below.

**HT/SP** 30–60 cm (1–2') / 45–60 cm (18–24")
**SOIL** Average to moist well-drained soil.
**BLOOM** September–November
**USES** ▼▲ Containers, Woodland garden

**'Aureomaculatum'** Leaves are punctuated with bright-yellow polka-dots that look like something out of Dr. Seuss. Begs to sit next to a gold-leafed Hosta!
**'Crested Leopard'** This combines the golden-yellow spots with heavily crimped and curled leaf edges. Completely unique and bizarre!

## FILIPENDULA ☼◐
## (Meadowsweet,
## Queen-of-the-Prairie)

These are mostly large and upright plants for moist to wet soils. Showy clusters of flowers are similar to Spirea. Foliage is jagged and bold.

### 'Kahome' ZONE 3
### (Dwarf Pink Meadowsweet)

Fluffy heads of raspberry-pink flowers are held above the dark green jagged-edged leaves. Likes a moist or wet site. In hot summer regions or during drought stress this selection is rather prone to powdery mildew infections.

**HT/SP** 20–30 cm (8–12") / 30–45 cm (12–18")
**SOIL** Rich moist to wet soil.
**BLOOM** July–August
**USES** ✂▼ Edging, Waterside

### *purpurea* ZONE 4
### (Japanese Meadowsweet)

One of the most eye-catching species, forming a tall upright clump of jagged maple-shaped leaves. Branching red stems hold sprays of rich pink flowers during the summer. Happiest where the

soil remains evenly moist, like at the waterside.

**HT/SP** 90–120 cm (3–4') / 60–75 cm (24–30")
**SOIL** Rich moist to wet soil.
**BLOOM** June–August
**USES** ✂ Specimen, Borders

**'Elegans'** More often seen than the species, this selection has airy white flowers with red stamens, which gives an overall soft-pink glow from any distance. Slightly shorter in habit, but still bold and beautiful when well grown.

**HT** 90–100 cm (36–40")

### *rubra* 'Venusta' ZONE 3
### (Martha Washington's Plume,
### Queen-of-the-Prairie)

A bold accent plant, forming a sturdy bushlike mound of coarsely divided green leaves. Large panicles of deep pink flowers make for a show-stopping display. One of the showiest perennials for moist sites. This is a selection of a native North American wildflower.

**HT/SP** 120–180 cm (4–6') / 90–120 cm (3–4')
**SOIL** Prefers a rich, moist to wet soil.
**BLOOM** July–August
**USES** ✂ Specimen, Borders

### *ulmaria* ZONE 3
### (European Meadowsweet, Queen-
### of-the-Meadow)

A mid-sized species, this produces the usual divided or jagged leaves, topped with fragrant clusters of creamy-white flowers in summer. The species itself is not often grown, but several interesting selections exist. These prefer average to moist soils, the coloured-leaf forms growing best in part shade, otherwise they are prone to sunburn and spider mites.

**HT/SP** 75–120 cm (30–48") / 45–60 cm (18–24")
**SOIL** Average to moist soil.
**BLOOM** June–July
**USES** ✂ Borders, Woodland gardens

**'Aurea'** (Golden European Meadowsweet) An outstanding foliage accent plant for moister parts of the garden, the leaves are a soft buttery-gold colour. Like the variegated form below, whether you allow the plants to bloom or you trim the flower stems off is entirely your choice. A hard trim back to 15 cm (6") will rejuvenate the plant if it happens to scorch during summer drought. Best in shade or morning sun.

**HT** 75–90 cm (30–36")

**'Variegata'** (Variegated European Meadowsweet) Mostly grown for the foliage, the pointy dark-green leaves have a handsome blotch of creamy-yellow in the centre. Short spikes of white flowers are a bonus, but nobody would notice if you decided to just cut them off. This collector's plant appreciates afternoon shade. Remove any reverting all-green shoots as they appear.

*Filipendula ulmaria* 'Aurea'

Best used towards the border front, or in containers.

HT     60–75 cm (24–30″)

### *vulgaris* 'Plena'                ZONE 2
### (Double Dropwort)

This species prefers average to dry soils, unlike its taller cousins. Forms a handsome, low rosette of finely-cut ferny leaves that radiate out in a perfect circle. Long-lasting creamy-white flowers make an appearance in early summer. Nice edging plant for the border and short enough for the rock garden.

HT/SP     40–50 cm (16–20″) / 30–45 cm (12–18″)
SOIL     Average well-drained soil.
BLOOM May–July
USES     △✄🌱 Borders, Edging

# FRAGARIA ☼ ◐
## (Strawberry)

Garden strawberries, grown for their large fruit, are usually relegated to the vegetable garden, but a few forms are appreciated for their ornamental features. They adapt well to average garden conditions, and most are tolerant of part shade.

### Hybrids                ZONE 2
### (Ornamental Strawberry, Flowering Strawberry)

A unique and ornamental group with large, brightly-coloured flowers that appear on and off throughout the season. Ideal for edging or planting as a groundcover, also excellent in containers and hanging baskets. Tasty bright red fruits are of medium size and really more of a bonus. Plants send out lots of runners, spreading quickly just like any normal garden strawberry, so don't be afraid to pull out any unwanted plants every year or two just to keep the patch under control. Fairly shade-tolerant.

HT/SP     10–15 cm (4–6″) / 30–90 cm (1–3′)
SOIL     Average to moist well-drained soil.
BLOOM May–October
USES     △◠▲🌱 Edible fruit, Hanging baskets

**Pink Panda ['Frel']** The first to be developed and introduced, bearing loads of soft to medium-pink flowers. Vigorous habit.

**Red Ruby ['Franor']** A darker-flowered selection, more of a deep rose-pink to near red.

### *vesca*                ZONE 2
### (Alpine Strawberry)

A runnerless, small-fruited strawberry with an everbearing habit and that elusive wild-strawberry flavour. Both the pointy fruits and tiny white flowers are ornamental. Makes for a unique edible edging.

HT/SP     15–25 cm (6–10″) / 25–30 cm (10–12″)
SOIL     Average to moist soil.
BLOOM May–October
USES     △🌱 Edible fruit, Edging

**'Rügen'** The classic red-fruited European strain, known in France as *Fraises des Bois*.

**'Yellow Wonder' ['Fructo Albo']** Bizarre but tasty creamy-white fruit. If I could only grow one kind of strawberry, this would be it – visitors are always amazed when they see and taste these.

# FRANCOA ☼◐
## (Chilean Bridal Wreath)

### *sonchifolia*                ZONE 7

Native to Chile, this is seldom seen in North American gardens. Plants form a low rosette of fuzzy, dark-green leaves, bearing upright spikes of soft-pink orchid-like flowers, each marked with a rose coloured blotch. Stems are produced from mid summer through the fall. Best in a mild winter climate with cool summers. An unusual and attractive cut flower. *Francoa* is sometimes grown as an annual in cold-winter regions. Prefers an evenly-moist soil and some protection from the hot afternoon sun. Evergreen.

HT/SP     60–70 cm (24–28″) / 30–40 cm (12–16″)
SOIL     Average to moist, well-drained soil.
BLOOM July–September
USES     △✄🌱▲ Borders

# FUCHSIA ☼◐●
## (Fuchsia)

Most gardeners are familiar with the tender types of Fuchsia, popular for hanging baskets. In regions with mild winter climates , however, there are scores of hardy, shrubby selections that make superb plants for shadier parts of the garden. A few of these will handle surprisingly cold winters, but even in harsh climates they are worth growing in containers and are easily wintered in a cool basement.

### *magellanica*                ZONE 6
### [*F.* 'Ricartonii']
### (Hardy Fuchsia)

Although truly woody shrubs, these associate well with perennials in the border, and benefit from a hard clipping back in early spring. Plants form an upright bush and bear many dangling tubular flowers, crimson with a purple centre. More delicate in appearance than the fancy hanging-basket types, but with a tougher constitution. These should survive in Zone 6 with a deep winter mulch.

HT/SP     60–120 cm (2–4′) / 60–90 cm (2–3′)
SOIL     Average to moist, rich soil.
BLOOM June–October
USES     ✄🌱 Borders

**'Aurea'** Bright chartreuse-yellow leaves set the stage for the crimson and purple flowers. The habit is compact.

HT     60–90 cm (2–3′)

**'Hawkshead'** A hybrid selection, making an upright bush with a grand display of pure-white bells.

# GAILLARDIA ☼
## (Blanket Flower)

### × *grandiflora* Hybrids                ZONE 2

These feature brightly-coloured daisy flowers, often with a contrasting central eye. All are long blooming and especially so if faded flowers are removed every week or two. Taller forms are excellent for cutting, the more compact types make ideal edging or container subjects. Blanket Flower is a good choice for hot, dry areas since plants are very drought-tolerant. Two to four years is a typical lifespan – to encourage longevity, cut plants back hard in early September. This forces new leaf growth from the base and helps to prevent plants from blooming themselves to death.

SP     30–45 cm (12–18″)
SOIL     Average to dry, well-drained soil.
BLOOM June–September
USES     ✄🌱▼🦋 Borders, Meadows

**Burgundy ['Burgunder']** Deep flamed-red flowers, nice tall stems for cutting.

HT     60–90 cm (2–3′)

**Goblin ['Kobold']** Red petals with golden-yellow tips. Compact habit.

HT     20–30 cm (8–12″)

**Golden Goblin ['Goldkobold']** Solid yellow flowers, also compact.

HT     20–30 cm (8–12″)

**'Mandarin'** A colourful British selection, the deep flame-orange petals are flushed with gold on the tips. Medium sized.

HT     50–60 cm (20–24″)

*Fragaria vesca* 'Ruegen'

*Francoa sonchifolia*

*Fuchsia magellanica*

*Gaillardia* Goblin

Monarch Group Mixed shades of yellow, orange, and red, including solids and bicolours. A superb cutting strain. May require some support.

HT      60–90 cm (2–3′)

## GALIUM ☼•
(Sweet Woodruff)

***odoratum***                          ZONE 3
[*Asperula odorata*]
Attractive, whorled green leaves set off tiny clusters of starry white flowers in mid to late spring. An excellent fast-spreading groundcover. This is best in a moist, shady location; plants will survive and tolerate drier conditions under thirsty trees but may become shabby-looking in mid to late summer. Said to be evergreen in mild climates but a hard trim in late winter is worth the extra effort. Sweet Woodruff shines as an underplanting to spring-blooming bulbs, a clever way of disguising that awkward shrivelling bulb foliage. Spreads quickly, but not to the point of being uncontrollable.

HT/SP   10–20 cm (4–8″) / 30–60 cm (1–2′)
SOIL    Average to moist soil.
BLOOM April–May
USES    M▾☙ Woodland gardens

## GAURA ☼•
(Gaura)

***lindheimeri***                       ZONE 5
(Butterfly Gaura)
A native North American wild-flower, now familiar to legions of gardeners from coast to coast. Plants bloom for months on end, with loose and delicate sprays of flowers, the species itself being white with a very light pink tinge. In the breeze these move constantly, looking like a cloud of small butterflies. Because

these are so difficult to photograph, I always find a picture never quite does them justice. Gardeners are often underwhelmed by photos of the plant, but nearly always admire them in real life.

Trim plants lightly after the first flush of blooms begin to wane. Gaura are very drought and heat tolerant. Plants may be short-lived in wet winter regions. A winter mulch is recommended in Zones 5–6. The straight species itself seeds freely, so even if the parent plants die out, new seedlings will often appear the following year. Most of the selections listed below do not self sow.

HT/SP   90–120 cm (3–4′) / 60–90 cm (2–3′)
SOIL    Average to dry, well-drained soil.
BLOOM June–October
USES    ✂☙❦ Borders, Meadows

**'Blushing Butterflies'** A brand new Australian selection, with clouds of soft-pink flowers and a compact, bushy habit. Should prove to be a superb container plant.

HT/SP   30–45 cm (12–18″) / 45–60 cm (18–24″)

**'Corrie's Gold'** An interesting variegated selection, the mid-green leaves are blotched with creamy-yellow. Flowers are white with a pale pink flush.

HT      60–90 cm (2–3′)

**'Crimson Butterflies'** Another new form from Australia, which provides interest not only from the fine display of rich pink flowers, but also makes a stunning low mound of crimson-red foliage. Beautiful both in and out of flower.

HT/SP   30–45 cm (12–18″) / 45–60 cm (18–24″)

**'Siskiyou Pink'** An excellent form with deep-pink blossoms. Fairly compact habit.

HT      60–70 cm (24–28″)

**'Sunny Butterflies'** Rounding out the trio of new Australian selections, this forms a low mound of green leaves, edged in creamy white. Flowers are a delicate pink shade. Quite an improvement on 'Corrie's Gold' in terms of habit and vigour.

HT/SP   50–60 cm (20–24″) / 45–60 cm (18–24″)

**'Whirling Butterflies'** A mid-sized selection, reported to be sterile and therefore able to flower more freely. Blooms are like the species, white with a pink cast.

HT      60–90 cm (2–3′)

## GAZANIA ☼
(Hardy Gazania)

***linearis* 'Colorado Gold'**           ZONE 5
It may come as a surprise to see *Gazania* listed in a perennial book, but this species is rather distinctive. Plants were originally collected in the high mountains of South Africa by the staff of

the Denver Botanic Garden and this has proven to be hardy in regions with cold and dry winters. It forms a low mound of leathery dark-green leaves, bearing golden-yellow daisies all season long. Deadhead regularly to encourage more buds to form. Needs excellent winter drainage to prevent rotting, so best grown in a well-drained rock garden or even in containers. Drought tolerant once established.

HT/SP   15–20 cm (6–8″) / 20–30 cm (8–12″)
SOIL    Requires a very well-drained site. Dislikes wet, heavy clay.
USES    ▲△❦ Rock gardens, Containers, Edging

## GENTIANA ☼•
(Gentian)

Best known are the dwarf, alpine varieties, with their bluer-than-blue trumpet-shaped flowers. This is a large group of plants; many of the taller species are useful in the perennial garden, and are generally a lot easier to grow than the fussy alpine types.

***acaulis***                            ZONE 2
(Trumpet Gentian, Spring Gentian)
Native to the European Alps, this spring-flowering Gentian is a much-loved alpine plant and a challenge to grow. Plants form a low, slow-spreading mat of pointed green leaves, bearing large upfacing funnel-shaped flowers in the most amazing shade of deep, true blue. Requires a rich, acidic and evenly moist soil, and has a distinct preference for cool-summer climates. Often performs best in a rock garden situation, where the roots can stay cool and moist. Protect from hot afternoon sun. Consider this plant as a challenge to the more advanced gardener.

HT/SP   10–15 cm (4–6″) / 25–30 cm (10–12″)
SOIL    Prefers a rich, evenly moist but well-drained acidic soil.
BLOOM April–May
USES    ▲△☙ Rock garden, Scree bed

**Blue Herald**                          ZONE 4
['Blauer Herold']
(Autumn Gentian)
Autumn Gentians are a very special group of plants, highly treasured for their rich display of flowers in late summer and fall. Plants are low-growing, the fresh green foliage forming a mound that bears large upfacing trumpet flowers for many weeks. This selection has deep-blue flowers, and a bushy habit. An excellent edging plant for the border, in the rock garden or alpine trough. Easier to grow than many of the other fall flowering types. Does best in cool summer regions.

HT/SP   15–30 cm (6–12″) / 25–30 cm (10–12″)
SOIL    Prefers a rich, evenly moist but well-drained soil.
BLOOM August–October
USES    ▲△☙ Rock garden, Edging

Galium odoratum

Gaura lindheimeri 'Crimson Butterflies'

Gaura lindheimeri

Gentiana acaulis

Gazania l. 'Colorado Gold'

*cruciata* ZONE 3
(Cross Gentian)

Unlike many species, this Gentian is so foolproof that most gardeners should enjoy success with it. Plants form a low, bushy clump of large dark green leaves, bearing small bright blue flowers that are held along arching stems in late summer. Nice edging plant for the border or woodland. Prefers an evenly moist soil. Clumps may be easily divided in early spring.

HT/SP  20–30 cm (8–12") / 30–45 cm (12–18")
SOIL  Prefers a rich, moist but well-drained soil.
BLOOM August–September
USES  ✂⋖⚠☷ Edging, Rock garden

*septemfida* ZONE 2
(Summer Gentian, Every-man's Gentian)

One of the easier low-growing Gentians, this species is a reasonable substitute for the more finicky alpine types. Plants form a sizable clump and are nice along the front of a border. Flowers are a good true blue, blooming in mid to late summer but with an unfortunate tendency to hide among the leaves.

HT/SP  15–30 cm (6–12") / 30–45 cm (12–18")
SOIL  Prefers a rich, moist but well-drained soil.
BLOOM July–September
USES  ⚠☷ Edging, Walls, Slopes

# GERANIUM ☼ ◐
(Cranesbill)

These are hardy perennial relatives of the annual Geraniums (more correctly known as *Pelargoniums*) that are commonly used for summer bedding and window boxes. Cranesbills come in a huge range of heights, forms and colours, to suit most garden purposes. For convenience they are indicated below as either *alpine* (short) or *border* (medium to tall) varieties.

All have similar divided or lobed leaves, forming either a mound or mat of foliage. Cup-shaped flowers generally appear in early summer, most often in lovely soft pastel shades of pink, blue, purple or white. Like so many other early-summer flowering perennials, most of the Cranesbills benefit from a hard pruning back as soon as the flowers have finished, a simple and quick technique that rejuvenates the foliage so it remains attractive for the rest of the season. Some varieties take on brilliant red foliage colouring in the fall.

'Ann Folkard' ZONE 4
Border type. Unusual chartreuse-yellow foliage, contrasting against a display of bright magenta-purple flowers, each with a black eye. A long-blooming hybrid. This is inclined to burn in full sun, particularly in warm-summer regions. Extremely useful for its habit of weaving among other plants near the front of the border, or even scrambling through a nearby shrub.

HT/SP  30–60 cm (1–2') / 70–90 cm (30–36")
SOIL  Average to moist, well-drained soil.
BLOOM June–August
USES  ⋗⚠☷ Edging, Borders, Massing

'Brookside' ZONE 4
Border type. Clumps of lacy green leaves, bearing large cup-shaped clear violet-blue flowers with a cream eye. A newer hybrid first discovered in England. Good vigour, and a long season of bloom. Likely hardy in Zones 2–3.

HT/SP  50–65 cm (20–24") / 60–70 cm (24–28")
SOIL  Average to moist, well-drained soil.
BLOOM June–August
USES  ☷ Borders, Massing

× *cantabrigiense* ZONE 4
(Cambridge Cranesbill)

Alpine or Border type. These are low-growing plants with trailing stems and glossy green, fragrant foliage. Flowers are sterile, and will repeat bloom for most of the summer. Plants have a neat and tidy appearance with a minimal need for maintenance. This make them a good choice as a vigorous ground-cover for either dry or moist locations. Evergreen.

HT/SP  15–20 cm (6–8") / 30–45 cm (12–18")
SOIL  Tolerates a wide range of soil conditions.
BLOOM May–August
USES  ⋖⋗⚠☷☇ Edging, Borders, Massing

'Biokovo' A natural hybrid selection discovered growing wild in Yugoslavia. Loads of small off-white flowers with a flush of pink in the middle.
'Cambridge' Bred at Cambridge University, with bright magenta-pink flowers.

*cinereum* ZONE 4
(Dwarf Cranesbill)

Alpine type. Dense, low mounds of foliage, with large flowers resting on the trailing stems for many weeks. Excellent in the rock garden, especially among dwarf conifers. The varieties listed have good vigour, preferring a gravelly soil, especially in regions with wet winters.

HT/SP  10–15 cm (4–6") / 25–30 cm (10–12")
SOIL  Average to dry, well-drained soil.
BLOOM May–September
USES  ⋖⋗⚠☷☇ Scree, Troughs

'Ballerina' Soft-pink flowers with exotic dark-purple veins and centre. Greyish leaves. An outstanding British selection.
'Purple Pillow' Bright magenta-purple flowers rest on the trailing stems of grey-green leaves.
'Splendens' Dayglo magenta flowers with a black eye.

*endressii* ZONE 3
(Pink Cranesbill)

Border type. Forms a vigorous, dense mound of shiny evergreen leaves, with clusters of small bright-pink flowers in summer. Excellent groundcover. May need a hard clipping in midsummer to rejuvenate the foliage.

HT/SP  40–50 cm (16–20") / 45–60 cm (18–24")
SOIL  Average to moist, well-drained soil.
BLOOM May–August
USES  ⋗⚠☷ Borders, Edging

*himalayense* ZONE 2
(Himalayan Cranesbill)

Border type. Mounding clumps of bold leaves and very large, deep violet-blue flowers with a reddish-pink cast. Red foliage in fall. Clip back hard after blooming.

HT/SP  40–50 cm (16–20") / 60–70 cm (24–28")
SOIL  Average to moist, well-drained soil.
BLOOM June–July
USES  Borders, Woodland gardens

'Johnson's Blue' ZONE 2
Border type. The best-known of all the blue selections, though many collectors of *Geraniums* no longer lavish it with the praise they once did. Plants produce large lavender-blue flowers that are sterile, so self-seeding is not a problem. The one major fault of this variety is its tendency to flop all over the place at flowering time, a trait that some of the newer selections do not share. 'Johnson's Blue' should always be sheared back hard as soon as the flowers have faded.

HT/SP  50–60 cm (20–24") / 60–70 cm (24–28")
SOIL  Average to moist, well-drained soil.
BLOOM June–July
USES  Borders, Massing

× *lindavicum* 'Apple Blossom' ZONE 5
Alpine type. This cute little Cranesbill features a summer-long display of soft-pink flowers that seem to rest on the low clump of small grey-green leaves. Best in the rock garden or alpine trough or for edging well-drained areas. Dislikes hot and humid summer regions.

Geranium endressii

Geranium × cantabrigiense 'Biokovo'

Geranium 'Brookside'

**HT/SP** 10–15 cm (4–6") / 20–45 cm (8–18")
**SOIL** Prefers a well-drained soil.
**BLOOM** June–August
**USES** ◭ ⋀⋎ ♥ ❦ Edging, Rock garden

### *macrorrhizum*    ZONE 2
### (Bigroot Cranesbill)

Border type. Extremely fragrant leaves form a dense, vigorous groundcover. Clusters of pink flowers appear in early summer. Heat tolerant. This is the best species of *Geranium* for large ground-cover plantings in sun or shade. Even succeeds in dry shade under thirsty trees. Good fall foliage colour.

**HT/SP** 25–30 cm (10–12") / 45–60 cm (18–24")
**SOIL** Tolerates a wide range of soil conditions.
**BLOOM** June–July
**USES** ⋀⋎ ♥ ❦ Borders, Massing

**'Bevan's Variety'** Deep magenta-pink flowers, bright and cheery.

### *maculatum*    ZONE 4
### (Spotted Cranesbill)

Border type. This is a woodland species, performing well in shady areas with reasonably good moisture. Flowers appear in late spring over a mound of deeply divided medium-green leaves.

**HT/SP** 45–60 cm (18–24") / 45–60 cm (18–24")
**SOIL** Prefers a rich, moist soil.
**BLOOM** April–June
**USES** Borders, Woodland

**'Chatto'** Soft porcelain-pink, green-eyed flowers appear early. Good repeat bloomer if sheared back after the first flush is over, particularly in cool summer regions.

**'Espresso'** Rich, dark coffee-brown foliage contrasts beautifully with a display of soft-pink flowers, which age to white.

**HT** 30–40 cm (12–16")

### × *magnificum*    ZONE 2
### (Showy Cranesbill)

Border type. Produces an abundant display of large violet-blue flowers with dark veins. Attractive divided green leaves usually have good red fall colour. Sterile. Better than 'Johnson's Blue' in most border situations.

**HT/SP** 45–60 cm (18–24") / 60–70 cm (24–28")
**SOIL** Average to moist, well-drained soil.
**BLOOM** June–July
**USES** Borders, Massing

### 'Nimbus'    ZONE 3

Border type. One of the most interesting newer hybrids. This forms a mound of feathery leaves that are tinged with gold early in the season, becoming green in summer. Bright amethyst-purple flowers have a contrasting white eye and a subtle pink flush. Said to be a good repeat-bloomer.

**HT/SP** 60–75 cm (24–30") / 60–70 cm (24–28")
**SOIL** Average to moist, well-drained soil.
**BLOOM** June–August
**USES** ♥ Borders, Massing

### *oxonianum*    ZONE 3
### (Pink Cranesbill)

Border type. Plants make a broad mound of glossy green leaves. Flowers are various shades of pink with dark veins. These are vigorous selections, excellent for using on a large scale as a weed-proof groundcover or for mingling among other perennials towards the front of a border. Best in a moist setting. Trim back hard after the first flush of bloom, as these will often repeat later.

**HT/SP** 45–60 cm (18–24") / 60–75 cm (24–30")
**SOIL** Prefers a rich moist, well-drained soil.
**BLOOM** May–September
**USES** ⋀⋎ ▲ ♥ Borders, Massing

**'Luzie'** Distinctive leaves are marked with black in the middle. Clumps produce very large lipstick-pink flowers with a white eye, appearing throughout most of the summer. An exciting new Canadian introduction, released in 2001 by Elke and Ken Knechtel at The Perennial Gardens in British Columbia.

**HT/SP** 30–45 cm (12–18") / 50–60 cm (20–24")

**'Phoebe Noble'** Also a Canadian selection, named after a noted Victoria-area gardener and educator. This is a vigorous grower, well-suited to mass plantings and quickly making the rounds world wide. Flowers are hot pink, appearing on and off through out the whole season. Trim back hard in mid to late June.

**HT/SP** 40–45 cm (16–18") / 80–90 cm (30–36")

### 'Patricia'    ZONE 4

Border type. I confess to being a non-lover of Cranesbills, but 'Patricia' knocked me over when I first saw her, and I continue to be impressed. The

deeply-cut green foliage makes a size-able mound that sets the stage for the most amazing display of big, black-eyed magenta-pink flowers. There is nothing at all subtle about this plant, which is exactly why I love it.

**HT/SP** 60–75 cm (24–30") / 60–70 cm (24–28")
**SOIL** Average to moist, well-drained soil.
**BLOOM** June–August
**USES** ♥ Borders, Massing

### *phaeum*    ZONE 4
### (Mourning Widow)

Border type. Dark, nodding maroon-purple flowers set this woodland species quite apart from all the others. Plants flower early and tolerate dry shade fairly well, although they really prefer moist conditions. A good vigorous habit, for filling in awkward empty spaces.

**HT/SP** 60–75 cm (24–30") / 60–70 cm (24–28")
**SOIL** Tolerates a wide range of soil conditions.
**BLOOM** May–July
**USES** Borders, Massing

**'Album'** Large clear-white flowers are showy in gloomy, dark corners.
**'Samobor'** Although the deep purple, white-eyed flowers are nice enough, the real reason to grow this is for the foliage. The deeply cut dark-green leaves carry spots and blotches of rich chocolate maroon. Elke Knechtel suggests combining this with gold-leaved Hosta or *Filipendula ulmaria* 'Aurea'. Either one sounds smashing to me!

### 'Phillipe Vapelle'    ZONE 4

Alpine type. With *G. renardii* as one of its parents, this selection inherited the same knubby, grey-green foliage that forms a low, rounded mound. Clusters of rich violet-blue flowers appear in late spring, with darker purple veining. Best in the rock garden or a container.

**HT/SP** 25–30 cm (10–12") / 30–45 cm (12–18")
**SOIL** Average to dry, well-drained soil.
**BLOOM** May–July
**USES** ◭ ♥ ❦ Rock garden, Edging

### 'Pink Spice'    ZONE 7

Alpine type. An interesting selection from New Zealand, one of the first dwarf hybrids with dark foliage. The low, bushy mound of rounded purple-black leaves is studded with soft-pink flowers for a good part of the season. Evergreen where hardy. Ideal in the rock garden, or in alpine troughs as well as containers. Plants may be wintered indoors in a sunny window. Has made it through Zone 5 winters with mulching.

**HT/SP** 10–20 cm (4–8") / 30–40 cm (12–16")
**SOIL** Well-drained soil that won't dry out.
**BLOOM** June–October
**USES** ◭ ♥ ▲ Rock garden, Edging

### *pratense*    ZONE 3
### (Meadow Cranesbill)

Border type. A nice display of good-sized violet-blue flowers is produced in

*Geranium m.* 'Bevan's Variety'

*Geranium* 'Johnson's Blue'

*Geranium maculatum* 'Chatto'

*Geranium × oxonianum* 'Luzie'

*Geranium* 'Patricia'

early summer. Deadhead after blooming and plants may flower a second time. Has a tendency to self-seed. Several terrific selections of this species have recently become available.

**HT/SP** 60–90 cm (2–3') / 60–70 cm (24–28")
**SOIL** Average to moist well-drained soil.
**BLOOM** May–June
**USES** Borders, Massing

**'Midnight Reiter'** Stunning plum-purple leaves hold their colour throughout the season. The violet-blue flowers are the perfect final touch. Very compact habit. Excellent at the border edge, in containers or in the rock garden, although mildew can result in plants going dormant early.

**HT/SP** 20–25 cm (8–10") / 25–30 cm (10–12")

**'Mrs Kendall Clark'** An older selection, but excellent for its display of soft baby-blue flowers with subtle white streaks.

**HT** 60–75 cm (24–30")

**'Victor Reiter Jr.'** Larger than 'Midnight Reiter' in habit, this strain produces deeply-cut deep purple leaves in the spring, which later age to green. Sprays of violet-blue flowers.

**HT/SP** 45–60 cm (18–24") / 45–60 cm (18–24")

*psilostemon*       ZONE 4
[*G. armenum*]
**(Armenian Cranesbill)**
One of the tallest Cranesbills, this plant will be a focal point in the border when its black-eyed magenta-purple flowers appear in early summer. Leaves are very large and deeply cut, with good red fall colour. Plants may require a little extra support and should be placed out of the wind. It should come as no surprise that this is one of the parents of the recent hybrid 'Patricia'.

**HT/SP** 90–120 cm (3–4') / 75–90 cm (30–36")
**SOIL** Average to moist, well-drained soil.
**BLOOM** June–August
**USES** Borders

**'Rozanne'**       ZONE 4
Border type. Recently introduced from Britain, this hybrid shows much promise for edging, borders or grown in containers. The mounding clump of green leaves bears wiry, upright stems that hold cup-shaped soft violet-blue flowers, each with a tiny white eye. Good repeat-blooming habit. May need a hard trim back in midsummer.

**HT/SP** 40–50 cm (16–20") / 45–60 cm (18–24")
**SOIL** Average to moist, well-drained soil.
**BLOOM** May–September
**USES** Border

**'Salome'**       ZONE 6
Border type. With a scrambling or rambling habit not unlike 'Ann Folkard', this recent selection has felty chartreuse-yellow foliage, especially in the spring. Flowers are a unique dusky lavender-pink shade with darker

veining, the centre a contrasting purple-black. May need afternoon shade.

**HT/SP** 30–40 cm (12–16") / 90–120 cm (3–4')
**SOIL** Average to moist, well-drained soil.
**BLOOM** May–July
**USES** Borders

*sanguineum*       ZONE 3
**(Bloody Cranesbill)**
Border type. Low, spreading mats of finely-cut leaves make this species well-suited to edging or groundcover use. Flowers are very showy, bright magenta-purple in the species, or various other shades in the many selections. Fairly drought-tolerant.

**HT/SP** 30–40 cm (12–16") / 45–60 cm (18–24")
**SOIL** Tolerates a wide range of soil conditions.
**BLOOM** May–August
**USES** Borders, Massing

**'Album'** Clear white flowers, with a taller habit than most selections. Many gardeners love this as a filler plant in the border.

**HT/SP** 45–60 cm (18–24") / 60–75 cm (24–30")

**'Max Frei'** Very compact habit and a great display of magenta-pink blooms.

**HT** 15–20 cm (6–8")

**'New Hampshire Purple'** Quite deep magenta-purple flowers, one of the best for massing.

**HT** 20–30 cm (8–12")

**var. *striatum*** ['Lancastriense'] Pale blush-pink flowers with dark crimson veins. Excellent for edging.

**HT** 15–20 cm (6–8")

**'Spinners'**       ZONE 3
Border type. One of the best new blue-flowered hybrids, worth considering instead of the older 'Johnson's Blue'. Foliage is deeply cut, forming a large sized mound with better standing power. Clusters of large violet-blue, white-eyed flowers make a great show in early summer, sometimes repeating in the autumn.

**HT/SP** 75–90 cm (30–36") / 75–90 cm (30–36")
**SOIL** Average to moist, well-drained soil.
**BLOOM** May–July
**USES** Borders

*sylvaticum*       ZONE 2
**(Wood Cranesbill)**
Border type. Good in woodland conditions. Forms a broad clump of divided leaves, with upfacing mauve-pink flowers with a white eye. One of the earliest to bloom. Trim back foliage to 10 cm (4") after flowering.

**HT/SP** 60–75 cm (24–30") / 60–70 cm (24–28")
**SOIL** Average to moist, well-drained soil.
**BLOOM** May–June
**USES** Borders, Woodland gardens

**'Album'** Large white flowers. Perhaps the best white-flowered Cranesbills in existence. Foliage is sturdy for most of the season.

**'Mayflower'** Bright violet-blue with a white eye.

*wlassovianum*       ZONE 3
**(Siberian Cranesbill)**
Border type. An interesting edging or woodland type, the foliage is velvety green with brown markings. Leaves develop good red and bronzy-orange tones in the autumn, which is the main reason for including this in the fall border. Flowers are dark violet-purple and appear much later than most other types.

**HT/SP** 25–30 cm (10–12") / 30–45 cm (12–18")
**SOIL** Prefers a moist, well-drained soil.
**BLOOM** August–September
**USES** Edging, Borders

# GEUM ☼ ☀
**(Avens)**
These bright and cheerful perennials are always popular in the sunny border, and are valued for their long season of bloom. Branching stems of flowers rise up from a bushy clump of hairy leaves. Good for cutting. Protect from hot afternoon sun. The flowers always remind me a bit of the Cranesbill Geraniums, but have hot colour tones rather than cool pastels.

**Hybrids**       ZONE 5
**(Hybrid Avens, Hybrid Geum)**
[*G. chiloense, G. quellyon*]
The well-branched stems of flowers are valuable for cutting. Nice filler plant in the summer border. These tend to be short-lived selections and also are not reliably hardy in all winters, but perform very well even if grown as annuals. Dividing these every year or two in the spring will help to keep plants young and vigorous. They usually hate hot, humid summer regions. Dead-

Geranium 'Pink Spice'
Geranium p. Midnight Reiter
Geranium p. Victor Reiter Jr.
Geranium s. 'New Hampshire Purple'
Geranium wlassovianum
Geranium 'Spinners'

heading works wonders to keep Geums in flower for longer.

**SP**   30–45 cm (12–18″)
**SOIL**   Average well-drained soil. Dislikes winter wet.
**BLOOM** June–August
**USES** ✄ ▲ ⚘ Borders, Massing

**'Blazing Sunset'** Fully double tangerine-red blooms. Long bloomer.

**HT**   50–60 cm (20–24″)

**× borisii** see 'Werner Arends'

**'Double Bloody Mary'** A new European Fleuroselect winner, with double blood-red flowers.

**HT**   60–70 cm (24–28″)

**'Lady Stratheden'** Deep canary-yellow semi-double flowers. An older seed strain, and somewhat variable, but still one of the best yellow forms.

**HT**   60–75 cm (24–30″)

**'Mrs J. Bradshaw'** A scarlet-orange counterpart to 'Lady Stratheden', featuring semi-double flowers.

**HT**   60–75 cm (24–30″)

**'Red Wings'** Also with scarlet-orange semi-double flowers, this is a vegetatively propagated form with better hardiness and a more compact habit. Zone 4.

**HT**   45–60 cm (18–24″)

**'Rijnstroom'** Also a little hardier, this unique selection has large, single coppery-orange flowers and a compact form. Zone 4.

**HT**   45–50 cm (18–20″)

**'Starker's Magnificum'** Lovely soft apricot-orange double flowers, a shade that contrasts beautifully with violet or purple-flowered neighbours. Zone 4.

**HT**   40–45 cm (16–18″)

**'Werner Arends'** Probably the most reliably hardy of the hybrids, featuring bright-orange single flowers in late spring, often reblooming in fall. Clip off flower stems after blooming. This is an excellent low-maintenance plant that is deserving of much wider use. Short enough for the border edge, containers, or even a large rock garden. Formerly known as *G. × borisii.* It seems that the correct name for this plant has finally been settled upon! Zones 2–9.

**HT**   30–40 cm (12–16″)

## GLECHOMA ☼ ◐
### (Ground Ivy, Creeping Charlie)

**hederacea 'Variegata'**   ZONE 4
**[Nepeta hederacea 'Variegata']**
A popular cascading foliage plant for hanging baskets, the round green leaves are handsomely dappled in creamy white. Spikes of violet-blue flowers appear in spring. An aggressive creeper, good as a lawn substitute but keep this out of beds, borders and lawns. Easily increased by allowing stems to trail along the ground and root along their length. New plants can be moved in spring or early fall. Mow or prune back hard in early spring.

**HT/SP**   5–10 cm (2–4″) / 45–75 cm (18–30″)
**SOIL**   Average to moist, well-drained soil.
**BLOOM** April–May
**USES** ⋀⋁ ⚘ Groundcover, Containers, Walls

## GONIOLIMON ☼
### (German Statice, Dumosa)

**tataricum**   ZONE 2
Tiny silvery-white flowers are held in prickly panicles, forming a dome-shaped mound towards late summer. Used mainly for cutting and drying, but also interesting as an edging plant. Prefers a hot sunny site. Excellent for drying. Attractive to butterflies.

**HT/SP**   25–40 cm (10–16″) / 30–45 cm (12–18″)
**SOIL**   Well-drained soil. Dislikes winter wet.
**BLOOM** July–August
**USES** △ ✄ ⚘ Edging, Borders

## GUNNERA ☼ ◐
### (Giant Rhubarb, Prickly Rhubarb)

**manicata**   ZONE 7
### (Giant Gunnera)
Enormous rhubarb-like leaves rise from the ground on thick, thorny stalks. Often seen in large gardens and parks in the Pacific Northwest, where these truly thrive as bold waterside specimens. Flowers appear in midsummer as bizarre bristly cones almost hidden at the base under the leaf canopy. In colder areas plants can be brought through the winter by covering with a very deep mulch piled inside a 1.2 m (4′) square wooden box in late fall, as I

once witnessed in a Halifax, Nova Scotia garden. Some gardeners report good results wintering in large containers in a cool basement, keeping the soil constantly moist.

**HT/SP**   180–300 cm (6–10′) / 150–180 cm (5–6′)
**SOIL**   Rich moist to wet soil.
**BLOOM** July–August
**USES** Waterside specimen

## GYPSOPHILA ☼
### (Baby's Breath)

These all have the familiar misty clouds of flowers, but come in a variety of sizes and colours. They flower best in cool-summer areas, but are fairly carefree.

**paniculata**   ZONE 2
### (Common Baby's Breath)
A widely grown cut flower, used by florists fresh or dried. Often recommended to fill gaps left by summer-dormant plants such as Bleeding Hearts or Oriental Poppies, and the plant serves this function well. Clumps resent being moved once established. They dislike winter wet but show good drought tolerance.

  In Manitoba this species has been placed on the bad list as a nuisance weed; mature plants can act as a tumbleweed and infest pasture land. Although this seems unlikely to happen in an enclosed garden area, one must still obey provincial or state regulations. Double-flowered varieties rarely set seed.

**SP**   80–90 cm (30–36″)
**SOIL**   Average well-drained soil.
**BLOOM** June–September
**USES** ✄ ⚘ Dried Flower, Borders

**'Alba'** Basically this is the species form, with classic single white flowers. Plants are fertile and will set seed.

**HT**   75–90 cm (30–36″)

**'Bristol Fairy'** Double white flowers, the best type for cutting.

**HT**   60–90 cm (2–3′)

**'Pink Fairy'** Large, double light-pink flowers. Compact habit.

**HT**   30–45 cm (12–18″)

**repens**   ZONE 2
### (Creeping Baby's Breath)
These are low, creeping plants suitable for edging or rock gardens. Mats are smothered with flowers in early summer. Not invasive or weedy in any way and moderately drought-tolerant.

**HT/SP**   10–15 cm (4–6″) / 30–45 cm (12–18″)
**SOIL**   Well-drained soil. Heat tolerant.
**BLOOM** June–July
**USES** △⋀⋁ ⚘ Walls, Slopes, Edging

**'Alba'** Pure white single flowers.
**'Rosea'** Soft-pink single flowers.

### HEDYOTIS see HOUSTONIA

Gunnera manicata

Glechoma hederacea 'Variegata'

Geum 'Werner Arends'

Gypsophila paniculata 'Pink Fairy'

# HELENIUM ☼
**(Sneezeweed, Helen's Flower)**
Relatively unknown in North America, although ironically enough the wild species forms are native to this continent. These are valuable perennials for their late-summer display of bright daisy-type flowers, and are also excellent for cutting. Widely grown in European gardens and commercially as a cut flower. Pinch plants back by half in May or early June to encourage bushiness. Staking may be required. Attractive to butterflies.

### *autumnale* Hybrids          ZONE 4
**(Fall Helenium)**
Reliable performers for the late summer border. Large clusters of flowers are held on tall stems for an impressive background display, although breakthroughs are now being made in the development of shorter cultivars with bushier habits. These are waterhogs, so give plenty of moisture in the summer. There are many named selections. Powdery mildew is often a problem when plants feel drought stress; use a preventative fungicide containing sulphur.
HT/SP   90–120 cm (3–4') / 45–60 cm (18–24")
SOIL   Prefers a rich, moist but well-drained soil.
BLOOM July–September
USES   ✂🦋 Borders, Massing

**'Bruno'** Deep crimson-mahogany flowers. Late-blooming and superb.
HT   100–120 cm (39–48")

**'Coppelia'** Flaming coppery-orange flowers. A rich and rare tone for those of us who thrive on hot colours.
**Pipsqueak ['Blopip']** Quite new on the scene, this new compact selection does not require staking or pinching to stay upright. Plants produce loads of bright-yellow flowers, the petals drooping gracefully around a brownish centre.
HT   45–60 cm (18–24")

**Red and Gold ['Rotgold']** A variable seed strain offering a mixture of shades, including yellow, orange, red, and gold. A good choice for the cutting garden or naturalizing in a meadow.

### *hoopesii*          ZONE 2
**(Orange Helenium)**
Earlier to bloom, this species produces shaggy golden-orange daisies with a deeper centre. Foliage is grey-green and somewhat glossy. When grown in rich soil this plant often collapses under the weight of the flowers, so short stakes might be in order. Prune back to 15 cm (6") after blooming.
HT/SP   60–90 cm (2–3') / 45–60 cm (18–24")
SOIL   Average to moist well-drained soil.
BLOOM June–August
USES   ✂🦋 Borders, Meadows

# HELIANTHEMUM ☼
**(Rock Rose, Sun Rose)**

### Hybrids          ZONE 4
These are not really roses, but versatile evergreen creepers, forming a low spreading mat of green or silvery-grey leaves. Flowers are like small wild roses, blooming for several weeks in summer. An excellent choice for edging, rock gardens and walls, or in containers. Some varieties may survive to Zone 2 with adequate protection. These all require very good drainage to prevent rotting out in wet winters. Shear plants lightly after the first flush of bloom is over. Drought-tolerant.
HT/SP   10–30 cm (4–12") / 45–60 cm (18–24")
SOIL   Well-drained soil. Dislikes winter wet.
BLOOM May–July
USES   ⛰🌿▲🌱 Walls, Slopes

**'Annabel'** Double soft-pink flowers. Bushy form, green foliage.
HT   15–30 cm (6–12")

**'Ben Ledi'** Lovely single rose-pink flowers, with a darker eye. Green foliage.
HT   20–30 cm (8–12")

**Double Apricot** Double button flowers in an interesting peachy-orange shade, green leaves. A common variety around the continent, but without a real name so far as I have been able to uncover.
HT   10–20 cm (4–8")

**'Fireball' ['Mrs C.W. Earle']** Double crimson-red flowers, green leaves.
HT   10–20 cm (4–8")

**'Fire Dragon'** Single flame-orange flowers, a superb contrast to the silvery-grey foliage.
HT   10–20 cm (4–8")

**'Henfield Brilliant'** Large orange-red single flowers, deep green foliage.
HT   15–20 cm (6–8")

**Single Yellow** Large chrome-yellow flowers, green leaves. A very vigorous and hardy form, unfortunately lacking a real name.
HT   15–30 cm (6–12")

**'The Bride'** Large single white flowers with a golden eye, silvery foliage.
HT   10–15 cm (4–6")

**'Wisley Pink'** Large, single soft-pink flowers, silvery-grey leaves. Outstanding!
HT   15–30 cm (6–12")

**'Wisley Primrose'** Pale primrose-yellow blooms over silvery-grey foliage.
HT   15–30 cm (6–12")

# HELIANTHUS ☼
**(Sunflower)**
Hardy perennial relatives of the annual birdseed and snack-food varieties. The selections listed are happiest in a moist sunny location where they will form sizable non-invasive clumps. All are excellent for cutting.

### *decapetalus* 'Plenus'          ZONE 4
**[*H.* × *multiflorus* 'Plenus']**
**(Double Perennial Sunflower)**
Fully double golden-yellow daisy flowers, making an appearance in late summer and fall. Plants are upright and bushy, although staking may be necessary if soils are rich. This needs a good moist site or powdery mildew may become a problem.
HT/SP   120–150 cm (4–5') / 60–90 cm (2–3')
SOIL   Prefers a rich moist soil.
BLOOM August–September
USES   ✂🦋 Borders, Meadows

### 'Lemon Queen'          ZONE 4
**['Limelight']**
A number of years ago I stumbled upon this amazing plant in the gardens at Sissinghurst Castle in England. Before me was a sunflower of enormous height, without the least hint of floppiness, and with flowers in a gorgeous soft lemon-yellow shade. Finally it seems to have reached this side of the pond, and I predict 'Lemon Queen' will quickly become a favourite in fall borders from coast to coast. In our warmer summer regions the clumps may well need some staking, particularly when grown in rich soils. Like most of the late-blooming daisies, pinching in May or June should work well to reduce the height. Superb for cutting.
HT/SP   180–210 cm (6–7') / 75–90 cm (30–36")
SOIL   Prefers a rich moist soil.
BLOOM August–October
USES   ✂🦋 Borders, Meadows

### *salicifolius*          ZONE 4
**(Willow-leaf Sunflower)**
A most unique back-of-the-border subject that has been described aptly as

*Helianthemum* 'Ben Ledi'
*Helenium* Pipsqueak
*Helianthemum* 'Fireball'
*Helianthemum* 'Wisley Pink'     *Helianthemum* 'Henfield Brilliant'

a giant asparagus fern. Stems are clothed in drooping, willowy leaves, with an almost tropical appearance. Single yellow daisies appear at the top in late fall and have a charm of their own. An interesting texture plant. Almost always needs to be staked. Native North American wildflower.

Another selection has made the rounds for years under this name, a plant with a more compact habit and finely-textured foliage, bearing a grand display of golden daisies in very late fall. The puzzle seems to have been finally solved, the correct name for the imposter being *H. angustifolius* 'Gold Lace'.

**HT/SP** 180–240 cm (6–8') / 90–120 cm (3–4')
**SOIL** Prefers a rich moist soil.
**BLOOM** October–November
**USES** ✂🌷 Specimen, Borders

## HELIOPSIS ☼
### (False Sunflower)

**helianthoides**  ZONE 2
Probably the longest flowering of the tall daisy-flowered perennials, with large single or double golden heads that bloom in succession over several months. The strong, sturdy stems are excellent for cutting. These are terrific background plants for summer and fall colour. Although reliable and long-lived plants, their one bad habit is a tendency to need extra support when grown in rich garden soil. The species itself is a native North American wildflower, but generally the garden selections are grown.

**HT** 90–120 cm (3–4')
**SOIL** Average well-drained soil.
**BLOOM** June–October
**USES** ✂🌷 Borders, Massing

**'Hohlspiegel'** A German selection, the name refers to a concave shaving

mirror – some names just don't translate well! This was developed as a commercial cut flower, producing the largest single golden-yellow flowers that I have seen.

**HT** 90–120 cm (3–4')

**Loraine Sunshine ['Helhan']** Unique and outstanding for its variegated foliage, which is creamy-white with an intricate netting of dark green veins. Large golden-yellow daisies are a bonus, but this is worth growing for the foliage alone. Interestingly, a large proportion of the seedlings maintain the variegated habit.

**HT** 90-100 cm (3')

**'Prairie Sunset'** A brand new selection from Prairie Nursery in Wisconsin. Single flowers are bright golden-yellow with red centres at first, later becoming all gold. The foliage is rather unique, green with distinctive purple veins that are echoed in the dark purple flower stems. Bushy habit, long blooming season from July until frost. In rich soils this might need extra support.

**HT** 120–150 cm (4–5')

**'Midwest Dreams'** A seed-grown mixture of yellow and orange shades, producing large single daisies. Has a fairly compact habit.

**HT** 80–90 cm (30–36")

**Summer Sun ['Sommersonne']** Semi-double golden daisies. The most widely-grown form, and a garden classic.

**HT** 90–120 cm (3–4')

## HELLEBORUS ◐●
### (Hellebore)

Much sought-after by perennial enthusiasts everywhere, the Hellebores are currently enjoying great popularity from coast to coast. These are invaluable for their mid-winter or early spring display of nodding, cup-shaped flowers. The foliage is leathery and somewhat coarse in texture, and reliably evergreen in most cases. Although they grow best in Zones 6–9, Hellebores are worth a try in colder regions, where the blooming season will be delayed until March or April. A winter mulch of loose leaves or straw is a good idea in very cold or windy areas.

The different species all require moisture early in the year during their flowering period, but later in the season will tolerate moderate summer drought. Also in common, all species hate being disturbed once they are established; plants will sulk for six months or so just to let you know how unhappy they are. Starting with nursery-grown container plants produces excellent results. In

time you may even find that your own plants will self-seed!

It's worth mentioning that gardening books and magazines often entice us all with pictures of named cultivars of Hellebores. Since increasing these by division is costly and slow, most growers offer strains produced from seed – the resulting plants varying a fair bit in their flower colour and even foliage characteristics. If you desire flowers of a certain colour it's best to purchase plants in bloom whenever possible, so you know what you're getting. That being said, I have seldom seen a Hellebore that I didn't like, so it's hard to really go wrong! **CAUTION: All are harmful if eaten/skin irritant.**

**argutifolius**  ZONE 6
**[H. corsicus]**
**(Corsican Hellebore)**
This unique species produces branching sprays of small apple-green flowers. Plants form an outstanding clump of grey-green leathery foliage, slightly vicious looking in appearance, with coarsely-toothed edges. More sun-tolerant than some of the other types. Do not trim until after flowering, or not at all.

**HT/SP** 45–60 cm (18–24") / 45–60 cm (18–24")
**SOIL** Average to moist, well-drained soil.
**BLOOM** February–April
**USES** ✂◭▲🌷 Specimen, Borders

**'Pacific Frost'** This is a unique and hard-to-find strain, the grey-green leaves are mottled all over light green and creamy-white. Flowers are the typical apple green. Quite stunning when well placed as a shade specimen. **'Janet Starnes'** is a seed strain of the Corsican Hellebore with a similar appearance.

**'Atrorubens'**  ZONE 5
**[H. orientalis abchasicus Early Purple Group]**
A magnificent plant when in bloom. The flowers are dusky maroon-purple, blooming between the Christmas and Lenten Rose. Similar in habit to *H. ×hybridus*, this benefits visually from trimming off the old foliage in late winter, just before the buds arise.

**HT/SP** 30–40 cm (12–16") / 30–45 cm (12–18")
**SOIL** Well-drained loamy soil.
**BLOOM** February–May
**USES** ◭▲♣✂🌷 Borders, Specimen

**foetidus**  ZONE 5
**(Stinking Hellebore)**
Small soft-green flowers appear in branching sprays, the petals often edged in reddish purple. The botanical name alludes to a slightly skunky odour given off by the plant, but I have always found this to be very mild, at least in an outdoor setting. The foliage is sturdy and evergreen; flowers appear quite early. Although this species seems to be

Helianthus salicifolius

Helianthus 'Lemon Queen'

Heliopsis h. Summer Sun

Helleborus argutifolius 'Pacific Frost'

Helleborus argutifolius

best adapted to regions with maritime conditions, some gardeners in places like the Midwest report amazing success. Fairly tolerant of heat and humidity. Plants will self seed better than most other Hellebores. Pruning, if required at all, should only be done immediately after blooming. A number of named strains are available through specialist nurseries or seed houses.

**HT/SP** 45–60 cm (18–24″) / 30–45 cm (12–18″)
**SOIL** Average to moist, well-drained soil.
**BLOOM** February–May
**USES** ✂△♠✿ Specimen, Borders

### *niger*                                   ZONE 4
### (Christmas Rose)

This species is the one most well-known to gardeners. Plants form a sturdy clump of leathery, evergreen leaves, not unlike a dwarf peony in appearance. Flowers are large and cup-shaped, pure white or sometimes tinged with pinkish green, appearing anytime from Christmas to Easter – depending on the climate. Plants sometimes even bloom under the snow. Slow to establish, but well worth the wait. Christmas Rose should rarely need to be pruned, aside from removing any dead or diseased leaves.

In my own experience the Christmas Rose has not been nearly as forgiving in my garden as the Lenten Rose hybrids. I made the classic mistake of planting it in dry shade, which it hated, and also way at the end of the garden. A path quickly became worn in the lawn from me running out every other day to check and see if it was blooming yet. My word of advice is to plant this up close to the house where you can best enjoy it without getting mud on your shoes!

**HT/SP** 25–30 cm (10–12″) / 25–40 cm (10–16″)
**SOIL** Rich, well-drained loamy soil.
**BLOOM** December–March
**USES** △♠✂✿ Borders, Specimen

### *orientalis* Hybrids                      ZONE 5
### [*H. hybridus*]
### (Lenten Rose)

These superb and vigorous hybrids form tough clumps of leathery, evergreen leaves. Flower stalks appear in early spring, holding large nodding flowers in shades of white, cream, pink, rose, red or maroon, often with contrasting spots. Plants are nearly always raised from seed, resulting in mixed colours. If you want a specific shade, try to purchase plants that are in flower.

Although plants bloom later than the Christmas rose, many gardeners consider this group of hybrids to be the nicer of the two, and certainly the easiest to please. Excellent under trees or shrubs. Cut off all the old leaves in late winter before the buds pop out of the ground; this simple task is the only

maintenance required, other than watering during dry periods.

**HT/SP** 40–60 cm (16–24″) / 45–60 cm (18–24″)
**SOIL** Rich, well-drained loamy soil.
**BLOOM** February–May
**USES** △✂♠✿ Borders, Woodland gardens

**Royal Heritage™ Strain** An exceptionally good strain from Brigg's Nursery in Washington state. It produces a wide range of shades from white through to pink, red, maroon, near-black and even green! Petals overlap well, creating distinctive cup-shaped blooms. Some plants produce flowers with richly contrasting blotches or freckles. To find your own perfect designer colours it's best to purchase plants when they're blooming.

### × *sternii*                               ZONE 6
### (Hybrid Hellebore)

This is a variable group of hybrids. With *H. argutifolius* as one of the parents, it has similar cultural requirements and general habit. The foliage usually has a distinctive greyish-green colour, with spiny or toothed edges to the leaflets. Flowers are in clusters or sprays, usually chartreuse or green but flushed with purple. Like other Hellebores with small sprays of flowers, pruning should only be done immediately after blooming, or not at all.

**HT/SP** 45–60 cm (18–24″) / 30–45 cm (12–18″)
**SOIL** Average to moist, well-drained soil.
**BLOOM** February–May
**USES** ✂△♠✿ Specimen, Borders

## HEMEROCALLIS ☼◑
### (Daylily)

Extensive breeding over the last fifty years has brought the Daylily to the top ranks of modern garden perennials. Plants form a sturdy clump of grassy leaves, bearing stiff stems that rise above and hold a succession of large lily-shaped flowers, each lasting for about a day. By choosing varieties that bloom at different times you can easily extend the flowering season from May through late August. Lack of choice is not a valid complaint with this enormous group of plants – literally thousands of selections are in existence, with more added to the list each year.

Daylilies are suitable for planting in perennial and shrub borders, massing as a groundcover, or for planting in large containers. All prefer full sun or part shade, and an average well-drained soil. Plants are very long-lived, and seldom need to be divided. Once established, Daylilies are also moderately heat and drought tolerant. As cut flowers, Daylilies are not great from a commercial standpoint, but they will make it through a dinner party just fine. After dinner you can nibble on the

petals, since the flowers of all Daylily varieties and species are edible!

In addition to the named hybrids there are some excellent old species forms that are still of value in perennial gardens. The Tawny Daylily (*H. fulva*) which grows all over the roadsides of eastern North America is probably best left there. Its spreading tendencies and brief season of bloom do not make it a first choice for gardens.

### NAMED HYBRIDS                            ZONE 2

This is but a short listing from the enormous number of named selections in existence. In recent years there have been many new colour breakthroughs, particularly with whites, purple and pinks. Some breeders are working on more dwarf varieties with reliable repeat blooming, others are selecting for new flower shapes or markings. For those gardeners with a serious passion for Daylilies there are many specialist nurseries in both the USA and Canada that carry the newest and latest (and most expensive!) selections.

Daylily breeders have developed their own shorthand and terms to describe specific plant habits. Some of these include:

- **Dormant** – foliage goes completely dormant in winter. This sometimes indicates superior winter hardiness.
- **Semi-evergreen** – leaves remain attractive well into late fall. In northern regions this is not always especially noticeable. Plants may not be quite as hardy as dormant types.
- **Evergreen** – foliage remains green through the winter in mild regions. Evergreen selections are seldom the best for cold winter areas, below about Zone 6.

*Helleborus niger*

*Helleborus* 'Atrorubens'

*Helleborus* × *sternii*

*Helleborus foetidus*

- **Diploid** - plants have the normal number of chromosomes.
- **Tetraploid** – plants have twice the normal number of chromosomes. Tetraploid varieties often have very thick, waxy petals and especially sturdy foliage. Don't worry too much about this term – for most of us it makes little difference, we just want "pretty" daylilies!
- **Extended** – this refers to flowers that last for at least 16 hours.
- **Repeat blooming** – varieties that continue to produce buds over a long season. Sometimes these varieties will rest briefly after the main flush of bloom, developing new buds later in the season.
- **Nocturnal** – buds open in late afternoon and last through the night.

Daylilies are among the most forgiving perennials one could ever grow. Plants adapt readily to a range of different soil conditions, although their preference is for a rich, well-drained loam. Disease problems are minimal. The foliage is occasionally bothered by thrips during summer droughts, best controlled by an insecticidal spray combined with regular watering.

There have been recent warnings about Daylily rust – a newly introduced fungal disease that can severely set back or even kill plants. Symptoms are very similar to a thrips infestation, so be sure to have plants tested in a laboratory before taking extreme measures, like destroying them. Cleaning up and discarding (in the garbage!) all the dead foliage in the fall will go far in helping to prevent the spread of Daylily rust. This will help to reduce numbers of overwintering insects at the same time.

| | |
|---|---|
| **SP** | 60–90 cm (2–3') |
| **SOIL** | Average well-drained soil is best, but tolerant of a wide range of conditions. |
| **BLOOM** | *Extra Early*: Late May to early June |
| | *Early*: Mid to late June |
| | *Midseason*: Mid July |
| | *Late*: August |
| **USES** | ✂ M ❦ 🦋 🌱 ❀ Borders, Massing, Containers |

### BICOLOUR SHADES　　ZONE 2

**'Janice Brown'** Big soft-pink flowers with a deep-rose eye and contrasting green throat. Repeat blooming. Early/Midseason. Diploid. Winter dormant.

**HT**　45–52 cm (18–21")

**'Moonlit Masquerade'** Creamy-white petals and an amazing dark-purple eyezone, green throat. Repeat blooming. Early/Midseason. Tetraploid. Semi-evergreen.

**HT**　55–65 cm (22–24")

**'Siloam Merle Kent'** Large blooms, orchid-pink petals with a deep purple eye. Extended blooming. Midseason/Late. Diploid. Winter dormant.

**HT**　40–45 cm (16–18")

**'Strawberry Candy'** Coral-pink flowers, delicious strawberry-red eye. Repeat blooming. Early/Midseason. Tetraploid. Semi-evergreen.

**HT**　60–65 cm (24–26")

**'When My Sweetheart Returns'** Constant repeat blooming habit from June until frost. Dwarf form, large blooms of a soft creamy-apricot with a rich rose-pink eye and bright lemon throat. Early/Midseason. Diploid. Winter dormant.

**HT**　35–40 cm (14–16")

### GOLD AND ORANGE SHADES ZONE 2

**'Apricot Sparkles'** Constant repeat blooming habit. Deep apricot-yellow flowers have a delightful diamond-dusted finish. Dwarf clumps are a great choice for massing. Extra early. Diploid. Winter dormant.

**HT**　30–40 cm (12–16")

**'Corky'** Charming small golden-yellow flowers, petals flushed with bronze on the reverse. Unusual near-black stems. Midseason. Diploid. Winter dormant.

**HT**　75–80 cm (30–32")

**'Scentual Sundance'** Blooms constantly from May until frost. Exceedingly fragrant, with large golden-yellow flowers. Colour is similar to 'Stella de Oro' but with much bigger blooms. Extra early. Diploid. Winter dormant.

**HT**　40–45 cm (16–18")

**'Siloam Dave McKeithen'** Large blooms in a lovely yellow and gold blend. Midseason. Diploid. Winter dormant.

**HT**　50–60 cm (20–24")

**'Stella de Oro'** An extremely popular repeat-blooming dwarf selection. Small golden-yellow flowers with a slightly darker throat. Fragrant. Blooms June-September. Excellent for edging or massing. Early. Diploid. Winter dormant.

**HT**　25–30 cm (10–12")

### LAVENDER AND PURPLE SHADES
　　　　　　　　　　　　　　ZONE 2

**'Little Grapette'** Light grape-purple with a green throat, dwarf habit. An award-winning miniature. Early. Diploid. Semi-evergreen.

**HT**　25–30 cm (10–12")

**'Regal Heir'** Very large lavender-purple flowers with a lemon throat, repeat blooming. Midseason. Diploid. Winter dormant.

**HT**　50–55 cm (20–22")

**'Russian Rhapsody'** Rich plum-purple flowers, deep purple eye. Midseason. Tetraploid. Semi-evergreen.

**HT**　70–75 cm (28–30")

**'Woodside Rhapsody'** Sun-fast wine-purple blooms with a green throat. Large and fragrant. Midseason/Late. Diploid. Winter dormant.

**HT**　70–80 cm (28–32")

### PINK SHADES　　　　　ZONE 2

**'Catherine Woodbery'** Fragrant. Pale orchid-pink and yellow blend, lime-green throat. A popular older selection. Midseason/Late. Diploid. Winter dormant.

**HT**　80–90 cm (30–36")

**'In the Flesh'** Delicate, very soft pink with a mustard throat. Extended blooming. Late season. Diploid. Winter dormant.

**HT**　40–45 cm (16–18")

**'Jolyene Nichole'** Very large medium-pink ruffled flowers with a lemon throat. Dwarf habit and a good repeat bloomer. Early/Midseason. Diploid. Winter dormant.

**HT**　30–35 cm (12–14")

**'Luxury Lace'** Creamy-pink petals with lavender ribs and a green throat. Nicely ruffled edges and good fragrance. Repeat bloomer. Midseason. Diploid. Winter dormant.

**HT**　70–75 cm (28–30")

**'Pastures of Pleasure'** Fragrant, ruffled orchid-pink flowers with a lemon throat. Nice tall scapes and high bud count. Early/Midseason. Diploid. Winter dormant.

**HT**　80–90 cm (30–36")

**'Preppy Pink'** Fragrant blooms of medium pink with a greenish throat. Extended and very good repeat blooming. Midseason. Diploid. Winter dormant.

**HT**　75–80 cm (30–32")

*Hemerocallis 'Corky'*　　*H. 'Regal Heir'*　　*H. 'Jolyene Nichole'*

*H. 'Strawberry Candy'*　*H. 'Innocent Bystander'*　*H. 'Moonlight Masquerade'*

*H. 'Siloam Dave McKeithem'*　*H. 'Siloam Justine Lee'*　*H. 'Preppy Pink'*

**'Rosy Returns'** Constant repeat blooming habit from June through frost. Good-sized bright rose-pink blooms with a deeper rose-red eyezone and yellow throat. Early. Diploid. Winter dormant. Shows terrific potential for northern climate regions.

HT    30–35 cm (12–14")

**'Velveteen'** Solid cerise-pink with a yellow throat. Midseason. Diploid. Winter dormant.

HT    70–75 cm (28–30")

**'Vivacious'** Silvery rose-pink, ruffled petals. Midseason. Diploid. Winter dormant.

HT    45–50 cm (18–20")

### RED SHADES                    ZONE 2
**'James Marsh'** Large, thick and waxy blooms of bright scarlet-red. Truly outstanding! Early/Midseason. Tetraploid. Winter dormant.

HT    65–70 cm (24–30")

**'Pardon Me'** Small, ruffled cranberry-red flowers with a yellow throat. Fragrant. Reliable repeat bloomer. Award winning. Midseason. Diploid. Winter dormant. This is quickly gaining in popularity as an alternative to 'Stella de Oro'. Unfortunately, this variety is highly prone to daylily rust infections.

HT    40–45 cm (16–18")

**'Red Hot Returns'** Constant repeat blooming habit from June through frost. Large flowers of rich, true red with a contrasting lemon-yellow throat. One of the most exciting new breakthroughs. Early/Midseason. Diploid. Semi-evergreen.

HT    50–60 cm (20–24")

**'Siloam Justine Lee'** Bright cherry-red flowers with a green throat, large blooms. Early/Midseason. Diploid. Winter dormant.

HT    30–40 cm (12–16")

**'Woodside Ruby'** Large, ruffled ruby-red flowers with a lemon throat. Midseason/Late. Diploid. Semi-evergreen foliage.

HT    75–85 cm (30–33")

### WHITE AND CREAM SHADES ZONE 2
**'Innocent Bystander'** Big, ruffled ivory-white blooms over a long season. Repeat blooming. Midseason. Diploid. Semi-evergreen.

HT    80–90 cm (30–36")

**'Joan Senior'** Large, ruffled creamy-white flowers, lime-green throat. Repeat-blooming. Fragrant. Early/Midseason. Diploid. Evergreen.

HT    55–60 cm (22–24")

### YELLOW SHADES                 ZONE 2
**'Big Time Happy'** Like a larger-flowered version of 'Happy Returns'. Soft lemon-yellow blooms with ruffled edges and a green throat. Blooms constantly from May until frost. Extra early. Diploid. Winter dormant.

HT    40–50 cm (16–20")

**'Bitsy'** Loads of small but charming lemon-yellow flowers over a long season. Extended and repeat blooming. Extra early. Diploid. Semi-evergreen.

HT    45–50 cm (18–20")

**'Happy Returns'** Prolific display of small but fragrant canary-yellow flowers. Repeat blooms consistently from May to frost! Very widely used for massed landscape plantings. Extra early. Diploid. Winter dormant.

HT    40–45 cm (16–18")

**'Hyperion'** Large and fragrant lemon-yellow flowers, extended blooming. Repeat blooming habit. An older selection but a true classic. Award winning. Midseason. Diploid. Winter dormant.

HT    90–100 cm (36–40")

**'Pudgie'** Double petals of electric yellow, large blooms that open in the evening. Extremely sturdy foliage and a nice compact habit. Midseason. Diploid. Winter dormant.

HT    35–40 cm (14–16")

**'Siloam Amazing Grace'** Huge, ruffled bright-yellow flowers, extended blooming. Early/Midseason. Diploid. Winter dormant.

HT    55–60 cm (22–24")

**'Siloam Harold Flickinger'** Large blooms of solid yellow. Early/Midseason. Diploid. Winter dormant.

HT    55–65 cm (22–24")

**'Sunny Honey'** Good-sized ruffled flowers in a soft honey-yellow shade. Terrific repeat blooming habit. Early. Diploid. Semi-evergreen.

HT    50–60 cm (20–24")

**'Sunset Returns'** Constant repeat blooming habit from June until frost. Dwarf habit, large flowers of deep yellow to apricot, kissed with gold and melon tints. Early. Diploid. Winter dormant.

HT    30–40 cm (12–16")

## HERNIARIA ☼◐
(Rupturewort)

***glabra***                        ZONE 5
**(Rupturewort, Green Carpet)**
Known to be nearly indestructible, this is an excellent choice for growing between flagstones or using as a lawn substitute. The tiny leaves create a dense evergreen carpet, becoming bronze in winter. Insignificant green flowers. Easily divided in spring. Tends to need watering during periods of extreme drought. Sometimes used in formal carpet bedding schemes. Growth rate is fairly slow and easy to control. This is a relatively unknown perennial that deserves to be used more often in our gardens.

HT/SP    1–3 cm (½–1") / 25–30 cm (10–12")
SOIL     Average to moist, well-drained soil.
BLOOM June–July
USES    〰▲▼🌱 Groundcover, Rock gardens

## HESPERIS ☼◐
(Sweet Rocket, Dame's Rocket)

***matronalis***                    ZONE 2
Produces heads or branching spikes of sweetly-scented purple, mauve or white flowers, resembling Summer Phlox – and plants are often called Wild Phlox in error. A real old-fashioned garden plant for the early summer border. Generally performs as a self-seeding biennial. Naturalized throughout much of eastern North America.

HT/SP    60–90 cm (2–3') / 45–60 cm (18–24")
SOIL     Average to moist soil.
BLOOM May–July
USES    ✂🦋 Borders, Meadows

## HEUCHERA ☼◐
(Coral Bells, Alumroot)
Not that many years ago the Coral Bells in gardens were mainly the old-fashioned flowering types, with their low clumps of rounded green leaves and upright sprays or loose spikes of red, pink or white flowers. A lot of breeding work has happened with the Coral Bells, transforming them into one of the most widely-used groups of perennials. Many of the newer types have been selected more for their outstanding

*H. 'Amazing Grace'*

*H. 'Janice Brown'*

*Herniaria glabra*

*H. 'Pastures of Pleasure'*

*H. 'Pardon Me'*

*Hemerocallis 'Hyperion'*

foliage, in previously unimaginable shades of purple, brown, red and near-black, often with exotic metallic silver markings to rival the best Rex begonia! Lately the breeding work has made some great strides in combining the marvellous foliage effect with bright and showy flowers, so we are now able have the best of both worlds all in one plant.

All types are most effective when featured towards the front of a border or in a rockery where their delicate sprays of flowers or attractive leaves can be seen up close. Flowers are excellent for cutting. Selections with pink or red flowers are usually attractive to hummingbirds.

### *americana* Hybrids          ZONE 4
### (Fancy-leaved Coral Bells)

Crosses involving the native North American species *H. americana* and others have resulted in an overwhelming number of hybrid selections. These were at first grown primarily for their beautiful foliage, available in a wide range of colours, sizes and shapes, but recent efforts in breeding have brought colourful flowers into this tribe. The older selections usually produce sprays of greenish-white bells – a nice complement to the leaves, but not much to write home about. Newer forms with scarlet, pink or red flowers are truly impressive in the garden, both for their foliage and flowers.

Most of these dislike hot afternoon sun but are tolerant of hot, humid summers. The exotic leaf textures and rich tones seem to associate especially well with ferns and other woodland plants. Foliage stays near-evergreen in mild winter areas. Foliage should be left alone in the fall, then tidied up in the

spring before new growth resumes. One odd habit many of these share is a tendency to develop a woody base that gets taller each season. Left alone, the plants end up looking like tufts of leaves on stilts. Don't be afraid to cut these awkward stems back hard every couple of years (in the spring), to a height of around 5–8 cm (2–3″). New shoots and leaves will develop from the remaining dormant buds.

Some gardeners in cold regions (like the Canadian prairies) are reporting good success with a number of different Coral Bell hybrids. By choosing a sheltered location (out of the drying winter winds) or one with reliable snow cover, gardeners in Zones 2 and 3 stand a good chance of finding these to be reliable. NOTE: the height ranges below are intended to indicate the foliage height first, followed by the flower height.

**SOIL** Rich average to moist soil.
**BLOOM** June–July
**USES** ✂📐🌿🐦 Borders, Edging, Specimen

**'Amber Waves'** Truly amazing, this rather recent introduction produces a mound of amber-gold leaves, flushed with butter yellow, and is completely unlike any other selection. Sprays of soft rose-pink flowers are nice enough. This new designer colour is going to be even better than gold Hostas for brightening up shady corners. Compact habit. Recommended for part shade to morning sun.

**HT/SP** 20–40 cm (8–16″) / 45–60 cm (18–24″)

**'Can-can'** One of the first ruffled types, featuring bright silvery-grey foliage with darker green veining. The wine reverse peeks out from under the skirts in a teasing sort of way. Foliage takes on rich plum overtones during cooler weather. Sprays of creamy flowers.

**HT/SP** 25–65 cm (1–2′) / 45–60 cm (18–24″)

**'Checkers'** Silvery-metallic leaves are intricately veined with green. As an added bonus plants produce a showy display of large ivory-white flowers held well above the foliage. One of my personal favourites.

**HT/SP** 30–60 cm (1–2′) / 30–45 cm (12–18″)

**'Cherries Jubilee'** One of the newer forms, combining a stunning display of cherry-red flowers with ruffled bronzy-brown leaves. Said to be a good repeat bloomer. Best foliage colour develops in partial shade.

**HT/SP** 20–45 cm (8–18″) / 30–45 cm (12–18″)

**'Chocolate Ruffles'** Enormous ruffled leaves. Foliage is dark chocolate-brown on top, burgundy below. Flowers are creamy, held up on tall purple stems. Nearly evergreen in milder areas. Good heat tolerance. The catchy name has

helped to make this one of the most popular selections worldwide.

**HT/SP** 25–75 cm (10–30″) / 45–60 cm (18–24″)

**'Crimson Curls'** Quite new on the scene, this is one of the best ruffled forms to date. Deep crimson-red to red-black leaves are intensely crimped and curled along the edges. Has sprays of creamy flowers.

**HT/SP** 20–45 cm (8–18″) / 45–60 cm (18–24″)

**Dale's strain** This strain is a seed-grown form of *H. americana*, selected for its blue-green leaves, mottled with silvery-white and showing dark-red veining during cold weather. Spikes of greenish-white flowers. A tough "grow anywhere" kind of plant, suitable for edging in sun or shade. Somewhat variable.

**HT/SP** 20–45 cm (8–18″) / 30–45 cm (12–18″)

**'Green Spice' ['Eco-improved']** Silvery-green leaves with contrasting beet-red veining that is especially good during colder months. Spikes of creamy flowers are nothing special. Despite its subtle nature, this remains my absolute personal favourite of the whole group.

**HT/SP** 25–70 cm (10–30″) / 45–60 cm (18–24″)

**'Pewter Veil'** New leaves are coppery pink, changing to silvery-pewter with darker veins. Leaves are very large, flowers creamy. Outstanding!

**HT/SP** 20–70 cm (8–30″) / 45–60 cm (18–24″)

**'Plum Pudding'** Rich plum-purple leaves with a shimmering metallic finish. Creamy flowers. Compact habit.

**HT/SP** 20–65 cm (8–24″) / 45–60 cm (18–24″)

**'Purple Sails'** Creamy flowers appear over a mound of maple-shaped leaves, in a cool smoky lavender-purple shade.

**HT/SP** 30–65 cm (1–2′) / 45–60 cm (18–24″)

**'Rachel'** Cheery deep coral-pink flowers are a grand contrast to the foliage, which is deep green overlaid with rich purple-black.

**HT/SP** 25–60 cm (1–2′) / 45–60 cm (18–24″)

**'Ruby Veil'** Huge leaves are metallic ruby-violet mottled with silver. Rich effect. Creamy flowers. Good sun tolerance.

**HT/SP** 15–65 cm (6–24″) / 45–60 cm (18–24″)

**'Shamrock'** A unique departure from the usual, featuring very tall sprays of chartreuse-green flowers over a mound of silver-kissed green leaves. Terrific as a cut flower. Deadhead to encourage repeat blooming. Good sun tolerance.

**HT/SP** 30–90 cm (1–3′) / 45–60 cm (18–24″)

**'Silver Scrolls'** Rounded leaves begin silver and burgundy in the spring, later deepening to silver with near-black highlights. Sprays of soft ivory-pink

*Heuchera* 'Amber Waves'

*Heuchera* 'Green Spice'

*Heuchera* 'Purple Sails'

flowers are held on beet-red stems. Said to be fairly sun tolerant.

**HT/SP**  45–60 cm (18–24″) / 45–60 cm (18–24″)

**'Smokey Rose'** Smoky-bronze foliage with a ruffled edge. Nice display of rose-pink flowers in mid-summer. Heat tolerant.

**HT/SP**  20–50 cm (8–20″) / 45–60 cm (18–24″)

**'Stormy Seas'** Ruffled leaves are a combination of pewter, silver, lavender and charcoal. Excellent vigour and full habit, making this one of the best for general landscape use. Flowers are creamy.

**HT/SP**  40–80 cm (16–30″) / 60–75 cm (24–30″)

**'Veil of Passion'** Showy sprays of bright-red flowers with contrasting bronzy-black leaves, mottled with metallic pewter. Maintains reliable leaf colour in partial shade. Deadhead for continued blooming.

**HT/SP**  25–65 cm (1–2′) / 30–45 cm (12–18″)

**'Velvet Night'** Perhaps the darkest form, with huge near-black leaves overlaid in metallic purple-grey. Creamy flowers. Dan Heims, the originator, suggests planting beside a gold-leaved Hosta for a knock-out combination.

**HT/SP**  20–65 cm (8–24″) / 45–60 cm (18–24″)

#### × *brizoides* Hybrids          ZONE 3

This is a kind of catch-all group that includes most of the green-leaved forms that are grown mainly for their colourful flowers. Plants form a low clump of rounded leaves, the tiny bells held well above in airy sprays that are a magnet to hummingbirds. The low, mounding habit makes these ever-popular for edging borders and in rock gardens. Flowers are superb for cutting. A preference for full sun to part-day sun sets these apart from the more shade-loving types with colourful foliage. Divide plants every 2–3 years to maintain vigour.

**SP**   30–45 cm (12–18″)
**SOIL**   Average to moist well-drained soil.
**BLOOM** May–July
**USES**   ✂✕△☂▲ Borders, Edging

**Bressingham Hybrids** An attractive seed-grown mixture of pink, coral and red flowers, with the occasional white.

**HT**   60–75 cm (24–30″)

**'Canyon Pink'** An exceptionally long-blooming selection, with clouds of deep-pink bells on a tidy, compact plant. One of the very best for edging. Introduced by the Santa Barbara Botanic Garden in 1985. Performed well recently in trials at the University of Georgia.

**HT**   20–30 cm (8–12″)

**'Rosada'** Unusually tall spikes of rose-pink flowers are featured here. A massed planting of this is truly an incredible sight. Excellent for cutting.

**HT**   70–75 cm (28–30″)

**'Yeti'** Another rather tall selection, with bells of snowy white.

**HT**   60–75 cm (24–30″)

#### *hirsutissima* 'Santa Rosa'   ZONE 4 (Dwarf Coral Bells)

This cute little plant is the tiniest form that I have ever seen, well suited to the alpine garden or planting in troughs with other miniature plants. Dainty spikes of soft-pink flowers appear quite early, over a low mound of tiny green leaves. Best in sun.

**HT/SP**  10–15 cm (4–6″) / 15–20 cm (6–8″)
**SOIL**   Average to moist soil, but very well drained.
**BLOOM** May–June
**USES**   △☂▲ Rock gardens, Troughs

#### *micrantha* var. *diversifolia*   ZONE 4 (Purple-leaved Coral Bells, Small-flowered Alumroot)

The species itself is native to the West Coast of North America, and from it some excellent purple-leaved selections have been made. Foliage is large and crinkly with an ivy or maple-leaf shape, in shades of deep purple-red. Stems of small whitish-pink flowers appear in early summer but are not very showy. Excellent at the border front, especially when massed. Evergreen in Zones 7–9.

**HT/SP**  30–60 cm (1–2′) / 30–45 cm (12–18″)
**SOIL**   Average to moist well-drained soil.
**BLOOM** June–July
**USES**   △▲☂ Borders, Edging

**Bressingham Bronze ['Absi']** An improvement on 'Palace Purple', with outstanding beet-red foliage that maintains its colour reliably throughout the season. Contrasts beautifully with blue fescue – at least, it once did in my own garden.

**'Palace Purple'** A seed-grown strain, the foliage is deep purple in spring, fading to bronzy-brown for the summer. Plants maintain their colour best with afternoon shade. Rogue out any green-leaved seedlings that might appear. Selected as *Perennial Plant of the Year* for 1991.

#### *sanguinea*          ZONE 3 (Red Coral Bells)

An important parent to many of the modern garden hybrids, this species still deserves to be grown, as the flowers appear a bit earlier than most, extending the season a bit. Flowers are usually in saturated shades of true red, and a magnet to hummingbirds. Leaves are small and rounded, forming a compact mound of deep green, although occasionally mottled with silver, or heavily variegated in some of the newer types. Great for edging. Dead-heading faded flowers will encourage continued

blooming. Divide every 2–3 years in spring. In my experience the variegated forms don't seem to be especially vigorous and might require a little extra coddling. Good drainage may be the key.

**HT/SP**  30–45 cm (12–18″) / 25–30 cm (10–12″)
**SOIL**   Average to moist well-drained soil.
**BLOOM** May–July
**USES**   △✂☂▲ Borders, Edging

**'Frosty'** Creamy-white leaves are dappled with soft mint green. The cherry-red flowers truly stand out.

**'Snow Storm'** Extremely bright variegation, the near-white leaves are veined in deep green and nicely ruffled. Flowers are a good strong red. Especially effective in groups.

**'Splendens'** Bright vermilion-red flowers over a low mound of green leaves. A good compact seed strain for edging or in the rock garden.

### × HEUCHERELLA ☼ ◐ (Foamy Bells)

#### Hybrids          ZONE 3

Interesting intergeneric hybrids between various *Heuchera* and *Tiarella* species and selections. The result combines the dense foliage mound and early blooming of Foamflower with the showier flower spikes of Coral Bells. Plants are generally vigorous and hardy and more or less evergreen. Outstanding in a woodland garden, appreciating part shade in warm-summer regions. Long flowering, due to the fact that the blossoms are sterile. Like the Foamflowers, these dislike summer drought and the competition of thirsty tree roots. Many selections have been introduced as of late.

*Heuchera* 'Stormy Seas'

*Heuchera hirsutissima* 'Santa Rosa'

*Heuchera* 'Velvet Night'

HT/SP   20–45 cm (8–18″) / 25–40 cm (10–16″)
SOIL    Rich, moist well-drained soil.
BLOOM May–July
USES    ⛰⋀⋅▲✂ Edging, Borders

*alba* **'Bridget Bloom'** Mounding habit, great display of shell-pink flowers for many weeks. Foliage is bright green. An older hybrid raised by Alan Bloom in England.
HT      25–35 cm (10–14″)

**'Burnished Bronze'** Large and deeply-cut leaves in a rich bronzy-purple shade with a glossy finish. Taller black stems hold sprays of soft-pink flowers. One of the best forms.
HT      20–45 cm (8–18″)

**'Kimono'** Leaves are so deeply cut as to be nearly star-shaped, mid-green in colour with a spidery purple-black centre and silvery flush. In summer the foliage becomes more full and rounded in outline. Flowers are pale pink. Exceptional winter effect, when the leaves take on a rose-purple cast.
HT      20–45 cm (8–18″)

*alba* **'Rosalie'** [*Tiarella* **'Rosalie'**] A Canadian introduction featuring dark green leaves with a prominent bronzy-red centre. Rose-pink flowers appear for many weeks in late spring. Beautiful in a woodland setting. Compact habit.
HT      20–30 cm (8–12″)

**'Silver Streak'** Maple-leaf shaped foliage is metallic silver in colour, heavily veined in bronzy-purple. Loose sprays of very pale lavender-pink flowers appear in late spring, and repeat again in fall. The black stems contrast beautifully.
HT      20–50 cm (8–20″)

**'Viking Ship'** Foliage is green and maple-shaped, with a heavy flush of silver during the spring. Rather tall stems of deep coral-pink blooms show a branching habit, flowers for a longer season. Tolerates heat and humidity. Good sun tolerance also.
HT      20–45 cm (8–18″)

# HIBISCUS ☼
## (Rose Mallow)

*acetosella*        ZONE 10
### (Red Shield Hibiscus)
Although more of a tender perennial, other than in frost-free regions, this species is being seen with more frequency in botanical garden and arboretum displays. Plants have deeply cut maple-shaped leaves in a dusky beet-red shade, sometimes producing small burgundy flowers in late fall. It makes a bold statement in containers, which then easily wintered indoors. Cut plants back hard to 15–30 cm (6–12″) in late winter or train them as standards. New plants may be started from tip cuttings.
HT/SP   90–150 cm (3–5′) / 75–90 cm (30–36″)
SOIL    Average to moist, well-drained soil.
BLOOM September–October
USES    ♟ Specimen, Containers

*moscheutos* **Hybrids**    ZONE 4
### (Hardy Hibiscus)
A whole lot of new Hibiscus selections have hit the market in recent years. All of these form substantial, shrub-like plants with foliage similar to the tropical or indoor Hibiscus. Flowers are also similar in shape, round and saucer-shaped with a prominent central stamen, ranging in colour from white through to pink and red. Gardeners in regions with hot summers succeed best with these heat-lovers. In regions like the Pacific Northwest the plants themselves are hardy enough, but more often than not fail to flower before fall frosts cut them to the ground.

These appreciate good drainage, yet must not be allowed to dry out in summer droughts. A thick mulch for the first winter is advised and planting before midsummer will increase survival. Hardy Hibiscus is always very late to resume growth in the spring, often not making an appearance until after the middle of May. Old stems should be cut to the ground before the new growth appears. Selected forms may be either propagated by dividing the woody roots in spring or by taking cuttings.
SP      75–90 cm (30–36″)
SOIL    Rich, moist soil.
BLOOM July–October
USES    🦋 Borders, Specimen

**'Fantasia'** The Fleming brothers of Nebraska worked for many years to improve Hibiscus, developing a number of good garden hybrids along the way. 'Fantasia' is a bushy and compact selection with distinctive maple-shaped green leaves. Huge, ruffled rose-pink flowers are produced in great numbers.
HT      90–100 cm (36–40″)

**'Kopper King'** A bit of a departure from the norm, this Fleming hybrid features unusual coppery-red leaves with a distinctive maple shape. Flowers are soft lavender to white with a deep purple-red eye that streaks out into the petals. Enormous blooms, sometimes up to 30 cm (12″) wide.
HT      90–105 cm (36–42″)

**'Lord Baltimore'** One of the best red forms to date, with big, ruffled blooms in a brilliant clear scarlet shade. Tall habit.
HT      120–150 cm (4–5′)

**'Plum Crazy'** Good dark-purple maple shaped foliage, courtesy of the Fleming breeding program. Flowers are an unusual lavender-plum shade, with purple veining.
HT      90–120 cm (3–4′)

**'Southern Belle'** An older strain, but exceedingly popular for the dinner-plate sized flowers, in a catchy mixture of red, pink, rose and white. Most flowers show a contrasting crimson eye. Selected colours are easily increased by dividing plants when growth appears in the spring. Plants are big and bushy. 'Dixie Belle' is another common mixture, with a similar range of shades but a more compact habit.
HT      90–120 cm (3–4′)

## HOLLYHOCK see ALCEA

# HOSTA ❀•
## (Hosta, Plantain Lily)
Hostas hold the trophy for being the most popular shade perennials of all time. Their lush clumps of bold, exotic leaves are the main feature, the stalks of mauve or white lily-like flowers an added bonus. Most varieties are easy, reliable plants that adapt well even to densely shaded sites. Both the foliage and flowers are of interest to floral designers.

With extensive breeding work still being undertaken there seems to be no end in sight to the number of Hosta varieties; well over two thousand are circulating among the specialists and collectors, from 1.5 m (5′) giants to 10 cm (4″) miniatures. Gardeners with a passion for these shade-lovers are advised to join their local chapter of the **American Hosta Society**.

Hostas are easily divided in spring or early fall but most varieties can be left alone for years before they become

*Heucherella* × **'Burnished Bronze'**

*Hibiscus moscheutos* **'Southern Belle'**

*Heucherella alba* **'Bridget Bloom'**

crowded and start to decline. Slugs and snails are often troublesome, particularly the monster slugs in the Pacific Northwest. Aside from hand-picking, trapping or baiting slugs, an alternative approach is to select those Hosta varieties marked "slug-resistant"; these have especially thick and waxy leaves that slugs find difficult to eat. Using a mulch of gravel or coarse sand around your Hosta plants is reported to be a big help in deterring these voracious feeders. Collectors are also reporting good results with a mulch of pine needles.

**LOCATION:** Rich, moist but well-drained soil. Golden-leaved and variegated varieties are generally more sun tolerant than green or blue-leaved types.

**USES:** Each variety has been placed in one of the categories listed below. This should help you to choose the best Hosta for your landscape situation. As a general rule most varieties grow about as wide as the height of the foliage, or perhaps half again. See below regarding heights.

**HEIGHTS** given are for the *foliage*, the flower stems usually rising 30–45 cm (12–18″) above that. Each variety is placed into one or more of the following groups, largely based on height.

- **Dwarf:** 20 cm (8″) or less. Suitable for rock gardens or containers. Usually slow growing.
- **Edging:** 30 cm (12″) or less, vigorous growth.
- **Groundcover:** 60 cm (24″) or less, very vigorous growth. Excellent for massing in low-maintenance plantings.
- **Background:** 75 cm (30″) or taller.
- **Specimen:** Good choice for a closely-viewed focal point. Interesting leaf texture, colour, shape, or flowers. Does not always indicate the monstrously huge types.

## SPECIES and VARIETIES    ZONE 2

Included here is a good cross-section of some of the latest selections available, as well as the more standard older varieties. Hosta breeders are still very much at work all over the world, trying to come up with even more spectacular specimens, so always keep an eye out for selections that may not be listed here. A word of warning is in order regarding prices: in general the newest and most exotic selections command a steep price for the first few years after they are released. Thanks to the modern technique of micro-propagation (also known as tissue-culture) many of these will become widely available and much more reasonable in price after just a few short years!

**'Abiqua Drinking Gourd'** SPECIMEN. Leaves are frosty blue-green in colour, the edges curling upwards into a cup that will actually hold water. Pale lavender to near-white flowers in July. Makes a broad mound in time. Good slug resistance.
HT/SP   45–60 cm (18–24″) / 90–120 cm (3–4′)

**'Aphrodite'** see *H. plantaginea 'Aphrodite'*

**'Aspen Gold'** SPECIMEN or GROUNDCOVER. Rounded bright-gold leaves are beautifully puckered or quilted all over. Plants form a medium-large mound in time, bearing white flowers in July. Excellent slug-resistance, with its thick waxy texture.
HT/SP   45–50 cm (18–20″) / 75–90 cm (30–36″)

**'August Moon'** GROUNDCOVER. Large and somewhat crinkled bright-yellow leaves, forming a medium to large mound. Pale lavender to near-white flowers appear in July. An excellent older selection, particularly for massing. Some direct sun will really bring out the yellow tones. Good slug resistance.
HT/SP   45–50 cm (18–20″) / 75–90 cm (30–36″)

**'Big Daddy'** SPECIMEN or BACKGROUND. Huge, heavily quilted deep-blue leaves that sometimes have a cupped shape, forming a large broad mound. Near-white flowers in late June. The very thick texture ensures that slug-resistance is excellent!
HT/SP   60–65 cm (24–26″) / 90–120 cm (3–4′)

**'Birchwood Parky's Gold'** GROUNDCOVER. Forms a compact and dense mound of chartreuse to soft gold heart-shaped leaves, with a somewhat powdery finish. Good gold autumn colour. Showy mauve flowers in July are held above on tall stems. Fairly sun-tolerant and fast-growing.
HT/SP   30–42 cm (12–18″) / 75–90 cm (30–36″)

**'Blue Angel'** SPECIMEN or BACKGROUND. Award-winning, enormous-growing selection with big powdery-blue leaves and a wide, mounding habit. Tall stems of near-white flowers appear in early July. Faster to mature than most other large blue varieties. Leaves show their best blue tones early in the season, changing to dark green later in the summer. Good slug resistance.
HT/SP   75–80 cm (30–32″) / 90–120 cm (3–4′)

**'Blue Boy'** EDGING or GROUNDCOVER. Forms a rounded mound of small frosted blue-green leaves. Nice for edging. Pale lavender flowers appear in July.
HT/SP   30–45 cm (12–18″) / 60–75 cm (24–30″)

**'Blue Dimples'** GROUNDCOVER or SPECIMEN. Regarded as one of the bluest selections ever introduced. Thick-substanced, waxy leaves with an intense

powdery-blue colour that lasts well late into the summer. Plants form a medium-sized mound with pale lavender flowers in late July. Good slug resistance.
HT/SP   40–45 cm (16–18″) / 75–90 cm (30–36″)

**'Blue Mammoth'** SPECIMEN. A highly-regarded and enormous mounding selection with huge powdery-blue leaves. Good substance and slug resistance. Near-white flowers in early July. Heavily quilted texture. This selection makes a superb focal point or specimen.
HT/SP   75–85 cm (30–33″) / 90–120 cm (3–4′)

**'Blue Shadows'** GROUNDCOVER or SPECIMEN. A stunningly variegated selection, found as a sport of 'Tokudama Aureonebulosa'. Rounded leaves are pale green in the centre, with a wide, streaky blue-green margin. Near-white flowers appear in July. Good slug resistance. Not a particularly fast grower.
HT/SP   35–45 cm (12–18″) / 75–90 cm (30–36″)

**'Blue Umbrellas'** BACKGROUND or SPECIMEN. Huge downward-cupping leaves form a giant mound. The colour is a decent blue in spring, later becoming shiny dark green. Near-white flowers appear in July. One of the most popular monster Hostas.
HT/SP   75–80 cm (30–32″) / 120–150 cm (4–5′)

**'Blue Wedgwood'** EDGING or GROUNDCOVER. Excellent slug-resistance. Vigorous habit, forming a medium-sized mound of thick, powdery blue-grey leaves. Regarded as one of the bluest selections ever developed. Soft-lavender flowers in August.
HT/SP   35–45 cm (12–18″) / 60–75 cm (24–30″)

**'Blue Whirls'** SPECIMEN. Narrow, pointed leaves are frosted blue-green in colour. Leaves are arranged like the spokes of a wheel when viewed from

*Hosta 'August Moon'*

*Hosta 'Blue Boy'*

*Hosta 'Blue Angel'*

above. Vase-shaped habit, forming a medium-sized mound. Pale lavender flowers in July. Good slug resistance.

**HT/SP**  50–55 cm (20–22″) / 75–90 cm (30–36″)

**'Bold Ruffles'** SPECIMEN. Large blue-grey leaves are heavily corrugated, with ruffled and unruly edges, becoming green by midsummer. Near-white flowers appear in July. Forms a big, broad mound in time, but not a fast grower. Excellent slug-resistance.

**HT/SP**  60–65 cm (24–26″) / 90–120 cm (3–4′)

**'Bressingham Blue'** SPECIMEN or BACKGROUND. Deeply ribbed, powdery blue-green leaves, upwardly cupped. Taller stems of white flowers in June. Closely related to *H. sieboldiana* 'Elegans'.

**HT/SP**  60–75 cm (24–30″) / 90–120 cm (3–4′)

**'Bridegroom'** SPECIMEN or GROUNDCOVER. This interesting selection has dark-green leaves that are shiny and slightly wavy, the tips upturned in a unique way. Purple flowers appear in July. Forms a medium-sized mound.

**HT/SP**  30–40 cm (12–16″) / 60–90 cm (2–3′)

**'Brim Cup'** EDGING. Unusual cupped habit, especially unique in a smaller Hosta. Leaves are deep green with a wide creamy-yellow to white margin. Pale lavender flowers in July. Collectors report that the leaf margins often tear or rip, and best results may be had by growing this in a container.

**HT/SP**  30–35 cm (12–14″) / 60–75 cm (24–30″)

**'Canadian Shield'** GROUNDCOVER. Discovered and introduced a few years ago by The Perennial Gardens in British Columbia. This is a sport of 'Halcyon', featuring dark green shiny foliage and a very sturdy habit. Pale lavender flowers in August. Good slug resistance.

**HT/SP**  40–45 cm (16–18″) / 75–90 cm (30–36″)

**'Candy Hearts'** EDGING or GROUNDCOVER. Plants quickly form a perfectly rounded clump of grey-green heart-shaped leaves. Pale-lavender flowers in July.

**HT/SP**  35–40 cm (14–16″) / 75–90 cm (30–36″)

**'Cherry Berry'** EDGING or SPECIMEN. This ranks high on my own list of personal favourites. The leaves are long and pointy with a streaky green margin, the centre starting out yellow in the spring then ageing to creamy white. In August, soft-purple flowers are held on burgundy-red stems that are amazingly showy. Some direct sun will encourage excellent leaf colour and good vigour. Substance is average.

**HT/SP**  25–30 cm (10–12″) / 60–75 cm (24–30″)

**'Chinese Sunrise'** GROUNDCOVER. An older selection with glowing spring effect. Glossy, narrow foliage begins with a golden centre and green edges, later becoming light green with a deep green margin and finally solid green towards fall. Good display of mauve flowers in late summer. Poor slug resistance. A sport of *H. lancifolia*.

**HT/SP**  35–45 cm (14–18″) / 75–90 cm (30–36″)

**'Choko Nishiki'** see 'On Stage'

**'Christmas Tree'** GROUNDCOVER or SPECIMEN. Forms a medium-large clump of corrugated deep-green leaves with a creamy-white edge, more yellow in the spring. Leaves continue up the flower stems. Lavender flowers in July. Good slug resistance.

**HT/SP**  50–55 cm (20–22″) / 90–120 cm (3–4′)

**'Dorset Blue'** EDGING. An outstanding dwarf blue type. Rounded and cupped powdery-blue leaves have excellent slug-resistance. Pale-lavender flowers in August. This is not a fast-growing selection.

**HT/SP**  20–25 cm (8–10″) / 45–60 cm (18–24″)

**'Elisabeth'** GROUNDCOVER. A popular form in Europe, especially valued for its outstanding display of purple flowers in late summer. Leaves are medium-green, oval shaped and ruffled.

**HT/SP**  60–65 cm (24–26″) / 75–90 cm (30–36″)

**'Elvis Lives'** SPECIMEN. Long and pointy blue-green leaves are lightly ruffled along the edges. Plants form an arching mound, best used to specimen effect, surrounded by a low groundcover. Lavender flowers appear in July. Gaining popularity quickly!

**HT/SP**  40–45 cm (16–18″) / 80–100 cm (30–40″)

**'Fall Bouquet'** EDGING. One of the newer red-stemmed selections, with glossy dark-green leaves. Flowers are lavender, appearing in autumn, and held on deep-red stems.

**HT/SP**  25–30 cm (10–12″) / 60–75 cm (24–30″)

**'Fire and Ice'** SPECIMEN or GROUNDCOVER. Leaves have a pattern opposite to 'Patriot', with white centres and a streaky dark-green margin. This makes for a rather bold effect when the clump matures. Medium-large in habit. Mauve flowers appear in late July.

**HT/SP**  50–55 cm (20–22″) / 90–100 cm (36–40″)

*fluctuans* **'Variegated'** see 'Sagae'

**'Fortunei Albopicta'** [*H. fortunei* 'Albo-picta'] GROUNDCOVER. An older selection but still worthy of growing. Outstanding spring foliage, bright yellow with a dark green margin, fading to all green by summer. Forms a medium-large mound. Pale lilac flowers in late July.

**HT/SP**  45–55 cm (18–22″) / 80–100 cm (30–40″)

**'Fortunei Aureomarginata'** ['Gold Crown'] GROUNDCOVER. A very popular older form. Attractive dark-green leaves have a strong yellow-gold edging, retained throughout the season. Pale lilac flowers in July. Fairly good sun tolerance. This selection is inexpensive and well suited to large landscape plantings.

**HT/SP**  50–55 cm (20–22″) / 90–120 cm (3–4′)

**'Fortunei Hyacinthina'** [*H. fortunei* 'Hyacinthina'] GROUNDCOVER. Silvery-green pointed leaves with a thin white pencil-margin, powdery white on the underside. Forms a handsome arching mound when young, later developing a broad habit. Pale purple flowers in August.

**HT/SP**  50–55 cm (20–22″) / 80–100 cm (30–40″)

**'Fragrant Blue'** SPECIMEN or GROUNDCOVER. Heart-shaped powdery blue-green leaves, forming a medium-large mound, and retaining a semblance of blue tone well into the summer. Pale lilac flowers appear in August and are particularly fragrant in warm-summer regions. Good slug resistance.

**HT/SP**  45–50 cm (18–20″) / 90–100 cm (36–40″)

**'Fragrant Bouquet'** SPECIMEN or GROUNDCOVER. Bright chartreuse-green leaves with a neat creamy-white to yellow margin. Plants make an outstanding display of large, fragrant pale-lilac to white flowers in August, held well above the leaves where they can be enjoyed. Vigorous habit. Fair slug resistance.

**HT/SP**  50–55 cm (20–22″) / 90–120 cm (3–4′)

**'Francee'** GROUNDCOVER. Forms a tidy mound of dark green leaves with a perfect white edge; refined and elegant in effect. Lilac flowers in late July. Widely regarded as one of the best all-purpose white edged selection, terrific for massing.

**HT/SP**  45–50 cm (18–20″) / 90–120 cm (3–4′)

*Hosta* 'Brim Cup'

*Hosta* 'Blue Umbrellas'

*Hosta* 'Canadian Shield'

*Hosta* 'Fortunei Aureomarginata'

*Hosta* 'Chinese Sunrise'

**'Frances Williams'** [*H. sieboldiana* 'Frances Williams'] SPECIMEN or BACKGROUND. Long considered to be one of the best Hosta of all time, and certainly still one of the most popular. Round, puckered leaves are blue-green with a wide yellow margin. Near-white flowers in June and July. Sometimes scorches around the edges unless grown in full shade and with plenty of moisture. Spectacular when well grown!
HT/SP  60–70 cm (24–28″) / 120–150 cm (4–5′)

**'Fresh'** DWARF or EDGING. A cute little miniature type, with wavy golden-yellow leaves edged in creamy white. Lavender flowers appear in July. A little sun will really bring out the strong colour. Somewhat slug prone.
HT/SP  15–25 cm (6–10″) / 25–30 cm (10–12″)

**'Fried Green Tomatoes'** GROUND-COVER. A good, vigorous form – like a dark-green version of 'Fragrant Bouquet'. Large heart-shaped leaves, mounding habit. Very pale lilac flowers in late summer. Fair slug resistance.
HT/SP  60–65 cm (24–26″) / 90–120 cm (3–4′)

**'Fringe Benefit'** GROUNDCOVER. Large powdery blue-green leaves with a creamy-yellow margin that later becomes creamy white. Good substance and a vigorous grower. Pale lavender flowers are held on tall stems in late July. Fairly sun-resistant.
HT/SP  50–55 cm (20–22″) / 90–120 cm (3–4′)

**'Frosted Jade'** BACKGROUND. Powdery-green leaves with a rippled white margin, forming a large, broad mound. Pale lavender flowers appear in July. Shade is best, to retain the powdery finish. Leaves are often slightly cupped. This selection needs plenty of room!
HT/SP  75–80 cm (30–32″) / 120–150 cm (4–5′)

**'Ginko Craig'** EDGING. Now one of the most popular edging selections. Forms a low clump of narrow dark-green leaves, with slightly wavy white margins. Excellent vigour but unfortunately rather slug prone due to the thin leaves. Mid-purple flowers appear in late August.
HT/SP  30–35 cm (12–14″) / 60–75 cm (24–30″)

**'Gold Standard'** GROUNDCOVER or SPECIMEN. All-green in spring, the leaves slowly changing to bright yellow with a green margin, the centres may become nearly white by fall. Lavender flowers in July. Should receive a few hours of direct sun each day for best colouring to develop. Good vigorous habit.
HT/SP  50–55 cm (20–22″) / 90–120 cm (3–4′)

**'Golden Scepter'** EDGING or GROUND-COVER. An all-gold version of 'Golden Tiara', colours up early, losing some of the punch later in the season. Lavender-purple flowers in July.
HT/SP  30–40 cm (12–16″) / 60–75 cm (24–30″)

**'Golden Sunburst'** [*H. sieboldiana* 'Golden Sunburst'] GROUNDCOVER. An all-yellow version of 'Frances Williams', best planted in the shade for bold effect. Huge leaves, good heavy texture. Near-white flowers appear in early July. Good slug resistance, but an unfortunate tendency to develop brown spots on the leaves unless protected from direct sunlight during the spring.
HT/SP  45–50 cm (18–20″) / 90–120 cm (3–4′)

**'Golden Tiara'** EDGING or GROUND-COVER. Perhaps the most popular edging variety. Light green heart-shaped leaves have a distinctive yellow to chartreuse edge. Fast growth habit. Purple flowers in July are rather showy. Somewhat slug prone.
HT/SP  30–40 cm (12–16″) / 75–90 cm (30–36″)

**'Great Expectations'** SPECIMEN. A stunning introduction that originated as a mutation of *H. sieboldiana* 'Elegans'. The deep blue leaves have an unusual bold centre variegation of golden-yellow, later changing to creamy-white. Truly exotic in appearance, and a must for the collector. Near-white flowers in late June. Needs some sun for best colouration. Extremely slow growing, but with regular watering and fertilizing a significantly sized plant will be achieved in 5–6 years.
HT/SP  50–70 cm (20–28″) / 75–120 cm (30–48″)

**'Ground Master'** GROUNDCOVER. Valued for its stoloniferous habit, this variety is excellent for massed plantings as a ground cover. Leaves are medium-green with a creamy-yellow margin that later fades to white. Bright purple lavender flowers in August. Prone to slug damage.
HT/SP  30–40 cm (12–16″) / 60–90 cm (2–3′)

**'Guacamole'** GROUNDCOVER or SPECI-MEN. A relatively new arrival, originally a sport of 'Fragrant Bouquet' and giving the same late-summer display of big fragrant near-white flowers. Leaves are large and heart-shaped, chartreuse in the middle, with a streaky dark-green margin. Centres may become bright gold in summer if given some direct sun. Fair slug resistance.
HT/SP  55–60 cm (22–24″) / 90–120 cm (3–4′)

**'Halcyon'** GROUNDCOVER. Deep blue-green leaves form a dense mound, making this one of the better blue types for landscape situations. Thick substance ensures good slug-resistance.

Tall stems of pale lavender flowers are produced in August. Not particularly fast to establish.
HT/SP  40–45 cm (16–18″) / 80–100 cm (30–40″)

**'Honeybells'** GROUNDCOVER. Fragrant pale-mauve flowers appear in August and September, held on tall stems well above the foliage mound. Large light-green leaves form a sturdy clump and are fairly sun tolerant. Vigorous habit but fairly slug prone. Good for massed landscape plantings.
HT/SP  55–60 cm (22–24″) / 90–120 cm (3–4′)

**'Invincible'** GROUNDCOVER. Pointed green foliage with a shiny, highly-polished finish. Showy display of fragrant pale-lavender flowers in August. Despite the name, this is not a particularly slugproof nor sun tolerant selection, but the shiny leaves are interesting for their "wet-look".
HT/SP  45–50 cm (18–20″) / 80–100 cm (30–40″)

**'June'** SPECIMEN. A much sought-after variegated form of 'Halcyon'. Leaves are chartreuse-yellow to gold with a streaky blue-green margin. Needs some sun in spring to develop good colouration. Pale lavender flowers appear in August. Very highly rated! Good slug tolerance.
HT/SP  30–40 cm (12–16″) / 75–90 cm (30–36″)

**'Kabitan'** [*H. sieboldii* 'Kabitan'] DWARF or EDGING. Long, narrow yellow leaves are edged in green and slightly ruffled. Rich purple flowers are a lovely contrast in August. Best with morning sun. Very bright and cheery but rather prone to slug damage. Nice in the rock garden.
HT/SP  20–35 cm (8–12″) / 30–60 cm (1–2′)

**'Krossa Regal'** SPECIMEN or BACK-GROUND. Upright vase-shaped habit. Outstanding powdery grey-blue leaves.

*Hosta* 'Fragrant Bouquet'
*Hosta* 'Francee'
*Hosta* 'Gold Standard'
*Hosta* 'Invincible'
*Hosta* 'Golden Tiara'

Stems of lavender flowers in August can reach up to 5'! Good slug-resistance. Very highly rated.

**HT/SP**  75–80 cm (30–32″) / 90–150 cm (3–5′)

**'Lakeside Black Satin'** GROUNDCOVER. Exceptionally dark-green, heart-shaped leaves have a shiny finish and nice rippling along the edges. Plants form a medium to large mound, bearing medium purple bell-shaped flowers in August. Reasonably slug tolerant.

**HT/SP**  50–55 cm (20–22″) / 90–100 cm (36–40″)

*lancifolia* **(Narrow-leaved Plantain Lily)** EDGING or GROUNDCOVER. Glossy dark green spear-shaped leaves, forming a tidy mound. Lilac-purple flowers are produced in August on taller stems. Tolerates drier, sunnier sites better than most other varieties. This species is probably the most common older type seen in gardens, introduced into North America in the nineteenth century. Leaves are prone to slug damage.

**HT/SP**  30–45 cm (12–18″) / 80–100 cm (32–40″)

**'Leather Sheen'** EDGING or GROUNDCOVER. Narrow, lance-shaped leaves are dark green with the most amazing glossy, polished finish. Good substance and slug tolerance. Mauve-purple flowers are held on taller stems in July. A versatile plant for edging or massing, and one of my personal favourites.

**HT/SP**  35–40 cm (14–16″) / 75–90 cm (30–36″)

**'Lemon Lime'** EDGING or GROUNDCOVER. Small clumps of chartreuse-green leaves and a good, vigorous habit make this selection ideal for edging. Good display of bright-purple flowers in July, held well above the leaves. One of the few Hosta that sometimes repeat blooms again in the fall.

**HT/SP**  25–30 cm (10–12″) / 60–90 cm (2–3′)

**'Little Sunspot'** GROUNDCOVER or SPECIMEN. A gorgeous gold-centred selection that forms a small clump, but very bright and showy. Rounded leaves remain a glowing golden-yellow, with a contrasting deep-green margin. Near-white flowers appear in July on taller stems. Find a prime spot for this winner. Somewhat slug tolerant.

**HT/SP**  30–35 cm (12–14″) / 60–90 cm (2–3′)

**'Love Pat'** SPECIMEN or GROUNDCOVER. Outstanding frosty-blue leaves in spring, later becoming dark green. Foliage is rounded with heavy quilting and often cup-shaped. A very highly rated variety. Near-white flowers in July. Excellent slug resistance. Quickly becoming a classic!

**HT/SP**  40–45 cm (16–18″) / 75–100 cm (30–40″)

**'Middle Ridge'** EDGING or GROUNDCOVER. Very similar in effect to 'Undulata Univittata', forming a low mound of wavy green leaves with a narrow streak of white in the centre. Rather slug prone.

**HT/SP**  30–45 cm (12–18″) / 60–90 cm (2–3′)

**'Minuteman'** SPECIMEN or GROUNDCOVER. Now one of the most popular white-edged forms, 'Minuteman' was found as a sport of 'Francee'. It forms a medium-large mound of heart-shaped leaves, dark green in the centre with a wide, streaky white margin. Mauve flowers make an appearance in late July. Terrific for massing or using as a pathway edging. Also stunning in containers. Somewhat slug tolerant.

**HT/SP**  50–55 cm (20–22″) / 75–100 cm (30–40″)

**'Moonlight'** GROUNDCOVER. Chartreuse-green in spring, later changing to bright golden-yellow and later creamy-yellow with a white margin. Pale lavender flowers in late July. Needs morning sun for best colouring to develop. Dense mounding habit. Average substance, so somewhat slug prone.

**HT/SP**  45–50 cm (18–20″) / 90–120 cm (3–4′)

**'Mr Big'** BACKGROUND or SPECIMEN. An apt name for this selection, which in time will form a huge mound of heavily-quilted blue-green leaves. Near-white flowers appear in August. Takes a few years to settle in and reach a mature size.

**HT/SP**  75–80 cm (30–32″) / 120–150 cm (4–5′)

**'Night Before Christmas'** SPECIMEN or GROUNDCOVER. Leaf centre is pure white, with a wide dark-green margin, a rather eye-catching combination. Flowers are pale lavender, appearing in late July. This will form a remarkable large mound in time. Good vigour, and some Hosta collectors consider this to be one of the best white-centred forms.

**HT/SP**  55–65 cm (22–24″) / 120–150 cm (4–5′)

**'Northern Halo'** [*H. sieboldiana* **'Northern Halo'**] SPECIMEN or BACKGROUND. Heavily corrugated blue-grey leaves have a creamy-white margin that later becomes creamy-green. This is a white-margined *H. sieboldiana* 'Elegans', so plants are somewhat slow to establish, but unforgettable when mature! White flowers appear in late June. Unlike 'Frances Williams' this does not usually develop burned edges. Excellent slug resistance.

**HT/SP**  65–70 cm (24–30″) / 120–150 cm (4–5′)

**'On Stage'** SPECIMEN. Much talked-about in Hosta circles! Bright yellow leaves with irregular green edging and streaking, later the centres fade to cream. Reported to tolerate full sun. Slow-growing. Pale lavender flowers appear in July. Whether the Japanese selection 'Choko Nishiki' and the American 'On Stage' are truly identical (or not) is something we prefer to let the Hosta experts argue about for a while longer.

**HT/SP**  45–55 cm (18–22″) / 90–120 cm (3–4′)

**'Pacific Blue Edger'** EDGING or GROUNDCOVER. Heart-shaped blue-green leaves form a medium-sized mound, bearing taller stems of lavender flowers in July. Nice vigorous habit.

**HT/SP**  30–40 cm (12–16″) / 60–75 cm (24–30″)

**'Pandora's Box'** DWARF or EDGING. This cute little Hosta forms a tiny mound of small white-centred leaves with a streaky green margin. Taller spikes of mauve flowers appear in late June. Quite sharp looking when used as a low edging.

**HT/SP**  10–15 cm (4–6″) / 25–40 cm (10–16″)

**'Paradigm'** SPECIMEN or GROUNDCOVER. One of my favourite newer selections, forming a medium-large mound of rounded leaves. Foliage is gold-centred with a bold blue-green margin. Good slug tolerance. Near-white flowers appear in late June.

**HT/SP**  50–55 cm (20–22″) / 80–90 cm (30–36″)

**'Patriot'** SPECIMEN or GROUNDCOVER. Truly one of the best variegated forms around, the medium-green leaves are widely edged in creamy-yellow to white, the margins streaking a bit towards the centre. Lavender flowers appear in August. Really stands out!

**HT/SP**  55–60 cm (22–24″) / 90–120 cm (3–4′)

**'Paul's Glory'** SPECIMEN or GROUNDCOVER. Gold-centred Hosta always seem to get my attention, this one probably more than any other. The beautiful golden heart-shaped leaves are boldly streaked with blue-green on the margins, the centre later fading sometimes to parchment white, especially with some direct sun. Pale lavender

Hosta 'Moonlight'

Hosta 'Krossa Regal'

Hosta 'Northern Halo'

Hosta 'On Stage'

Hosta 'Minuteman'

flowers appear in late July. Excellent vigour, and good slug resistance.

HT/SP  55–65 cm (22–26″) / 90–120 cm (3–4′)

**'Pearl Lake'** GROUNDCOVER. Profuse bloomer. Pale lavender flowers form in July, over a mound of heart-shaped grey-green leaves. Vigorous grower. One of the best forms for edging or massed plantings. Somewhat prone to slug damage.

HT/SP  35–45 cm (14–18″) / 80–100 cm (32–40″)

**'Pineapple Upsidedown Cake'** GROUNDCOVER or SPECIMEN. The narrow, rippled leaves start out green in the spring, later developing a gold centre with green margins. Lavender flowers make an appearance in August. Good slug tolerance.

HT/SP  45–50 cm (18–20″) / 90–120 cm (3–4′)

*plantaginea* **(Fragrant Plantain Lily, August Lily)** GROUNDCOVER or SPECI-MEN. Very fragrant, huge white flowers in August are held just above the leaves. Exceptionally showy. Clumps produce shiny light-green foliage with good heat and sun-tolerance. This is one of the original Hosta species first planted in North American gardens. Needs a warm summer climate to bloom reliably. Prone to slug damage.

HT/SP  55–65 cm (22–26″) / 90–120 cm (3–4′)

*plantaginea* **'Aphrodite' (Double Fragrant Plantain Lily)** SPECIMEN. An unusual double-flowered selection which arrived from China a number of years ago. The foliage mound is virtually identical to the plain species, but with larger flowers that are completely double and sterile. Exceptionally fragrant. Needs a warm summer climate to bloom reliably. This is perhaps of interest mainly to the serious Hosta collector.

HT/SP  50–60 cm (20–24″) / 90–120 cm (3–4′)

**'Queen Josephine'** GROUNDCOVER or SPECIMEN. Plants form a medium-sized mound of thick leaves that show good slug tolerance. Foliage is dark green in the centre, with a neat creamy-yellow to bright yellow margin and a shiny finish. Pale lavender flowers appear in August.

HT/SP  35–45 cm (14–18″) / 80–100 cm (32–40″)

**'Regal Splendor'** SPECIMEN or BACK-GROUND. A terrific sport of 'Krossa Regal' sharing the same upright, vase-shaped habit. The powdery grey-blue leaves are edged in creamy white. Very tall stems of lavender flowers in August. Excellent slug resistance.

HT/SP  75–80 cm (30–32″) / 90–150 cm (3–5′)

**'Revolution'** SPECIMEN or GROUND-COVER. A rather unique newer form, this makes a medium-sized mound of creamy-white centred leaves that have

dark-green speckles, and a streaky green margin. Pale lavender flowers in July.

HT/SP  45–50 cm (18–20″) / 60–75 cm (24–30″)

**'Royal Standard'** GROUNDCOVER or SPECIMEN. An older selection from the 1960's, 'Royal Standard' still has great popularity for its showy display of fragrant white flowers in August. Foliage is bright green and shiny, tolerant of more sun than most, particularly when given sufficient moisture. In time this forms a substantial mound. Prone to slug damage but still excellent for massed landscape plantings.

HT/SP  55–65 cm (22–26″) / 90–120 cm (3–4′)

**'Sagae'** [*H. fluctuans* **'Variegated'**] SPECIMEN. Very highly-rated among collectors, considered by many to be the finest variegated Hosta ever! Large grey-green leaves with wide, bright yellow margins. Forms an upright and arching mound. Lavender flowers in July. Find a prime spot for this baby.

HT/SP  75–80 cm (30–32″) / 120–150 cm (4–5′)

**'Sea Dream'** GROUNDCOVER. Leaves start out light green, later becoming yellow to bright gold, with a creamy-white edging. Lavender flowers in July are held on rather tall stems. Regarded as one of the best white-edged yellows. Prone to slug damage.

HT/SP  45–50 cm (18–20″) / 100–150 cm (40–60″)

**'Sea Lotus Leaf'** GROUNDCOVER or SPECIMEN. Thick blue-green foliage is upwardly cupped like a lotus leaf, with heavy quilting. In time this makes an impressive mound. Near-white flowers in July. Excellent slug resistance.

HT/SP  55–65 cm (22–26″) / 100–150 cm (40–60″)

**'Sea Octopus'** DWARF or EDGING. Narrow mid-green leaves, heavily ruffled and rippled. A nice late show of mauve flowers. Most unusual! Grow on a ledge or in a trough so it can be easily seen. Plants should be divided every three years or so to maintain the maximum ruffled effect. In mature clumps the foliage becomes more relaxed and much less interesting.

HT/SP  20–30 cm (8–12″) / 45–60 cm (18–24″)

**'Sea Thunder'** SPECIMEN. An outstanding selection with superb centre-variegation. Creamy-white pointed leaves are bordered and streaked with dark green. Deep lavender flowers appear in late July. Good vigour. This does have a bit of a reversion problem, so be sure to remove any all-green shoots that might appear or they might well take over the clump. Somewhat slug prone.

HT/SP  35–40 cm (14–16″) / 60–80 cm (24–30″)

**'September Sun'** GROUNDCOVER or SPECIMEN. This is a green-edged version of 'August Moon', forming a

medium-large clump in time. Leaves are bright golden-yellow with a wide mid-green margin. Morning sun really makes the colours come to life. Pale lavender flowers in July. Good slug resistance.

HT/SP  50–55 cm (20–24″) / 90–120 cm (3–4′)

**'Shade Fanfare'** GROUNDCOVER. A rather popular selection, the soft-green leaves have a margin that changes from pale yellow to creamy-white. A vigorous grower, forming a medium-large mound rather quickly. Pale mauve flowers in late July are held on tall stems. Fair slug tolerance.

HT/SP  45–55 cm (18–22″) / 80–100 cm (30–40″)

*sieboldiana* **'Elegans'** SPECIMEN or BACKGROUND. The original, and still one of the best large-leaved true blue Hostas. Frosted powdery-blue leaves are heavily corrugated, becoming more of a dark green by mid to late summer. Short stems of almost-white flowers appear in late June. Not quick to establish, but after 4–5 years this forms an enormous clump. Excellent slug resistance.

HT/SP  65–75 cm (24–30″) / 120–150 cm (4–5′)

**'Snow Cap'** SPECIMEN or GROUND-COVER. This is similar in appearance to 'Northern Halo'. Leaves are rounded and blue-green in colour, with wide creamy-white margins. Said to be prone to tearing on the edges. Best in full shade. Near-white flowers appear towards late June. Excellent slug tolerance.

HT/SP  45–50 cm (18–20″) / 80–100 cm (32–40″)

**'So Sweet'** GROUNDCOVER. Good display of very fragrant pale-lavender flowers in August. The shiny leaves are medium-green with a narrow margin that begins yellow and changes to creamy white. This is a vigorous

Hosta 'Patriot'

Hosta plantaginea

Hosta 'Regal Splendor'

Hosta 'Sagae'

Hosta 'Sea Thunder'

Hosta sieboldiana 'Elegans'

grower, quickly forming a substantial clump. Said to flower best with a little sun. Somewhat slug prone.

**HT/SP** 45–55 cm (18–22″) / 90–120 cm (3–4′)

**'Stiletto'** DWARF or EDGING. An outstanding dwarf selection, with narrow, grass-like foliage, mid-green with a rippled white margin. Rich display of lavender-purple flowers in August. Good vigorous habit and one of the very best for edging. Dividing plants every 4–5 years will help to maintain the rippled appearance.

**HT/SP** 20–30 cm (8–12″) / 45–60 cm (18–24′)

**'Striptease'** GROUNDCOVER or SPECIMEN. Leaves are a pleasing combination of wide, dark-green margins with a streak of golden-yellow in the middle. Pale lavender flowers rise above in late July. Plants form a mound of medium size. Morning sun brings out the best colour in this 'Gold Standard' sport. Somewhat prone to slug damage.

**HT/SP** 45–50 cm (18–20″) / 90–120 cm (3–4′)

**'Sugar and Cream'** BACKGROUND. Forms a big clump fairly quickly, with large wavy mid-green leaves with white to creamy-yellow margins. Fragrant near-white flowers in August are quite showy. This is a variegated sport of 'Honeybells'. Somewhat prone to slug damage.

**HT/SP** 70–80 cm (30–32″) / 90–120 cm (3–4′)

**'Sum and Substance'** SPECIMEN or BACKGROUND. Enormous golden-chartreuse leaves, among the largest of any Hosta, forming a huge mound up to 6′ wide, so be sure to give this plenty of room. Very highly rated. Pale lavender flowers are held on even taller stems in August. Excellent slug-resistance. Sun tolerant, with plenty of moisture.

**HT/SP** 75–90 cm (30–36″) / 150–180 cm (5–6′)

**'Summer Fragrance'** SPECIMEN or GROUNDCOVER. Quickly forms a large, upright mound of white-edged green leaves, the margin more of a creamy-yellow in spring. Very fragrant pale-mauve flowers are held on tall stems in August. Prefers a little sun for best blooming. Somewhat prone to slug damage.

**HT/SP** 60–65 cm (24–26″) / 90–120 cm (3–4′)

**'Summer Music'** SPECIMEN or GROUNDCOVER. A unique white-centred sport of 'Shade Master', the leaves are medium green on the edges, the middle soft yellow to creamy-white by summer. Pale lavender flowers are produced in July. A nice alternative to 'Undulata Univittata', this can be used for massing or edging. Somewhat prone to slug damage.

**HT/SP** 40–45 cm (16–20″) / 80–90 cm (30–36″)

**'Sun Power'** SPECIMEN or BACKGROUND. Brilliant golden-yellow leaves are lightly ruffled and twisted, quickly forming a substantial mound. This is a highly regarded gold form with an upright vase-shaped to arching habit. Pale-lavender flowers in July. Good slug resistance.

**HT/SP** 70–75 cm (30–32″) / 120–150 cm (4–5′)

**'Super Nova'** [*H. sieboldiana* 'Super Nova'] SPECIMEN or GROUNDCOVER. In effect this is like the reverse of 'Frances Williams', with a golden-yellow centre and wide blue-green margin. Leaves are thick and waxy, with heavy corrugation and a noted tendency to be more resistant to scorching. Near-white flowers appear in June. Good slug resistance.

**HT/SP** 60–70 cm (24–28″) / 90–120 cm (3–4′)

**'Tattoo'** SPECIMEN or EDGING. A much-talked about sport of 'Little Aurora', currently sought after by ardent collectors. The heart-shaped leaves are gold in the centre with a chartreuse margin and a unique maple-shaped pattern of darker green, almost like a watermark or dye stain. Plants form a small and tidy mound best used towards the garden edge or in containers. Near-white flowers in July. Somewhat slug tolerant.

**HT/SP** 25–30 cm (10–12″) / 45–60 cm (18–24″)

**'Tokudama'** [*H. tokudama*] SPECIMEN or GROUNDCOVER. Thick, waxy foliage is an intense powdery-blue shade in spring with attractive quilting, later deepening to dark green. Still considered to be one of the best blue forms, but slow to establish. Near-white flowers in July. Useful where *H. sieboldiana* 'Elegans' might be too large. Excellent slug resistance.

**HT/SP** 40–45 cm (16–18″) / 90–110 cm (36–42″)

**'Tokudama Aureonebulosa'** [*H. tokudama* 'Aureo-nebulosa'] SPECIMEN or GROUNDCOVER. This features rich central variegation. Leaves are thick with streaky blue-green margins, the middle chartreuse in spring then later becoming golden yellow. This is a very choice, slow-growing variety for the enthusiast. Clusters of near-white flowers in July. Excellent slug-resistance.

**HT/SP** 40–45 cm (16–18″) / 90–100 cm (36–40″)

**'Undulata'** [*H. undulata*] EDGING. Another older selection, but not as commonly seen in landscapes as 'Undulata Univitatta' The main difference is that this one has a broader area of white in the centre, covering about two thirds of the leaf surface. Lavender flowers appear in July, and then the foliage becomes more mottled or even all-green in appearance. Remove spent flowers to tidy up the clumps. If slugs make a big mess this plant responds well to being cut back hard.

**HT/SP** 25–30 cm (10–12″) / 60–80 cm (24–30″)

**'Undulata Albomarginata'** [*H. undulata* 'Albo-marginata'] GROUNDCOVER. Slightly wavy leaves, two-tone green with a broad creamy-white margin. Pale-lilac flowers in July are held on taller stems. This is the old standard white-edged hosta commonly seen everywhere. Especially valuable for mass planting, and not to be sneezed at despite the usual problems with slugs and snails.

**HT/SP** 40–45 cm (16–18″) / 80–100 cm (32–40″)

**'Undulata Univitatta'** EDGING or GROUNDCOVER. Without a doubt the most commonly encountered white-centred Hosta in North American gardens. Wavy, twisted leaves are green on both sides, with about one third of the middle creamy-white in tone, with a few pale green streaks in between. Lilac flowers appear in early July. This somewhat unstable variety will lose some variegation as plants mature in the garden. Divide every three years for the best colour.

**HT/SP** 30–45 cm (12–18″) / 60–90 cm (2–3′)

***ventricosa*** **'Aureomarginata'** SPECIMEN or GROUNDCOVER. An older yet highly-regarded form. Leaves are deep green with irregular wide margins, yellow in spring, changing to creamy-white by summer. Forms a large mound in time. Showy bell-shaped purple flowers in July. Susceptible to slug damage.

**HT/SP** 45–55 cm (18–22″) / 90–110 cm (36–42″)

**'Whirlwind'** GROUNDCOVER or SPECIMEN. Another of my favourites, forming a medium-large mound fairly quickly. Leaves are pointy with a dark green margin, the centre ivory-white in

*Hosta* 'Stiletto'

*Hosta* 'Super Nova'

*Hosta* 'Sum and Substance'

spring, gradually fading to light green, then dark green in summer. Lavender flowers tower over top in August. Good slug tolerance. Nice as a specimen plant in a large tub.

**HT/SP** 45–50 cm (18–20") / 80–100 cm (32–40")

**'Wide Brim'** GROUNDCOVER or SPECIMEN. Quickly forms a medium-sized mound, the rounded dark-green leaves have wide creamy-white to gold margins, and light corrugation. Lots of pale lavender flowers appear in late July. A highly-rated selection that deserves much wider use in our landscapes. Good slug tolerance.

**HT/SP** 40–45 cm (16–18") / 80–100 cm (32–40")

**'Zager's White Edge'** GROUNDCOVER. An excellent green-leaved form with a crisp pure-white edging. Produces lavender flowers in July. Somewhat slug prone.

**HT/SP** 40–45 cm (16–18") / 80–100 cm (32–40")

**'Zounds'** SPECIMEN or GROUND-COVER. Outstanding bright golden-yellow corrugated foliage, stands out like a beacon. One of the best gold-leafed forms for shady situations. Pale lavender flowers appear in late June. Makes a big, broad clump in time. Excellent slug tolerance.

**HT/SP** 50–55 cm (20–22") / 90–120 cm (3–4')

## HOUSTONIA ☼ ◐
(Mountain Bluets)

*caerulea* **'Millard's Variety'**   ZONE 3
[*Houstonia michauxii* 'Fred Mullard', *Hediotis caerulea*]
This cute little creeper forms a low mat of tiny green leaves, smothered by little blue star flowers in late spring. An easy rock garden perennial that will sometimes self-seed around. Likes a moist soil while blooming, but doesn't mind drying out in the summer. Dislikes lime. Native to eastern North America, generally growing in regions with acidic soil.

**HT/SP** 10–15 cm (4–6") / 20–30 cm (8–12")
**SOIL** Moist to wet lime-free soil.
**BLOOM** April–June
**USES** △ M• ▼ Between flagstones, Containers

## HOUTTUYNIA ☼ ◐
(Chameleon Plant)

*cordata* **'Chameleon'**   ZONE 4
Forms a thick patch of brightly-coloured leaves splashed with a bold combination of green, red, yellow and cream, and with an intense fragrance of copper and tangerines that is not appealing to everyone. Plants spread quickly by underground rhizomes, especially in moist locations, and should be kept out of most borders due to its aggressive nature. The star-shaped white flowers are fairly insignificant. A

useful groundcover although very late to come up in spring. Nice in containers or at the waterside. Plants will spread more slowly in dry locations. This is eaten as a vegetable in Japan and some other Asian countries.

**HT/SP** 15–40 cm (6–16") / 60–90 cm (2–3')
**SOIL** Prefers a rich, damp to wet soil.
**BLOOM** July–August
**USES** M• ▼ Waterside

## HUMULUS ☼ ◐
(Hops)

*lupulus*   ZONE 2
A vigorous climbing vine, useful as a fast cover for a screen or fence. These can be trained up pergolas or trellises, or allowed to clamber up a shrub. Foliage is large and handsomely lobed. The cone-shaped dried fruits are used in beer making, but only the female plants produce usable fruit. If beer is what you crave, be sure to seek out a named selection (there are several) that is a true female clone. Specialty herb nurseries sometimes carry these.

Hops are herbaceous vines, growing back from the ground each year. Remove the tops completely in late fall or early spring but be sure to wear gloves and eye protection, since the rough stems can cause cuts. Clumps can become somewhat invasive, spreading by underground roots.

**HT/SP** 3–6 m (10–20') / 90–120 cm (3–4')
**SOIL** Prefers a rich, moist soil.
**BLOOM** July–August
**USES** ▼ Climbing vine

**'Aureus'** (Golden Hops) With bright chartreuse-golden leaves, this selection is the best form for ornamental effect. Plants are vigorous climbers, although they may sit there for a couple of years before taking off. Plenty of moisture is required, and even so a little bit of afternoon shade will help to prevent leaf scorch in hot-summer regions. Appears to be hardy in cold winter areas like the Canadian Prairies.

## HUTCHINSIA ☼ ◐
(Hutchinsia)

*alpina*   ZONE 4
[*Pritzelago alpina*]
Hutchinsia is not so common in gardens, but it's a reliable spring-blooming species best suited to the rock garden or for edging a well-drained border. Plants form a low, creeping mat of ferny evergreen leaves, smothered for several weeks by short sprays of tiny white flowers. Great in walls or trough gardens. Prefers part shade in hotter regions. Clumps may be easily divided in late summer.

**HT/SP** 5–10 cm (2–4") / 20–30 cm (8–12")
**SOIL** Prefers an evenly moist soil.
**BLOOM** April–June
**USES** △ ▲ ▼ Rock garden, Trough gardens

## HYPERICUM ☼ ◐
(St. John's-Wort)
This is a large group of plants, including several common shrubs and woody groundcovers as well as some truly herbaceous types. What they all share in common is a long display of yellow flowers, star-shaped to rounded, usually with a cluster of stamens sticking out from the centre. Most are of easy care and fairly long lived.

*androsaemum* **'Albury Purple'** ZONE 5
(Tutsan, Purple St. John's-Wort)
A woody species, best cut back hard to 15 cm (6") in the spring to encourage good bushy growth from the base. The foliage of this selection is a rich dusky-purple shade, a nice backdrop to the yellow flowers in midsummer. These are followed in turn by berry-like fruits that mature in the fall to deep chocolate brown. Selections of this species are grown commercially for the berried stems, which are used by florists. 'Albury Purple' makes a nice accent in the perennial border or in containers. Gardeners in Zones 5–6 should mulch plants well in late fall.

**HT/SP** 70–90 cm (30–36") / 45–60 cm (18–24")
**SOIL** Average to moist, well-drained soil.
**BLOOM** July–August
**USES** ✂ ▼ Borders, Massing

*calycinum*   ZONE 5
(Aaron's Beard, St. John's-Wort, Rose of Sharon)
A popular evergreen groundcover, with large golden-yellow flowers appearing throughout the summer and fall. Plants have upright stems of powdery-green

*Houstonia caerulea* 'Millard's Variety'

*Houttuynia cordata* 'Chameleon'

*Humulus lupulus* 'Aureus'

*Hypericum androsaemum* 'Albury Purple'

leaves, forming a dense weed-proof patch fairly quickly. Especially useful for stabilizing slopes. Excellent among shrubs and trees. Quite drought-tolerant once established. To encourage a bushy habit, pinch the growth tips in the spring for the first two to three seasons. Space at 5–10 plants per square yard.

**HT/SP** 30–45 cm (12–18″) / 30–60 cm (1–2′)
**SOIL** Tolerates a wide range of soil conditions.
**BLOOM** May–October
**USES** ⋔⋏▲▼Ӿ Massing

### cerastioides                    ZONE 5
### (Trailing St. John's-Wort)
A small species, best suited to the rock garden or as a groundcover. Plants form a mound of finely-textured olive-green leaves that become smothered by small golden-yellow flowers in late spring. Fairly drought-tolerant once established. Clip plants back lightly after blooming to keep them bushy. Deciduous habit.

**HT/SP** 15–25 cm (6–10″) / 30–45 cm (12–18″)
**SOIL** Average to dry, well-drained soil.
**BLOOM** May–July
**USES** ⟁⋔▼Ӿ Rock garden, Edging

### × moserianum 'Tricolor'      ZONE 6
### (Tricolor St. John's-Wort)
This selection is semi-woody in habit, at its best when cut back to 15 cm (6″) each spring. The foliage is rather showy, soft green with splashes of cream and pink. The flowers are quite large and of the usual golden yellow. This really shines as a container plant but also fits into the rock garden or front of the border. Protect from hot afternoon sun in warmer regions. Gardeners in Zone 6 should mulch plants well in late fall.

**HT/SP** 30–60 cm (1–2′) / 30–45 cm (12–18″)
**SOIL** Average to moist, well-drained soil.
**BLOOM** July–August
**USES** Ӿ▼ Borders, Edging

### olympicum minus               ZONE 6
### [H. polyphyllum]
### (Olympic St. John's-Wort)
Another small mound-forming species that is most at home as an edging or rockery plant. Flowers are quite large for the mound size, in a bright golden-yellow shade. Leaves are fine in texture, olive in colour and generally evergreen. Drought tolerant.

**HT/SP** 10–15 cm (4–6″) / 25–30 cm (10–12″)
**SOIL** Tolerates a wide range of soil conditions.
**BLOOM** May–July
**USES** ⟁⋔▲▼Ӿ Rock garden, Edging

**'Variegatum'** The tiny leaves are splashed and speckled with creamy-white early in the season, later becoming olive green. Flowers are the usual golden yellow.

### perforatum                    ZONE 4
### (Common St. John's-Wort)
This is the medicinal species of St. John's-Wort – oil from the plant is widely used in the pharmaceutical industry. Plants form a narrow upright clump of green leaves, bearing small yellow starry flowers in summer. Best suited to naturalizing in meadows. Drought tolerant, once established. An interesting addition to the herb garden. Naturalized throughout much of North America. I frankly think of this as more of a weed than an ornamental garden perennial.
**CAUTION: Harmful if eaten.**

**HT/SP** 30–60 cm (1–2′) / 25–30 cm (10–12″)
**SOIL** Average to dry, well-drained soil.
**BLOOM** June–August
**USES** Ӿ Herb gardens, Meadows

## IBERIS ☼◐
## (Candytuft)

### sempervirens                  ZONE 3
### (Evergreen Candytuft)
A spring-blooming favourite, usually seen cascading over rocks and walls or used as a groundcover. The tiny evergreen foliage forms a compact mat or bush, smothered with white flowers for many weeks in spring. Plan to shear plants back by about half immediately after flowering, which keeps them bushy and full. Fairly drought-tolerant once established. Because they most often grow from a single woody stem at the base, plants are difficult or impossible to divide.

**SP** 30–60 cm (1–2′)
**SOIL** Average to dry, well-drained soil.
**BLOOM** April–June
**USES** ⟁⋔▲▼Ӿ Walls, Slopes, Edging

**'Alexander's White'** Fairly tall and bushy in habit. Loads of white flowers

in spring and a tendency to repeat bloom in the autumn.

**HT** 20–25 cm (8–10″)

**Little Gem ['Weisser Zwerg']** Especially compact and tidy. Masses of small white flowers.

**HT** 15–20 cm (6–8″)

**'Purity'** Midsized in habit, with especially glossy foliage. Flowers are white.

**HT** 15–20 cm (6–8″)

**Snowflake ['Schneeflocke']** Larger form, good for edging borders. Clean white flowers in good-sized clusters.

**HT** 20–25 cm (8–10″)

## INCARVILLEA ☼◐
## (Hardy Gloxinia, Garden Gloxinia)

### delavayi                      ZONE 5
Not really a true Gloxinia, but the large rose-purple trumpet-shaped flowers slightly resemble the real thing. This forms a mound of coarsely divided green leaves, bearing stems of flowers for many weeks if faded blooms are deadheaded regularly. Winter protection is recommended in Zones 5–6. Worth growing as a container plant in Zones 1–4, bringing indoors for the winter, or treating as an annual. The fleshy roots are inclined to rot out where soils are heavy or stay wet during the winter. Excellent for cutting.

**HT/SP** 45–60 cm (18–24″) / 30–45 cm (12–18″)
**SOIL** Well-drained soil. Dislikes winter wet.
**BLOOM** May–July
**USES** Ӿ▼ Borders

## IRIS ☼◐
## (Iris, Flag)
Irises are a huge, wonderful and diverse group of plants, with flowers in virtually every colour of the rainbow. Few gardens would seem complete without at least one representative from the Iris ranks. All have grassy, sword-shaped leaves forming a clump. Most prefer a rich, well-drained soil with plenty of water during the blooming season.

Certain types, most notably the modern hybrid Bearded Irises, are susceptible to the Iris Borer. This nasty pest lays its eggs inside the leaves, which hatch and develop quickly into green worms that tunnel their way down to the fleshy rhizomes. See the section on *Pests & Diseases* at the end of this guide for more information.
**CAUTION: All are harmful if eaten.**

### Bearded Iris Hybrids          ZONE 3
### [I. germanica hybrids]
By far the Bearded Iris hybrids are the most popular with gardeners, particularly the taller forms. Their large satiny flowers put on a short but spectacular display in spring and early summer.

Incarvillea delavayi
Hypericum × moserianum 'Tricolor'
Iberis sempervirens

Modern Bearded Iris flowers come in nearly every colour and combination imaginable, including blue, bronzy-brown, maroon-black, orange, peach, pink, purple, white, and yellow – about the only colour missing is clear fire-engine red. There are over twenty thousand named varieties that have been selected over the last fifty years or so. Since most growers handle just a small selection of cultivars, gardeners wishing to build up a collection should consider joining one of the chapters of the American Iris Society or contacting a specialist Iris grower by mail-order.

Bearded Irises are grouped by height into several categories; Tall, Border, Intermediate, Standard Dwarf and Miniature Dwarf. The Tall Bearded selections are the most popular, although the foliage has a tendency to look tired after flowering, remaining rather shabby through the rest of the season. They are heavy feeders, requiring additional fertilizer in early spring, again before blooming-time and once more in mid-August.

Divide plants every 3–4 years in July–August, making sure each division has at least one fan of leaves. Plant into rich well-prepared soil with excellent drainage and in a sunny location. It is very important that the top of the horizontal rhizome should be just showing at the surface of the soil, not too deep nor too shallow. Modern Bearded Iris are terribly overbred and seem to be susceptible to various insects and diseases, most notably Iris borers, aphids and various kinds of leaf spots and rots. See the *Pests & Diseases* section for some ideas on controlling these.

**SOIL** Rich, well-drained loamy soil, better on the dry side.
**BLOOM** April–June
**USES** ✂ Borders

**TALL BEARDED (TB)** The giants of this group, bringing the Bearded Iris season to a close in May–June. Stems may need to be staked to prevent the heavy blooms from snapping off in the wind. Flowers are big, and sometimes delightfully ruffled. A sampling of selections are listed here.
**HT** 70–100 cm (30–40″)

**'Babbling Brook'** Ruffled powder-blue flowers, soft-yellow beards.
**'Breakers'** Big flowers of mid to deep blue, heavily ruffled petals.
**'Camelot Rose'** Soft orchid-pink standards, contrasting burgundy-red falls.
**'Champagne Elegance'** Ivory-white standards with ruffled falls in a blend of peachy-apricot.

**'China Dragon'** Ruffled tangerine-orange petals, contrasting rusty-red beards.
**'Cranberry Ice'** Big blooms in a solid, velvety wine-red.
**'Immortality'** Fragrant and ruffled white flowers, often repeat blooms in autumn.
**'Memory of France'** Creamy-white standards and soft buttery-yellow falls. Big and ruffled.
**'Rave On'** Glowing orange blooms with darker tangerine beards.
**'Snow Cloud'** Early blooming. Ruffled white standards, subtle soft grey-blue falls.
**'Superstition'** Amazing black-purple flowers with just a hint of maroon. Good fragrance.
**'Well Endowed'** Tall and stately stems of ruffled golden-yellow blooms.

**INTERMEDIATE BEARDED (IB)** Mid-sized in habit, many gardeners claim these make better all around border plants. Stems are sturdy and should not need to be staked. Nicest when several clumps are grown together.
**HT** 40–70 cm (16–30″)

**'Appleblossom Pink'** Soft-pink petals, blending to cream in the centre, white beards.
**'Batik'** White flowers are boldly streaked with rich royal purple, yellow beards.

**STANDARD DWARF BEARDED (SDB)** Particularly useful at the border front, but also short enough for the rock garden. This is a large group with a broad scope of colours and blends available. Among the easiest to grow.
**HT** 20–38 cm (8–15″)

**MINIATURE DWARF BEARDED (MDB)** [*I. pumila*] True miniatures, and superb in the rock garden. Clumps are effective, but where these really shine is when used to edge long borders, or planted in drifts of different colours. Flowering is in mid spring, beginning the Bearded Iris season. Plants are tough and of very easy care so long as they get lots of sun and good drainage. Drought tolerant. The number of named selections in this group is not nearly so extensive. Generally sold by colour, which ranges from purple to blue, lavender, bronze, pink, peach, yellow or white.
**HT** 10–20 cm (4–8″)

**ensata** ZONE 4
[*I. kaempferi*]
**(Japanese Iris)**
Their large and flattened, crepe-textured blooms appear over tall grassy clumps that somewhat resemble cat-tails. These have been selected and bred in Japan for hundreds of years. Plants must have plenty of moisture until they bloom, followed by a drier period for the rest of the growing season. Also, they are not tolerant of lime soils or hot, dry conditions. Japanese Irises are set in their ways, and without the specific conditions just mentioned they will seldom thrive. There are now hundreds of named selections but growers often sell them by colour only, so try to buy plants in flower whenever possible to be sure of what you are getting. Flowers come in shades of blue, pink, purple and white, in both single and double forms.
**HT/SP** 75–120 cm (30–48″) / 45–60 cm (18–24″)
**SOIL** Evenly moist rich soil, see above.
**BLOOM** June–July
**USES** ✂ ▼ Waterside, Borders

**'Imperial Magic'** ['Murakomo'] A gorgeous selection, the petals are medium-purple, exotically dappled and streaked with soft mauve.
**HT** 80–90 cm (30–36″)

**Mount Fuji** ['Haku-botan'] Cascading white petals with a tiny yellow eye.
**HT** 75–90 cm (30–36″)

**Royal Robe** ['Agoga-kujyo'] Large, drooping flowers of rich, velvety deep purple.
**HT** 75–90 cm (30–36″)

**'Variegata'** Grown more for its excellent foliage, boldly striped lengthwise with green and creamy-yellow, fading to green during the summer months. Flowers are violet-purple. Beautiful at the waterside.
**HT** 70–75 cm (28–30″)

*Iris* Tall Bearded

*Iris* 'Champagne Elegance'

*Iris* 'Batik'

*Iris ensata*

### *foetidissima* ZONE 6
### (Scarlet-berry Iris, Gladwyn Iris)

An evergreen species, grown for its clusters of colourful scarlet fruit, which look attractive in fall and winter and are sometimes used in dried arrangements. The small mauve-purple flowers are fairly insignificant. Tolerates part shade. Another name is "Stinking Iris", as the leaves give off a bad smell when crushed.

**HT/SP** 45–60 cm (18–24") / 30–45 cm (12–18")
**SOIL** Average to moist, well-drained soil.
**BLOOM** May–July
**USES** ✂❦▲ Borders, Winter interest

**'Fructu Albo'** A rare and seldom-grown form, the berries turn pearly white in fall. Very nice when combined with the scarlet form.

### *pallida* ZONE 3
### (Sweet Iris, Sweet Flag)

The species itself is seldom grown, but the striped forms listed below are very popular both for their handsome foliage, and showy lavender-blue flowers. Both forms are good for edging, or anywhere a splash of bright foliage would be effective in the border. These are reliable and disease-resistant. Evergreen in mild areas. Divide like Bearded Iris, in July or August.

**HT/SP** 55–60 cm (22–24") / 30–45 cm (12–18")
**SOIL** Average well-drained loamy soil.
**BLOOM** May–July
**USES** ✂❦ Borders, Edging

**'Argentea Variegata'** (Silver-variegated Sweet Flag) The more commonly seen form. Leaves are striped lengthwise with silvery-white and grey-green.

**'Aureo Variegata'** (Gold-variegated Sweet Flag) Attractive stripes of creamy-gold and olive green leaves.

### *pseudacorus* ZONE 2
### (Yellow Flag Iris)

This forms husky cattail-sized clumps, attractive at the waterside or in ponds but also happy in the border with plenty of moisture. The bright crayon-yellow flowers are small, but put on a nice display. Naturalized in many parts of North America along lakes and rivers. Forms with double flowers or variegated foliage are also well worth growing.

**HT/SP** 90–120 cm (3–4') / 60–75 cm (24–30")
**SOIL** Rich average to wet soil.
**BLOOM** May–June
**USES** ✂❦ Border, Waterside

### × *pumila* see Bearded Iris Hybrids (Miniature Dwarf Bearded)

### *setosa* var. *arctica* ZONE 2
### (Arctic Iris)

Finally becoming popular and widely known, this species makes a low, grassy mound of foliage that is perfect at the border edge or in the rock garden. Good-sized lavender-blue flowers are veined in silvery-white, looking vaguely similar to the Siberian Iris. A very hardy species native to Siberia and Alaska. Could be massed effectively as a groundcover in Zones 2–6, much the way *Liriope* is used in the southern States. The dried seedheads have rather good winter interest. Plants may be easily divided in late summer. Best in a moisture-retentive soil.

**HT/SP** 15–30 cm (6–12") / 20–30 cm (8–12")
**SOIL** Average to moist, well-drained soil.
**BLOOM** May–June
**USES** ▲❦✂ Borders, Edging

### *sibirica* ZONE 2
### (Siberian Iris)

These form strong clumps of grassy leaves that remain attractive all season. Delicate-looking flowers rise above on slender stems in late spring. They tolerate shade better than most Irises as well as poorly-drained soils. Siberian Iris are very long-lived and need to be divided only when the flowers start to become small or few in number, or when clumps begin to open up in the middle. Division is usually carried out in the autumn but doing it in the spring won't cause much harm.

Blooms are generally in shades of blue to rose, purple and white, with many named cultivars in existence at a variety of heights. Flowers are nice for cutting, the seed-pods have good winter interest and are sometimes cut for dried arrangements.

**HT/SP** 60–100 cm (24–40") / 45–60 cm (18–24")
**SOIL** Rich, average to moist (or wet) soil.
**BLOOM** May–June
**USES** ✂❦ Borders, Waterside

**'Baby Sister'** Soft violet-blue flowers on very compact clumps.

**HT** 30–40 cm (12–16")

**'Butter and Sugar'** Award-winning selection in a white and soft butter-yellow combination. Said to be a good repeat bloomer.

**HT** 65–70 cm (24–30")

**'Caesar's Brother'** Deep royal-blue flowers with a gold throat. An excellent older introduction.

**HT** 90–100 cm (36–40")

**'Chartreuse Bounty'** Bicoloured flowers of chartreuse-yellow and white. Tall and stately.

**HT** 90–100 cm (36–40")

**'Chilled Wine'** Rich wine-red flowers with a blue cast. Not a true fire-engine red.

**HT** 90–95 cm (3–3')

**'Dance Ballerina Dance'** Nice mid-sized habit. Flowers are a combination of mauve-pink and soft creamy-pink, with yellow streaking in the throat.

**HT** 55–60 cm (22–24")

**'Ego'** A pleasing blend of light and medium blue.

**HT** 70–80 cm (28–32")

**'Ewen'** Rich wine-red flowers with creamy-yellow markings. Mid-sized.

**HT** 70–75 cm (28–30")

**'Papillon'** Large blooms in a soft lavender-blue shade.

**HT** 85–90 cm (33–36")

**'Persimmon'** Bright, rich medium-blue flowers.

**HT** 85–90 cm (33–36")

**'Pink Haze'** Soft lavender-pink flowers, petals flecked with crimson. Unusual.

**HT** 80–90 cm (30–36")

**'Ruffled Velvet'** Deep velvety-purple flowers with gold veining. Mid-sized.

**HT** 60–75 cm (24–30")

**'Silver Edge'** Rich sky-blue flowers, the petals edged in silver.

**HT** 70–75 cm (28–30")

**'Sky Wings'** Small and delicate blooms, soft lavender-blue with yellow veins.

**HT** 80–85 cm (30–33")

**'Snow Queen'** [*I. sanguinea* 'Snow Queen'] White blooms with a contrasting yellow throat.

**HT** 75–90 cm (30–36")

**'White Swirl'** Heavy-blooming selection, with loads of clean white flowers.

**HT** 95–100 cm (36–40")

### *unguicularis* ZONE 8
### [*I. stylosa*]
### (Algerian Winter Iris)

Totally unlike any of the other Iris, this species opens its blossoms one by one from late fall to early spring. Plants make an evergreen grassy clump, the fragrant lavender flowers hiding among

*Iris setosa*

*Iris sibirica* 'Ruffled Velvet'

*Iris sibirica* 'Silver Edge'

*Iris sibirica* 'Ego'

*Iris pallida* 'Aureo Variegata'

them for some extra protection. Prefers a hot, dry site – like you might find against a wall or house. Performs especially well in the Pacific Northwest. Plants resent being disturbed; divide or move only if absolutely necessary, doing so in late summer.

| HT/SP | 30–45 cm (12–18″) / 30–45 cm (12–18″) |
| SOIL | Average to dry, well-drained soil. |
| BLOOM | December–March |
| USES | ✂◀▲ Borders |

### *versicolor*     ZONE 2
### (Blue Flag Iris)
Native to eastern North America, this species is like a bright blue-flowered version of *I. pseudacorus*. The bold, upright clumps of green foliage are attractive beside a pond or stream. Plants also adapt well to average border conditions.

| HT/SP | 90–120 cm (3–4′) / 60–75 cm (24–30″) |
| SOIL | Prefers rich, moist to wet soil. |
| BLOOM | May–June |
| USES | ✂◀ Wildflower, Borders, Waterside |

## ISOTOMA ☀◐
## (Blue Star Creeper)

### *fluviatilis*     ZONE 6
### [*Laurentia fluviatilis*]
A beautiful little mat-forming plant, the tiny green leaves bear light blue starry flowers all summer long. Ideal for planting between paving stones, putting up with light traffic once established. Worth growing even as an annual in colder regions for its all-season display. Proving to be hardier than we first thought, it may winter in Zone 5 with snowcover. Plants are easily increased by ripping apart into pieces about 5 cm (2″) in diameter, best done in spring.

| HT/SP | 2–4 cm (1–2″) / 15–30 cm (6–12″) |
| SOIL | Average to moist well-drained soil. |
| BLOOM | May–September |
| USES | ▲◣M▲▼ Patios, Walkways |

**'Kelsey Blue'** Even more beautiful than the species, with a rich display of bright-blue starry flowers.

## JASIONE ☀◐
## (Shepherd's Bit, Shepherd's Scabious)

### *laevis*     ZONE 4
### [*J. perennis*]
Plants form a low, bushy mound of grey-green leaves, with ball-shaped heads of violet-blue flowers appearing for most of the summer. A nice frontal or edging plant. Related to the Bellflowers, these are especially effective when combined with summer-blooming heathers, since they both enjoy similar conditions. Flowers are good for cutting.

| HT/SP | 25–30 cm (10–12″) / 25–30 cm (10–12″) |
| SOIL | Well-drained light soil, preferably acidic. |
| BLOOM | May–August |
| USES | ▲✂◀ Borders, Heather beds |

## KALIMERIS ☀◐
## (Japanese Aster, Kalimeris)
These are close cousins to our native *Boltonia* and *Aster*, native to Japan and other eastern Asian countries. Most are long-flowering and compact plants, well suited to the front of a sunny border. Some types have been better-known under the name *Asteromoea*.

### *yomena*     ZONE 4
I have yet to encounter the green-leaved species form, but two excellent variegated selections have recently been introduced in North America. Plants are bushy in habit, spreading to form a patch. Small mauve-pink daisy flowers appear in early fall, lasting for several weeks in the cool autumn weather. These promise to be versatile plants, excellent towards the border edge but especially nice when planted as a foliage accent in mixed containers. Attractive to butterflies.

| SOIL | Average to moist, well-drained soil. |
| BLOOM | September–October |
| USES | ✂▼◀ Edging, Containers |

**'Fuji Snow'** Leaves are boldly splashed with green, creamy-white and pink. Quite stunning. More compact than 'Shogun'.

| HT/SP | 20–30 cm (8–12″) / 25–30 cm (10–12″) |

**'Shogun' ['Variegata']** Olive-green leaves are edged and splashed with golden-yellow in spring, later aging to green and creamy white.

| HT/SP | 40–60 cm (16–24″) / 45–60 cm (18–24″) |

## KIRENGESHOMA ◐
## (Waxbells)

### *palmata*     ZONE 5
### (Yellow Waxbells)
A first-rate foliage plant, with exotic-looking upright clumps of toothed green maple-like leaves. Flowers are pendulous soft-yellow bells rising above on purple-black stems in late summer and fall. A good candidate for cool, moist woodland gardens where they mingle perfectly with other shade-lovers like *Rodgersia*, ferns or *Tricyrtis*. Somewhat slow to establish but well-behaved and durable.

| HT/SP | 90–120 cm (3–4′) / 75–90 cm (30–36″) |
| SOIL | Rich, moist woodland soil, preferably acidic. |
| BLOOM | August–October |
| USES | ✂◀ Shady borders, Woodland gardens |

**Koreana Group [*K. koreana*] (Korean Waxbells)** Very similar in habit and overall appearance, although the soft lemon-yellow bells open a little bit wider and are held in a more upright fashion, resulting in a showier flower effect. Stems are plain green with the maple-shaped leaves slightly smaller.

## KNAUTIA ☀
## (Scabious)

### *macedonica*     ZONE 4
### [*Scabiosa rumelica*]
### (Crimson Scabious, Balkan Scabious)
A bushy-growing border perennial, valued for its long succession of crimson red, double pincushion flowers. Excellent for cutting. This is a good filler plant for summer schemes, and one of the few perennials available in this rich shade of deep red. Sometimes performs as a biennial or short-lived perennial, but nearly always comes back by self seeding. Plants often benefit from a hard clip back to about 20 cm (8″) in mid-summer. Attractive to butterflies. Drought tolerant.

| HT/SP | 60–90 cm (2–3′) / 45–60 cm (18–24″) |
| SOIL | Average to dry, well-drained soil. |
| BLOOM | June–September |
| USES | ✂◀▼ Borders |

**'Melton Pastels'** A delightful blend of shades, including the usual crimson as well as baby pink and mauve.

## KNIPHOFIA ☀
## [*Tritoma*]
## (Red-hot Poker, Torchlily)
Tufts of sword-shaped leaves form a broad clump that remains evergreen in milder regions. Flowers are arranged in a bottle-brush shaped head, held on strong upright stems. Recent hybrids have extended the range of colours beyond the old red and yellow combination. In Zones 5–6 the leaves should be tied up and the plants mulched for the winter to protect the sensitive crown. Trim back any damaged leaf-tips in early spring. These demand excellent drainage, yet appreciate a good supply

*Isotoma fluviatilis* 'Kelsey Blue'
*Knautia macedonica*
*Kirengeshoma palmata*

of moisture when blooming. Planting before midsummer is recommended. Selections with red or orange flowers may attract hummingbirds.

### Hybrids         ZONE 5

Much breeding work and selection has happened over the last few decades, aiming to produce a wider range of colours on sturdy cold-hardy plants. A great deal of variation in plant heights, blooming times, and hardiness has resulted. Quite drought-tolerant once established.

SP    45–60 cm (18–24")
SOIL  Average to rich well-drained soil. Dislikes winter wet.
BLOOM June–September
USES  ✂❦▲➵❦ Borders

**'Cobra'** Great big spikes are held on tall stems. Flowers begin a bronzy-copper shade, ageing to an orange and creamy-white bicolour. Superb for cutting. July–September.

HT    90–120 cm (3–4')

**'Flamenco'** A recently introduced strain, producing a riot of bloom in shades of yellow, orange and flame red. Good height for cutting.

HT    75–90 cm (30–36")

**'Percy's Pride'** One of the biggest, with enormous spikes of soft sulphur-yellow flowers. August–October.

HT    90–110 cm (36–42")

**Pfitzer's Hybrids [Stark's Early Hybrids]** A blend of yellow, orange and red shades, often bicoloured. Early blooming. May–August.

HT    80–90 cm (30–36")

**'Royal Castle'** An older strain, producing a mixture of the usual yellow, orange and red shades. May–August.

HT    80–90 cm (30–36")

**'Shining Sceptre'** Glowing golden-orange flowers. Very tall and robust. July–September.

HT    90–100 cm (36–40")

## LAMIASTRUM ☼ ●
### (False Lamium, Yellow Archangel)

***galeobdolon***    ZONE 2
**[*Lamium galeobdolon*]**
At one time included under *Lamium*, then segregated and now possibly moving back. Regardless of the name, these are attractive groundcover plants for shady areas, the foliage remaining evergreen in mild winter regions. Small but showy yellow flowers appear briefly in the spring. Great in containers.

SOIL  Tolerates a wide range of soil conditions.
BLOOM April–June
USES  ↝▲➵❦ Shady borders, Woodland

**'Florentinum' ['Variegatum']** A very fast-spreading mat of handsome green and silver striped foliage, the stems running and rooting where they touch the ground. Fairly easily controlled by removing runners or clipping, but invasive enough to be kept out of most borders. An especially good groundcover for difficult shady areas, like under trees. I often recommend this plant for growing under shallow-rooted trees like Norway Maples. Beautiful bronze appearance in winter. Great for masking dying bulb foliage in late spring. Plants also cascade nicely out of window boxes or planters. Drought tolerant.

HT/SP  20–30 cm (8–12") / 60–90 cm (2–3')

**'Hermann's Pride'** A totally non-running habit in contrast to the selection above. This rates high on my list of favourite shade plants, with attractive pointy leaves that are heavily veined in metallic silver. Forms a neat mound, well-behaved and excellent for edging. Clumps may be easily divided in spring or early fall. Drought tolerant. Not as inclined to stay evergreen, in fact totally herbaceous in my Zone 6 garden.

HT/SP  25–30 cm (10–12") / 30–45 cm (12–18")

## LAMIUM ☼ ●
### (Creeping Lamium, False Salvia)

***maculatum***    ZONE 2
One of the most handsome and sturdy groundcover plants for shady areas. Quickly forms a low patch of small leaves, in various combinations of green and silver, depending on the selection. Clusters of flowers appear in mid-spring then sporadically until late fall. Perfect for edging, between shrubs or in containers, but a bit too vigorous for the rock garden. Gardeners in regions with cool nights can often succeed with these in full sun.

Although evergreen in mild regions, plants often benefit from a hard cutting back (or even mowing) in early spring. These are drought tolerant once established, but happiest in an evenly moist soil. Like *Lamiastrum*, I often recommend Creeping Lamium for the difficult dry shade conditions found under greedy trees. The various selections have become extremely popular in recent years, particularly for massed landscape plantings. Also a good mask for dying bulb foliage. Easily divided by ripping the clump apart into pieces, in spring or early fall.

HT/SP  15–20 cm (6–8") / 30–60 cm (1–2')
SOIL  Tolerates a wide range of soil conditions.
BLOOM April–September
USES  ↝▲➵❦ Edging, Massing

**'Aureum'** Chartreuse-yellow leaves with faint silvery stripes, mauve-pink flowers. Will not tolerate direct sun without burning. Much less vigorous than other selections.

**'Beedham's White'** Chartreuse-yellow leaves, better vigour than 'Aureum' and less inclined to burn from the sun. Clear white flowers.

**'Chequers'** Very vigorous variety. Leaves are dark green with a central silver stripe. Clusters of deep rosy-purple flowers appear early, continuing on and off. Habit is a little more upright than most. New leaves become tinged with red during the summer, particularly with direct sun.

HT    20–30 cm (8–12")

**'Orchid Frost'** Leaves of this new selection are silvery with a wide blue-green edge. The distinctive two-tone effect is different from any of the other silver forms. Rose-pink clusters of flowers contrast well and are said to appear more reliably through the summer months.

**'Pink Pewter'** Silvery leaves with a narrow green edge. Similar to 'White Nancy', but with soft salmon-pink flowers. Good vigour. This is a good substitute for the older selection 'Beacon Silver', which has developed production problems in recent years for many nurseries.

**'Red Nancy'** The foliage is virtually identical to 'White Nancy', with flowers in a cherry-red to purple shade. Still a far cry from Popsicle red.

**'Shell Pink'** Green and white striped foliage (similar to 'Chequers'), with soft-pink flowers.

**'White Nancy'** Leaves are almost completely silver, with just the narrowest blue-green edge. Clear white flowers appear to almost float on top. The habit is dense and low. An excellent choice for covering large or small areas.

*Kniphofia* 'Percy's Pride'

*Lamiastrum g.* 'Hermann's Pride'

*Lamium m.* 'Beedham's White'

*Lamium m.* 'Orchid Frost'

*Kniphofia* 'Flamenco'

*Lamium m.* 'Chequers'

## LATHYRUS ☀
**(Sweet Pea)**

### *latifolius*　　ZONE 3
**(Everlasting Pea)**

A trailing perennial vine, this will climb on fences and trellises, or clamber over slopes. Flowers are in lovely shades of rose, pink, and white. Good cut-flower, fresh or dried, but unfortunately lacking the fragrance of the annual Sweet Pea. This species has naturalized throughout much of North America and there is some concern about its invasive potential in the Pacific Northwest. Plants spread primarily by seed, although this is not generally a problem in a garden setting.

**HT/SP** 30–240 cm (1–8′) / 60–90 cm (2–3′)
**SOIL** Average to dry, well-drained soil.
**BLOOM** June–September
**USES** ✂ ⋔ 🦋 Slopes, Climbing vine

### *vernus*　　ZONE 3
**(Spring Vetchling)**

Not at all like a climbing Sweet Pea, this species forms a low clump and is most at home in the shady woodland garden. Light-green shoots burst out of the ground in spring, producing clusters of pea-like flowers in shades of pink to magenta purple. Inclined to become dormant in summer, so tolerant of drought conditions. Performs best in regions with cool nights. Clumps dislike being moved once established. Propagation by seed is best, sown directly outdoors in the fall.

**HT/SP** 30–40 cm (12–16″) / 30–45 cm (12–18″)
**SOIL** Prefers a rich, moist woodland soil.
**BLOOM** March–May
**USES** ⚭△✂ Woodland, Rock garden

**'Spring Melody'** A gorgeous selection with bicoloured flowers of soft-pink and rose.

## LAURENTIA see ISOTOMA

## LAVANDULA ☀
**(Lavender)**

A group of low woody shrubs from the Mediterranean, often grown with perennials in borders and mixed plantings. Lavenders are native to areas with hot dry summers and mild winters, so they are extremely happy in the Pacific Northwest (with good winter drainage), but there are some varieties of English Lavender that adapt well right across the country. All types have that same unmistakable sweet fragrance and spikes of showy flowers in summer. Shearing the bushes back lightly after flowering or in early spring will keep them dense and compact. Most types are quite drought-tolerant once established. Attractive to butterflies.

### *angustifolia*　　ZONE 4
**(English Lavender, Common Lavender)**

An old-fashioned plant with a long history as a scented herb, but always appreciated for its showy spikes of flowers and attractive greyish leaves. Lavender is especially effective when planted around shrub roses. Acting as an evergreen shrub in milder regions, Lavender can be used to make a low hedge. Mulch for the winter in very cold areas. Good drainage is essential to success. Several forms of this species exist.

**SP** 30–60 cm (1–2′)
**SOIL** Average to dry, very well-drained soil.
**BLOOM** June–August
**USES** ✂⚭▲🍷🦋 Borders, Edging, Herbal crafts

**Blue Cushion ['Schola']** One of the shortest forms, with grey-green foliage and deep violet-blue flowers over a long season. Ideal for the rock garden or edging.
**HT/SP** 30–40 cm (12–16″) / 30–45 cm (12–18″)

**Goldburg ['Burgoldeen']** An odd name, considering the foliage is brightly striped with grey-green and creamy-white. Deep lavender-blue spikes are a lovely contrast. Well suited to containers.
**HT/SP** 30–60 cm (1–2′) / 40–60 cm (16–24″)

**'Hidcote'** Dark violet-purple flower spikes, and a good compact habit. A seed-grown strain so somewhat variable.
**HT** 30–60 cm (1–2′)

**'Hidcote Pink'** Soft baby-pink spikes, compact habit with grey-green leaves.
**HT** 30–45 cm (12–18″)

**'Jean Davis'** Olive-green foliage, with spikes of pale pink.
**HT** 30–35 cm (10–12″)

**'Munstead'** Bright lavender-blue flowers. Grey-green leaves form a nice compact mound. The most commonly-grown seed strain, and somewhat variable. Often said to be the hardiest form.
**HT** 30–40 cm (12–16″)

**'Twickel Purple'** A taller form, with long arching stems of deep-purple spikes. Foliage is olive green. Very showy.
**HT** 45–60 cm (18–24″)

### *dentata*　　ZONE 7
**(French Lavender, Fringed Lavender)**

The grey-green leaves of this species are finely toothed along the edges, giving a feathery appearance. Plants form a bushy mound, bearing short stems of mauve-lavender flowers in summer. Although not hardy over a wide region this is one of the best forms for container growing, often clipped or trained into interesting topiary shapes. One point of confusion – this plant is

also sometimes referred to as Spanish Lavender, a name better used for *Lavandula stoechas*.

**HT/SP** 60–90 cm (2–3′) / 60–70 cm (24–28″)
**SOIL** Average to dry, very well-drained soil.
**BLOOM** July–August
**USES** ✂⚭▲🍷🦋 Containers, Topiary

**'Goodwin Creek Grey'**　　ZONE 7
Outstanding silvery-grey foliage, forms a medium-sized bushy mound. Taller stems with big deep-purple spikes are produced over an extremely long season. This claims *L. dentata* as one of its parents, inheriting its less hardy nature but also the ability to withstand growing in containers and being clipped into shapes. Discovered at Goodwin Creek Gardens, a herb nursery in Oregon.

**HT/SP** 45–60 cm (18–24″) / 60–75 cm (24–30″)
**SOIL** Average to dry, very well-drained soil.
**BLOOM** June–September
**USES** ✂⚭▲🍷🦋 Containers, Topiary

### × *intermedia*　　ZONE 5
**(Lavendin)**

These hybrids had their origins in France, first developed for growers supplying essential oils to the perfume industry. Plants generally are more vigorous and disease-free than the *L. angustifolia* types, and a little larger in habit. They also tend to bloom a bit later.

**HT/SP** 60–75 cm (24–30″) / 45–60 cm (18–24″)
**SOIL** Average to dry, very well-drained soil.
**BLOOM** July–September
**USES** ✂⚭▲🍷🦋 Borders, Herbal crafts

**'Fred Boutin'** Excellent foliage in a bright silvery-grey, with long spikes of bright-purple flowers.
**HT** 60–75 cm (24–30″)

**Walburton's Silver Edge ['Walvera']** Another interesting new variegated selection, with wide grey-green leaves that sport a creamy-white edge. Spikes are

*Lamium maculatum 'White Nancy'*

*Lathyrus latifolius*

*Lathyrus vernus 'Spring Melody'*

*Lavandula angustifolia 'Munstead'*

long, medium-blue in colour. Promises to have good interest in the garden year round.

HT      60–70 cm (24–28″)

### 'Richard Gray'                    ZONE 7
An extremely silver selection, with a mid-sized habit. Flower spikes are dark-blue and really stand out because of the foliage. Perhaps best in a container.

HT/SP   45–50 cm (18–20″) / 45–60 cm (18–24″)
SOIL    Average to dry, very well-drained soil.
BLOOM   July–September
USES    ✂❦▲❦❦ Containers, Borders

### 'Sawyers'                         ZONE 7
A newer British hybrid selection with a tight, compact habit. Perhaps the most silvery form, with short spikes of mauve-purple flowers.

HT/SP   50–60 cm (20–24″) / 45–60 cm (18–24″)
SOIL    Average to dry, very well-drained soil.
BLOOM   July–August
USES    ✂❦▲❦❦ Containers, Borders

### *stoechas*                        ZONE 7
(Spanish Lavender,
Butterfly Lavender)
Although this is sometimes called French Lavender, I find that name only causes confusion and is better applied to *L. dentata*. This species is bushy and fairly compact, with fat, deep-purple flower spikes. Most often seen in the butterfly-flowered forms, as listed below.

HT/SP   45–60 cm (18–24″) / 45–60 cm (18–24″)
SOIL    Average to dry, very well-drained soil.
BLOOM   July–August
USES    ✂❦▲❦❦ Borders, Containers

**'Otto Quast' ['Quasti']** Spikes are fat, dark purple at the base, with interesting waving "flags" of bright mauve at the tips. Extremely showy. Foliage is silvery-grey

HT      60–70 cm (24–28″)

## LAVATERA ☼
(Tree Mallow)
The Tree Mallows are a mainstay of British gardens throughout the summer months, giving endless colour and substantial structure. Gardeners in similar climates – like the Pacific Northwest – have also discovered how valuable and easy these are to grow. Their funnel-shaped flowers bring to mind a Rose-of-Sharon or a small single hollyhock, and all of these plants are close relatives. Lavatera are in constant bloom summer through fall, and combine effectively with so many other flowers. These are not long-lived plants but generally last three to five years before dying out. For those of us in cold-winter regions, Tree Mallows are well worth growing as container plants, wintered in a cool protected porch or down in the basement.

### Hybrids                           ZONE 6
(Tree Mallow)
Plants form a large mound of lobed grey-green leaves, covered in bright hollyhock-type flowers from midsummer to frost. These are actually woody shrubs but should be cut back hard each spring to 15 cm (6″), forcing new bushy growth from the base. The various colour selections look equally at home with both perennials and shrubs. Planting before midsummer is recommended. Use a deep winter mulch in colder areas.

HT/SP   120–180 cm (4–6′) / 90–120 cm (3–4′)
SOIL    Average to moist, well-drained soil.
BLOOM   June–October
USES    ✂❦ Borders, Containers

**'Barnsley'** White flowers with a pink blush, aging to soft-pink. Remove any stems that revert to deep pink. Reported to be hardy to Zone 5 with a heavy winter mulch and plenty of snow cover.

HT      120–210 cm (4–7′)

**'Bredon Springs'** Beautiful clear rose-pink flowers, foliage is soft grey-green.

HT      120–180 cm (4–6′)

**'Candy Floss'** Soft-pink flowers with a white eye over grey-green leaves.

HT      120–210 cm (4–7′)

**'Eye Catcher'** Brilliant magenta-pink blooms, one of the showiest forms.

HT      150–180 cm (5–6′)

## LEONTOPODIUM ☼
(Edelweiss)

### *alpinum*                         ZONE 2
A well-known rockery plant from the Swiss Alps. Foliage is silver-grey, bearing woolly white flowers that are sometimes used for dried arrangements. Best in a well-drained rock garden or gravel scree bed. Interesting

and unique, particularly if you like the song. Extremely drought-tolerant.

HT/SP   15–20 cm (6–8″) / 20–30 cm (8–12″)
SOIL    Very well-drained soil.
BLOOM   June–July
USES    ✂❦▲❦❦ Rock garden, Troughs

## LEPTINELLA ☼ ◐
[*Cotula*]
(Brass Buttons)

### *gruveri*                         ZONE 7
(Miniature Brass Buttons)
The minute leaves of this flat carpeting perennial are the perfect filler for cracks between flagstones in moist, shady areas. Tiny greenish flowers appear in summer. Runners quickly fill in and help to keep weeds out. May be used as an evergreen lawn substitute over small areas. Easily divided at any time by digging up the clump and ripping apart into small pieces. May become dormant during summer droughts, greening again once watered. Best in partial to full shade.

HT/SP   1–2 cm (½–1″) / 20–30 cm (8–12″)
SOIL    Prefers moist, well-drained soil.
BLOOM   June–July
USES    ▲∧∧▲❦ Between flagstones, Lawn substitute

### *squalida*                        ZONE 5
(Green Brass Buttons)
An interesting little subject for filling in the gaps between flagstones, growing on walls or in the rock garden. Soft, feathery green leaves form a tight mat or low mound and turn an attractive bronze colour in winter. The yellow-green button-like flowers are fairly insignificant. Easily divided by ripping the patch apart in spring. This seems to resent drying out during the heat of summer. Evergreen.

HT/SP   2–5 cm (1–2″) / 25–30 cm (10–12″)
SOIL    Average to moist, well-drained soil.
BLOOM   May–June
USES    ▲∧∧▲❦ Between flagstones, Lawn substitute

**'Platt's Black'** (Black-leaved Brass Buttons) *Feathery leaves are an especially appealing bronzy-black shade. Shows up particularly well against light-coloured stone. Habit is identical to the species.*

## LEUCANTHEMUM ☼ ◐
(Shasta Daisy)

### × *superbum*                      ZONE 4
(Shasta Daisy)
No sunny border would seem complete without including at least one of these familiar, sturdy white daisies. Recent breeding has resulted in a good selection of flower types and plant heights. All varieties will bloom for much longer when the faded flowers are removed weekly. Good drainage in winter is essential to success. Since these tend to

Leptinella squalida

Lavandula intermedia Walburton Silver Edge

Lavatera 'Barnsley'

Leontopodium alpinum

be short-lived, dividing the clumps every two years in spring is a good idea. Aphids are often a problem, so watch for signs of attack in early summer. Taller selections may need to be staked.

Gardeners often mistake the weedy **Ox-eye Daisy** for a Shasta, but they are different plants. Ox-eye Daisy (*L. vulgare*) is a prolific self-seeder, and has become a serious weed of pastures and waste places in a number of states and provinces. True Shasta Daisies will seldom self-sow and there is very little chance of plants becoming a pesky weed.

**SP**    45–60 cm (18–24″)
**SOIL**    Average well-drained soil.
**BLOOM** June–September
**USES**    ✄◄ 🦋    Borders, Cutting garden

**'Aglaia'** The true form has large, frilly double flowers with a crested white centre. Hardier than 'Esther Read'. Beware of single-flowered seed-grown impostors.
**HT**    60–75 cm (24–30″)

**'Alaska'** Classic single white flowers with a yellow eye. This is the most common strain available. Hardy to Zone 3.
**HT**    60–90 cm (2–3′)

**'Becky'** From the southern U.S., this variety has quickly made the rounds and is receiving loud applause for its sturdiness and free-flowering habit, even in hot humid areas. It features very large single flowers, tall stems and fresh-looking foliage. Despite the height, this often does not require staking. Re-blooming stems become shorter in the heat of summer. Selected as the 2003 *Perennial Plant of the Year.*
**HT**    90–105 cm (36–42″)

**'Crazy Daisy'** A rather new strain. Flowers have narrow petals with a finely-cut or fringed appearance ranging from single to semi- or fully-double heads. Quite variable in form, hence the "crazy" part of the name.
**HT**    60–70 cm (24–28″)

**'Esther Read'** Fully double flowers, almost like a florist's mum. Slightly less hardy, Zones 5–9. This was the first double cultivar to be developed.
**HT**    30–60 cm (1–2′)

**'Phyllis Smith'** A seldom-offered British introduction, and hands-down my own personal favourite. The petals are very finely fringed, surrounding a bright golden-yellow centre. The height is perfect for along the front of the border or in containers. Good repeat-flowering habit.
**HT**    45–60 cm (18–24″)

**Silver Princess ['Silberprinzesschen']** Compact, mounding plants with masses of single white flowers.
**HT**    25–30 cm (10–12″)

**'Silver Spoons'** Single, yellow-eyed flowers, the narrow white petals flare into tiny spoons on the ends. Quite tall. May require staking.
**HT**    90–120 cm (3–4′)

**'Snowcap'** Probably the best of the compact forms. Good-sized single white daisies on a mounding plant that blooms for weeks on end. Ideal for massing or edging along the front of the border.
**HT**    30–35 cm (10–12″)

**'Snowdrift'** A mid-sized strain, featuring semi- to fully-double white flowers. Nice for cutting.
**HT**    60–70 cm (24–28″)

**'Sunny Side Up'** An interesting new double form, flowers have a large knobby or crested eggyolk-yellow centre, surrounded by a double row of white petals. Resembles some sort of exotic florist's mum. Mid-sized habit.
**HT**    65–75 cm (24–30″)

**'Summer Snowball'** A terrific fully-double variety, the round, fluffy flowers are pure white, the size of tennis balls. Great for cutting.
**HT**    70–75 cm (28–30″)

# LEWISIA ☼
## (Lewisia)

***cotyledon***                          ZONE 3
A challenging but rewarding plant for the rock garden. Forms a flat rosette of ever-green foliage, sprays of brightly-coloured starry flowers are held above in early summer. Modern hybrid strains produce both solid-coloured and striped flowers, from pink through salmon, orange, yellow and white shades. Lewisia demands perfect drainage, best achieved by placing plants almost vertically between rocks in a wall or planting in a scree garden. A mulch of gravel around the crown is required to keep plants high and dry. Very showy!

**HT/SP** 15–20 cm (6–8″) / 15–20 cm (6–8″)
**SOIL**    Requires excellent drainage.
**BLOOM** May–June
**USES**    ⛰▲🌱 Troughs, Screes

**'Little Plum'** A rather new hybrid strain, this produces compact and heavy blooming plants. The star-shaped flowers are a pleasant shade of cotton-candy pink, with a flush of salmon-orange when they first open. Will often repeat bloom in the autumn.
**HT**    10–15 cm (4–6″)

# LIATRIS ☼
## (Blazing Star, Gayfeather)
These are popular as commercial cut flowers, valued for their tall, long-lasting spikes. Excellent border peren-

nials and also easy to naturalize in a meadow planting. Blazing Stars are tough, drought-tolerant North American native wildflowers. Clumps should be divided every 3–4 years to keep them flowering well.

***spicata***                          ZONE 2
Plants form a low grassy clump of leaves, with taller spikes of rosy-purple flowers appearing in midsummer. An easy, reliable border perennial. Attractive to butterflies.

**HT/SP** 75–90 cm (30–36″) / 30–45 cm (12–18″)
**SOIL**    Tolerates a wide range of soil conditions.
**BLOOM** July–September
**USES**    ✄◄ 🦋 🌱 Borders, Meadows

**Floristan Violet ['Floristan Violett']** Developed for the cutflower industry. Tall spikes of magenta purple flowers.
**Floristan White ['Floristan Weiss']** Spikes of fluffy white flowers, especially nice together with the purple.
**'Kobold'** Good compact habit, mauve flowers. An ideal size for containers or the border front.
**HT**    45–60 cm (18–24″)

# LIGULARIA ☼◐
## (Ligularia)
Also sometimes known as Elephant Ears. These are bold background or specimen plants, forming big clumps of large, rounded leaves with upright spikes or clusters of yellow daisy flowers in summer. Ligularias are at their best in a cool, moist location, especially beside water. Avoid planting these under trees where they will have to compete for moisture. During periods of heat or drought the leaves may look sad and wilted towards the end of the day, only to bounce back fresh and perky by morning. These are

Leptinella s. 'Platt's Black'    Leucanthemum × 'Becky'    Leucanthemum × 'Esther Read'

Leucanthemum × 'Snowcap'

Lewisia 'Little Plum'    Lewisia cotyledon

long-lived plants that seldom need to be divided. Growing in containers will greatly reduce the damage done by slugs and snails.

SP     70–90 cm (30–36″)
SOIL    Rich, moist to wet soil.
BLOOM June–August
USES   ✂💐 Borders, Waterside, Specimen

### *dentata*        ZONE 3
### [*L. clivorum*]
The most commonly seen species with its large, rounded rhubarb-like leaves that form a substantial clump. Tall spikes of golden-yellow flowers put on a great show at the back of the summer border. Excellent waterside specimen. Heat tolerant.
**'Desdemona'** Large handsome dark-green leaves, rich purple on the backside. The branching heads of bright golden-orange daisies create a vibrant contrast.

HT      90–120 cm (3–4′)

**'Othello'** Slightly taller than 'Desdemona', blooms a bit earlier.

### **'Gregynog Gold'**     ZONE 3
### [*L.* × *hessei* 'Gregynog Gold']
Pyramidal spikes of golden-orange flowers over an impressive mound of large wavy green leaves. Nice for cutting.
HT      90–150 cm (3–5′)

### **'Sungold'**         ZONE 4
The foliage forms a medium-sized bright-green mound, with much taller spikes of golden-yellow daisies held well above the leaves. Consider moving this out towards the middle or even the front of the border, surrounded by lower-growing neighbours.
HT      120–150 cm (4–5′)

### **'The Rocket'**       ZONE 4
### [*L. stenocephala* 'The Rocket']
Purple-black stems end in long bottle-brush spikes of yellow flowers. Leaves are deeply toothed or divided, lighter in appearance and reportedly more slug-resistant. Excellent as a background plant.
HT      120–180 cm (4–6′)

### *wilsoniana*       ZONE 2
### (Giant Groundsel)
Probably the best form of all for floral display, with very tall candelabra-like spikes of chrome-yellow daisies in mid-summer. Leaves are large and rounded, forest green. Extremely hardy. Blooms earlier than the rest.
HT      150–180 cm (5–6′)

# LILIUM ☼◑
# (Lily)
Lilies can provide bold effect in the summer border with their large flowers. The various types offer a wide range of colours, shapes, and blooming times from which to choose. As cut-flowers they are strong stemmed and long-lasting. Divide the clumps every few years in late fall, separating the bulbs and replanting in a different site. Gardeners interested in building up a collection of lilies might consider joining one of the many regional Lily societies.

Most Lilies are susceptible to botrytis infection, which causes the leaves to turn brown and sometimes affects the flowers. Good sanitation is the key, removing the dead stems and any fallen leaves in the autumn. Lily Beetles are quickly gaining ground in some regions, and these can completely defoliate plants within a matter of days. See the section on *Pests & Diseases* for more information.

### **Asiatic Hybrids**       ZONE 2
Easy to grow, early blooming and very hardy. Flowers open wide, either upfacing, outfacing, or nodding, in an incredibly wide range of colours and blends. Some of the newer selections are free of spots or have bold splotches (brush-marks) of a contrasting colour on each petal. The general range includes orange, pink, red, white, and yellow, with many pastels, bicolours and in-between shades – there are literally hundreds of named varieties available. For many years these have been the mainstay of summer borders in regions like the Canadian Prairies. Unfortunately, Asiatic Lilies have no fragrance.
HT/SP   60–120 cm (2–4′) / 30–45 cm (12–18″)
SOIL    Average well-drained soil.
BLOOM June–July
USES   ✂💐 Borders, Massing

**'Lollypop'** Big upfacing blooms, the white petals boldly flushed with rose-red towards the tips. Sure to attract attention!
HT      60–70 cm (24–28″)

**Pixie Series** Excellent new dwarf selections, developed for commercial greenhouse growers but truly ideal towards the border front or in mixed containers. Flowers are upfacing. Shades include: **'Buff Pixie'** (gorgeous soft orange), **'Butter Pixie'** (soft butter-yellow), **'Crimson Pixie'** (rich crimson-red, very compact), **'Orange Pixie'** (bright orange), **'Pink Pixie'** (bright pink), **'Reinesse'** (ivory-white).
HT/SP   30–50 cm (12–20″) / 25–30 cm (10–12″)

### *lancifolium*       ZONE 2
### [*L. tigrinum*]
### (Tiger Lily)
A classic garden species, with tall stems that are great for cutting. Out-facing or nodding bright-orange flowers are spotted with black and held on strong stems in a long branching raceme. Petals curl back attractively behind the flowers. The tiny little black bulbils held along the stems can be planted like seeds; these will form blooming-size bulbs in about three years. One occasionally can find Tiger Lilies available with double flowers or blooms of pink, yellow or white.
HT/SP   120–150 cm (4–5′) / 30–45 cm (12–18″)
SOIL    Average well-drained soil.
BLOOM May–September
USES   ✂💐 Borders, Cutting

### **Oriental Hybrids**     ZONE 4
### (Oriental Lily)
Late-blooming and very fragrant, their large star-shaped flowers are superb for cutting. These deserve a place in every border. Oriental lilies have a reputation for being a bit fussy and short-lived, probably the result of gardeners treating them the same as the Asiatic hybrids. They are often planted near Rhododendrons as the requirements for growing each are similar; light sandy-loam soils that are rich in compost or peat, preferably on the acidic side. Gardeners in mild coastal climates most often succeed with these, but they are well worth trying in other areas. Winter mulching is recommended in Zones 4–5. There are many named selections of Oriental Lilies ('Casa Blanca' is the most famous) but in a fairly small range of colours – mostly in shades of white, pink or red, sometimes attractively banded or spotted.
HT/SP   90–180 cm (3–6′) / 30–45 cm (12–18″)
SOIL    Prefers a moist, well-drained acidic soil.
BLOOM August–September
USES   ✂ Borders, Woodlands

*Liatris spicata* Floristan White

*Ligularia dentata* 'Othello'

*Ligularia* 'Gregynog Gold'

*Lilium* 'Lollypop'

***speciosum* var. *rubrum***    ZONE 4
**(Red Japanese Lily)**
A late-blooming species with branching stems of fragrant ruby-red flowers with a soft-pink margin. An old-fashioned favourite for lime-free soils. Very popular flower in wedding bouquets. Prefers a cool exposure.

**HT/SP** 120–150 cm (4–5') / 30–45 cm (12–18")
**SOIL** Prefers a moist, well-drained acidic soil.
**BLOOM** August–September
**USES** ✂🌿 Borders, Woodland gardens

**Trumpet Lily Hybrids**    ZONE 4
Immense flaring trumpet flowers, excellent as a background planting in the border or massed among shrubs. Blooms are strongly fragrant. These will require staking but otherwise are easy and trouble-free. The choice of named cultivars is not nearly as extensive as the Asiatics but includes a good range of colours. Gardeners on the Prairies are wise to mulch these well in late fall or grow near a house foundation. Said to attract hummingbirds.

**HT/SP** 120–180 cm (4–6') / 30–45 cm (12–18")
**SOIL** Average to moist, well-drained soil.
**BLOOM** July–August
**USES** ✂🌿 Borders, Cutting

**'African Queen'** Apricot-orange trumpets, a shade that blends well in the garden.
**'Golden Splendor'** Not really gold, but a deep-yellow shade with maroon stripes on the petal reverse.
**'Pink Perfection'** Pink and white striped petals, greenish throat.
***regale*** (Regal Lily) A species type of Trumpet Lily. Big white blooms are marked with maroon on the outside, yellow throat. Gorgeous.

# LIMONIUM ☀
**(Sea Lavender, Statice)**

***latifolium***    ZONE 2
**[*L. platyphyllum*]**
**(Sea Lavender)**
Dainty lavender-blue flowers are borne in large panicles. Plants form a rounded bush, with up to a dozen flowering stems. This is a showy, attractive border perennial. Moderately drought-tolerant. Excellent for drying or cutting fresh. Attractive to butterflies.

**HT/SP** 60–75 cm (24–30") / 60–70 cm (24–28")
**SOIL** Average to dry, well-drained soil.
**BLOOM** July–August
**USES** ✂🌿🌸 Dried Flower, Borders

# LINUM ☀
**(Flax)**

***perenne*** **Blue Sapphire**    ZONE 2
**['Blau Saphir']**
**(Blue Flax)**
Small heavenly-blue flowers appear in early summer on an upright arching clump. Makes a particularly nice

display when planted in groups. Prune hard after flowering to encourage a second flush. Needs excellent winter drainage. Short-lived, but readily self seeds. Very drought-tolerant. An old-fashioned favourite!

**HT/SP** 25–30 cm (10–12") / 45–60 cm (18–24")
**SOIL** Average to dry, well-drained soil.
**BLOOM** May–August
**USES** ✂🌿🌸 Borders, Meadows

# LIRIOPE ☀☀●
**(Lily-turf)**
Widely used as a groundcover in the southern US, this is a sturdy group of plants valued for their heat-tolerance and resistance to pests and diseases. The grassy evergreen leaves form a dense clump or mat, with short spikes of showy flowers in late summer. *Liriope* prefer a shady exposure, particularly in hot summer areas. Although tolerant of a wide range of sites their preference is for a moist but well-drained soil with plenty of humus, preferably on the acidic side. A light trim in early spring will tidy up any brown tips caused by winter winds. These also perform surprisingly well in many parts of Canada and the northern US.

***muscari***    ZONE 6
**(Blue Lily-turf)**
Plants quickly develop into dense evergreen clumps. Showy spikes of flowers are followed by black berries that remain throughout the winter months. This is the species most used as a groundcover or edging, with close to one hundred named varieties in existence.

**HT/SP** 20–50 cm (8–20") / 30–40 cm (12–16")
**SOIL** Average to moist well-drained soil, preferably acidic.
**BLOOM** July–September
**USES** 🔺🌿🌸 Massing, Edging

**'Big Blue'** Large spikes of blue flowers, held well above the leaves.
**'Royal Purple'** Flowers of deep royal purple, green foliage.
**'Silvery Sunproof'** Light green leaves, striped lengthwise with yellow to creamy white. Blue flowers.
**'Variegata'** Leaves brightly striped with green and cream. Lavender-violet flowers.

***spicata***    ZONE 4
**(Creeping Lily-turf)**
This hardier species spreads to form a dense patch of grassy, dark-green foliage, changing to bronze in colder months. Short spikes of small, pale-lavender flowers appear in late summer but these are not as showy as the varieties listed above. Benefits from a hard trimming back in spring – use a mower or string trimmer if the planting is large.

**HT/SP** 20–30 cm (8–12") / 30–60 cm (1–2')
**SOIL** Average to moist well-drained soil, preferably acidic.
**BLOOM** July–August
**USES** 🔺🌿🌸 Massing, Edging

**Silver Dragon ['Gin-ryu']** Dark green leaves are edged in silvery white. Pale lavender flowers. Possibly not as hardy, perhaps Zone 6.

**HT** 10–15 cm (4–6")

# LITHODORA ☀☀
**(Lithospermum)**

***diffusa*** **'Grace Ward'**    ZONE 5
**(Blue Lithospermum)**
An excellent groundcover or rockery plant with brilliant sky-blue flowers all summer long. Foliage is evergreen, an attractive grey-green colour, forming a low creeping mat. Very popular in the Pacific Northwest where it seems to grow especially well. Inclined to be fussy and short-lived in cold-winter areas; use a winter mulch in Zones 5–6. Must have acidic conditions and perfect drainage to thrive. **'Heavenly Blue'** is a very similar selection.

**HT/SP** 10–15 cm (4–6") / 30–45 cm (12–18")
**SOIL** Well-drained acid soil. Dislikes lime.
**BLOOM** May–August
**USES** 🔺🌿🌸 Slopes, Walls

# LOBELIA ☀☀
**(Lobelia)**
Showy late-summer blooming perennials with large upright spikes of flowers, not at all like the more familiar trailing annual types grown in hanging baskets. These short-lived perennials appreciate a moist site and look perfect growing beside a stream or pond where they will often naturalize by self-seeding. Flowers are excellent for cutting. Use a winter

*Lilium* Oriental selection

*Lilium speciosum* var. *rubrum*

*Linum perenne* Blue Sapphire

*Liriope m.* 'Silvery Sunproof'

*Liriope muscari* 'Variegata'

mulch in cold regions, or treat as annuals. **CAUTION: All selections are harmful if eaten.**

### *cardinalis*     ZONE 4
### (Cardinal Flower)
A native wildflower over much of eastern North America, growing alongside streams and ponds. Plants have bright-green coarse foliage that forms a low clump. Bears upright spikes of scarlet-red flowers beginning in midsummer. Typically this is a short-lived species which self-seeds in a good moist spot. Hummingbirds love it.

HT/SP   90–120 cm (3–4') / 45–60 cm (18–24")
SOIL     Rich, moist to wet soil.
BLOOM July–September
USES    ✂ ➤ ✿ ❦ Borders, Waterside

### 'Queen Victoria'     ZONE 7
### (Red-leaved Cardinal Flower)
Rich maroon-red foliage, contrasts well with spikes of scarlet-red flowers. Superb for mass planting or use in containers, this is widely considered to be one of the best perennials for foliage colour. Not reliably hardy in all areas, but worth growing even as an annual.

HT/SP   75–90 cm (30–36") / 30–45 cm (12–18")
SOIL     Prefers a rich, moist but well-drained soil.
BLOOM July–September
USES    ✂ ➤ ✿ ❦ Borders, Waterside

### *siphilitica*     ZONE 4
### (Giant Blue Lobelia)
Stately upright spikes of flowers, from dark blue to white over leafy clumps of green foliage. Great for cutting. This is a native North American wildflower, easy to naturalize in any moist sunny area where it will happily self-seed. Deadheading will keep this in flower for weeks on end.

HT/SP   60–90 cm (2–3') / 30–60 cm (1–2')
SOIL     Average to moist or wet soil.
BLOOM July–October
USES    ✂ ➤ ✿ ❦ Borders, Waterside

### × *speciosa* Hybrids     ZONE 6
This is a complex hybrid group, including a number of recent selections that produce flowers in the most amazingly rich jewel tones. The clumps of bright green or bronze leaves have good strong stems. Many gardeners in Zones 5–6 are enjoying success with these plants – it seems to depend so much on the amount of winter snow cover. If snow is not reliable, a heavy mulch in late fall should make a big difference. At any rate, the long blooming season makes these useful even as bedding annuals. Divide every 2–3 years in spring, to maintain vigour.

SP      45–60 cm (18–24")
SOIL     Rich moist, well-drained soil.
BLOOM July–October
USES    ✂ ➤ ✿ ❦ Borders, Massing

**Compliment Series ['Kompliment']**
Midsized plants with nice strong stems, developed for the floral industry. Foliage is bright green, with spikes of deep red, scarlet, blue or purple flowers, depending on the strain.

HT      70–75 cm (28–30")

**'Cotton Candy'** A recent colour break, this strain produces blooms in a soft cotton candy pink shade. Dark green leaves. Zone 5.

HT      60–70 cm (24–28")

**Fan Series** Plants are a little more compact and bushy, making them ideal for using in mixed containers or massed plantings. Some strains have bronzy-red leaves, others green. Flowers are in shades of burgundy, cinnabar-rose, soft pink, deep rose and scarlet, usually sold according to colour.

HT/SP   50–60 cm (20–24") / 30–40 cm (12–16")

**'Grape Knee-Hi'** Quite new on the scene, this compact plant has deep grape-juice purple spikes over dark green leaves. Flowers are sterile, so blooming continues strong for weeks on end. Zone 5.

HT      50–60 cm (20–24")

**'La Fresco'** This one is my own favourite, with tall stems of rich magenta-purple blooms over a mound of green leaves. Plants seem to be reliable and carefree. Zone 5.

HT      70–75 cm (28–30")

**'Pink Flamingo'** A narrow, upright form with spikes of bright-pink flowers. Green leaves.

HT      75–90 cm (30–36")

**'Rose Beacon'** Large spikes of rich rose-pink over green foliage.

HT      70–75 cm (28–30")

## LOTUS ☼
### (Golden Bird's-foot)

### *corniculatus* 'Plenus'     ZONE 2
### (Bird's-foot Trefoil)
Forms a low creeping green mat, smothered with double golden pea-flowers in early summer. A good groundcover for difficult sunny areas. Not overly invasive, tolerant of very poor soils. Nice in the rock garden.

HT/SP   8–10 cm (3–4") / 30–60 cm (1–2')
SOIL     Tolerates a wide range of soil conditions.
BLOOM May–July
USES    ◭ ∿ ▲ ❦ Walls, Slopes

## LUNARIA ☼◐
### (Money Plant, Honesty)

### *annua*     ZONE 2
### [*L. biennis*]
This is most often grown for the coin-shaped, papery seed heads but the sprays of pretty purple or white flowers in late spring are also delightful. The branches of papery dried pods are popular for indoor decoration. A biennial, useful in the shade garden where it will self-seed all over the place.

HT/SP   60–90 cm (2–3') / 30–60 cm (1–2')
SOIL     Rich average to moist soil.
BLOOM May–June
USES    ✂ ✿ Woodland gardens, Meadows

## LUPINUS ☼◐
### (Lupine, Lupin)
The tall spires of Lupines are an unforgettable sight in the late spring garden. Excellent for cutting, the flowers are available in a rainbow of colours. Plants grow best in a deep, rich soil on the neutral to acidic side. Good drainage is essential. Use a winter mulch in cold regions. Since Lupines are short-lived, renew plantings every other year. Cutting plants back to the base after blooming may encourage them to live an extra year. Lupines often look scruffy after blooming; plant something in front that will get big later in the summer to hide them. Aphids have a special liking for them. **CAUTION: Harmful if eaten.**

### Russell Hybrids     ZONE 3
Extensive breeding has created a wide choice of colours as well as plant heights. Spikes can now be had in shades of blue, pink, rose, red, white, or yellow, sometimes attractively bi-coloured. Plants will self-seed if allowed but seedlings will usually revert to mixed colours.

In recent years growers have been experiencing regular crop failures due to a seed-borne disease that kills the young seedlings. If you have a difficult time locating container-grown plants, consider purchasing seed instead and sowing it right in the garden. Sow seeds in May or June, after soaking in warm

*Lobelia* Fan Deep Red

*Lotus corniculatus* 'Plenus'

*Lunaria annua*

water overnight. Plants will flower the following year.

**HT/SP**  75–100 cm (30–40″) / 30–45 cm (12–16″)
**SOIL**   Deep rich, well-drained soil, preferably acidic.
**BLOOM** June–July
**USES**   ✂✈ Borders

**'Gallery' Series** Plants have a compact habit, with slightly shorter spikes in a wide range of bright shades. Stems are sturdier than other hybrids.

**HT**     45–60 cm (18–24″)

# LYCHNIS ☀
## (Campion)

Related to *Dianthus*, the Campions have flowers in bright pink, magenta, red or orange shades – mostly vibrant colours that don't easily fit into soft pastel schemes. However, they are hardy, easy-to-grow plants mostly for the summer border. Gardeners inclined towards a daring sense of colour design will find these interesting and useful. Attractive to butterflies.

### *alpina*                    ZONE 1
### (Arctic Campion)

From short tufts of grassy leaves, clusters of bright pink flowers appear in late spring. Short-lived but readily self-seeds. An easy little rock garden plant, especially useful in brand-new rock gardens or walls.

**HT/SP**  10–15 cm (4–6″) / 15–20 cm (6–8″)
**SOIL**   Average to dry, well-drained soil.
**BLOOM** May–June
**USES**   △✿✈ Rock garden, Troughs

### *chalcedonica*             ZONE 2
### (Maltese Cross)

One of my earliest childhood memories is attempting to break the tough stems of this plant, which my mother calls Cross-of-Jerusalem. I guess my eye has always been attracted to "hot" colours, like the flaming scarlet-orange heads these never fail to provide. This is an old-fashioned, long-lived cottage garden plant. Shearing the stems back hard after flowering may encourage a repeat bloom in fall.

**HT/SP**  90–120 cm (3–4′) / 30–45 cm (12–18″)
**SOIL**   Average to moist, well-drained soil.
**BLOOM** June–August
**USES**   ✂✈ Borders

**'Carnea'** Heads are a little smaller, in a soft shrimp-pink to Atlantic salmon shade – especially for you orange-haters out there!

### *coronaria*                ZONE 3
### (Rose Campion)

The attractive rosettes of felty silver-grey leaves are reason enough to grow this. Branching stems of bright magenta-rose flowers bloom throughout the summer. Not a long-lived species, but readily self-seeds. Can be used for cutting. Several colour variations exist.

**HT/SP**  60–90 cm (2–3′) / 40–50 cm (16–20″)
**SOIL**   Average to dry, well-drained soil.
**BLOOM** June–August
**USES**   ✂✿✈🐝 Borders, Meadows

**'Angel's Blush'** Flowers have white petals with a blush of soft baby-pink in the centre. Perfect for those pastel gardens.

### *flos-jovis* **'Peggy'**    ZONE 3
### (Flower-of-Jove)

This species is quite similar to the Rose Campion but slightly more compact in habit and usually longer lived. Rosettes of felty silver-grey leaves bear taller stems of bright rose-red flowers in early summer. Low enough to use for edging, in containers or the rock garden. Plants will self seed.

**HT/SP**  25–30 cm (10–12″) / 30–45 cm (12–18″)
**SOIL**   Average to dry, well-drained soil.
**BLOOM** May–July
**USES**   ✂✿✈🐝 Edging, Containers

### **'Molten Lava'**          ZONE 3

Clusters of large scarlet-orange flowers really stand out over a compact mound of rich burgundy-bronze leaves. Very showy for the border front. Nice in containers whether it's in bloom or not.

**HT/SP**  20–25 cm (8–10″) / 25–30 cm (10–12″)
**SOIL**   Average well-drained soil.
**BLOOM** June–July
**USES**   ✂△✿✈ Edging, Containers

# LYSIMACHIA ☀•
## (Loosestrife)

These are *not* the same as Purple Loosestrife (*Lythrum*). Most are moisture-loving perennials, typically with short spikes of white or yellow flowers. They vary from low creeping types to taller border varieties. Most share the trait of spreading fairly quickly, so some extra consideration should be given to their placement. However, none have the potential to set copious amounts of seed and invade our wetlands.

### *ciliata* **'Firecracker'**      ZONE 2
### ['Atropurpurea', Steironema ciliata]
### (Fringed Loosestrife)

A species native over most of North America, this select form has rich bronze-purple leaves, forming a loose upright clump. The nodding yellow flowers contrast beautifully even though the leaves fade a bit in the heat of summer. This does spread quickly to form a patch so growing it in a planter or large tub might be wise unless you have plenty of space. There was a planting of this on my street one year, combined with late-blooming tulips in an apricot-peach shade, that looked gorgeous.

**HT/SP**  75–90 cm (30–36″) / 75–90 cm (30–36″)
**SOIL**   Prefers a rich moist soil.
**BLOOM** June–August
**USES**   ✂✿✈ Borders, Planters

### *clethroides*              ZONE 3
### (Gooseneck Loosestrife)

Unusual spikes of white flowers are crooked or bent just like a goose's neck, and highly valued by designers. The coarse green foliage can develop rich red fall colour. It quickly spreads to form a patch and may swamp out slower-growing neighbours. Best at the waterside or a similar moist location. Tolerates semi-shade. Great for massing.

**HT/SP**  60–90 cm (2–3′) / 75–90 cm (30–36″)
**SOIL**   Prefers a rich, moist soil.
**BLOOM** July–September
**USES**   ✂✈ Borders, Waterside

### *ephemerum*               ZONE 5
### (Milky Loosestrife)

A completely non-invasive species that is seldom seen in gardens. Forms a bushy, upright clump of powdery-green leaves and later tall tapering spikes of silvery-white flowers appear. Excellent for cutting. Grown as a commercial cut flower.

**HT/SP**  90–120 cm (3–4′) / 45–60 cm (18–24″)
**SOIL**   Rich, average to moist soil.
**BLOOM** July–August
**USES**   ✂✈✿ Borders, Waterside

### *nummularia*              ZONE 2
### (Creeping Jenny)

Low trailing stems quickly form a bright green carpet. Golden-yellow flowers appear among the leaves from spring to fall. Nice as a groundcover in any moist, shady area but is also excellent in hanging baskets. Remains evergreen in mild climates. Can become invasive but runners are easily removed or weeded out. Quite tolerant of heavy shade, but dislikes dry soils.

Lychnis alpina

Lychnis chalcedonica

Lysimachia ciliata 'Firecracker'

Lysimachia clethroides

**HT/SP**　5–10 cm (2–4") / 45–60 cm (18–24")
**SOIL**　Prefers a rich moist soil.
**BLOOM** May–August
**USES**　Lawn substitute, Waterside

**'Aurea' (Golden Creeping Jenny)** The rounded golden-yellow leaves seem to almost have a luminous glow. Must be planted in the shade to avoid scorching. This form is not nearly as aggressive as the plain green species. In my own garden this was a knockout, scrambling under and around a clump of blue *Pulmonaria*, but it eventually straggled away. Divide every 2–4 years to maintain vigour.

### *punctata*　ZONE 2
### (Yellow Loosestrife)

Upright, bushy clumps spread over time to form a large patch. Star-shaped yellow flowers appear in leafy spikes in summer. A good waterside plant, this also adapts well to the border and will even grow in shade under trees. Excellent for cutting. Trim stems back hard after blooming to renew the foliage.

**HT/SP**　60–90 cm (2–3') / 60–90 cm (2–3')
**SOIL**　Average to moist, well-drained soil.
**BLOOM** June–August
**USES**　Borders, Woodland gardens

**'Alexander'** This excellent British selection is finally starting to catch on. The green leaves are boldly edged with cream, the fresh new growth in spring vibrantly tinged with pink. Yellow flowers are an added bonus, but it is worth growing for the foliage alone.

**HT**　45–60 cm (18–24")

**'Golden Alexander'** A brand-new colour form, the foliage is edged in a deeper creamy-yellow. Somehow this combination seems to work better with the starry bright-yellow flowers.

**HT**　45–60 cm (18–24")

## LYTHRUM
## (Purple Loosestrife)

### *salicaria*　ZONE 2

Included here for sake of information only, *Lythrum* is now widely considered to be a serious and invasive weed of natural wetland habitats over large parts of North America. Not that many years ago it was speculated that the hybrid garden selections such as 'Morden Pink', 'Morden Purple' and 'Dropmore Purple' would prove to be sterile and therefore incapable of producing seed, but this has since been proven wrong. Several provinces and states have now placed *Lythrum* on the **noxious weed** list, which outlaws the sale of plants. Gardeners are strongly encouraged to remove and destroy Purple Loosestrife plants to help prevent further spread.

Consider any of these as reasonable substitutes in the garden: *Astilbe chinensis* var. *taquetii*, *Chelone obliqua*, *Lavatera* hybrids, *Liatris spicata*, *Lobelia* hybrids, *Perovskia atriplicifolia*, *Physostegia virginiana*, *Sidalcea* hybrids.

## MACLEAYA
## (Plume Poppy)

### *cordata*　ZONE 2

A giant background plant with handsome, deeply lobed blue-green leaves, topped in summer by cream-coloured plumes. Plants will spread fairly quickly to make a large patch and can become a tad invasive unless restrained each spring – plan to control, rather than fear it. Otherwise, this is a good bold specimen plant.

**HT/SP**　180–300 cm (6–10') / 90–120 cm (3–4')
**SOIL**　Prefers a deep, rich soil.
**BLOOM** July–August
**USES**　Borders, Specimen

**M. microcarpa 'Kelway's Coral Plume'** A more compact form, with slightly bluer leaves and plumes of bronzy-purple flowers.

**HT**　180–240 cm (6–8')

## MALVA
## (Mallow)

With their satiny pink or white flowers, the Mallows can immediately be recognized as cousins to the Hollyhock and Hibiscus. These are short-lived perennials but often come back by self-sowing. They have a very long blooming season and are sometimes treated as bedding annuals. Like Hollyhocks, the plants may succumb to rust infections on the foliage.

### *moschata*　ZONE 3
### (Musk Mallow)

Small rounded pink or white flowers are borne all summer long on a bushy

mound of deeply-cut green leaves, which are said to have a pleasant musky smell when crushed. As filler plants in the sunny border these are true workhorses, especially among pastel-flowered neighbours. Cut these back in early fall before they bloom themselves to death. Short-lived but will usually self seed.

**HT/SP**　60–90 cm (2–3') / 45–60 cm (18–24")
**SOIL**　Average to moist, well-drained soil.
**BLOOM** July–September
**USES**　Borders, Meadows

**'Appleblossom Pink'** More compact habit, blooms of soft pink.

**HT**　45–70 cm (18–30")

**var. *rosea*** A range of soft to deep pink shades.

**'Park Allee'**　ZONE 5
This will form a bushy, upright clump, probably requiring staking if grown in rich soil. The medium-sized flowers are a gorgeous soft creamy-apricot shade with contrasting salmon-peach stamens, blooming over a long season. Likely to perform best in regions with mild maritime winters, otherwise grow it as a specimen annual.

**HT/SP**　120–150 cm (4–5') / 60–70 cm (24–28")
**SOIL**　Average to moist, well-drained soil.
**BLOOM** July–October
**USES**　Specimen, Containers

### *sylvestris*　ZONE 6
### (Tree Mallow)

This has foliage that closely resembles a Hollyhock, being large and fairly coarse, the edges gently wavy in outline. The species itself produces good-sized blooms of mauve-purple, but it's the striped selections below that are most often encountered. References sometimes claim these to be hardy down to Zones 3–4, but after several attempts to winter this in my Zone 6 garden, I have determined that they are annuals here – at least in my heavy clay soil. Nevertheless, I would not be without them, and every visitor to the garden wants to know what they are. Plants flower nonstop from midsummer to very late fall. Pinching the tips when the stems reach about 30 cm (12") will help to form a bushy clump, otherwise plan to get out the bamboo stakes. These will sometimes come back by self seeding, or save your own seed and start them early indoors.

**HT/SP**　90–150 cm (3–5') / 45–60 cm (18–24")
**SOIL**　Average to moist, well-drained soil.
**BLOOM** July–October
**USES**　Borders

**'Brave Heart'** Flowers are bright mauve, striped heavily with rich royal purple. They almost appear to have a purple eye.

**HT**　120–150 cm (4–5')

*Lysimachia nummularia*

*Lysimachia n. 'Aurea'*

*Lysimachia punctata*

*Lysimachia p. Golden Alexander*

*Malva moschata rosea*

*Macleaya cordata*

**'Mystic Merlin'** A bright purple and lilac-mauve bicolour. Plants make a big, tall specimen.

HT     150–180 cm (5–6')

**'Zebrina'** (Striped Mallow, Zebra Mallow) Soft lavender-purple flowers, exotically striped with deep maroon veins. An old European cottage garden plant.

HT     60–120 cm (2–4')

# MAZUS ☼ ◑
(Mazus)

*reptans*                ZONE 5
(Creeping Mazus)
Forms a ground-hugging green mat, studded with yellow-spotted lavender flowers that always remind me a bit of a tiny snapdragon. This is charming when grown between paving stones, in the rock garden or as a lawn substitute. Dislikes drying out, but tolerant of summer heat. Reliably evergreen in Zones 7–9.

HT/SP   5–10 cm (2–4") / 30–45 cm (12–18")
SOIL    Average to moist, well-drained soil.
BLOOM April–June
USES    ⬲⋀⋔⛉⬆ Between flagstones, Lawn substitute

**'Albus'** (White Creeping Mazus) Classy looking evergreen carpet, studded with small white flowers for weeks on end. Habit is nearly identical to the species or slightly more compact.

# MECONOPSIS ◑
(Himalayan Poppy)
Probably the most over-promoted perennial of all time, the amazing sky-blue flowers are often featured on the covers of gardening magazines, causing the plant to instantly shoot to the top of every gardener's "want list". Please heed my warning – unless you live in a region with cool nights and virtually no hot, humid summer weather, you are doomed to fail with *Meconopsis*. Where these plants will grow well are in regions like the Pacific Northwest, parts of the Canadian Maritimes, northern Quebec and Ontario, and the Canadian Prairies.

Even in climates to their liking, these are not long-lived perennials. Most species live for 2–3 years, flower heavily, set seed and then die. Seed germinates fairly well indoors under lights, but then the trouble starts when a large proportion of the promising crop dies from damping-off disease – at least, that's always been my experience. Choose a site with rich soil (plenty of compost) that is evenly moist (or can be regularly watered) with morning sun or dappled all-day shade. Have I talked

you out of trying these yet? I didn't think so.

*betonicifolia*                ZONE 3
[*M. baileyi*]
(Blue Himalayan Poppy)
The most famous species, with big satiny flowers of electric blue petals, surrounding a tuft of yellow stamens. Leaves are coarse and hairy. Forms a low rosette the first year, then produces flower stems in the second or third summer. Usually the plants then set seed and die, although some gardeners cut off the finished flower stems in an effort to push yet one more year of life from them.

HT/SP   75–120 cm (30–48") / 30–45 cm (12–18")
SOIL    Rich, evenly moist soil, preferably acidic.
BLOOM May–July
USES    ⋀⛉ Moist woodland garden

× *sheldonii*                ZONE 3
Perhaps some of the hybrid vigour found in this group will help more gardeners to succeed. Flowers are said to be the bluest of all forms. Foliage forms a substantial rosette with a distinctly upright habit, the tall stems branching to give several large blooms. Perhaps longer lived than most.

HT/SP   90–120 cm (3–4') / 30–45 cm (12–18")
SOIL    Rich, evenly moist soil, preferably acidic.
BLOOM May–July
USES    ⋀⛉ Moist woodland garden

# MELISSA ◑
(Lemon Balm)

*officinalis* **'All Gold'**        ZONE 4
(Golden Lemon Balm)
Green Lemon Balm is usually relegated to the herb or vegetable garden, but this distinctive form is a gorgeous foliage plant for any moist, shady site. It forms a low, bushy clump of bright golden-yellow leaves with an intense lemon fragrance and flavour. The mauve flowers are insignificant and should be clipped off to prevent self seeding. Easier still, just hack the whole plant back to 10 cm (4") in midsummer. Nice for edging or in tubs. Protect from hot afternoon sun. Evergreen in mild winter regions.

HT/SP   30–60 cm (1–2') / 45–60 cm (18–24")
SOIL    Prefers a rich, moist soil.
BLOOM June–July
USES    ⋔⛉⬆ Edging, Containers

# MENTHA ◑
(Mint)
Most forms of mint are too invasive to consider letting out of containers or planting in the perennial garden, even though some of them have good ornamental features.

*requienii*                ZONE 7
(Corsican Mint)
Tiny green leaves create a flat carpet with the fragrance of creme-de-menthe. Minute mauve flowers appear in July. Grows nicely in between flagstones or on pathways, even as a self-seeding annual. Looks a bit like Baby-tears. This species is one that should not be feared.

HT/SP   1–2 cm (½–1") / 15–30 cm (6–12")
SOIL    Average to moist, well-drained soil.
BLOOM July–August
USES    ⬲⋀⋔⛉ Pathways, Containers

# MERTENSIA ◑
(Bluebells)

*pterocarpa* var. *yezoensis*   ZONE 4
(Japanese Bluebells)
Similar in effect to our native species (see below), the foliage of this Japanese cousin lasts throughout the season instead of leaving an awkward gap. Leaves are grey-green, with clusters of violet-blue bells. Useful for edging in the woodland, or in containers. Dislikes summer drought.

HT/SP   15–30 cm (6–12") / 30–45 cm (12–18")
SOIL    Prefers a rich, moist woodland soil.
BLOOM April–May
USES    ⋀⋇⋖⛉ Woodland garden

*virginica*                ZONE 2
[*M. pulmonarioides*]
(Virginia Bluebells)
A favourite native woodland perennial, this blooms in mid to late spring and shortly thereafter sets seed and becomes completely dormant for the rest of the year. Flowers are large dangling sky-blue bells, held in a loose cluster over powdery blue-green leaves. In favoured sites the plants will increase by self-seeding. These are often harvested from the wild, so make sure the plants you purchase are nursery propagated!

Mazus reptans 'Albus'

Meconopsis × sheldonii

Melissa officinalis 'All Gold'

Mentha requienii

Clumps may be divided any time they are dormant. Tolerant of summer drought.

**HT/SP** 30–60 cm (1–2′) / 30–45 cm (12–18″)
**SOIL** Average to moist, well-drained soil.
**BLOOM** April–May
**USES** 〰️ Woodland garden

# MIMULUS ☼ ◐
## (Monkey Flower)

Little-known in North America, aside from the seed-grown mixes usually sold as bedding plants in the spring. There are several excellent species and hybrids in existence. Flowers are flaring funnels, with a snapdragon look about them. In colder regions these may be treated as half-hardy perennials wintered indoors in a pot. Constantly wet soils beside a pond or splashing fountain suit these perfectly.

### 'Puck'                                ZONE 6

Selected in England, this has bright nasturtium-yellow flowers heavily speckled with red in the throat. Mounding, spreading habit. Benefits from a hard shearing back in midsummer.

**HT/SP** 10–15 cm (4–6″) / 25–30 cm (10–12″)
**SOIL** Prefers a rich, moist to wet soil.
**BLOOM** June–September
**USES** 〰️ Waterside

# MONARDA ☼ ◐
## (Bee-Balm, Bergamot)

Tall, bushy plants with aromatic mint-like foliage. Their bright shaggy flower heads attract bees and butterflies. Plants are suited to the border or wildflower garden, having been developed from native North American species. A good range of colours is available and there are some exciting new dwarf selections now that allow gardeners to use these at the border front.

Plants spread quickly to form a vigorous patch, eventually thinning out in the middle; divide every couple of years and replant only the younger outside pieces. Powdery mildew on the foliage is often a problem. See the section on *Pests & Diseases* for some ideas on controlling this. If, however, your plants are plagued by mildew every year, my advice is to discard them and replace with some of the newer mildew-resistant selections. Growing Beebalm in evenly-moist soil will help to prevent mildew infections from taking hold.

### Hybrids                              ZONE 3

The varieties listed below are mostly tall growing, long-flowering and excellent for cutting. They grow best with a moist, rich soil and full sun. The leaves and flowers of all Beebalms are edible and fun to add to salads or use as a garnish. Very attractive to hummingbirds and butterflies.

**HT/SP** 75–120 cm (30–48″) / 60–75 cm (24–30″)
**SOIL** Rich, moist well-drained soil.
**BLOOM** July–September
**USES** 〰️ Borders

**Blue Stocking ['Blaustrumpf']** Large, shaggy heads of bright violet-purple. Good heat tolerance.

**HT** 80–100 cm (30–40″)

**'Gardenview Scarlet'** Brilliant-red flowers, very tall. An older variety but with excellent mildew resistance.

**HT** 100–120 cm (39–48″)

**'Jacob Cline'** Big scarlet-red flowers, tall stems. Excellent mildew resistance.

**HT** 90–120 cm (3–4′)

**'Marshall's Delight'** Developed by Agriculture Canada in Morden, Manitoba. Heads of hot-pink flowers on tall stems. Excellent mildew resistance. Probably the best hardy selection for cold regions.

**HT** 75–120 cm (30–48″)

**'Mohawk'** Dusky mauve-purple flowers with brownish bracts. Tall. Good mildew resistance.

**HT** 90–120 cm (3–4′)

**'Panorama' Strain** A mixed seed-strain, producing a pleasing range of scarlet, bright red, pink, salmon, and crimson shades. Quite variable. Some plants may be prone to mildew.

**HT** 75–120 cm (30–48″)

**'Petite Delight'** A real breeding breakthrough, this was the first dwarf selection, raised by Agriculture Canada in Morden. Clear lavender-pink flowers appear over a mound of grey-green mildew-resistant leaves. Terrific for edging and in containers. I have found this selection to perform best in well-drained soil that is not overly moist.

**HT/SP** 25–30 cm (10–12″) / 30–45 cm (12–18″)

**'Petite Wonder'** The newest dwarf selection, also from Agriculture Canada. Clumps are very similar to 'Petite Delight' in appearance, with flowers in a lovely soft-pink shade. Mildew resistant.

**HT/SP** 25–30 cm (10–12″) / 30–45 cm (12–18″)

**Prairie Night ['Prärienacht']** A tall German selection, featuring flowers of deep mauve to rosy-purple. Average mildew tolerance.

**HT** 90–120 cm (3–4′)

**'Raspberry Wine'** Gorgeous wine-red flowers, among the darkest of any. Excellent mildew resistance.

**HT** 90–120 cm (3–4′)

**'Scorpion'** Shaggy heads of purple-red flowers. Good mildew resistance.

**HT** 90–120 cm (3–4′)

**'Violet Queen'** Deep purple flowers, excellent mildew resistance.

**HT** 100–120 cm (39–48″)

### 'Lambada'                            ZONE 8
### (Lemon Beebalm)

This *M. citriodora* hybrid is quite different from the Beebalms listed above. Plants form a bushy, upright clump of lemon-scented leaves, with tiers of flowers arranged in a whorl or ring around the stem. Blossoms are a soft lavender-rose shade with white spots. Terrific for cutting, fresh or dried. May act as an annual or short-lived perennial. Best in full sun.

**HT/SP** 75–100 cm (30–40″) / 60–75 cm (24–30″)
**SOIL** Average to moist, well-drained soil.
**BLOOM** June–September
**USES** 〰️ Borders, Containers

# MYOSOTIS ☼ ◐ ●
## (Forget-me-not)

### *sylvatica*                          ZONE 3
### (Woodland Forget-me-not)

Few other flowers can match the true sky-blue of Forget-me-nots. Their long display combines perfectly with all sorts of spring-blooming bulbs and perennials. These are ideal "tuck-in" plants for the spring garden, self-seeding anywhere that pleases them. This is a true biennial that will almost always perenniate by self-seeding – in fact, ruthless thinning out of seedlings in the fall will allow the remaining plants to perform their best. I like to do this in late September, allowing about 15 cm (6″) between plants. Fairly shade tolerant, especially below deciduous trees. There are strains available in various shades of blue as well as pink and white.

**HT/SP** 15–20 cm (6–8″) / 15–30 cm (6–12″)
**SOIL** Average to moist, well-drained soil.
**BLOOM** March–June
**USES** 〰️ Borders, Woodland gardens, Bedding

*Mimulus* 'Puck'

*Monarda* Blue Stocking

*Monarda* 'Scorpion'

*Monarda* 'Gardenview Scarlet'

*Monarda* 'Raspberry Wine'

# MYRRHIS ☼ ◑
(Sweet Cicely, Myrrh)

### *odorata*                          ZONE 4
Sweet Cicely is grown in the garden both as an herb and flowering perennial. Foliage is bright green and almost fernlike in appearance, with a strong flavour and smell of sweet licorice. Large umbels of tiny white flowers appear in early summer, followed by shiny black seeds. Prune back hard after flowering to rejuvenate the foliage, or if you don't want seedlings all over the place. Excellent for specimen effect in the June border. The seeds can be used to propagate more plants but must be sown immediately when fresh, in late summer. Germination takes place the following spring.

**HT/SP** 90–120 cm (3–4') / 75–90 cm (30–36")
**SOIL** Prefers a rich moist, well-drained soil.
**BLOOM** June–July
**USES** ✂ Borders, Woodland gardens

# NEPETA ☼
(Catmint)

Showy, fragrant relatives of the mints, most of the garden forms are clumping and well-behaved. They have a preference for sunny sites and will tolerate poor soil – in fact, some of them perform their best when grown in a not-too-rich site. These give us a good range of blues to use in the summer border, combining so nicely with the flashier border plants. Taller types are useful for cutting. Catnip (*N. cataria*) is the best-known species but it lacks much ornamental value and has a tendency to self seed all over the place. Perhaps it's best to relegate Catnip to the back alley or vegetable garden. And yes, cats will sometimes be attracted to other selections and species.

### 'Dropmore Hybrid'                ZONE 2
['Dropmore Blue']
A Canadian hybrid of exceptional merit, bred by Dr. Frank Skinner in Manitoba, and introduced by him in 1932. This is a superb choice for edging or mass planting, with clusters of sterile bright blue flowers that appear throughout the summer. The dense, fragrant grey-green foliage stands up well to heat, although plants often benefit from clipping back in early July. Great in containers, also an effective companion to roses. Quite drought-tolerant once established. Clumps may be easily divided in spring or early fall.

**HT/SP** 25–30 cm (10–12") / 30–45 cm (12–18")
**SOIL** Tolerates a wide range of soil conditions.
**BLOOM** May–September
**USES** ✂ ⋏ ♟ ☙ 🦋 ⚘ Edging, Borders, Massing

### *grandiflora*                     ZONE 4
(Showy Catmint, Large-flowered Catmint)
The foliage of this species is very similar to that of 'Dropmore Blue', grey-green in colour with small, rounded leaves. Plants are a fair bit taller, with loose spikes of flowers that are great for cutting. I find these do best when grown in lean soil, otherwise plan to provide some sort of support. Deadheading will encourage repeat blooms, or simply cut the clump back hard in midsummer. Not particularly drought tolerant. Will probably prove hardy to at least Zone 3.

**SP** 45–60 cm (18–24")
**SOIL** Average to moist, well-drained soil.
**BLOOM** June–August
**USES** ✂ ☙ 🦋 Borders

**'Dawn to Dusk'** Spikes of soft-pink flowers, quite different from the other Catmints. Creates a remarkable combination with white or deep-pink roses.

**HT** 60–90 cm (2–3')

**'Pool Bank'** Rich blue flowers are held in bracts of a darker violet-blue. A beautiful shade for the pastel border scheme.

**HT** 75–90 cm (30–36")

### *racemosa* 'Walker's Low'        ZONE 3
[*N. mussinii* 'Walker's Low']
(Blue Catmint)
Very similar in habit to 'Dropmore Hybrid', the mounds are slightly larger in size. Flowers are a rich lavender-blue shade, appearing over several weeks. Deadhead to encourage more buds to form.

**HT/SP** 30–40 cm (12–16") / 45–60 cm (18–24")
**SOIL** Tolerates a wide range of soil conditions.
**BLOOM** May–September
**USES** ✂ ⋏ ♟ ☙ 🦋 ⚘ Edging, Borders, Massing

### 'Six Hills Giant'                 ZONE 2
Nice long spikes of violet-blue flowers are produced over a bushy mound of grey-green, fragrant leaves. One of the best forms for cutting. Fits well into the middle of the sunny border. Deadhead to encourage continued blooming. May need to be staked if grown in rich soil.

**HT/SP** 60–70 cm (24–28") / 45–60 cm (18–24")
**SOIL** Average to moist, well-drained soil.
**BLOOM** May–August
**USES** ✂ ☙ 🦋 Borders

### *subsessilis*                     ZONE 3
(Japanese Catmint)
A relative newcomer to the scene, this is a mounding species with glossy green foliage and nice-sized heads of tubular violet-blue flowers. Has proven to be reliable on the Prairies. Stems are a nice height for cutting. Deadhead to promote more buds to form.

**HT/SP** 45–60 cm (18–24") / 45–60 cm (18–24")
**SOIL** Prefers a rich moist, well-drained soil.
**BLOOM** June–August
**USES** ✂ ☙ 🦋 Borders

### *yunnanensis*                     ZONE 4
(Chinese Catmint)
Newly introduced from China, this is a mid-sized species with grey-green foliage and nice spikes that bloom over a long season. Flowers are rich blue, with an overtone of lavender-pink. Deadhead to promote more buds to form. Destined to become popular. Will likely prove hardy in Zone 3.

**HT/SP** 60–90 cm (2–3') / 45–60 cm (18–24")
**SOIL** Prefers a rich moist, well-drained soil.
**BLOOM** June–September
**USES** ✂ ☙ 🦋 Borders

# NIPPONANTHEMUM ☼ ◑
(Montauk Daisy, Nippon Daisy)

### *nipponicum*                      ZONE 5
[*Chrysanthemum nipponicum*]
A nearly shrubby type of daisy, with thick leathery green leaves. Plants grow fairly tall and can be used to good specimen effect. Yellow-eyed white daisy flowers appear in late fall, remarkably fresh-looking and a bit surprising for so late in the season. Prune plants back to 10 cm (4") in spring, then pinch in midsummer if you want a bushier mound. Tolerant of ocean-side conditions. Evergreen in very mild winter regions.

**HT/SP** 60–90 cm (2–3') / 60–75 cm (24–30")
**SOIL** Average to moist, well-drained soil.
**BLOOM** October–November
**USES** ✂ ☙ 🦋 Specimen, Borders

*Myosotis sylvatica* 'Victoria Blue'

*Nepeta racemosa* 'Walker's Low'

*Myrrhis odorata*

*Nepeta subsessilis*

## OENANTHE ☼ ☼
(Oenanthe)

### *javanica* 'Flamingo'  ZONE 4
(Flamingo Creeper)

This arrived from Korea not too long ago and is grown as a spreading foliage plant. Related to parsley, the lacy blue-green leaves are dappled with cream and lavender pink. Umbels of white flowers are held above, although not particularly showy. This forms a fast-spreading mat that roots wherever it touches the ground but can be fairly easily controlled by tearing off the runners. Interesting in a hanging basket or window box. I don't recommend re-leasing this to run all through your borders – frankly, it scares me a little.

**HT/SP**  10–15 cm (4–6") / 45–75 cm (18–30")
**SOIL**  Prefers a rich, moist soil.
**BLOOM** July–August
**USES**  ⋀⋁♥ Containers, Fast-spreading groundcover

## OENOTHERA ☼
(Evening Primrose, Sundrops)

Sun-loving plants, very tolerant of hot sites and lean dry soils. Flowers are poppy-shaped, with a soft satiny texture. Sundrops are daytime blooming, while Evening Primroses open late in the day and close before the next morning. All types are originally native North American wildflowers.

### 'Cold Crick'  ZONE 4

A brand new hybrid that is going to be enormously popular. Plants form a non-spreading mound of green leaves, absolutely loaded with bright chrome-yellow flowers in early summer. Being sterile, this won't even spread around by self-sown seedlings. My guess is that deadheading will encourage a repeat

*Oenothera fruticosa*

*Oenothera versicolor* 'Sunset Boulevard'

*Oenothera macrocarpa*

round of blooms. This is probably the best form for edging and general border use.

**HT/SP**  25–30 cm (10–12") / 30–45 cm (12–18")
**SOIL**  Average, well-drained soil.
**BLOOM** June–July
**USES**  ♥♦ Edging

### *fremontii* 'Lemon Silver'  ZONE 4
[*O. missouriensis* ssp. *fremontii* 'Lemon Silver']

A beautiful Canadian introduction. Huge lemon-yellow crepe-textured flowers that seem to rest right on top a low mat of silvery-blue leaves. Blooms over a very long season. Superb in the sunny rock garden. Drought tolerant.

**HT/SP**  10–15 cm (4–6") / 30–45 cm (12–18")
**SOIL**  Average to dry, well-drained soil.
**BLOOM** June–August
**USES**  ⋀♥♦ Edging

### *fruticosa*  ZONE 3
[*O. tetragona*]
(Yellow Sundrops)

Flowers begin as red buds, opening into lemon-yellow blossoms over several weeks. Plants eventually spread to form a wide patch. Divide or reduce the clump every other year to maintain control. These are reliable, long-lived garden perennials. Several named varieties exist. Very drought-tolerant.

**HT/SP**  45–60 cm (18–24") / 45–60 cm (18–24")
**SOIL**  Average to dry, well-drained soil.
**BLOOM** June–August
**USES**  ♥♦ Borders, Massing

Summer Solstice ['Sonnenwende'] An excellent German selection. Bronzy-red tinged foliage forms a sturdy upright clump. Large, bright yellow flowers over a long season. A great improvement.

### *macrocarpa*  ZONE 3
[*O. missouriensis*]
(Ozark Sundrops)

Large yellow blossoms with a crepe-like texture. With low, sprawling stems this is best suited to the rock garden or for edging. Very drought-tolerant.

**HT/SP**  15–30 cm (6–12") / 25–30 cm (10–12")
**SOIL**  Average to dry, well-drained soil.
**BLOOM** June–August
**USES**  ⋀♥♦ Edging

### *pallida*  ZONE 4
(White Evening Primrose)

Large white crepe flowers, ageing to shell pink. A short-lived perennial, but will self-seed if happy. Needs excellent drainage. Very drought-tolerant.

**HT/SP**  25–30 cm (10–12") / 25–30 cm (10–12")
**SOIL**  Average to dry, well-drained soil.
**BLOOM** June–August
**USES**  ⋀♥♦ Walls, Slopes

### *speciosa*  ZONE 5
(Showy Evening Primrose)

A vigorous and extremely floriferous species, with upfacing cup-shaped flowers that begin white, then age to rose-pink. Leaves are a low mat of

olive-green. An excellent landscaping plant with a long season of bloom, so long as plants are given plenty of space. Because of its wandering habit, this should probably be restrained or edged regularly. Very drought-tolerant.

**HT/SP**  15–40 cm (6–16") / 60–75 cm (24–30")
**SOIL**  Average to dry, well-drained soil.
**BLOOM** June–September
**USES**  ⋀⋁♥♦ Containers, Massing

### 'Siskiyou' [*O. berlandieri* 'Siskiyou']
Big satiny flowers in a deep-pink shade. Compact but spreading.

**HT**  15–30 cm (6–12")

### 'Woodside White' Large white flowers
with a greenish eye, aging to soft pink.

**HT**  30–40 cm (12–16")

### *versicolor*  ZONE 7
(California Evening Primrose)

Bushy, upright clumps of olive-green leaves bear a long display of blooms that begin soft-yellow and age to deeper tones throughout the day. This California native might be best treated as an annual in cold or wet winter regions. Superb in containers. Needs excellent drainage.

**HT/SP**  35–45 cm (12–18") / 25–40 cm (10–16")
**SOIL**  Very well drained soil.
**BLOOM** July–September
**USES**  ♦♥♦ Containers, Rock garden

'Lemon Sunset' Flowers open soft yellow, ageing to deep orange-red.
'Sunset Boulevard' Soft orange and yellow flowers deepen to scarlet and orange.

## OMPHALODES ☼•
(Navel-seed)

### *cappadocica*  ZONE 6
(Navel-seed, Blue-eyed Mary)

Finally becoming widely available, these delightful spring bloomers remind me of something in between a Forget-me-Not and a Jacob's Ladder. Plants form a low mound of long, narrow leaves with a hairy texture. Loose sprays of bright-blue flowers appear around the same time as many early woodlanders and bulbs are blooming. Does best in a rich soil that remains moist through the season. Some gardeners in Zones 4–5 report good success where snow cover is reliable. Navel-seed is a true perennial that performs best in regions with cool summers. Several selections exist.

**HT/SP**  15–20 cm (6–8") / 20–30 cm (8–12")
**SOIL**  Prefers a rich moist, well-drained soil.
**BLOOM** April–June
**USES**  ⋀⋀♥ Edging, Woodland

'Cherry Ingram' Especially large flowers open deep-blue, ageing to violet.
'Starry Eyes' Star-shaped sky-blue flowers, flushed white on the petal edges. Unique.

## OPHIOPOGON ☼◗
**(Mondo Grass, Lilyturf)**
Several different Mondo Grasses are commonly used in the Southern US as groundcovers. Generally these are not quite as hardy as the closely related *Liriope*. A winter mulch of evergreen boughs is recommended in Zones 5–6. These form evergreen grassy tufts, the small stems of flowers almost hidden among the leaves.

### *planiscapus* 'Nigrescens'     ZONE 6
**(Black Mondo Grass)**
With its nearly jet-black leaves this makes a most unique specimen for edging or mass planting. Short spikes of pale-pink flowers are followed by black berries in the fall. At its best when contrasted with yellow or silver foliage, such as *Lysimachia nummularia* 'Aurea' or *Lamium* 'White Nancy'. This is not a fast grower. Prefers a sheltered, partly shaded location.

HT/SP   10–15 cm (4–6″) / 20–30 cm (8–12″)
SOIL    Average to moist, well-drained soil.
BLOOM July–August
USES    △M◗▲♥ Massing, Edging

## ORIGANUM ☼
**(Oregano)**
In addition to the more herbal, pizza-flavouring varieties, there are several types of Oregano that make showy perennials worthy of a bright sunny spot. Attractive to butterflies.

### *laevigatum* 'Herrenhausen' ZONE 4
**(Ornamental Oregano)**
Fragrant, bushy clumps bear many clusters of mauve-pink flowers through late summer and fall. A recent German hybrid gaining much attention here. This is most effective when allowed to romp or trail through and over other border plants. Good for cutting.

HT/SP   30–60 cm (1–2′) / 30–45 cm (12–18″)
SOIL    Average to dry, well-drained soil.
BLOOM August–October
USES    ✂❮♥♥╀ Borders, Walls

### *vulgare*     ZONE 4
**(Common Oregano, Pot Marjoram)**
The plain green species form is often included in the herb garden, although the flavour is not nearly as strong as Greek Oregano. I prefer to grow some of the coloured-leaved selections instead, using them in sunny parts of the garden as low edging or groundcover plants. These work very well in containers, forming a low mound of rounded leaves with clusters of soft-pink flowers in early summer. After blooming, get the hedge shears and trim these back to about 5 cm (2″) tall. This forces nice low growth and renews the colour for the rest of the season. Clumps are easily divided in spring. Tolerant of hot, dry sites. All forms below are edible

(although very mild in flavour) and it's fun to sometimes include snippings in salads just for the colour.

HT/SP   15–30 cm (6–12″) / 45–60 cm (18–24″)
SOIL    Average to dry, well-drained soil.
BLOOM June–July
USES    △M◗▲♥♥╀ Borders, Edging, Walls

**'Aureum' (Golden Oregano)** Excellent bright-yellow foliage forms a low, spreading mat. A terrific edging plant in the border. Seems to colour up well in either sun or shade. For sure this selection should be trimmed back hard after blooming or it looks scruffy later on.
**'Gold Tip'** Chartreuse-green foliage, the leaves on the stem tips are bright golden-yellow and really stand out. Cut back mid-season to rejuvenate the effect.
**'White Anniversary' ['Country Cream']** More compact in habit, the leaves are bright green, strongly dappled with creamy white. Likely not as hardy, but Zone 6 at least.

## OXALIS ☼◗
**(Wood Sorrel)**

### *crassipes* 'Alba'     ZONE 6
**(White Wood Sorrel)**
A delightful Japanese selection with a non-weedy habit. Plants form a low mound of bright-green clover-like leaves. Bears a display of small white star-shaped flowers for literally months on end, especially in cool summer regions. Tolerates a wide range of conditions, including summer drought. Excellent in containers, rock gardens, or as an edging. Gardeners in colder regions can easily winter this indoors. Prune back hard in midsummer if the mound becomes untidy. Flowers are sterile.

HT/SP   15–20 cm (6–8″) / 25–30 cm (10–12″)
SOIL    Tolerates a wide range of soil conditions.
BLOOM May–October
USES    △M◗♥╀ Edging

## PACHYSANDRA ◗●
**(Spurge, Pachysandra)**

### *terminalis*     ZONE 3
**(Japanese Spurge)**
An extremely well-known evergreen groundcover plant, the dark-green and glossy foliage forms a dense, spreading patch. Clusters of white flowers appear briefly in the spring. Very tolerant of poor, dry soils and deep shade. Despite its popularity this is notoriously slow to become established. Requires very close spacing, 15–20 cm (6–8″), to achieve a solid fill in about three years. No pruning is usually required, but any disfigured leaves may be trimmed in early spring. Some gardeners mow their Japanese Spurge every few years, which might help to encourage an especially dense habit or rejuvenate an old patch. Several outstanding selections exist –

any of these are more interesting to look at than the plain old green species, in my opinion.

HT/SP   15–20 cm (6–8″) / 15–30 cm (6–12″)
SOIL    Tolerates a wide range of soil conditions.
BLOOM April–May
USES    M◗▲♥╀ Massing, Difficult shady areas

**'Green Sheen'** Leaves are a little smaller than the species, but amazingly glossy as if coated in lacquer. Said to have good heat tolerance.
**'Variegata'** Foliage is medium-green with a creamy-white edging. An extremely slow spreading form.

## PAEONIA ☼
**(Peony)**
Peonies are old favourites for the late spring border, prized for their large satiny flowers and so terrific for cutting. The handsome foliage remains attractive all season, particularly when hoops or rings are used to hold clumps together. Breeding has created thousands of named cultivars, many of which are available only through specialist growers. A number of excellent varieties are listed below, giving a sense of the range of colours and styles.

Herbaceous peonies prefer a deep, rich well-drained loamy soil and full sun exposure. New plants take several years to become established, and resent being disturbed at any time. Many years can go by before Peonies actually require dividing, as many as ten or fifteen. When necessary, divide plants in the early fall only; be sure that each division has several growth points or eyes, and that they are planted no deeper than they were originally growing. Established plants should be fertilized in the early spring and again immediately after blooming. Peonies

*Omphalodes cappadocica* 'Cherry Ingram'

*Ophiopogon planiscapus* 'Nigrescens'

*Origanum vulgare* 'White Anniversary'

*Pachysandra terminalis* 'Green Sheen'

can easily be damaged by rain, especially the double-flowered forms, unless adequately staked or grown in special peony hoops.

These are tough plants, but certain diseases sometimes cause trouble. Botrytis is the most common, causing buds to turn to a mess of fuzzy grey spores instead of gorgeous flowers. This fungus may also cause stems to wilt or spots to form on the foliage. Leaf spots of various kinds are not uncommon. Most of these can be fairly easily controlled using a fungicidal spray every two weeks, beginning when the new shoots are about 15 cm (6″) tall. Good sanitation in the fall can go a long way to preventing disease the next season. Remove dead stems right to the ground and clean up any fallen leaves on the ground. Throw these out, rather than add them to the compost pile.

Gardeners sometimes panic about ants crawling over the buds of peonies. Ants feed on the sticky sap but don't do any actual damage to the plants. Some peony growers feel that ants are actually beneficial to certain varieties of peonies, and without them the flowers might not open in their normal manner.

## Complex Hybrids        ZONE 3
### (Hybrid Garden Peony)
This is a group of complex hybrids, involving a number of species and cultivars. Modern breeders are on a constant quest to broaden the colour range and style of flowers. Because these have not been widely tested in cold climates the hardiness range is approximate and may vary widely from one variety to the next, particularly with any that have tree peony blood in them. Many of these have a compact habit and

should not require staking. Culture is the same as for the regular Garden Peony selections with one exception: any that appear to form a woody base should be pruned carefully, leaving the woody parts alone rather than pruning right back to the ground in autumn. If in doubt, wait until spring.

**HT/SP**  60–90 cm (2–3′) / 75–90 cm (30–36″)
**SOIL**  Rich, well-drained loamy soil.
**BLOOM** May–June, divided into Early, Midseason and Late.
**USES**  ✂ Borders, Massing

**'Buckeye Belle'** Semi-double; deep mahogany-red petals surrounding yellow stamens; Midseason.
**HT**    70–75 cm (28–30″)

**'Claire de Lune'** Single; creamy-yellow to ivory petals, yellow stamens; Very Early.
**HT**    85–90 cm (33–36″)

**'Dancing Butterflies'** Japanese; bright lipstick-pink petals, small yellow centre; Midseason.
**HT**    75–80 cm (30–32″)

**'Flame'** Japanese; fiery scarlet-red petals, yellow stamens. Compact; Midseason.
**HT**    55–60 cm (22–24″)

**'Nymphe'** Semi-double; delicate small flowers, lavender-pink petals, yellow centre. Compact; Midseason.
**HT**    60–65 cm (24–26″)

**'Paula Fay'** Semi-double; hot-pink petals, yellow centre. Early/Midseason.
**HT**    80–85 cm (30–33″)

## *lactiflora* Hybrids        ZONE 2
### (Garden Peony)
The very large number of named cultivars have been categorized into Single, Japanese, Semi-double, and Double forms, each category basically having more petals than the one previous. Flowers vary tremendously in size, bloom time, and fragrance, with the basic range of shades including pink, magenta, red, white and cream. As some nurseries sell by colour only, it is wise to buy plants in flower whenever possible, or else look for named varieties.

**HT/SP**  75–100 cm (30–40″) / 80–90 cm (30–36″)
**SOIL**  Rich, well-drained loamy soil.
**BLOOM** May–June, divided into Early, Midseason and Late.
**USES**  ✂ Borders, Massing

**'Bowl of Beauty'** Japanese; bright rose-pink with creamy-yellow stamens; Midseason. Compact.
**HT**    60–65 cm (24–26″)

**'Catherine Fontijn'** Double; soft pink with white blush; Early.
**HT**    80–85 cm (30–33″)

**'Charles' White'** Double; white outer petals, full middle of creamy-yellow stamens; Early.
**HT**    85–90 cm (33–36″)

**'Dia Jo Kuhan'** Japanese; dainty small flowers, magenta petals edged in pink, yellow stamens; Early.
**HT**    75–90 cm (30–36″)

**'Festiva Maxima'** Double; white petals are flecked with red, exceptionally fragrant; Early/Midseason.
**HT**    85–90 cm (33–36″)

**'Inspecteur Lavergne'** Double; deep-red petals, subtle white pencil edge; Early/Midseason.
**HT**    75–80 cm (30–32″)

**'Jan van Leeuwen'** Japanese; satiny white petals, contrasting yellow stamens, compact habit; Midseason.
**HT**    55–60 cm (22–24″)

**'Karl Rosenfield'** Double; bright magenta-red with a tiny yellow centre; Early/Midseason.
**HT**    90–95 cm (3–3′)

**'Mr G.F. Hemerik'** Japanese; deep rose-pink petals, yellow stamens. Compact; Midseason.
**HT**    60–65 cm (24–26″)

**'Okinawa'** Japanese; rich carmine red, yellow stamens; Midseason.
**HT**    75–90 cm (30–36″)

**'Pink Hawaiian Coral'** Double; salmon to coral-pink petals; Early.
**HT**    80–90 cm (30–36″)

**'Primevère'** Double; incredible creamy-white outer petals, sulphur-yellow centre; Early.
**HT**    85–90 cm (33–36″)

**'Prince of Darkness'** Double; amazing dark midnight-red; Midseason.
**HT**    80–90 cm (30–36″)

**'Romance'** Japanese; rose-pink petals, yellow stamens; Midseason.
**HT**    75–90 cm (30–36″)

**'Sarah Bernhardt'** Double; soft apple-blossom-pink, exceptional fragrance; Late.
**HT**    85–90 cm (33–36″)

**'Shirley Temple'** Double; white petals are dappled and blushed with soft pink; Midseason/Late.
**HT**    80–85 cm (30–33″)

**'Sorbet'** Double; alternating layers of soft-pink and ivory petals; Midseason.
**HT**    70–75 cm (28–30″)

**'Sword Dance'** Single; bright lipstick-red petals, yellow petaloids. Compact; Late.
**HT**    60–65 cm (24–26″)

Paeonia 'Paula Fay'

Paeonia l. 'Bowl of Beauty'

Paeonia 'Claire de Lune'

Paeonia lactiflora 'Jan van Leeuwen'

Paeonia l. 'Dia Jo Kuhan'

### *mlokosewitschii*    ZONE 4
### (Molly-the-Witch Peony)

Molly-the-Witch is a tongue and cheek reference to the unwieldy botanical name of this rare species. It forms a medium-sized mound of blue-green leaves, often veined or edged in purple. The single flowers are rounded in form, in an amazing clear yellow with darker stamens. This seems to need better-than-average drainage, particularly so in regions with wet winters. Will tolerate light shade. Propagation by seed is possible – germination may take two full years, and then another 3–5 years for plants to reach flowering size. Possibly hardy to Zone 2.

HT/SP   60–70 cm (24–28″) / 60–70 cm (24–28″)
SOIL     Average to dry, well-drained soil.
BLOOM May–June
USES    Borders, Rock gardens

### *officinalis*    ZONE 2
### (Common Peony)

The "common" part of the name is a bit deceptive, as these are no longer common at all. This was the peony native to countries surrounding the Mediterranean before plant hunters brought back new forms from China and Japan. They can occasionally be found in old gardens, but by and large are unknown here and deserve to be "rediscovered" in North America. Plants look similar to regular garden peonies, but only one flower is produced per stem, blooming a couple of weeks ahead of the main peony season.

HT/SP   70–75 cm (28–30″) / 70–80 cm (28–32″)
SOIL     Rich, well-drained loamy soil.
BLOOM May–June
USES    Borders

**'Alba Plena'** Double white flowers, compact habit. Early.

HT     60–70 cm (24–28″)

**'Anemoniflora Rosea'** Very compact plants. Single rose-pink petals surround an orange-yellow centre. Fragrant. Early.

HT     30–45 cm (12–18″)

**'Rosea Plena'** Fragrant double rose-pink blooms. Early.

HT     70–75 cm (28–30″)

**'Rubra Plena'** (Memorial Day Peony) Large, long-lasting double red flowers. Fragrant. Early.

HT     70–75 cm (28–30″)

**subsp.** *villosa* [*P. mollis*] A very early-blooming form, with big magenta-pink single flowers. Fragrant.

HT     45–60 cm (18–24″)

### *peregrina* 'Sunshine'    ZONE 4
### (Balkan Peony)

A rare single-flowered selection, featuring unusual salmon-coral petals with overtones of vermilion red, surround-

ing a yellow centre. A true collector's plant, best suited to the sunny border. Foliage is much like a regular garden peony. Early-blooming.

HT/SP   70–75 cm (28–30″) / 70–80 cm (28–32″)
SOIL     Rich, well-drained loamy soil.
BLOOM May–June
USES    Borders

### *suffruticosa* Hybrids    ZONE 4
### (Tree Peony)

Spectacular plants for the part-shade garden, differing considerably in habit and culture from the regular garden peonies. In my Zone 6 garden these are always the first Peonies to bloom, usually in early May. Tree Peonies develop a woody base, although truly they are small to medium-sized shrubs once maturity is reached – which can be easily ten years or more. These are not fast growers but fortunately they are not shy to flower while still young. The number of named selections commonly available is not nearly as large as with Garden Peonies. However, the range of colours includes shades of true yellow, salmon and deep purple that are just not seen in other types. If at all possible, buy Tree Peonies in bloom, because they are so often incorrectly labelled by offshore nurseries that you can never really be certain of the variety.

Most often, Tree Peonies have been grafted onto the roots of garden peonies. When planting, this graft union needs to eventually be about 15 cm (6″) below the soil surface. Plant container-grown specimens deep in their hole, adding 3 cm (1″) of soil every couple of months through the first season until the hole is filled in. The idea is to get the plant developing roots from above the graft union so, in case the main stem ever breaks off, the plant can develop new growth from underground that remains true to colour.

A site with all-day dappled shade or morning sun is best. Tree Peonies can scorch in hot afternoon sun. They prefer a nice, rich loamy soil with good drainage. Gardeners in Zones 4–5 are advised to mulch well around the base of the plants in late fall. Some gardeners prefer to wrap their plants with burlap. Pruning should seldom be required; broken branches may be removed at any time, but otherwise very little shaping or cutting-back is needed. Whatever you do, ensure that nobody accidentally prunes your Tree Peony back to ground level!

HT/SP   90–150 cm (3–5′) / 90–100 cm (36–40″)
SOIL     Rich, well-drained loamy soil.
BLOOM May
USES    Borders, Woodland

### *tenuifolia*    ZONE 2
### (Fernleaf Peony)

Always rare and much in demand, these are not quick to increase on a commercial scale. The finely-cut leaves make this quite unlike any other Peony. Delicate, crimson-red single flowers seem to rest on the leaves, appearing well before the main flush of Garden Peonies begins. Even more rare and expensive is the double red-flowered 'Plena', a collector's gem!

HT/SP   30–45 cm (12–18″) / 45–60 cm (18–24″)
SOIL     Rich, well-drained loamy soil.
BLOOM May–June
USES    Borders, Edging

## PAPAVER ☼
### (Poppy)

Satiny poppy flowers are a traditional favourite. They are useful for cutting if picked in bud, the cut ends then seared over a flame. Good drainage is crucial, particularly where winters are wet. Most species are short-lived perennials that happily self-seed in any sunny border, the exception to this is the longer-lived Oriental Poppy. All species prefer lighter soils and a warm, sunny location.

### *alpinum* Hybrids    ZONE 3
### (Alpine Poppy)

Short and graceful little poppies, in shades of yellow, orange, pink, and white, the petals sometimes intricately fringed. The ferny leaves form a low tuft. These are not long-lived but should self-seed into rock garden cracks and crevices. Best in regions with cool summers. Moderately drought-tolerant.

HT/SP   15–25 cm (6–10″) / 15–20 cm (6–8″)
SOIL     Average to dry, well-drained soil.
BLOOM May–August
USES    Screes, Troughs, Walls

*Paeonia officinalis* 'Anemoniflora Rosea'

*Paeonia officinalis* 'Rosea Plena'

*Paeonia tenuifolia* 'Plena'

*Paeonia* 'Festiva Maxima'

### *atlanticum*  ZONE 4
### (Atlas Poppy)

Low silvery-green tufts of hairy leaves are a pretty contrast to the soft sherbet-orange flowers. Short lived, but freely self-seeding. Nice scattered in a sunny border or rock garden. The occasional double-flowered plant will show up un-expectedly from the seedlings.

**HT/SP** 25–30 cm (10–12″) / 20–30 cm (8–12″)
**SOIL** Average to dry, well-drained soil.
**BLOOM** May–August
**USES** 🔺❄✂🌱 Borders, Rock garden

### *miyabeanum* 'Pacino'  ZONE 3
### (Sulphur Poppy)

A charming little alpine type. Plants make a low rosette of olive-green leaves, bearing short stems of cool sulphur-yellow flowers for many weeks. Even if you're a yellow hater this plant is hard to resist. Short-lived but will self seed like the Alpine Poppy. Moderately drought-tolerant.

**HT/SP** 15–20 cm (6–8″) / 20–30 cm (8–12″)
**SOIL** Average to dry, well-drained soil.
**BLOOM** May–July
**USES** 🔺❄🌱 Troughs

### *nudicaule*  ZONE 2
### (Iceland Poppy)

Tufts of light-green leaves, with cheerful flowers in shades of yellow, orange, red, pink, or white, sometimes strikingly bicoloured. Long blooming season. Usually biennial but freely self-seeding. Many strains exist, each with a slightly different range of colours. Good for cutting if picked in bud. Moderately drought-tolerant.

**HT/SP** 30–45 cm (12–18″) / 20–30 cm (8–12″)
**SOIL** Average to dry, well-drained soil.
**BLOOM** May–October
**USES** 🔺❄✂🌱 Borders

**'Champagne Bubbles'** A large-flowered hybrid strain, wide colour range.

*Papaver n. 'Champagne Bubbles'*

*Papaver nudicaule 'Flamenco'*

*Papaver orientale 'Flamingo'*

*Papaver o. 'Little Dancing Girl'*

*Papaver orientale 'Allegro'*

*Papaver o. 'Patty's Plum'*

**'Flamenco'** A European Fleuroselect winner, this strain produces a range of lovely pastel shades, the petal edges frosted or picoteed with contrasting tones.

### *orientale*  ZONE 2
### (Oriental Poppy)

Large clumps of coarse, hairy foliage, producing enormous satiny flowers in late spring. There are several good seed strains available in various shades, typically with a dark zone or eye in the middle. Many named hybrids also exist; these are propagated from root-cuttings and include both single and double-flowered forms in shades of orange, true pink, white, and deep red, sometimes bicoloured or with exotically fringed petals.

These are gorgeous in the border, but because the leaves usually go completely dormant after flowering plan to plant something nearby that gets bushy in the summer to fill in the gap — *Echinacea*, *Gypsophila*, *Perovskia*, and *Rudbeckia* all come to mind. Oriental Poppies are best divided about the same time as Bearded Iris, in July or August when the foliage is more or less dormant. Pieces of root about the size of a pencil will usually grow and produce flowering-sized plants within a year or two. Do not trim off the foliage in the fall. Any winter-damaged leaves may be pruned off in spring, but leave the healthy-looking ones alone.

**HT/SP** 75–100 cm (30–40″) / 45–60 cm (18–24″)
**SOIL** Well-drained soil, preferably sandy loam.
**BLOOM** May–June
**USES** ✂ Borders

**'Allegro'** Scarlet-orange blooms, compact. Seed strain.
**HT** 45–60 cm (18–24″)

**'Beauty of Livermere'** Deep ox-blood red. A tall seed strain.
**HT** 90–100 cm (36–40″)

**'Blackberry Queen'** Single petals in a gorgeous lavender-plum tone. Compact.
**HT** 50–60 cm (20–24″)

**'Brilliant'** Vivid, fiery scarlet-red with a black eye. Seed strain.
**HT** 80–100 cm (30–40″)

**'Carneum'** Shades of salmon to flesh pink with a dark eye. Seed strain.
**HT** 75–90 cm (30–36″)

**'Cedar Hill'** Dainty, small soft-pink blooms. Compact.
**HT** 55–60 cm (22–24″)

**'Double Tangerine Gem'** Double and semi-double petals in soft orange tones. Seed strain.
**HT** 75–90 cm (30–36″)

**'Flamingo'** Fringed white petals are edged in glowing orange, black centre.
**HT** 75–100 cm (30–40″)

**'Garden Glory'** Semi-double scarlet orange petals, fringed and ruffled edges.
**HT** 70–75 cm (28–30″)

**'Little Dancing Girl'** Soft-pink single flowers with maroon-purple spots. Very compact.
**HT** 45–50 cm (18–20″)

**'Patty's Plum'** I read about this plant for years before finally seeing it, and the deep maroon-plum flowers are every bit as wonderful as I had imagined. Almost too good to be true!
**HT** 70–75 cm (28–30″)

**'Perry's White'** Large white flowers, maroon-black base spots.
**HT** 70–90 cm (30–36″)

**'Picotée'** White petals, the edges ruffled and stained with soft orange.
**HT** 70–75 cm (28–30″)

**'Pink Ruffles'** Rich salmon-pink blooms, heavily ruffled edges.
**HT** 70–75 cm (28–30″)

**'Pinnacle'** Petals are scarlet-orange with a white base and brownish centre.
**HT** 65–75 cm (24–30″)

**'Pizzicato' mixture** A mid-sized strain, producing flowers in shades of white, pink, salmon, orange and scarlet.
**HT** 60–70 cm (24–28″)

**Princess Victoria Louise ['Prinzessin Victoria Louise']** Soft salmon-pink flowers, dark eye. Seed strain.
**HT** 75–90 cm (30–36″)

**'Raspberry Queen'** Glowing raspberry-pink flowers, maroon-black eye. Tall.
**HT** 90–100 cm (36–40″)

**'Royal Wedding'** Big blooms, white petals with a black-purple eyezone. Seed strain.
**HT** 75–80 cm (30–32″)

**'Türkenlouis'** Neatly fringed single petals in a fiery scarlet-orange.
**HT** 75–80 cm (30–32″)

## PELTIPHYLLUM see DARMERA

## PENSTEMON ☼
### (Beard-tongue)

A large and diverse group of plants, mostly wildflowers native to areas of North America with warm arid summers. Their showy, tubular flowers are usually held above the foliage in upright spikes. Taller types make excellent cut-flowers. Penstemon cannot tolerate wet feet, so very good drainage is a basic requirement. This is true for all types, especially so for the lower alpine species. Attractive to butterflies, the darker shades will also bring hummingbirds.

*barbatus* **Hybrids**  ZONE 3

These are among the hardiest Beard-tongues available. Plants typically form a low mound of green foliage, with spikes of trumpet flowers rising above in early summer. Taller selections are quite good for cutting. Divide plants every 2–3 years to keep them vigorous. Moderately drought and heat tolerant.

SP  30–45 cm (12–18")
SOIL  Average to dry, well-drained soil.
BLOOM June–August
USES  ✂🌡➳🦋🏵 Borders, Wildflower gardens

**'Elfin Pink'** Compact spikes of clear pink flowers. A good companion to 'Prairie Dusk', and just as reliable.

HT  30–45 cm (12–18")

**'Prairie Dusk'** Strong stems of vivid purple flowers over a long season. Very effective in combination with *Achillea* 'Moonshine'.

HT  50–60 cm (20–24")

*digitalis* **'Husker Red'**  ZONE 3
**(Smooth Beard-tongue)**

Originally selected at the University of Nebraska. Attractive upright clumps of maroon-red foliage are a wonderful contrast in the spring border, although fading to dark green during the warmer months. Flowers are very pale pink, held on stems well above the leaves. Especially effective when mass planted. Selected as the *Perennial Plant of the Year* for 1996, and now a classic.

HT/SP  75–90 cm (30–36") / 30–45 cm (12–18")
SOIL  Average to moist, well-drained soil.
BLOOM June–August
USES  ✂🌡🦋 Wildflower, Borders, Massing

**'Glacier'**  ZONE 5

A new hybrid strain, a European Fleuroselect winner. Plants form a low clump of green foliage with taller spikes of trumpet flowers in white or very soft blue, produced during the summer. First developed as a commercial cut flower, but also useful in the sunny border.

HT/SP  70–80 cm (28–32") / 45–60 cm (18–24")
SOIL  Average to dry, well-drained soil.
BLOOM June–July
USES  ✂🌡🦋🏵 Borders

# PEROVSKIA ☼
**(Russian Sage)**

*atriplicifolia*  ZONE 4
**(Russian Sage)**

Not really a sage at all, *Perovskia* forms an upright bush of fine-textured grey-green leaves that are pleasantly fragrant when rubbed. The plant becomes a haze of lavender-blue by midsummer when spikes of tiny flowers appear. These continue to bloom for weeks, contrasting beautifully with the various hot-coloured daisies of autumn. Russian Sage is an excellent filler plant for the

border, but can also make an effective display when mass planted on its own, or featured with waving ornamental grasses. Some of the woody stems must be left each year for new shoots to develop; prune plants back to 15 cm (6") in early to mid spring. Attractive to butterflies. Drought-tolerant. Selected as *Perennial Plant of the Year* for 1995.

HT/SP  90–150 cm (3–5') / 60–90 cm (2–3')
SOIL  Average to dry, well-drained soil.
BLOOM July–October
USES  ✂🌡🦋🏵 Borders, Massing

**'Filigran'** A hybrid selection from Germany. The foliage is even more lacy and finely cut, with the usual lavender-blue flowers. Plants have a distinctly narrow, upright habit.

HT  120–150 cm (4–5')

**'Lace'** Selected in Quebec a number of years ago, and distinctly shorter than the species. Makes a bushy, upright clump of silver-grey leaves with a soft texture. Typical lavender-blue flowers.

HT  80–100 cm (30–40")

**'Little Spire'** (Dwarf Russian Sage) This represents what I think of as the first significant breeding breakthrough. Plants look identical to the species but grow half the size. Sure to be a huge hit with gardeners and landscape designers everywhere.

HT/SP  60–75 cm (24–30") / 45–60 cm (18–24")

# PERSICARIA ☼ ◐
**[*Polygonum*]**
**(Fleece-Flower, Knotweed)**

Formerly known as *Polygonum*, these were recently split by botanists into *Persicaria* and *Fallopia*. A good number of these varieties are relatively new to North American gardens but can be depended on to attract attention with their showy late summer and fall display. Most feature spikes of pink or red poker flowers, usually held over top of the foliage.

*affinis* **'Dimity'**  ZONE 3
**['Superba']**
**(Dwarf Fleeceflower)**

Forms a low carpet of tough and leathery green leaves, turning beautiful shades of bronzy-red in fall. Short poker spikes of red flowers fade to pink as they age and appear over a very long season. A nice groundcover or rock garden plant, appreciating part shade. I once saw a knock-out combination with 'Dimity' weaving in and around a spreading turquoise-blue juniper. Extremely drought-tolerant. Flowers can be dried.

HT/SP  15–20 cm (6–8") / 30–60 cm (1–2')
SOIL  Tolerates a wide range of soil conditions.
BLOOM June–August
USES  ⛰◿🌡🏵 Borders, Edging

*amplexicaulis*  ZONE 4
**[*Polygonum amplexicaule*]**
**(Mountain Fleeceflower)**

Quite new to North American gardens, these upright bushy plants are ideal for massed landscape plantings but yet not too invasive for including in the border. They are covered with showy poker flowers from midsummer on. A good choice for difficult wet sites. Spikes are nice for cutting and may also be dried.

HT/SP  90–120 cm (3–4') / 90–120 cm (3–4')
SOIL  Prefers a rich, moist soil.
BLOOM July–October
USES  ✂◿🌡 Massing, Borders, Waterside

**'Firetail'** Long crimson-red spikes, with a full and bushy habit.

**'Taurus'** Rich rosy-red to crimson pokers on a fairly compact bush. This gets to about half the size of 'Firetail', lending itself to a multitude of garden uses.

HT  60–75 cm (24–30")

*bistorta* **'Superba'**  ZONE 3
**[*Polygonum bistorta*]**
**(Pink Bistort)**

Large bright-pink bottlebrush spikes are held well above the dense green foliage, turning to soft pink as they age. Deadhead the spent spikes to promote continual blooming. This forms a large mound, but I wouldn't consider it to be invasive. Especially good for cutting. Nice at the waterside.

HT/SP  60–75 cm (24–30") / 60–70 cm (24–28")
SOIL  Average to moist or even wet soil.
BLOOM June–August
USES  ✂🌡 Borders, Massing

*microcephala* **'Red Dragon'**  ZONE 6

This new selection seemed to appear out of nowhere a couple of years back. I think it's one of the most impressive new foliage plants, particularly effective in mixed containers but also interesting

*Perovskia atriplicifolia*

*Penstemon digitalis* 'Husker Red'

*Penstemon* 'Elfin Pink'

*Penstemon* 'Prairie Dusk'

when weaving through the border. Leaves are long and pointy, dark-green to bronzy in colour with a black-purple centre and a silvery V-shaped marking. Tiny white flowers appear in early summer. Hardiness is not yet fully determined, but Zone 4 or 5 might be possible with good snow cover. Plants may also be wintered indoors in a pot.

**HT/SP** 60–90 cm (2–3') / 45–60 cm (18–24")
**SOIL** Average to moist, well-drained soil.
**BLOOM** June–July
**USES** ✂❦⚘ Borders, Containers

### polymorpha    ZONE 5
### (White Fleeceflower)

Renowned designer Wolfgang Oehme first introduced this to North America, and he recommended it as a well-behaved, non-spreading species with a long season of display. Plants have proven him right time and again, and these are now becoming a standard part of the designer's bag of tricks. This forms a tall, bushy clump with huge fluffy spikes of creamy-white flowers that remain attractive for weeks on end. The green leaves are coarse in texture but I find this to be in scale with the overall size. Hardiness is not yet fully tested but so far this appears to grow fine in parts of Zone 4 with reliable snowcover. Seems to be fairly shade tolerant.

**HT/SP** 90–120 cm (3–4') / 80–90 cm (30–36")
**SOIL** Average to moist well-drained soil.
**BLOOM** July–September
**USES** ✂❮ Borders, Specimen

### vacciniifolia    ZONE 4
### [Polygonum vacciniifolia]
### (Small-leaved Fleeceflower)

This is a relatively unknown rock garden perennial, forming a low, creeping mound of tiny green leaves and looking overall like a dwarf blueberry bush. In early summer the plant is liter-

ally smothered with short spikes of rose-pink flowers, particularly in regions with cool nights. Although spreading, this is a well-behaved species in the garden, suitable for edging as well as in the rockery. Foliage develops bright red and gold tints later in the fall. An excellent ground cover for around shrubs. Tolerates a fair bit of shade.

**HT/SP** 15–20 cm (6–8") / 60–75 cm (24–30")
**SOIL** Average to moist, well-drained soil.
**BLOOM** June–July
**USES** ⏃⌂ᨒ⚘ Massing, Edging

### virginiana 'Painter's Palette'    ZONE 5
### [Persicaria filiformis, Polygonum filiforme, Tovara virginiana]
### (Tovara)

Grown mostly for its colourful foliage, the oval leaves are variegated with cream and green, with an unusual V-shaped chocolate-brown marking. Sometimes massed as a groundcover for moist areas but at its best when shown off as a bushy specimen plant. Although I have read about this plant being a wanderer I've found it to be completely clumping and non-invasive. Airy sprays of pinkish flowers in late summer age to deep red seed-heads that are delightful in the fall garden. Seedlings may appear near the clump – many of these will be true to type, others without the brown chevron or lacking variegation. Some patience is require in the spring since this always comes up very late.

**HT/SP** 60–120 cm (2–4') / 45–75 cm (18–30")
**SOIL** Prefers a rich, moist soil.
**BLOOM** August–October
**USES** ✂ᨒ⚘ Massing, Containers

## PETASITES ☼◐
## (Butterbur)

### japonicus var. giganteus    ZONE 4
### (Giant Japanese Butterbur)

A monster plant for the waterside, bearing enormous rounded leaves, not unlike rhubarb at first glance. Greenish flowers appear on naked stems in very early spring. This is a bold textural plant that looks great beside a pond or stream. Place carefully, as this is an aggressive spreader and difficult to eradicate. I prefer to grow this plant inside of a large plastic tub. The leaf-stems are edible, if you are adventurous!

**HT/SP** 120–180 cm (4–6') / 90–120 cm (3–4')
**SOIL** Moist to wet soil, even in shallow water.
**BLOOM** March–April
**USES** Waterside specimen

## PETRORHAGIA ☼
## (Tunic Flower)

### saxifraga    ZONE 2
### [Tunica saxifraga]

A low-growing rock garden plant, producing a misty cloud of white or pale

pink flowers similar to Baby's Breath. Easy and reliable. Blooms over a long season. Sometimes self-seeds prolifically. Drought tolerant. A good choice for growing in low-maintenance gravel gardens or in stone walls.

**HT/SP** 15–20 cm (6–8") / 15–30 cm (6–12")
**SOIL** Average to dry, well-drained soil.
**BLOOM** May–August
**USES** △▽▲ᨒ Walls, Edging

## PHLOMIS ☼
## (Phlomis)

There are not yet many selections of these available here in North America, but all kinds of them are being grown in Britain and other parts of Europe. Most produce tall clumps with ball-shaped heads of flowers that are spaced in tiers along the upper ends of the stems. All are excellent for cutting.

### fruticosa    ZONE 5
### (Jerusalem Sage)

Gardeners in California and other mild regions have been growing this species for years as an evergreen shrub. Plants appear to be far hardier than most of us ever knew, although usually dying back to the ground in cold winter areas. The leaves are grey-green and felty to the touch, with balls of soft primrose-yellow flowers appearing in early summer. Cut plants back by half after flowering to encourage repeat bloom. In mild regions plants can get fairly large. May winter in Zone 4 with good snowcover.

**HT/SP** 60–120 cm (2–4') / 75–90 cm (30–36")
**SOIL** Average to dry, well-drained soil.
**BLOOM** May–July
**USES** ✂❮▲▽ᨒ Borders

### tuberosa 'Amazone'    ZONE 2
### (Sage-leaved Mullein)

Grown commercially in Europe as a cut flower, this makes a tough and sturdy perennial for the sunny border. Plants form a low mound of coarse grey-green leaves. Bears tall spikes of whorled mauve-pink flowers in the summer. Interesting in the middle of the sunny border, surrounded by lower plants. Drought-tolerant once established. The dead tops have good winter interest. This species grows amazingly well on the Canadian Prairies.

**HT/SP** 90–120 cm (3–4') / 45–60 cm (18–24")
**SOIL** Average to dry, well-drained soil.
**BLOOM** June–August
**USES** ✂❮▽ᨒ Borders

## PHLOX ☼◐
## (Phlox)

Among the most popular of garden perennials, these range in form from low creeping alpines to tall border plants. The flowers of most types have a heavy, sweet perfume, the taller vari-

Persicaria vacciniifolia

Persicaria microcephala 'Red Dragon'

Petrorhagia saxifraga

Persicaria polymorpha

Phlomis fruticosa

eties being especially valued for cutting. All are selections or hybrids of native North American wildflowers.

### *buckleyi*                    ZONE 5
**(Sword-leaved Phlox)**
Native to the Virginias, this species adapts to a wide range of garden conditions and climates. Plants form a bushy clump of long, willowy evergreen leaves. Bears clusters of bright rose-purple flowers beginning in late spring and remaining in bloom for weeks. An excellent choice for edging in sun or part shade, adapting well to both the border or woodland garden. Also a good choice for pots or mixed containers. Clip back by half after blooming, to encourage a low, bushy mound for the rest of the season. Easily divided in spring or early fall.

**HT/SP** 30–40 cm (12–16") / 30–45 cm (12–18")
**SOIL** Average to moist, rich soil.
**BLOOM** May–July
**USES** ✂△Ⓜ▲☂ Edging, Woodland gardens

### *carolina* Hybrids                    ZONE 3
**(Carolina Phlox)**
Similar to the Summer Phlox, these hybrids are less prone to powdery mildew and begin to bloom about a month earlier, forming bushy, upright clumps. Cut spent heads back to a main stem and these will nearly always give a good round of repeat bloom in late summer and fall. The colour range is white through pink and magenta.

**HT/SP** 75–90 cm (30–36") / 60–75 cm (24–30")
**SOIL** Average to moist well-drained soil.
**BLOOM** June–July
**USES** ✂☙➤ Borders, Meadow gardens

**'Miss Lingard'** Large heads of pure white flowers. Early-blooming and extremely fragrant, also a reliable repeat bloomer. This is one is high on my list of personal favourites.

### *divaricata*                    ZONE 3
**(Woodland Phlox)**
These medium-sized clumps are ideal for edging along a shady border. Loose clusters of flowers appear in spring. Nice groundcover under shrubs or trees, preferring partial shade. Shear plants lightly after blooming. There are a few named colour selections, ranging from white through pink to blue and purple.

**HT/SP** 15–20 cm (6–8") / 30–45 cm (12–18")
**SOIL** Rich, moist woodland soil.
**BLOOM** April–June
**USES** △✂Ⓜ☂ Woodland gardens

**'Louisiana Purple'** Rich violet-purple-blue flowers with a darker eye. Early.

### *douglasii*                    ZONE 2
**(Moss Phlox, Douglas' Phlox)**
Low, evergreen rockery types, these look very similar to *P. subulata* but with an even tighter habit. The dense

mound or carpet of needle-like leaves becomes smothered by tiny flowers in spring. A good choice for rock gardens or edging. More resistant to downy mildew and other disease problems that so often bother the *P. subulata* varieties. Best in full sun. Drought-tolerant.

**HT/SP** 5–10 cm (2–4") / 25–30 cm (10–12")
**SOIL** Average to dry, well-drained soil.
**BLOOM** April–May
**USES** △Ⓜ▲☂✶ Edging, Scree

**'Crackerjack'** Bright, starry flowers in a startling magenta-red shade. A reliable performer.
**'Rose Cushion'** Delicate soft baby-pink flowers. A slow-growing smaller selection best suited to the scree or rock garden.

### *kelseyi* 'Rosette'                    ZONE 2
**(Moss Phlox, Kelsey's Phlox)**
In habit this selection looks much like the *P. douglasii* selections, but with more of a mounding or tight bun shape. Starry rose-pink flowers appear at the same time as the other Mossy types. A true alpine, best in a scree or trough. Drought tolerant.

**HT/SP** 5–10 cm (2–4") / 25–30 cm (10–12")
**SOIL** Average to dry, well-drained soil.
**BLOOM** April–May
**USES** △Ⓜ▲☂✶ Trough, Rock garden

### *maculata* Hybrids                    ZONE 3
**(Meadow Phlox)**
This hybrid group is often recommended as a substitute for Summer Phlox in areas where powdery mildew is a problem. Plants have a similar upright habit, but the foliage is darker green and the cone-shaped flower heads appear a little bit earlier. Flowers are fragrant, excellent for cutting. Although mildew-resistance is excellent, the choice of colours is more limited.

**HT/SP** 60–90 cm (2–3') / 45–60 cm (18–24")
**SOIL** Average to moist well-drained soil.
**BLOOM** June–August
**USES** ✂☙➤⛊ Borders, Meadow gardens

**'Natascha'** A beautiful pink and white bicolour, the petals have a candystriped effect. Compact.

**HT** 50–60 cm (20–24")

### *paniculata*                    ZONE 3
**(Summer Phlox, Garden Phlox)**
The fragrant and luxurious heads of Summer Phlox can be spectacular in the summer border. There are many named selections, offering a wide choice of colours to match most any design scheme. Shades range from pink through salmon to orange, red, blue, mauve-purple and white. Some varieties have a contrasting eye in the centre of each flower. They make superb cut flowers. Attractive to butterflies, the deeper shades may also draw in hummingbirds.

Shorter plants should be placed in front of Summer Phlox, to hide the withering lower leaves at blooming time. Powdery mildew is often a problem, see the section on *Pests & Diseases* for some ideas on how to control it. Simply growing Summer Phlox on a moist site or keeping it well watered will help to prevent mildew. Varieties with especially good resistance to mildew infection are noted below. Fertilize Phlox in early spring and again just before flowering as they are heavy feeders. Plants should be divided about every three years in the spring. As with the Carolina Phlox, removing the faded flower heads back to a main stem will encourage side shoots to develop for a round of repeat bloom.

**HT/SP** 60–120 cm (2–4') / 60–75 cm (24–30")
**SOIL** Prefers a rich, moist well-drained soil.
**BLOOM** July–September
**USES** ✂☙➤ Cut flowers, Borders

**'Becky Towe'** A brand new variegated selection, featuring rose-pink flowers with a magenta eye. Foliage makes a mid-sized mound of green leaves with golden-yellow splashes in spring. Softens to a green and butter-yellow effect during summer.

**HT** 50-70 cm (18")

**'Blue Boy'** Big heads of mauve-blue flowers, very tall habit.

**HT** 90–100 cm (36–40")

**'David'** A superb, tall white-flowered selection with nice big fragrant heads. Exceptionally good mildew resistance. Selected as the *Perennial Plant of the Year* for 2002.

**HT** 90–100 cm (36–40")

*Persicaria virginiana* 'Painter's Palette'

*Phlox douglasii* 'Crackerjack'

*Phlomis tuberosa* 'Amazone'

**'Delta Snow'** A rather new selection, the white flowers have a contrasting purple eye. Mid-sized habit. Excellent mildew resistance.

HT    60–75 cm (24–30")

**'Eva Cullum'** Large heads, clear pink flowers with a dark red eye. Compact habit. Somewhat mildew resistant.

HT    60–75 cm (24–30")

**'Franz Schubert'** Soft lilac-blue flowers with a darker eye. Good mildew resistance.

HT    80–90 cm (30–36")

**'Harlequin'** As variegated plants go, this one is a real shocker. Green and creamy-yellow splashed leaves are topped by screaming magenta-purple flowers. Not subtle in the least, which is probably why I love it. Not especially vigorous.

HT    75–80 cm (30–32")

**'Juliet'** Pale-pink flowers, compact habit.

HT    50–60 cm (20–24")

**'Norah Leigh'** Probably the easiest of the variegated types to grow, with excellent vigour and mildew resistance. The foliage is dark green in the middle with broad creamy-white margins. Flowers are white, each with a bright rose-pink eye and combine rather well with the leaves. A little difficult to place in the border, but interesting all season long.

HT    70–75 cm (28–30")

**'Orange Perfection'** Brilliant heads of salmon orange. This is a rare colour that cries out to be used in a clever way.

HT    80–90 cm (30–36")

**'Shortwood'** Bright pink flowers with a darker rose eye. Very tall in habit so it combines well with other tall types like 'David'. Somewhat mildew resistant.

HT    90–110 cm (36–42")

**'Starfire'** Cherry-red flowers contrast well with the bronzy-green foliage. Still one of the best reds, but unfortunately rather mildew prone.

HT    80–90 cm (30–36")

**× *procumbens* 'Variegata'**    ZONE 3
**(Variegated Creeping Phlox)**
Grown as much for the charming foliage effect as for the flowers. Forms a low mound of green leaves, strongly splashed with creamy white. Mauve-pink flowers are held in upright clusters. A little gem for the woodland or rock garden, preferring part shade.

HT/SP   10–15 cm (4–6") / 20–30 cm (8–12")
SOIL    Average to moist, well-drained soil.
BLOOM April–June
USES    ◮▲❦ Edging, Woodland garden

***pulchra***    ZONE 4
**(Mountain Phlox, Alabama Phlox)**
An Appalachian native, and well adapted to regions with hot, humid summers. This species flowers in late spring, forming a low bushy mound that is the perfect size for the border front. Loose clusters of soft violet-blue flowers are pleasingly fragrant. Benefits from a hard clip back after blooming. Tolerates full sun to part shade, with good moisture. I accidentally planted this beside an olive-green coloured Tall Bearded Iris, and the combination was amazing!

HT/SP   30–40 cm (12–16") / 45–60 cm (18–24")
SOIL    Average to moist, well-drained soil.
BLOOM May–June
USES    ✄◮❦ Edging, Woodland gardens

**'Morris Berd'** [***P. glaberrima* 'Morris Berd'**] Fragrant clusters of rose-pink flowers. Outstanding. Excellent heat tolerance.

HT    30–60 cm (1–2')

***stolonifera***    ZONE 2
**(Creeping Woodland Phlox)**
Very different from the other spring-blooming varieties, these form a dense evergreen groundcover, tolerant of heavy shade. Small but showy clusters of flowers appear in late spring. Excellent under shrubs or in any shady area that doesn't go overly dry in summer. Keep out of full sun. Selections range in colour from blue to purple, pink or white. Selected as *Perennial Plant of the Year* for 1990.

HT/SP   15–20 cm (6–8") / 30–45 cm (12–18")
SOIL    Prefers a rich moist, well-drained soil.
BLOOM April–May
USES    ◮М▲❦ Edging, Woodland gardens

**'Blue Ridge'** Soft lilac-blue flowers.
**'Sherwood Purple'** Deep and vibrant purple-blue. Smashing when combined with yellow Leopard's-bane (*Doronicum*).

***subulata***    ZONE 2
**(Moss Phlox, Creeping Phlox)**
By far the most popular of spring-blooming alpines, these form low mats of needle-like evergreen leaves, smothered by tiny round flowers. Although often used for edging beds and borders, I don't recommended Moss Phlox as a groundcover for large areas because the plants thin out too quickly and allow weeds to invade. Divide clumps every 2–3 years to maintain vigour. Shear plants lightly after blooming to keep the habit thick. Various fungal infections can cause trouble in regions with wet winters; choose a sunny well-drained site to help avoid these. Drought-tolerant once established, these will even grow in gravel. Several colour selections are commonly available.

HT/SP   5–15 cm (2–6") / 30–45 cm (12–18")
SOIL    Average to dry, well-drained soil.
BLOOM April–May
USES    ◮М▲❦ Edging, Rock garden

**'Apple Blossom'** Lovely soft-pink blossoms, a nice change from the usual screaming pink.
**'Atropurpurea'** Bright rosy-red flowers.
**'Bonita'** ['Benita'] Soft mauve-blue with a darker eye.
**'Candy Stripe'** ['Tamaongalei'] A newer variety, the flowers are striped in rose-pink and white, with a crimson eye.
**'Coral Eye'** Soft baby-pink flowers with a coral-pink eye.
**'Crimson Beauty'** Bright rosy-red blooms, close to true red.
**'Ellie B.'** Tiny snow-white flowers, distinctly star-shaped. Very compact habit. Possibly the same as another selection, 'Tiny White'.
**'Emerald Cushion Blue'** Soft lavender-blue flowers. Lustrous dark-green foliage and a vigorous, disease-resistant habit. The best for groundcover purposes.
**'Emerald Pink'** ['Emerald Cushion'] Still the most popular and widely-grown variety, smothered with screaming pink flowers.
**'Fort Hill'** Notched, star-shaped flowers with deep rosy-pink petals.
**'Laura'** ['Millstream Laura'] Pale pink with a dark rose eye.
**'Nettleton Variation'** Leaves are striped with green and creamy-white, bright-pink flowers. A very slow-growing selection, best suited to the rock garden.
**'Oakington Blue Eyes'** Soft lavender-blue flowers.
**'White Delight'** An older white selection, larger in habit than 'Ellie B.' Snow-white flowers.

*Phlox paniculata* 'Becky Towe'
*Phlox paniculata* 'David'
*Phlox pulchra* 'Morris Berd'
*Phlox s.* 'Emerald Cushion Blue'
*Phlox paniculata* 'Shortwood'
*Phlox subulata* 'Bonita'

# PHORMIUM ☼
### (New Zealand Flax)

***tenax***                                ZONE 8

The *Phormium* craze is now upon us — you can't open a garden magazine anymore without reading about them or seeing pictures. These are first-class foliage plants for use as specimens or focal points in containers or dramatic border plantings. Their evergreen leaves are long and strap-shaped, a bit like a yucca in appearance, although not quite as stiff. Native to New Zealand, there are probably over a hundred selected forms offering a wide range of leaf colours, many with boldly contrasting stripes or margins. Where hardy, these can produce extremely tall branching stems that bear reddish flowers in late summer or fall.

Most of us must treat New Zealand Flax as a tender perennial. Grow it in a container and bring indoors before hard frost, placing in a bright window for the winter. Clumps may be divided after a couple of years, something best done in spring. Be sure to cut the leaf fans back to about 15 cm (6") when dividing. Otherwise, the only pruning required is to remove damaged or dead leaves and finished flower stems right at the base of the clump. Gardeners in California have good access to many of the newer forms, but availability promises to get much better now that plants are being cloned by tissue culture.

HT/SP   75–120 cm (30–48") / 75–120 cm (30–48")
SOIL   Average to moist, well-drained soil.
USES   ♥▲ Specimen

**Purpureum Group** Foliage is a rich bronzy-purple shade, although variable in colour since this strain is usually grown from seed.

# PHYGELIUS ☼ ◑
### (Cape Fuchsia)

Exotic and unique cousins to the common Fuchsia, these are bushy and upright plants from South Africa. The drooping, tubular flowers are arranged in loose heads on the ends of tall stems and always remind me a bit of exploding firecrackers. These act as semi-woody shrubs in the Pacific Northwest but usually die back to ground level in colder regions. Plants should be cut back hard to 15 cm (6") in early spring, and pinched occasionally throughout the season to maintain a more compact and bushy habit. Cuttings taken in fall will root fairly easily in a greenhouse or under lights, providing a backup to plants wintering outside. These make excellent container specimens for the patio or deck and can be wintered in a cool porch or basement. Flowers are nice for cutting. Red and orange forms may attract hummingbirds.

HT/SP   90–120 cm (3–4') / 60–90 cm (2–3')
SOIL   Average to moist well-drained soil.
BLOOM July–October
USES   ✄♥➤ Borders

***aequalis* 'New Sensation'**   ZONE 8
### (Dwarf Cape Fuchsia)

A terrific new compact selection from England, with glowing magenta-pink flowers and a dense, bushy habit. This is going to sweep across the country as an exciting new container subject. Where hardy, this will be terrific near the front of a sunny border. Should be smashing next to anything with dark-purple or bronze leaves.

HT/SP   30–40 cm (12–16") / 40–50 cm (16–20")

**× *rectus***                           ZONE 7
### (Hybrid Cape Fuchsia)

Recent crosses and hybrids, some in interesting new shades, with especially large heads of flowers.
**'African Queen'** Peachy salmon-orange flowers with a yellow throat.
**'Moonraker'** Big, loose spikes of soft creamy-yellow flowers, dark green leaves. Absolutely superb!
**'Winchester Fanfare'** Deep salmon-pink with a yellow throat.

# PHYSALIS ☼ ◑
### (Chinese Lantern Plant)

***alkekengi***                          ZONE 2
**[*P. franchetii*]**

Showy scarlet-orange inflated pods appear in September, and are useful for dried arrangements. The tomato-like white flowers are insignificant. This plant is an aggressive spreader, best kept in the cutting garden or back lane, or allowed to naturalize at the edge of a woodland. Whatever you do, keep a watchful eye that it does not spread beyond where you want it. Fertilize yearly for good-quality lanterns. For a little fun, try tucking a vase full of the cut lantern stems next to a large gold-leaved hosta! **CAUTION: all parts of this plant are poisonous, particularly the green berries inside each pod.**

HT/SP   60–90 cm (2–3') / 60–90 cm (2–3')
SOIL   Average to moist, well-drained soil.
USES   ✄♥

**Dwarf Strain** A compact form, with shorter stems of the usual orange lantern pods.
HT   30–45 cm (12–18")

# PHYSOSTEGIA ☼ ◑
### (Obedient Plant)

***virginiana***                         ZONE 2

Another terrific native North American wildflower. Tall wand-like spikes of flowers appear in mid to late summer. The common name comes from the fact that the individual flowers in the spikes will stay wherever you move them. Very useful as a background plant in the border or wild garden. Excellent cut flowers. These form a large clump that may be inclined to spread, but can be easily controlled with an edging spade — something that needs to be done each spring. All are superb for cutting. Attractive to butterflies.

SP   60–90 cm (2–3')
SOIL   Average to moist, well-drained soil.
BLOOM July–October
USES   ✄🦋 Borders, Waterside

**'Bouquet Rose' ['Pink Bouquet']** Nice large spikes of deep rose-pink.
HT   90–120 cm (3–4')

**'Miss Manners'** A recent breeding breakthrough, this is the first non-spreading selection. Flowers are white, held on strong stems that are an ideal height. The habit should regain some gardening fans who have banished spreading plants from their borders.
HT   75–90 cm (30–36")

**'Summer Snow'** Pure white flowers. Somewhat slower to spread, in my experience.
HT   75–90 cm (30–36")

**'Variegata'** Green leaves are heavily splashed in creamy-white. Soft lavender-pink blooms. Spreading is not a big problem with this selection, but it will run a little. I love the effect in large tubs or mixed containers.
HT   60–90 cm (2–3')

*Phlox subulata* Candy Stripe
*Phlox* × *procumbens* 'Variegata'
*Physalis alkekengi*
*Phlox subulata* 'Laura'
*Phormium tenax*
*Phygelius aequalis* 'New Sensation'

## PINELLIA ☼•
### (Green Dragon)

**cordata**                                ZONE 5
**(Miniature Green Dragon)**
A Chinese cousin to our familiar Jack-in-the-pulpit, this is not a well-known plant and deserves to be used more in shady woodland gardens. Plants form a low clump of glossy dark-green arrow-head-shaped leaves, backed in purple. Bizarre hooded green flowers have a long twirling tail, appearing in late summer. This is turning out to be hardier than first expected, particularly in regions with good winter snow cover. Tiny new plants will form from little bulbils that drop from the parent clump. These can be moved after a year or two.

**HT/SP** 15–30 cm (6–12") / 20–30 cm (8–12")
**SOIL** Prefers a rich moist, well-drained woodland soil.
**BLOOM** August
**USES** ▲🌱 Woodland, Shade borders

## PLATYCODON ☼ ◑
### (Balloon Flower)

**grandiflorus**                           ZONE 3
These are a real novelty in the garden when their inflated buds actually "pop" open into star-shaped flowers. The long-lived plants form an upright clump in the border, seldom needing to be divided. Flowers are available in shades of blue, pink or white. Because Balloon Flowers are very slow to make an appearance in spring they can be easily damaged by early weeding or digging; you can mark the spot by planting crocuses or other small bulbs underneath them. I have always found the habit of Balloon Flowers to be a wee bit lax and floppy. Fortunately, some of the more recent dwarf strains are much better.

**HT/SP** 60–75 cm (24–30") / 45–60 cm (18–24")
**SOIL** Average to moist, well-drained soil.
**BLOOM** June–August
**USES** ✂◀🌱 Borders

**'Fairy Snow'** Charming white stars, with a blue line running down the centre of each petal. Very compact.

**HT** 20–30 cm (8–12")

**'Fuji' Series** A mid-sized Japanese series, forming bushy mounds of medium habit. Flowers are available in blue, pink or white. Nice for cutting.

**HT** 45–60 cm (18–24")

**'Hakone Double Blue'** Fully double violet-blue flowers. Bushy, compact habit.

**HT** 40–60 cm (16–24")

**'Sentimental Blue'** A terrific new dwarf form with violet-blue flowers. Just the perfect height for the rock garden or containers.

**HT** 15–20 cm (6–8")

## PODOPHYLLUM ◑
### (May Apple)
Gardeners in the eastern part of the continent are probably familiar with our native May Apple, *P. peltatum*. These burst out of the ground in early spring, quickly forming a patch of umbrella-shaped leaves. Nodding white flowers are hidden among the leaves, later forming fleshy yellow fruit. The native May Apple is an aggressive spreader, favouring moist woodland conditions. There are a number of other species and forms native to China that make even better garden plants. These are not very easy to come by, but occasionally are offered by specialty nurseries. Grab them when you see them! **CAUTION: Harmful if eaten.**

**pleianthum**                             ZONE 9
**(Chinese May Apple)**
Upright stems appear in spring, bearing large starfish-shaped green leaves with a glossy sheen. Clusters of ill-smelling deep-red flowers change first to silver, then finally into yellow fleshy fruits. At home in the woodland garden, this requires a rich moist soil. Unusual and rare.

**HT/SP** 45–60 cm (18–24") / 75–90 cm (30–36")
**SOIL** Prefers a rich, moist woodland soil.
**BLOOM** May–June
**USES** ▲ Woodland, Shady rock garden

## POLEMONIUM ☼ ◑
### (Jacob's Ladder)
When not in flower, most species of Jacob's Ladder are easily mistaken for a fern. The divided green leaves form lush mounds. These range from good-sized clumps for the border or lightly-shaded woodland, to low alpine or groundcover species. Most types have small, round violet-blue flowers with a tiny yellow eye, looking a wee bit like Phlox.

**boreale 'Heavenly Habit'**              ZONE 3
**(Arctic Jacob's Ladder)**
Just recently introduced, this selection is nice in the rock garden, for border edging or in containers. Plants form a low mound of ferny green leaves, bearing loads of starry violet-blue flowers, each with a white eye. Flowers appear over a long season, but clipping in midsummer will encourage a low habit and possibly more blooms in late summer. May benefit from afternoon shade in warmer regions.

**HT/SP** 25–30 cm (10–12") / 30–45 cm (12–18")
**SOIL** Average to moist, well-drained soil.
**BLOOM** June–August
**USES** ✂▲🌱 Rock garden, Edging

**caeruleum**                              ZONE 2
**(Common Jacob's Ladder)**
An easy and reliable plant for an early summer display. Flowers are medium-blue through to white, held on stems well above the green foliage mound. These can be prolific self-sowers, unless the spent flower stems are removed to prevent seed formation. Flowering stems are nice for cutting. Foliage remains evergreen in mild winter regions.

**HT/SP** 45–80 cm (18–30") / 30–45 cm (12–18")
**SOIL** Average to moist, well-drained soil.
**BLOOM** May–July
**USES** ✂◀🌱▲ Borders, Woodland gardens

**Brise d'Anjou ['Blanjou']** This was all the rage a few years back when it first hit the market. The ferny leaves are brightly edged in creamy-white, and these really are the main feature. Clumps are shy to bloom in warmer regions, but may produce a display of violet-blue flowers. Many gardeners have tried and failed with this plant; an evenly-moist but freely draining soil and afternoon shade seem to be the key to success. Nowhere near as vigorous as the plain species.

**HT/SP** 45–60 cm (18–24") / 25–30 cm (10–12")

**'Snow and Sapphires'** A new variegated selection, said to have a stronger and more freely-blooming habit. The dark-green leaflets are edged in creamy white. Rich violet-blue flowers put on a grand show in early summer. Consider using this towards the border edge, or in containers.

**HT** 60–75 cm (24–30")

**cashmerianum**                           ZONE 4
**(Kashmir Jacob's Ladder)**
A less common species, the compact habit lends itself nicely to the rock garden or for edging. Clusters of soft-blue starry flowers appear for a few weeks in late spring and early summer.

*Pinellia cordata*

*Platycodon g. 'Sentimental Blue'*

*Physostegia virginiana 'Bouquet Rose'*

*Polemonium caeruleum*

*Podophyllum pleianthum*

Clip back in late June to rejuvenate the leaves.

**HT/SP** 30–40 cm (12–16″) / 25–30 cm (10–12″)
**SOIL** Average to moist, well-drained soil.
**BLOOM** May–June
**USES** ✄◁⚘ Rock garden, Edging

### *pauciflorum* 'Sulphur Trumpets'
ZONE 6
**(Yellow Jacob's Ladder)**
An interesting departure from the usual blue forms, with clusters of tubular creamy-yellow blooms with a salmon blush. Foliage is green and ferny, forming a medium-sized mound. Charming in the rock garden or moist woodland.

**HT/SP** 30–45 cm (12–18″) / 25–30 cm (10–12″)
**SOIL** Average to moist, well-drained soil.
**BLOOM** June–July
**USES** △✄◁⚘ Rock garden, Woodland

### *reptans* 'Blue Pearl'
ZONE 3
**(Creeping Jacob's Ladder)**
One of our native North American species. This makes a creeping mound of ferny green leaves, spreading at a reasonably slow rate – safe enough to include in the rock garden. Makes a charming small-area groundcover. The starry flowers are pale blue in colour. I find this benefits from a hard trim after blooming, the foliage then remains attractive all season long.

**HT/SP** 25–30 cm (10–12″) / 45–60 cm (18–24″)
**SOIL** Average to moist, well-drained soil.
**BLOOM** May–July
**USES** △⚘⚘ Rock garden, Edging

## POLYGONATUM ☼●
**(Solomon's Seal)**
Their graceful, arching stems add an exotic touch to the shade garden and are often described as being architectural. Delicate creamy bell flowers hang from the stems in late spring, usually followed later by black or blue berries. Solomon's Seal are the perfect woodland companions to Hostas, Astilbes, and ferns. These are highly regarded for cutting by flower arrangers. Seldom mentioned is the gorgeous buttery-yellow colour that the stems and leaves provide for a brief couple of weeks in late fall.

New plantings may take a couple of years to become established, but they will be reliable for many years with minimal maintenance. Established clumps may be divided in early fall. Simply cut the fleshy rhizomes into sections, each with at least a couple of stems attached.

The botanical nomenclature of Solomon's Seal has been extremely mixed-up for years, especially for the variegated selections. Finally some of these are being sorted out by specialists. One of the key features of the common garden forms is the number of individual flowers held in each cluster, should you care to tackle sorting out your own collection. **CAUTION: All are harmful if eaten.**

**SOIL** Best in a rich, moist woodland soil.
**BLOOM** May–June
**USES** ✄△⚘ Borders, Woodland gardens

### *commutatum*
ZONE 3
**(Giant Solomon's Seal)**
The tallest commonly-encountered species, native to eastern North America. The bold, arching stems of green leaves can form a wide clump in time, so a fair bit of room should be allotted at planting time. Flowers are fairly large dangling white bells, held in clusters of three to eight from the axils of the leaflets. Botanists are making moves to include this with the shorter species *P. biflorum*. In very rich soil the stems of Giant Solomon's Seal may reach as tall as 7′.

**HT/SP** 90–120 cm (3–4′) / 60–90 cm (2–3′)

### *falcatum* 'Variegatum' see *odoratum* var. *pluriforme* 'Variegatum'

### × *hybridum*
ZONE 2
**[*P. multiflorum*]**
**(Common Solomon's Seal)**
The true species *P. multiflorum* exists in the wild, but nearly always what is offered by nurseries or seen in gardens is considered part of the hybrid group *P.* × *hybridum*. Stems are arching and of medium height. Flowers are white bells with green tips, usually held in clusters of four and followed by black-blue berries. Clumps are vigorous and will spread to form a patch in time.

**HT/SP** 60–70 cm (24–28″) / 60–75 cm (24–30″)

**'Striatum'** This is a slower growing form and more compact in size. Leaflets are streaked with creamy-white, rather than edged along the margins like *P. odoratum* var. *pluriforme* 'Variegatum'.

**HT** 30–60 cm (1–2′)

### *odoratum*
ZONE 2
**(Fragrant Solomon's Seal)**
Native to Europe, this species has white bells that dangle in pairs from the leaf axils. Plants slowly colonize and are a suitable height for edging along a woodland path. The fragrance is sweet but often elusive.

**HT/SP** 60–75 cm (24–30″) / 60–75 cm (24–30″)

### *odoratum* var. *pluriforme* 'Variegatum'
ZONE 2
**[*P. falcatum* 'Variegatum']**
**(Variegated Japanese Solomon's Seal)**
Arching stems of green leaves are narrowly edged in creamy-white. White flowers are green on the tips, held in clusters of four and followed by dark blue berries. This form has been sold for many years under a variety of names. This is easy to tell apart from *P.* × *hybridum* 'Striatum', which has creamy streaks throughout the leaf, rather than just on the margins.

**HT/SP** 45–90 cm (18–36″) / 60–75 cm (24–30″)

## POLYGONUM see PERSICARIA

## POTENTILLA ☼
**(Cinquefoil)**
Although the Shrubby Cinquefoils (*P. fruticosa*) are familiar landscape plants, the herbaceous types listed here are not nearly so well known. Their wild-rose shaped flowers appear in shades of red, orange, yellow, or white. Most are happy in average sunny border conditions, the smaller types are nice in a sunny rock garden.

### *megalantha*
ZONE 2
**[*P. fragiformis*]**
**(Woolly Cinquefoil)**
Clumps of beautiful felty green strawberry-shaped leaves bloom in early summer with a bright display of chrome-yellow flowers. I love this as a rock garden or edging plant, the leaf texture invites everyone who passes by to stop and touch it. Cut back hard after blooming to rejuvenate the foliage. Drought tolerant.

**HT/SP** 25–30 cm (10–12″) / 25–30 cm (10–12″)
**SOIL** Average to dry, well-drained soil.
**BLOOM** May–June
**USES** △⚘⚘ Borders, Edging

### *neumanniana* 'Nana'
ZONE 3
**[*P. verna* 'Nana']**
**(Alpine Cinquefoil)**
A very low, slow-spreading rockery plant. Single yellow buttercup flowers nestle on a compact evergreen mound.

*Polygonatum commutatum*

*Polygonatum odoratum* 'Variegatum'

*Polemonium caeruleum* 'Snow & Sapphires'

Very showy in bloom. Fairly drought-tolerant. Ideal for planting between flagstones or in gravel screes.

**HT/SP** 5–10 cm (2–4″) / 15–30 cm (6–12″)
**SOIL** Average to dry, well-drained soil.
**BLOOM** April–June
**USES** ⛰〰▲♻ Troughs, Walls

### *thurberi* 'Monarch's Velvet'    ZONE 4
### (Red Cinquefoil)

This superb introduction forms a clump of strawberry-like leaves, bearing upright stems of rich, raspberry-red flowers with a black centre for weeks on end. Excellent for cutting. Well suited to the border, or in mixed containers. Clumps may be easily divided in spring or early fall. Drought tolerant once established.

**HT/SP** 30–40 cm (12–16″) / 30–45 cm (12–18″)
**SOIL** Average to dry, well-drained soil.
**BLOOM** June–September
**USES** ✄♻ Borders, Edging

### *tridentata*    ZONE 2
### [*Sibbaldiopsis tridentata*]
### (Three-toothed Cinquefoil, Shrubby Fivefingers)

Native to dry Prairie areas of the Midwest and Canada, this forms an indestructible low mat of shiny evergreen leaves. Clouds of small round white flowers appear in late spring and early summer. An excellent filler plant for the rock garden or border edge, also good as a groundcover. Foliage develops bronze shades in the colder months. Drought tolerant once established. Prune lightly in spring, as stems are somewhat woody.

**HT/SP** 10–25 cm (4–10″) / 25–30 cm (10–12″)
**SOIL** Average to dry, well-drained soil.
**BLOOM** May–June
**USES** ⛰〰▲♻ Edging, Massing

## PRATIA ☼◐
## (Pratia)

Tremendous confusion exists over the nomenclature of these plants, many references calling them *Laurentia* or *Isotoma*. Honestly, from a distance of 5′ it is rather hard to see distinct differences. The most obvious thing is that *Pratia* fruit is a deep red to purple-black berry, while the seed of *Isotoma* is a small dry capsule that splits open when ripe. For the record, the genus *Laurentia* is now made up only of erect-growing or semi-trailing annuals, mainly used in hanging baskets.

### *angulata* 'Treadwellii'    ZONE 7
### (Treadwell's Pratia, White Star Creeper)

A flat, creeping perennial that forms a carpet of tiny green leaves, studded with tiny starry white flowers all summer long. Flowers may be followed by small purplish berries in the autumn. Ideal for planting between paving stones, in the rock garden, or in containers. Plants are easily ripped apart into small pieces to make new plantings, and this should be done in early spring. Native to New Zealand and happiest in climates with a similar mild winters and temperate summers. Tolerates full sun if soil remains moist. Evergreen.

**HT/SP** 2–4 cm (1–2″) / 15–30 cm (6–12″)
**SOIL** Average to moist, well-drained soil.
**BLOOM** May–September
**USES** ⛰〰▼▲ Between flagstones, Rock gardens

### *pedunculata* 'County Park'    ZONE 6
### (Blue Star Creeper)

A slightly hardier species, making a flat green carpet and bearing tiny bright-blue star flowers all summer long. Prefers evenly moist soil, otherwise the needs and uses are the same as 'Treadwellii', listed above. Evergreen.

**HT/SP** 2–4 cm (1–2″) / 15–30 cm (6–12″)
**SOIL** Average to moist, well-drained soil.
**BLOOM** May–September
**USES** ⛰〰▼▲ Between flagstones, Lawn substitute

## PRIMULA ◐
## (Primrose, Cowslip)

Primrose flowers are a true sign of spring, associating well with all sorts of flowering bulbs. They are moisture-lovers, and seem to do best in cooler climates, particularly in coastal areas. Where winters are dry and windy apply a thick mulch in late fall. Certain species are even hardy on the Prairies.

### *auricula* Hybrids    ZONE 2
### (Auricula Primrose)

Rosettes of waxy, evergreen leaves bear clusters of flowers in muted shades of yellow, mauve, pink, red and wine, usually with a contrasting eye. These were extremely popular in Victorian England when hundreds of named varieties were selected and collected, but today they are usually only available in mixtures. The best clumps of Auricula that I know of are in Prairie gardens, where the plants seem to thrive. Those of us in wet-winter regions have a more difficult time keeping these happy.

**HT/SP** 15–20 cm (6–8″) / 15–20 cm (6–8″)
**SOIL** Prefers a moist but very well-drained soil.
**BLOOM** March–May
**USES** ⛰▲♣◄ Edging, Borders

### *beesiana*    ZONE 4
### (Bee's Candelabra Primrose)

The Candelabra Primroses are grown for their colourful display of flowers arranged in tiers or layers on tall, upright stems. This species features heads of rose-purple flowers with a yellow eye, appearing in late spring and early summer. Foliage is light green, held in a low rosette at ground level. All Candelabra type Primroses prefer a rich soil that is constantly moist, and dislike any hint of summer drought. A stream bank or pondside setting is ideal. Allow plants to self-sow. Will tolerate full sun in cool summer regions.

**HT/SP** 40–70 cm (16–30″) / 20–30 cm (8–12″)
**SOIL** Requires a rich, moist to wet soil.
**BLOOM** May–July
**USES** ✄◄▲▼ Moist borders, Waterside

### × *bulleesiana*    ZONE 4
### (Hybrid Candelabra Primrose)

A delightful hybrid group, generally grown from seed and giving a mixture of pastel shades from creamy-yellow through pink, red, salmon, orange, mauve and purple. Flowers are held in whorls (or tiers) on upright stems. These are definitely vigorous moisture lovers and will cope with wet soil beside a stream or pond. Not for average border conditions.

**HT/SP** 45–50 cm (18–20″) / 25–30 cm (10–12″)
**SOIL** Requires a rich, moist to wet soil.
**BLOOM** June–July
**USES** ✄◄▲▼ Moist borders, Waterside

### *denticulata*    ZONE 2
### (Drumstick Primrose)

Flowers are held in a ball-shaped cluster in jewel-toned shades of blue, lilac, pink, and white. These are vigorous, durable and tough garden plants; hardy almost anywhere with reliable snow cover or a light mulch. Plants go dormant in the winter, the buds bursting out of the ground in spring.

**HT/SP** 20–30 cm (8–12″) / 20–30 cm (8–12″)
**SOIL** Prefers a rich, moist soil.
**BLOOM** March–May
**USES** ✄◄▲▼ Borders, Woodland gardens

Potentilla neumanniana 'Nana'

Primula denticulata

Primula beesiana

Primula auricula Hybrids

## Double English Hybrids ZONE 4
(Double English Primrose]
[*P. vulgaris* Hybrids]

Double Primroses have been cherished in English cottage gardens for centuries. Their charming fully-double flowers put on a tremendous display over the spring season, always reminding me a bit of double African Violets in appearance. Many of the older selections nearly disappeared from gardens due to virus diseases that gradually took hold. Thanks to modern tissue culture techniques many of the best older types have been cleaned up of nasty viruses and are now vigorous, healthy and available for today's gardeners to once again enjoy.

These are among the easiest Primroses to succeed with, preferring a rich, moist soil with plenty of peat and composted manure. In my own heavy clay soil (in Zone 6) there are several clumps doing very nicely after five or six years, with little attention other than a drink of water during summer droughts. In warm summer regions it's wise to choose a site with protection from the hot afternoon sun. As with the single English Primroses below, try to divide these every 2–3 years – either after blooming or in early fall, in order to maintain good vigour. Gardeners in Zones 2–3 may well succeed with these in sheltered places.

**HT/SP**  10–15 cm (4–6″) / 15–20 cm (6–8″)
**SOIL**   Best in a rich moist, well-drained soil.
**BLOOM** March–May
**USES**   △▲♥ Moist borders, Woodland gardens

**'April Rose'** Deep ruby-red flowers.
**'Dawn Ansell'** Clear white petals surrounded by a green ruff or collar. This type of bloom is sometimes called "Jack-in-the-Green".
**'Freckles'** Deep velvety-red petals, spotted with silver-white.
**'Granny Graham'** Deep violet-blue flowers, like little jewels.
**'Ken Dearman'** Glowing salmon-orange to peachy-pink blooms.
**'Lilian Harvey'** Bright magenta-pink, flowers are like perfect little roses.
**'Marianne Davey'** Flowers of ivory-white with a kiss of yellow in the centre.
**'Marie Crousse'** Deep lilac-purple, petals are edged in silver.
**'Miss Indigo'** Dark violet-purple with a silvery-white edge.
**'Paragon'** Just recently available, with fluffy light-pink blooms.
**'Quaker's Bonnet'** ['Lilacina Plena'] Nearly always the first to flower, with perfect little mauve-purple blooms. Very dainty.
**'Red Giant'** Rather large blooms in a deep velvety-red shade.

**'Red Velvet'** Deep scarlet-red, leaves flushed with bronze on the margins.
**'Rosetta Red'** Bright rose-red flowers.
**'Roy Cope'** Deep crimson, ageing to purple-red.
**'Sue Jervis'** An early bloomer with soft flesh-pink petals. Good companion to 'Quaker's Bonnet'.
**'Sunshine Susie'** Bright buttercup-yellow. One of the best.
**'Val Horncastle'** Lovely soft sulphur-yellow. Beautiful with blue Forget-me-Nots.

## English Primrose Hybrids ZONE 4
(English Primrose)
[*P. × pruhoniciana, P. juliae*)

Although these appear similar to the modern Polyantha Primrose at first glance, plants are generally shorter in habit. They have a tougher constitution, growing readily in any reasonably moist, somewhat shady location, the clumps multiplying readily. Hundreds of selections have come and gone over the centuries, with both single and double flowers (see the listing above for Double English Hybrids). These are ideal for edging, growing in a shady rock garden or among ferns, bulbs and other woodland perennials. To maintain vigour, divide plants every 2–3 years, either right after blooming or in early fall. As with all Primroses, slugs are sometimes a concern.

**HT/SP**  10–15 cm (4–6″) / 20–30 cm (8–12″)
**SOIL**   Prefers a rich moist, well-drained soil.
**BLOOM** March–May
**USES**   △♥▲ Edging, Woodland gardens

**'Guinevere'** ['Garryard Guinevere'] Unusual bronzy-green leaves look good whether the plants are flowering or not. Blooms are soft-pink and contrast nicely. An old historical variety.
**'Mahogany Sunrise'** (Gold-laced Primrose) Gold-laced Primroses are an interesting and distinctive colour variation. This selection produces yellow-eyed deep mahogany-red flowers, each petal edged in golden-yellow. Flowers are held in clusters on a short stem. Plant near the border edge where these may be viewed from up close!

**HT/SP**  15–20 cm (6–8″) / 15–30 cm (6–12″)

**'Tie Die'** A real show-stopper, this produces deep denim-blue flowers veined in purple, with a cheery yellow eye. Probably a Polyantha Hybrid.
**'Wanda'** An extremely popular and very old historical variety. Magenta-purple flowers smother the bright green leaves in early spring. Perhaps the toughest Primrose of all, the plants quickly form a dense patch. Generally hardy in Zones 2–3 where snowcover is reliable.

**'Wanda' Hybrids** A series of strains developed from the original magenta 'Wanda'. These are vigorous selections in a wide range of jewel shades, from magenta and blue, to red, pink, yellow and white. They out-perform the Polyantha types in most regions.

## *florindae* ZONE 3
(Himalayan Cowslip)

A late-blooming Primrose, sending up loose ball-shaped umbels of fragrant, dangling yellow or orange flowers in the summer. Excellent for cutting. Long-lived if planted in a good moist site.

**HT/SP**  60–90 cm (2–3′) / 30–60 cm (1–2′)
**SOIL**   Prefers a rich, moist to wet soil.
**BLOOM** June–August
**USES**   ✂◄♥ Waterside, Bog gardens

## *japonica* ZONE 5
(Japanese Primrose)

A candelabra-flowered species, with several whorls of red, pink or white blossoms on each upright stem. Leaves form a low, cabbage-like clump of fresh green. This species prefers a constantly moist soil, perhaps beside a stream or pond, but will adapt to a semi-shaded border.

**HT/SP**  30–60 cm (1–2′) / 25–30 cm (10–12″)
**SOIL**   Prefers a rich, moist to wet soil.
**BLOOM** May–July
**USES**   ✂◄△♥ Moist borders, Waterside

**'Miller's Crimson'** Bright rosy-red flowers.
**'Postford White'** Showy stems of white flowers.

## *× polyantha* Hybrids ZONE 4
(Polyantha Primrose, Florist's Primrose)

The best-known Primroses because they are so widely available – sold everywhere from nurseries to florists and supermarkets from Christmas to

Primula 'Marianne Davey'  Primula 'Paragon'  Primula 'Quaker's Bonnet'

Primula 'Val Horncastle'  Primula 'Guinevere'  Primula pulverulenta

Primula 'Wanda' Hybrids  Primula vialii  Primula 'April Rose'

spring – basically intended to be enjoyed indoors and then discarded. These will often survive outdoors, thriving particularly well in mild-winter regions where they pop into flower during warm spells any time from November to April. In colder regions these should be planted away from drying north-west winds in a sheltered spot. A huge range of colours and bicolours are available. Generally short-lived unless divided every 2–3 years after blooming is over.

I've killed many of these on my windowsill before they ever made it out to the garden – the combination of warm house temperatures and erratic watering is not to their liking. After flowering is over, get the plants outside during the daytime whenever the temperature is above freezing, bringing inside at night when it turns frosty. Clean up any dead leaves and spent flowers, fertilize every two weeks and they should give you a beautiful second round of bloom and be ready for planting outdoors in April or May.

**HT/SP** 10–15 cm (4–6″) / 15–20 cm (6–8″)
**SOIL** Best in a rich moist, well-drained soil.
**BLOOM** November–May
**USES** ⛰∧⋀•▲☗ Edging, Woodland gardens

### *pulverulenta*                    ZONE 5
### (Magenta Candelabra Primrose)
Upright stems of flowers, the blooms are held in tiers or whorls varying in colour from magenta-pink to purple-red. A fairly late-blooming species, best in the bog garden or at the waterside. Nice for cutting.

**HT/SP** 40–70 cm (16–30″) / 30–45 cm (12–18″)
**SOIL** Prefers a rich, moist to wet soil.
**BLOOM** May–July
**USES** ✂❮∧☗ Waterside, Bog gardens

### *veris*                          ZONE 2
### (English Cowslip)
Without a doubt this is one of the easiest Primroses to grow, putting up with average conditions far better than the fussier types. Plants bear upright stems of nodding lemon-yellow flowers in mid-spring, occasionally ranging towards orange or red in colour. Flowers are very fragrant, making this an old favourite for gardeners in the know. Plants are usually happy in average to heavy soils with a partial shade exposure. These associate well with a wide range of spring flowering bulbs, as well as other rock garden species, especially blue *Pulmonaria* and *Brunnera*. Will tolerate full sun in cool summer regions. Clumps may be easily divided after blooming, or in early autumn.

**HT/SP** 20–25 cm (8–10″) / 25–30 cm (10–12″)
**SOIL** Prefers a rich moist, well-drained soil.
**BLOOM** April–May
**USES** ✂❮∧☗ Moist borders, Woodland gardens

**'Perth Sunrise'** Found in a garden in Perth County, Ontario, this selection and 'Perth Sunset' have stood the test of time. Both are hybrids but likely have *P. veris* blood in them. 'Perth Sunrise' produces upfacing umbels of large brick-red flowers with a golden-yellow eye.

**HT/SP** 20–30 cm (8–12″) / 30–45 cm (12–18″)

**'Perth Sunset'** A companion to 'Perth Sunrise', the flowers are a deeper burgundy-red, also with a golden-yellow eye. Both of these are fragrant, easy and carefree.

**HT/SP** 20–30 cm (8–12″) / 30–45 cm (12–18″)

**'Sunset Shades'** A lovely mixture of shades, including yellow, orange, red and some bicoloured forms.

### *vialii*                         ZONE 3
### (Chinese Pagoda Primrose)
With its bizarre-looking rocket-shaped spikes of dazzling mauve and scarlet flowers, this is unlike any typical Primrose in appearance. Plants usually form a green rosette in their first year, then flower for a year or two before dying from exhaustion. Will self seed in constantly moist locations, seems to prefer soils on the acidic side.

**HT/SP** 30–60 cm (1–2′) / 20–30 cm (8–12″)
**SOIL** Prefers a rich, moist to wet soil.
**BLOOM** May–July
**USES** ✂❮∧☗ Moist borders, Bog gardens

# PULMONARIA ☼•
## (Lungwort, Lords and Ladies)
Despite being stuck with such an unfortunate common name, these spring-blooming perennials are anything but unappealing. They create low mounds of handsome leaves, often heavily splotched or dotted with silvery-grey. Clusters of flowers are held above the leaves in various shades, from sky blue through to pink, purple, red, and white. These look at home in a woodland setting, growing very well beneath trees and shrubs. Trim off any tired-looking leaves in very early spring. Any of these combine beautifully with yellow primroses or Narcissus.

Powdery Mildew is sometimes a problem, particularly with older forms – cut the plants back hard immediately after bloom to rejuvenate the leaves and create healthier, happier clumps. All types are easily divided in early fall. Evergreen in mild-winter regions.

**SP** 40–60 cm (16–24″)
**SOIL** Best in a rich moist, well-drained soil.
**BLOOM** March–May
**USES** ✂∧⋀•▲☗ Edging, Woodland, Borders

### Hybrids                          ZONE 3
A number of new selections have been introduced in recent years. Breeders are developing excellent forms with not only new colours of flowers and foliage, but more importantly, better disease resistance and vigour. Just like with the *Heucheras,* things will surely reach a point of overkill, but some of the best selections will stand the test of time. Just remember – you don't need them all!

**'Berries and Cream'** Clusters of deep raspberry-pink bells, heavily silvered leaves have a green central vein and margins, sometimes dark green speckles. Compact habit.

**HT** 20–25 cm (8–10″)

**'Dark Vader'** Dark green leaves, heavily spotted with silver. Clusters of dark purple flowers, ageing to pinkish-red and held above the leaves.

**HT** 25–30 cm (10–12″)

**'Highdown'** ['Lewis Palmer'] Good clear bright-blue flowers, leaves lightly spotted in silver.

**HT** 20–30 cm (8–12″)

**'Majesté'** Solid silver foliage with a glossy sheen. Light-pink buds open to deep blue bells. Superb.

**HT** 20–25 cm (8–10″)

**'Purple Haze'** Upfacing clusters of violet-purple bells. Green leaves are lightly spotted in silver. Compact habit.

**HT** 20–25 cm (8–10″)

**'Raspberry Ice'** Clusters of glowing raspberry-pink bells, Long mint-green leaves are spotted in silver and edged in creamy-white. Makes a good-sized mound.

**HT** 30–35 cm (10–12″)

**'Raspberry Splash'** A true colour breakthrough, with large bells in a stunning magenta-pink shade. Foliage is

*Primula japonica* 'Postford White'

*Primula veris*

*Primula* 'Perth Sunset'

*Primula veris* Sunset Shades

fairly upright, dark green with lots of silver spots.

HT    30–35 cm (10–12")

**'Roy Davidson'** Clusters of soft powder-blue flowers held on arching stems. Dark green foliage is long and narrow with silver spots.

HT    25–30 cm (10–12")

**'Sissinghurst White'** One of the few white-flowered selections, and still excellent. Clear white bells are well displayed. Light-green foliage has soft silvery spotting. Really stands out when combined with any of the blue-flowered forms.

HT    25–30 cm (10–12")

**'Trevi Fountain'** Individual flowers are large, deep cobalt-blue in colour. Heavy silver spotting on long, dark-green leaves. Good summer heat tolerance.

HT    25–30 cm (10–12")

**'Victorian Brooch'** Clusters of upfacing bells in bright magenta-pink. Green leaves are lightly spotted in silver. Blooms for a long season. Compact.

HT    25–30 cm (10–12")

*longifolia*                    ZONE 3
(Long-leaved Lungwort)

This species is rather distinctive, with exceptionally long, narrow leaves that form a broad mound. Plants generally bloom a couple of weeks later than other types, extending the season. Adapts well to climates with hot, humid summers. Powdery mildew is sometimes a problem, but plants are quick to produce attractive new foliage when cut back hard. Flowers are held in clusters on long, arching stems.

**'Bertram Anderson'** ['E.B. Anderson'] Long, narrow dark-green leaves are well spotted in silver. Flowers are a bright gentian-blue colour, making this one of my personal favourites. Terrific for mass planting.

HT/SP  20–25 cm (8–10") / 45–60 cm (18–24")

**subsp. *cevennensis*** One of the largest forms, with very long leaves spotted with more silver than 'Bertram Anderson'. Flowers are perhaps a bit of a darker violet-blue shade. Excellent mildew resistance and heat tolerance.

HT/SP  30–45 cm (12–18") / 45–60 cm (18–24")

*mollis* **'Samobor'**          ZONE 3
(Mountain Lungwort)

The largest-growing form I have seen, the leaves are also rather distinct, with more of a velvety-green finish. Dangling pale-blue bells appear in mid-spring. Cut back hard immediately after blooming to rejuvenate. Said to tolerate heat and humidity.

HT/SP  30–60 cm (1–2') / 45–60 cm (18–24")

*rubra*                         ZONE 3
(Red Lungwort)

Usually the first species to flower in the spring, with blooms in a distinctive coral-red tone. Foliage is a lighter-green than most forms, sometimes plain or lightly spotted with silver, depending on the selection. Does not always hold up well to summer heat. Best in shade.

HT/SP  30–45 cm (12–18") / 45–60 cm (18–24")

**'David Ward'** The first truly variegated (rather than just spotted) form, the large mint-green leaves are strongly bordered in creamy white. Salmon-pink flowers really stand out. Unfortunately, the white edges often pucker, since they lack chlorophyll and grow more slowly than the centres. Foliage is also very prone to sun scorch, so plan to place this in lots of shade.

HT    30–40 cm (12–16")

*saccharata*                    ZONE 2
(Bethlehem Sage)

Low green foliage is usually heavily spotted with silver. Clusters of flowers open pink and soon turn to bright blue, depending on the particular selection. Evergreen in milder areas. An important parent of many of the new hybrids. Plan to cut the leaves back immediately after blooming. Powdery mildew can be a problem in humid regions.

HT/SP  25–30 cm (10–12") / 45–60 cm (18–24")

**'Leopard'** Light-pink buds open to reddish-pink bells. Green leaves have excellent silver spotting.

HT    25–30 cm (10–12")

**'Mrs. Moon'** Pink buds turn into bright-blue bells. Silver-spotted leaves. An older selection, often encountered in gardens.

HT    25–30 cm (10–12")

**'Reginald Kaye'** A vigorous selection, the dark green leaves have loads of big silver spots. Pinkish-purple buds open up into violet-blue bells. A nice compact habit, excellent for edging.

HT    15–20 cm (6–8")

# PULSATILLA ☼◑
(Pasque-flower, Prairie Crocus)

*alpina* **subsp. *apiifolia***   ZONE 4
[*Anemone sulphurea*]
(Yellow Pasque-flower)

Not as easy to please as the Common Pasque-flower below, this is best grown in gravel scree conditions similar to its native mountain environment. Flowers are like downy sulphur-yellow crocuses, held over a mound of ferny olive-green leaves. Drought-tolerant once established.

HT/SP  20–30 cm (8–12") / 15–20 cm (6–8")
SOIL    Well-drained rock garden or scree.
BLOOM March–May
USES   ✂◁▲❦ Rock garden, Troughs

*vulgaris*                      ZONE 2
[*Anemone pulsatilla*]
(Common Pasque-flower)

A favourite early spring bloomer with violet-purple flowers like the native Prairie Crocus, which is a close cousin. Showy in the rock garden or border, beautiful in a grassy meadow. Occasionally there are other colour forms of this available in red, pink or white. Flowers are followed by fuzzy seed-heads with a powder-puff appearance. Scatter the seeds around in late summer when they detach easily, and they might well naturalize through your garden. Drought-tolerant once established.

HT/SP  15–30 cm (6–12") / 20–30 cm (8–12")
SOIL    Tolerates a wide range of soil conditions.
BLOOM March–May
USES   ✂◁▲❦ Edging, Meadows

**'Alba'** Clear white petals surround a yellow centre.

**'Papageno'** A most interesting strain, the petal edges are deeply cut or fringed. A wide range of shades, including some amazing tones I have never seen before, like dusty-rose, salmon and mahogany red. Some flowers have extra petals.

**Red Clock ['Röde Klokke']** Shades of rose to bright-red around a yellow centre.

# RANUNCULUS ☼◑
(Buttercup)

Buttercups generally thrive in moist, sunny areas – not always an easy sort of spot to find in the average garden. There are not many types commonly seen in gardens. This is partly due to

*Pulmonaria* 'Dark Vader'

*Pulmonaria* 'Purple Haze'

*Pulmonaria longifolia* subsp. *cevennensis*

*Pulsatilla vulgaris*

their spreading reputation, but also because some of the better forms have not been available for long on this continent. Flowers are generally small and button-shaped, packed full of layered petals. Most gardeners are familiar with the Florist Ranunculus or Persian Buttercup (*R. asiaticus*), which come in a range of bright shades. These are not usually hardy except in the mildest-winter regions but the tuberous roots may be dug and stored free of frost for the winter. Tubers are available at garden centres in early spring at a reasonable price, so frankly it's easier to just treat them as annuals.

### *ficaria* ZONE 5
### (Celandine Buttercup, Lesser Celandine)

A European native Buttercup with dozens of garden selections, a few are now beginning to arrive here in North America. Plants bloom in early to late spring, forming a gorgeous low mound of small rounded leaves that are sometimes marked with silver or in various bronzed tones. The small buttercup flowers appear in great numbers, and can be single, semi-double or double buttons. Lesser Celandine blooms early in the season then becomes dormant during the warmth of summer. Plants will cope with the spring-moist/summer-dry woodland conditions that so many shade-loving plants dislike. Mounds form a tuberous root and spread fairly quickly or even aggresively to form a patch, although less so in summer-dry gardens. Tuck these gems in between Hostas or ferns or any other perennials that become dormant for the winter. Easily divided after blooming, or in early fall if you can find them. Toler-

*Ranunculus ficaria* 'Brazen Hussy'

*Rodgersia pinnata* 'Elegans'

*Raoulia australis*

ant of shade or sun – so long as they get plenty of moisture at bloom time.

**HT/SP** 10–15 cm (4–6") / 30–45 cm (12–18")
**SOIL** Prefers a rich moist, well-drained soil.
**BLOOM** March–May
**USES** ✂◣ Woodland, Waterside

**'Brazen Hussy'** Amazing purple-black foliage really sets the stage for a display of small starry golden-yellow flowers. Selected by British eccentric and perennial guru, Christopher Lloyd.

**'Double Mud'** A truly hilarious name, describing the double, soft primrose-yellow flowers, which have brown markings on the petals almost like mud stains. Foliage is green.

### *repens* ZONE 4
### (Creeping Buttercup)

A fast-spreading species, producing a trailing mat of glossy, fresh green leaves. The stems root where they touch the ground. Flowers appear in late spring and are quite showy against the foliage. These selections are a little too rampant for the border. A good choice as a groundcover in a sunny wet site, perhaps beside a stream or pond, or at the bottom of a ditch growing around any of the various water Iris. One other option is to grow them in a large container, set right into a pond or pool – the water should prevent these from escaping into the open garden. Evergreen in mild-winter regions.

**HT/SP** 15–30 cm (6–12") / 60–90 cm (2–3')
**SOIL** Rich, moist to wet soil.
**BLOOM** May–July
**USES** ✂ⵡ⚘▲ Waterside, Massing

**'Buttered Popcorn'** Single buttercups are a nice accent over the foliage, which makes an impressive mat of chartreuse-green leaves, pleasantly splashed in soft gold. Best colouring is with sun.

**var. *pleniflorus*** Loads of thumbnail-sized bright-yellow double buttercups appear for several weeks. I do admire this plant, but it needs careful placement since it's a quick spreader.

## RAOULIA ☼
### (Vegetable Sheep)

### *australis* ZONE 5
### (New Zealand Scab Plant)

A delightful and obscure little alpine plant from New Zealand. It forms an absolutely flat carpet of silver-grey foliage that will crawl in between and over rocks. An interesting choice for trough gardens and alpine screes. Flowers are tiny and insignificant. Must have perfect drainage. Plants will surely perish if planted in the border. In New Zealand there are several native species which form large hummocky colonies up on

the dry hills, resembling flocks of sheep from a distance.

**HT/SP** 1–2 cm (½–1") / 15–30 cm (6–12")
**SOIL** Very well-drained, gravelly soil.
**USES** ◬▲⚘ Troughs, Walls, Screes

## RATIBIDA ☼
### (Prairie Coneflower, Mexican Hat)

### *columnifera* ZONE 2
### (Prairie Coneflower)

As yellow daisies go, this species is quite distinctive. Flowers have very droopy golden-yellow petals, surrounding a long brown central cone. The effect is quite charming, particularly when plants are used towards the front of a sunny border. I find these can get a wee bit floppy in overly rich garden soil, but adapt well to difficult sites. Sometimes short-lived but generally self seeds and naturalizes well, without becoming troublesome. Native through large areas of the Prairie provinces and the Midwest and well adapted to summer drought conditions. A good candidate for gravel gardens. Nice for cutting.

**HT/SP** 60–90 cm (2–3') / 45–60 cm (18–24")
**SOIL** Average to dry, well-drained soil.
**BLOOM** July–September
**USES** ✂ⵡⵣ Borders, Meadows

**'Buttons and Bows'** Really unique, with ruffled double flowers of rusty-red, the petals edged in golden yellow. Each bloom looks like a tiny barmaid's skirt from some seedy Klondike saloon. Not likely to self sow, since the flowers are probably sterile.

**HT** 60–75 cm (24–30")

## RHEUM ☼◗
### (Rhubarb)

There are several ornamental species, all of them related to the common edible back-yard rhubarb (*R.* × *hybridum*), but with more exotic-looking leaves and blooming stalks. Impressive specimen plants for moist sites.

### *palmatum* var. *tanguticum* ZONE 3
### (Ornamental Rhubarb)

Large rhubarb leaves with deeply-lobed and pointy edges, almost like an enormous maple leaf. In the spring these are beautifully tinged with bronzy-red, later fading to dark green. Bizarre spikes of white to reddish-pink flowers appear in early summer on tall stems. An imposing specimen plant that looks great at the waterside. In warm regions this sometimes goes dormant by mid to late summer and is best grown in part shade. The best specimens I have ever seen are in Prairie gardens.

**HT/SP** 90–180 cm (3–6') / 90–100 cm (36–40")
**SOIL** Rich, moist soil.
**BLOOM** May–June
**USES** ✂ⵡ Specimen, Borders, Waterside

# RODGERSIA ☼☽
(Rodgersia)

These make exotic bold-leaved clumps for the waterside or moist woodland areas. Fluffy plumes of flowers rise above in the summer. Unique specimen plants, but not quick to mature, preferring the dappled shade of high trees.

**SOIL** Rich, moist soil.
**BLOOM** June–August
**USES** ✂❮❅ Dried Flower, Borders, Waterside

### *aesculifolia*  ZONE 3
(Fingerleaf Rodgersia)

Leaves are large and shaped like those of the horse chestnut, dark green with some bronzy overtones in spring. The creamy-white flowers are held above in a wide airy panicle, blooms later than other species.

**HT/SP** 90–100 cm (36–40″) / 90–100 cm (36–40″)

### *pinnata*  ZONE 4
(Featherleaf Rodgersia)

Fairly variable in form, and several good selections are now becoming available. Leaves are large and compound, often flushed with bronze during the cooler spring months. Big heads of white to soft-pink flowers are held well above the foliage. Both the blooms and showy red seed heads are interesting for cutting. Usually the first species to bloom, in early summer.

**HT/SP** 90–120 cm (3–4′) / 90–100 cm (36–40″)

**'Elegans'** Shades of creamy-pink to rose.

**'Superba'** Bronzed leaves in spring are particularly outstanding. Fluffy plumes of rose-pink blooms. One of the most impressive.

### *tabularis* see ASTILBOIDES

# ROSMARINUS ☼
(Rosemary)

### *officinalis*  ZONE 8
(Common Rosemary, Bush Rosemary)

Familiar at least in flavour and fragrance to most people, Rosemary is a common kitchen herb, the green needle-like leaves used in either fresh or dried form to flavour savoury dishes. Plants are native to Mediterranean regions and require a similar mild-winter climate to survive outdoors. Plants grow into woody, evergreen shrubs with good ornamental effect, studded with tiny soft-mauve flowers in late winter or very early spring. The fragrance is a bit pine-like but with something all its own that will make your mouth begin to crave really good Italian or Greek food.

Most of us can only hope to grow Rosemary as a container plant. Winter it in the sunniest possible spot indoors until spring weather settles and it can once again be moved outdoors. Good drainage is essential, and the key to success indoors seems to be even moisture – neither too wet nor too dry. A minimally heated porch is ideal, so long as the temperatures remain above freezing. Harvest the tips of the plant regularly and plants will remain compact and bushy. Some gardeners train these on a single stem as a standard. Where hardy outdoors, Rosemary is very drought tolerant once established.

**HT/SP** 60–120 cm (2–4′) / 30–70 cm (12–30″)
**SOIL** Average to dry, well-drained soil.
**BLOOM** February–April
**USES** ❅▲❮❅ Specimen

**'Arp'** This is reputed to be a more hardy form, wintering in Zones 6 or 7. I had it survive for one winter covered by a pile of snow next to my driveway, but really it's not going to stand for Canadian winters other than in the Pacific Northwest. That being said, gardeners in the southeastern states say this selection is not only hardy through the cold but also more tolerant of summer heat.

**Prostratus Group (Trailing Rosemary)** A low, spreading habit that lends itself to growing over sunny walls or in containers. A beautiful evergreen accent for the rock garden. Harvest and use the leaves just like regular Bush Rosemary.

**HT/SP** 10–15 cm (4–6″) / 60–90 cm (2–3′)

# RUDBECKIA ☼
(Coneflower, Black-eyed Susan)

For a long display of bright colour in the late summer border it's hard to beat this tough group of plants, all of them descending from native North American wildflower species. The name "Black-eyed Susan" describes these coneflowers well, their large golden daisies centred with a deep brown or black eye. All varieties prefer a warm sunny location with rich moist soil. Superb as cut flowers, some also have nice seed-heads for drying. Attractive to butterflies.

### Gold Fountain  ZONE 2
['Goldquelle']

The flowers and foliage of this hybrid are nearly identical to Golden Glow (listed below), but on a more compact and self-supporting plant. Forms a good-sized clump but lacks the invasive, spreading tendencies of its taller cousin. Despite the smaller size this may still require staking if grown in very rich soil.

**HT/SP** 90–100 cm (36–40″) / 60–70 cm (24–28″)
**SOIL** Average to moist, well-drained soil.
**BLOOM** July–September
**USES** ✂❮❅ Borders

### *fulgida*  ZONE 3
(Orange Coneflower)

Included in this species are some of the most popular perennials currently grown in gardens, especially in regions with hot, humid summers. Plants have a long season of bloom and a sturdy, self-supporting habit. Flowers are good-sized golden-orange daisies with a dark brown eye, held on branching stems and followed by black seed-heads that remain attractive throughout most of the winter. The seeds supply a source of winter food for finches and other small birds. Reliable and long-lived. Clumps are easily divided in spring. All of these will self-seed to a certain extent. Dead-heading them regularly and cutting down the dead stalks in fall will help to prevent seeding if this is a problem.

**SP** 45–60 cm (18–24″)
**SOIL** Average to moist well-drained soil.
**BLOOM** July–October
**USES** ✂❮❅ Borders, Massing

**var. fulgida (Autumn Orange Coneflower)** Said to be longer-blooming than 'Goldsturm', the heads are slightly smaller but continue until frost. Plant habit is similar.

**HT** 60–80 cm (24–30″)

**'Goldsturm' (Goldstorm Coneflower)** The most familiar variety, widely used in low-maintenance gardens, especially popular for mass planting with ornamental grasses and *Sedum 'Autumn Joy'*. Rates among the ten best perennials of all time!

**HT** 60–75 cm (24–30″)

**'Pot of Gold'** A Canadian introduction, with flowers nearly identical to 'Goldsturm' but on a more compact plant. Not exactly dwarf, but a better choice for the front of the border or in mixed

*Rodgersia aesculifolia*

*Rodgersia pinnata 'Superba'*

*Rudbeckia fulgida 'Pot of Gold'*

*Rudbeckia hirta 'Becky'*

*Rudbeckia hirta 'Indian Summer'*

containers. This is the best of the various compact types that I have seen.

HT          45–60 cm (18–24")

### 'Herbstsonne'          ZONE 2
### (Autumn Sun Coneflower)

A well-grown planting of this absolutely stops people in their tracks. It forms an enormous upright clump, bearing huge chrome-yellow daisies with drooping petals that surround a greenish-gold cone. Sensible advice would be to recommend this only for the back of a large border, but it's a fun plant to feature as a monstrous specimen in smaller areas also. Plants may require the support of a few stout bamboo canes, depending on the climate and soil. Appreciates a moist site. Long-lived.

HT/SP    150–240 cm (5–8') / 90–120 cm (3–4')
SOIL      Average to moist, well-drained soil.
BLOOM July–October
USES      ✂🦋 Borders, Specimen, Waterside

### *hirta* Hybrids          ZONE 5
### (Gloriosa Daisy)

Although more or less biennial, these hybrids are best treated as self-seeding annuals in most regions. Their large flowers put on a constant display from midsummer to very late fall, and they will grow in hot locations with only the occasional deep soaking. Excellent as filler plants in the summer border, also a good choice for containers. Some unusual deep bronze colours are to be found among the modern tetraploid seed strains. Deadheading every week or so will keep these in constant bloom until frost. Very drought-tolerant.

SOIL      Tolerates a wide range of soil conditions.
BLOOM July–October
USES      ✂🦋 Borders, Massing

**'Autumn Colors'** A new European strain with a great range of bright shades. Most flowers are single and bicoloured, in tones of yellow, gold, orange or bronzy-red. Mid-sized habit. Will probably replace the older 'Rustic Colors' strain.

HT/SP    50–60 cm (20–24") / 25–30 cm (10–12")

**'Becky'** An excellent and versatile mixture with a compact habit and nice big flowers. Ideal for edging or in mixed containers. Shades include yellow, gold, orange and a bronzy-red. The flowers are sometimes bicoloured.

HT/SP    25–40 cm (10–16") / 30–40 cm (12–16")

**Double Gold Strain** Extra-full golden-yellow flowers and a black eye. The original Gloriosa Daisy. In rich soils plants sometimes need some extra support.

HT/SP    75–90 cm (30–36") / 30–45 cm (12–18")

**'Indian Summer'** An absolutely outstanding All America Selection from a few years back. Huge golden-orange daisies are produced on tall stems but the habit is bushy and self supporting. One of the best forms for mass plantings. This self seeds nicely in my own garden.

HT/SP    90–110 cm (36–42") / 30–45 cm (12–18")

**'Irish Eyes'** Single yellow flowers with green centres, a nice departure from the usual black eyed forms. Terrific for cutting. Mid-sized habit.

HT/SP    70–80 cm (28–32") / 30–45 cm (12–18")

**'Prairie Sun'** An outstanding new selection, the single flowers are golden with yellow tips, surrounding a green central button or cone. Nice tall stems are great for cutting. Sort of an improvement on 'Irish Eyes'.

HT/SP    70–80 cm (28–32") / 30–40 cm (12–16")

**Rustic Colors** A mid-sized mixture of single blooms, in shades from yellow through to gold, orange, bronze and deep mahogany-red, often with contrasting tips.

HT/SP    45–60 cm (18–24") / 30–45 cm (12–18")

**'Sonora'** A nice change from the typical forms, the petals of this strain feature a ring of chocolate-brown surrounding the black centre, with tips of golden yellow. Compact habit.

HT/SP    30–40 cm (12–16") / 30–45 cm (12–18")

**'Toto' Series** A re-selected group of varieties, producing bushy plants with a compact habit that are ideal for containers or massed plantings. All have single flowers with a brown cone, including: **'Toto Gold'**, bright golden-orange; **'Toto Lemon'**, flowers of cheery true lemon-peel yellow; **'Toto Rustic'**, my personal favourite, with rich mahogany-red to brown petals tipped in gold.

HT/SP    30–40 cm (12–16") / 25–30 cm (10–12")

### *laciniata* 'Hortensia'          ZONE 2
### (Golden Glow, Outhouse Plant)

Lovingly referred to as the Outhouse Plant, this very old selection is extremely tall and rangy in habit. Has the ability to make a huge patch after only a couple of years. The double chrome-yellow pompon flowers are terrific for cutting. Plants are very wind-prone and need to be staked, also susceptible to powdery mildew – but it's a *must* for anyone serious about making an authentic period garden!

HT/SP    180–210 cm (6–7') / 90–120 cm (3–4')
SOIL      Average to moist, well-drained soil.
BLOOM July–September
USES      ✂🦋 Borders

### *maxima*          ZONE 4
### (Giant Coneflower)

This native of the southern states is quite new to gardens, but much hardier than everybody thought it would be. Plants first make a beautiful low clump of powdery-blue basal leaves, followed in midsummer by tall stems of drooping black-eyed Susan flowers, making this a plant of long-season interest. Seed heads remain attractive until beaten down by winter ice storms. I find this to be a worthwhile plant for the blue leaves alone. I like to place it up towards the border front where they may be seen, surrounded by a low groundcover.

HT/SP    150–240 cm (5–8') / 60–90 cm (2–3')
SOIL      Average to moist, well-drained soil.
BLOOM July–October
USES      ✂🦋 Specimen, Borders

### *occidentalis*          ZONE 4
### (Naked Coneflower)

Certainly the most bizarre species of Coneflower, the flowers feature a bristly cone but lack the familiar gold or orange petals. In bloom this always reminds me a bit of Teasel heads. Every few years this plant is rediscovered it seems, and it's currently enjoying another wave of popularity. At the very least it does make an unusual cut flower, either fresh or dried. There are a couple of selections around.

HT/SP    75–100 cm (30–40") / 45–60 cm (18–24")
SOIL      Average to moist, well-drained soil.
BLOOM July–October
USES      ✂🦋 Borders, Cut flower

**'Black Beauty'** Naked cones of deep brown to near-black, with contrasting yellow stamens. Flowers are larger than the species and rather unique in a sunny border if you can figure out a clever way to use them. Consider placing them against a light-coloured fence or wall.

**'Green Wizard'** Bright green cones or flower heads, later changing into chocolate-brown seed heads. This strain may simply be another name for the straight species.

*Rudbeckia hirta* 'Toto Gold'

*Rudbeckia* 'Herbstsonne'

*Rudbeckia hirta* 'Sonora'

*triloba*  ZONE 4
**(Many-flowered Coneflower, Three-lobed Coneflower)**
Although native over a large area of eastern North America, I first became aware of this species while visiting German gardens about ten years ago. There it was often combined with soft-blue Michaelmas Daisies to charming effect. This usually acts as a self-seeding biennial, forming a low rosette of leaves the first year. The second summer it produces upright branching stems that are absolutely loaded with thousands of tiny little brown-eyed golden daisies. Plants self-seed in large numbers but the seedlings are easy to move around or pull out while still small. Butterflies seem to adore this plant.

HT/SP  75–100 cm (30–40") / 60–75 cm (24–30")
SOIL  Average to moist, well-drained soil.
BLOOM July–October
USES  ✂❦ Borders, Meadows

# RUMEX ☼◐
**(Dock, Sorrel)**
This genus is mostly made up of roadside weeds, the best-known garden type being the edible Sorrel grown in the vegetable or herb garden. There are a couple of forms with good foliage interest in the perennial garden.

*acetosa* **'Rhubarb Pie'**  ZONE 5
**(Variegated Sorrel)**
An unusual accent plant for the moist border. Forms a clump of spinach-like leaves in a garish combination of coral-red, dark green and creamy yellow. Greenish flower spikes are insignificant and best removed to prevent self seeding. If foliage gets tired, cutting plants back in midseason will rejuvenate it. This shows good promise for creating stunning effects in containers or at the border edge, but it's not a combination of colours that will be to everyone's liking. Probably evergreen in mild winter regions. Likely hardy to Zones 2–3 with no trouble.

HT/SP  20–30 cm (8–12") / 30–60 cm (1–2')
SOIL  Prefers a rich, moist soil.
BLOOM June–July
USES  ♟▲ Edging

*sanguineus* var. *sanguineus*  ZONE 4
**(Bloody Dock, Red-veined Sorrel)**
Years ago I bought one of these and dragged it home in my suitcase. It thrived in the garden and remains one of my favourite foliage plants for tucking into odd places here and there – something it will accomplish all by itself since plants do tend to seed around some. The foliage forms a low clump, each dark-green leaf showing an intricate pattern of beet-red veins. Cutting off the insignificant green flowers will help prevent seedlings from

appearing. This deserves a spot right next to a pathway or in a raised bed where the rich foliage effect may be best appreciated. Gardeners often ask me if this is edible; I've been unable to find any reference to say for sure one way or another, but from personal experience I can tell you not to bother – the leaves taste about as interesting as lawn grass.

HT/SP  20–30 cm (8–12") / 20–30 cm (8–12")
SOIL  Prefers a rich, moist soil.
BLOOM June–July
USES  ♟ Edging

# SAGINA ☼◐
**(Pearl Wort)**

*subulata*  ZONE 3
**(Irish Moss)**
A creeping moss-like groundcover for small areas, sometimes used as a lawn substitute in cool-summer regions. Especially nice growing between flagstones or in the rock garden. The bright green foliage is studded with tiny white flowers in summer. Evergreen where hardy. Plants seem to dislike the extremes of overly dry or soggy-wet soils. In warm regions keep this out of hot afternoon sun. Clumps are easily divided by ripping apart into 3–5 cm (1–2") pieces in spring or early fall. Has proven to be fairly reliable in cold winter regions, including the Canadian Prairies.

HT/SP  1–2 cm (½–1") / 15–30 cm (6–12")
SOIL  Evenly moist but well-drained soil.
BLOOM May–August
USES  ▲⋀•▲♟ Pathways, Rock gardens

**'Aurea'** (Scotch Moss) Identical in habit, but with leaves of bright neon-yellow.

# SALVIA ☼
**(Perennial Sage, Hardy Salvia)**
Some of these are valued for their long summer display of flowers, others more for their handsome foliage. Salvia is a large and diverse group of hardy and tender perennials, annuals and herbs that includes the familiar Common Sage used in cooking. Almost all of these appreciate a warm sunny site and are fairly drought-tolerant. The flowers are attractive to butterflies and in many cases also to hummingbirds.

*argentea*  ZONE 5
**(Silver Sage)**
An unusual foliage plant, valued for its intensely silver-grey fuzzy leaves that are arranged in a low rosette. Spikes of creamy-yellow flowers will appear in the second year, rising to 3–4' but these are often removed. Plants are biennial or short-lived perennials. Place plants towards the front of the border where the impressive leaves can be easily viewed and touched. Drought tolerant.

HT/SP  30–45 cm (12–18") / 45–70 cm (18–30")
SOIL  Average to dry, very well-drained soil.
BLOOM June–July
USES  ▲⋀▲♟❦ Specimen, Borders

*azurea* var. *grandiflora*  ZONE 5
**[*S. pitcheri*]**
**(Azure Sage)**
Tall branching spikes of bright clear-blue flowers appear in late summer and fall. A native of the south-eastern U.S., tolerant of heat and humidity. This is fairly tall and may require staking if grown in rich soil, or allow the stems to flop frontward over something bushy. Plants burst into bloom late in the season, at a time when sky-blue flowers are a rarity. Beautiful when combined with *Solidago sphacelata* 'Golden Fleece'.

HT/SP  90–120 cm (3–4') / 45–60 cm (18–24")
SOIL  Tolerates a wide range of soil conditions.
BLOOM August–October
USES  ✂❦➤♟❦ Borders, Meadows

*nemorosa*  ZONE 3
**(Blue Sage, Perennial Salvia)**
An important parent to the various *S.* × *sylvestris* selections, these may be used interchangeably for all intents and purposes. Spikes of violet to blue flowers appear in early summer, overtop of a low mound of olive-green to slightly greyed, sturdy leaves. Taller forms are good for cutting.

SP  45–60 cm (18–24")
SOIL  Tolerates a wide range of soil conditions.
BLOOM June–July
USES  ✂❦➤❦❦ Borders, Massing

**East Friesland ['Ostfriesland']** Nice compact habit, spikes of deep violet-purple.

HT  40–45 cm (16–18")

**'Marcus'** A brand new dwarf selection, with showy spikes of deep violet-blue over a bushy grey-green mound. Flower

*Rumex sanguineus* var. *sanguineus*
*Salvia argentea*
Sagina moss checkers table

spikes are short and sort of chunky in appearance, which makes for a bright display. Great for edging, containers or even in the rock garden.

HT     25–30 cm (10–12″)

**Rose Wine ['Rosenwein']** A vast improvement on the older 'Rose Queen', which was always floppy. This has a good, bushy habit, with spikes of deep rosy-pink blooms.

HT     50–60 cm (20–24″)

### *nipponica* 'Fuji Snow'     ZONE 6
### (Variegated Japanese Sage)

Primarily a foliage plant, this Japanese woodlander forms a handsome clump of arrowhead-shaped green leaves, edged in snowy white. Taller stalks of soft creamy-yellow flowers appear around midsummer. This needs protection from hot afternoon sun, and seems to grow best in moist woodland conditions. A high proportion of seedlings should display variegation. Gorgeous as a foliage focal point in mixed containers.

HT/SP     45–60 cm (18–24″) / 45–60 cm (18–24″)
SOIL     Prefers a rich moist, well-drained soil.
BLOOM July–August
USES     ✂ ❦ ❦ Woodland garden

### *officinalis*     ZONE 4
### (Common Sage)

A favourite and familiar herb, worthy of a place in the perennial border. The fragrant, pebbly-textured leaves are a muted powdery-green colour, bearing taller stems of rich violet-blue flowers in summer. The coloured forms listed below are not quite as hardy, but gardeners often treat them as annuals or winter them indoors in pots. I find all types make outstanding edging plants in the ornamental kitchen garden, or in any sunny spot. Plants should be cut back to about 10 cm (4″) in spring to

maintain a compact bushy habit. Drought-resistant once established. Evergreen.

HT/SP     30–60 cm (1–2′) / 30–45 cm (12–18″)
SOIL     Average to dry, well-drained soil.
BLOOM June–July
USES     ✂ ❦ ❦ ❦ Herb gardens, Edging

**'Garden Gray'** Silvery-grey foliage, very similar to the straight species form.

**'Icterina'** Leaves are handsomely splashed in golden-yellow and green. Sometimes incorrectly called 'Aurea', which is another form with all-yellow leaves. Not as hardy, probably Zone 6.

**'Purpurascens'** Gorgeous purple-flushed leaves with dark violet stems. Zone 6.

**'Tricolor'** Dappled variegation of purple, pink, cream and green. Zone 6 or 7.

### *pratensis* 'Indigo'     ZONE 4
### (Meadow Sage)

Branching stems with spikes of deep lavender-blue flowers appear in early summer, held well above sturdy low foliage. The overall look is a bit coarser than the Blue Sage forms and hybrids, but I find plants to be more reliable about repeat flowering in the autumn. Cut back hard in early spring, even if the clump remains evergreen.

HT/SP     60–70 cm (24–28″) / 45–60 cm (18–24″)
SOIL     Average to moist, well-drained soil.
BLOOM June–July
USES     ✂ ❦ ❦ ➤ Borders, Meadows

### × *sylvestris* selections     ZONE 3
### (Hybrid Blue Sage, Perennial Salvia)

A sturdy group of hybrids, very similar in appearance and function to the *Salvia nemorosa* selections. These are very showy plants for the summer border. Said to possibly rebloom in the fall if dead-headed, I have never found this to be the case here in Zone 6. Fairly drought-tolerant once established.

SP     45–60 cm (18–24″)
SOIL     Tolerates a wide range of soil conditions.
BLOOM June–July
USES     ✂ ❦ ➤ ❦ ❦ Borders, Massing

**Blue Hill ['Blauhügel']** Mid-sized spikes with flowers that are close to true blue. An outstanding German introduction.

HT     45–50 cm (18–20″)

**'Caradonna'** Medium to tall selection, with flowers of deep violet-blue held on unusual blue-black stems. Spikes are open and graceful in habit. Excellent for cutting.

HT     50–75 cm (20–30″)

**Blue Queen ['Blaukönigin']** Medium-tall, with bright violet-blue flower spikes. Good heat tolerance.

HT     45–60 cm (18–24″)

**May Night ['Mainacht']** The darkest form commonly seen, with rich spikes of deep indigo-violet flowers. Good heat

tolerance. Selected as the *Perennial Plant of the Year* for 1997.

HT     45–60 cm (18–24″)

**Snow Hill ['Schneehügel']** Spikes of clean snow-white flowers, especially nice combined with blue or violet forms.

HT     45–50 cm (18–20″)

**The Dancer ['Tänzerin']** A really good taller selection, with long spikes of deep violet-blue. Excellent for cutting.

HT     60–75 cm (24–30″)

### *verticillata* 'Purple Rain'     ZONE 3
### (Whorled Sage)

This appeared on the scene not too many years ago and has quickly proven itself to be both long-blooming and very hardy. Plants form a low mound of fuzzy olive-green leaves. Short arching stems rise above, holding rich violet-purple flowers in clusters evenly spaced apart to the tip. Dead-head for continual bloom. I once saw this planted in front of Annabel Hydrangeas in Adrian Bloom's garden, and it was a dynamite combination that I someday hope to reproduce in my own garden. 'White Rain' is a newer white-flowered selection that should be equally useful and long-blooming.

HT/SP     40–45 cm (16–18″) / 30–45 cm (12–18″)
SOIL     Tolerates a wide range of soil conditions.
BLOOM June–September
USES     ✂ ❦ ➤ ❦ ❦ Massing, Borders

## SANGUISORBA ☼ ◐
## (Burnet)

Several "new" Burnets have appeared on the scene in recent years. All of them feature lacy-looking leaves held in a low clump, with taller spikes of bottlebrush-shaped flowers appearing above, often arching gracefully. They appreciate a rich, moisture retentive soil, most of them looking especially nice at the waterside. Salad Burnet (*S. minor*) is most often grown in the herb garden, but I've always liked it for edging, with its short spikes of red flowers in early summer and lacy leaves that taste of cucumber.

### *menziesii*     ZONE 2
### (Alaskan Burnet)

Native to parts of Alaska, where it grows in sunny areas with moist soil. The foliage mound is sturdy and bluish-grey in colour, with taller spikes of deep maroon-red flowers in summer. Like many Burnets, this is best featured towards the front of the border.

HT/SP     75–90 cm (30–36″) / 45–60 cm (18–24″)
SOIL     Prefers a rich moist, well-drained soil.
BLOOM June–August
USES     ✂ ❦ Borders

Salvia verticillata 'Purple Rain'

Salvia officinalis

Salvia × sylvestris May Night

Salvia × sylvestris Blue Hill

### obtusa  ZONE 4
(Japanese Bottlebrush)

This is the most common species, forming a tough clump of elegant lacy leaves with a grey-blue powdery finish. Arching spikes of fluffy rose-pink, or occasionally white flowers appear in early to mid-summer. Excellent for cutting. Tough and long-lived. Easily divided in early spring. Don't be afraid to chop the foliage back hard after blooming if it happens to get tired looking.
HT/SP 70–90 cm (30–36") / 60–75 cm (24–30")
SOIL Prefers a rich moist, well-drained soil.
BLOOM June–July
USES ✄❦ Borders

'Chatto' This compact selection features particularly blue foliage and spikes of soft ivory-white blooms.
HT/SP 40–45 cm (16–18") / 45–60 cm (18–24")

### officinalis 'Tanna'  ZONE 4
(Great Burnet)

Similar to S. menziesii, this is a mid-sized selection with dark-red ball-shaped spikes in early summer. The lacy foliage is grey-green in colour.
HT/SP 60–90 cm (2–3') / 45–60 cm (18–24")
SOIL Prefers a rich moist, well-drained soil.
BLOOM June–August
USES ✄❦ Borders

### tenuifolia 'Pink Elephant'  ZONE 4
(Chinese Burnet)

A big, tall specimen plant suited either to the back of the border or right up front, surrounded by a low groundcover. The foliage is lacy and green, with very tall stems of arching rose-pink bottlebrush spikes in late summer. This is like the Burnet impersonation of Meadow-Rue! Does best with moisture and plenty of sun. May need to be staked.
HT/SP 120–175 cm (48–69") / 60–75 cm (24–30")
SOIL ich moist, well-drained soil.
BLOOM July–August
USES ✄❦ Moist Borders

## SANICULA ✦•
(Sanicle)

### caerulescens  ZONE 5
(Blue Sanicle)

Blue Sanicle was just recently introduced from China where it grows in moist mountain woodlands. Plants form a low mound of divided bronzy-green leaves that look somewhat like Cryptotaenia. These are smothered by branching heads of small mauve-blue flowers that appear for weeks on end in the spring. The overall effect is airy, a bit like a dwarf Meadow-rue. Combines well with spring-flowering bulbs of all kinds, particularly yellow narcissus. Best in a rich, moist soil where it will romp nicely with Hostas or ferns. Plants will self seed but not in a troublesome way. Attractive to butterflies.

HT/SP 15–25 cm (6–10") / 25–30 cm (10–12")
SOIL Prefers a rich moist, well-drained soil.
BLOOM April–June
USES ▵❦❦ Woodland, Shady rock garden

## SANTOLINA ☼
(Lavender Cotton, Cotton Lavender)

### chamaecyparissus  ZONE 6
[S. incana]

Low bushes of soft feathery silver-grey leaves, sometimes used as a clipped miniature hedge or edging. Yellow button-flowers will appear in summer where plants are hardy, but are often clipped off. The entire plant has a pleasant camphor-like fragrance. Often treated as an annual or used for carpet bedding. Give plants a good hard clipping to 15 cm (6") in early spring to keep them bushy. Very drought-tolerant, but soggy soil in winter can easily cause root rot. Evergreen.
HT/SP 30–45 cm (12–18") / 30–60 cm (1–2')
SOIL Average to dry, very well-drained soil.
BLOOM June–July
USES ▵▲❦❦ Edging

## SAPONARIA ☼
(Soapwort)

The vigorous border species are best known, but there are also several cushion-forming types for the alpine enthusiast. The name Soapwort refers to S. officinalis or Bouncing Bet, which when beaten in water forms a mild soap that is still used to wash ancient tapestries in Europe.

### 'Bressingham'  ZONE 4
(Alpine Soapwort)

Slowly spreads to form a dome of green grassy-looking foliage, studded with big bright-pink rounded flowers in late spring. A choice alpine variety for the rock garden or trough. A half-and-half mixture of grit and compost is recommended for best results. Plants seem to prefer regular moisture but excellent drainage.
HT/SP 5–10 cm (2–4") / 15–20 cm (6–8")
SOIL Best in a special gritty scree-type soil.
BLOOM May–June
USES ▵▲❦ Troughs, Rock garden

### × lempergii 'Max Frei'  ZONE 3
(Hybrid Soapwort)

This Austrian hybrid is valuable for the summer rock garden, because it blooms in midsummer when many other alpines are over and done. Plants form a low, bushy mound of green leaves, bearing clusters of starry soft-pink flowers for many weeks. Excellent also for edging or in mixed containers. Not invasive. Appreciates good drainage, particularly in areas with wet soil in winter. Drought tolerant once established.

HT/SP 30–40 cm (12–16") / 45–60 cm (18–24")
SOIL Average to dry, well-drained soil.
BLOOM July–September
USES ▵▲❦ Rock garden, Edging

### ocymoides  ZONE 2
(Rock Soapwort)

The most common species, forming a vigorous trailing mound for the rockery or edging. The bright green foliage is smothered with pink flowers in late spring. Fine for tumbling over walls or as a groundcover on steep sunny slopes. Shear plants back hard after blooming. Fairly drought-tolerant. Occasionally forms with white flowers or variegated foliage are offered. Evergreen.
HT/SP 15–20 cm (6–8") / 30–60 cm (1–2')
SOIL Average to dry, well-drained soil.
BLOOM May–June
USES ▵❦▲❦❦ Walls, Slopes

### × olivana  ZONE 4
(Alpine Soapwort)

A delightful alpine hybrid, forming a tight dome of bright-green leaves. Starry hot-pink flowers are arranged in a circle around the edge of the clump. This is relatively easy to please in a gravel scree or rock garden but should be kept well away from more vigorous plants that might swamp it out. Evergreen. Drought tolerant once established.
HT/SP 5–10 cm (2–4") / 20–30 cm (8–12")
SOIL Best in a well-drained rock garden or gravel scree.
BLOOM May–June
USES ▵▲❦❦ Troughs, Rock garden

## SAXIFRAGA ☼
(Saxifrage, Rockfoil)

This huge group of plants includes many easy rock garden specimens and a whole lot of other types that are best left to the experienced alpine connoisseur. Their small starry flowers are usually held in airy sprays during late spring. Rosettes of

Sanguisorba obtusa

Santolina chamaecyparissus

Saponaria 'Bressingham'

Saponaria ocymoides

evergreen foliage develop into a neat clump. Most require excellent drainage and prefer a cool location, a rockery or scree providing the ideal conditions. Afternoon shade is a preference, particularly in hot summer regions.

### × *arendsii* hybrids    ZONE 4
### (Mossy Saxifrage)
These form lush-looking cushions of bright-green foliage, bearing short stems of upfacing cup-shaped blossoms in shades of white, cream, pink or red, making for a brief but showy display in late spring. The hundreds of selections all require a cool, evenly-moist location and will not tolerate drought. Does best in a shady rock garden or wall and growing in a half-and-half mixture of grit and compost. Choose a sheltered site away from drying winter winds. Not a good choice for regions with hot, humid summers. Often these are merely sold by flower colour, but several named forms may be readily acquired.

HT/SP   10–20 cm (4–8") / 15–30 cm (6–12")
SOIL     Best in an evenly moist mixture of grit and compost.
BLOOM April–June
USES   ⛰▲♛ Rock garden, Troughs

'Apple Blossom' Slightly wider, more succulent leaves than other mossy types. Flowers are soft appleblossom pink at first, ageing to ivory.
'Cloth of Gold' Forms a stunning small dome of golden-yellow foliage, with white flowers held on short stems.
Purple Carpet ['Purpurteppich'] A seed strain, featuring a range of flower shades from magenta-pink to reddish-purple.

### *cotyledon*    ZONE 3
### (Pyramidal Saxifrage)
Very wide, flat rosettes of leathery grey-green leaves. Tall, branching panicles of white flowers appear in early summer, best displayed when arching out from a wall or trough. Prefers acidic soil.

HT/SP   45–60 cm (18–24") / 15–20 cm (6–8")
SOIL     Prefers a moist, well-drained acidic soil.
BLOOM June
USES   ⛰ॐ﹤▲♛ Walls, Troughs

### *fortunei*    ZONE 6
### (Japanese Rockfoil)
These make nice little clumps of somewhat hairy, rounded leaves. There are hundreds of forms grown in Japan that are highly sought after by collectors. They prefer shaded woodland conditions and thrive in evenly moist soils. Taller sprays of tiny star-shaped white or pale pink flowers appear in late summer. Modern-day plant collectors have been bringing back the best of these to North America, and quantities are slowly becoming available. Those of us in cold-winter regions can try wintering these indoors in pots.

HT/SP   10–30 cm (4–12") / 15–30 cm (6–12")
SOIL     Prefers a rich moist, well-drained soil.
BLOOM August–October
USES   ⛰♛ Rock gardens, Woodland

Five Color ['Go Nishiki'] Rounded leaves with indented edges, appearing slightly maple shaped. The hairy foliage is brightly splashed with green, red, pink, cream and gold. Reported to have good slug resistance.
'Rubrifolia' Glossy, rounded leaves in a burnished bronzy-red shade. Gorgeous planted in front of Blue Corydalis.

### *paniculata*    ZONE 3
### (Encrusted Saxifrage)
Clusters of grey-green leathery rosettes form a neat tight mound, the leaf edges are trimmed with a curious silver deposit of lime. Short sprays of white starry flowers are produced in early summer. One of the easiest types to grow in sun or part shade, and much hardier than one might expect.

HT/SP   15–25 cm (6–10") / 25–30 cm (10–12")
SOIL     Average to moist well-drained soil.
BLOOM May–June
USES   ⛰ॐ﹤▲♛ Walls, Rock garden

### × *urbium*    ZONE 4
### (London Pride)
These generally have a vigorous habit, spreading into low evergreen mats of leathery rosettes. Short stems of airy pale pink flowers appear in late spring. They make excellent groundcover or edging plants for shady areas, even in the dense shade under evergreen trees or shrubs. Clumps may be easily divided in spring. The plain green form is common, but some delightful selections exist.

HT/SP   20–30 cm (8–12") / 15–30 cm (6–12")
SOIL     Average to moist, well-drained soil.
BLOOM May–June
USES   ⛰Ⲙᐱ▲♛ Edging, Rock garden

'Aureopunctata' (Golden London Pride) Leaves are heavily spotted with gold. A unique and reliable edging plant. I think this is one of the best little plants to tuck in odd corners here and there, like at the base of a wall or in gaps between flagstones.
HT     20–30 cm (8–12")

*primuloides* (Dwarf London Pride) A miniature variety, with small rosettes of green leaves. Nice in a shaded rock garden and perfect for troughs.
HT     10–15 cm (4–6")

## SCABIOSA ☼
### (Pincushion Flower, Scabious)
Best-known are the taller, old-fashioned *S. caucasica* selections, especially valued for cutting. These seem to perform best in regions with cool summers, but a number of others types have proven themselves more versatile in warm regions. Plants produce rounded button-like flowers in a range of soft pastel shades. Dead-heading will encourage continued blooming well into the fall. Foliage is grey green and somewhat lacy. All types are attractive to butterflies.

### *caucasica*    ZONE 2
### (Common Pincushion)
This is the most familiar species, which is surprising since the plants don't usually perform all that well if grown in regions with warm summers. The lacy flowers are large and excellent for cutting, produced in a range of shades from blue through to lavender, lilac-pink and white. Deadheading will encourage plants to continue producing buds, at least in cooler climates. These are easily lost in a border unless several plants are grouped together.

HT/SP   45–75 cm (18–30") / 30–45 cm (12–18")
SOIL     Average well-drained soil.
BLOOM June–October
USES   ॐ﹤♥♛ Borders

### *columbaria* selections    ZONE 4
### (Dwarf Pincushion Flower)
Small flowers are produced in large quantities and over an extremely long season, making these an excellent choice for borders or containers. Tolerance to heat and humidity is good, but plants also perform well in areas with harsh winters. All of the selections below give the best impact when planted in groups of five or more. I recommend dividing these every 2–3 years in spring, since plants are not generally long lived. Drought-tolerant once established.

Saxifraga cotyledon

Saxifraga fortunei 'Rubrifolia'

Saxifraga × urbium 'Aureopunctata'

Scabiosa caucasica

**SP** 30–45 cm (12–18")
**SOIL** Average to dry, well-drained soil.
**BLOOM** June–October
**USES** ⛰❀❮❤🦋 Massing, Edging, Borders

**'Butterfly Blue'** This is now the most popular *Scabiosa*, flowering virtually all season long with a copious display of small lavender-blue pincushions over mounding ferny grey-green leaves. Selected as the *Perennial Plant of the Year* for 2000.
**HT** 30–45 cm (12–18")

**var. ochroleuca** [*S. ochroleuca*] (Yellow Scabious) An unusual colour for this genus, with small round pincushions of soft primrose yellow. Flowers are held above the foliage on wiry stems, appearing over many weeks. A short-lived perennial, but will often self-seed. Beautiful in combination with the crimson *Knautia macedonica*.
**HT/SP** 60–80 cm (24–30") / 45–60 cm (18–24")

**'Pink Mist'** Soft lavender-pink flowers, originally found as a sport of 'Butterfly Blue'. Remove any stems that revert to blue, which happens fairly often.
**HT** 30–45 cm (12–18")

**japonica var. alpina** ZONE 4
[*S. alpina*]
(Dwarf Pincushion Flower)
A cute little summer-blooming species for the rock garden, flowering for months if regularly deadheaded. Forms a mound of grey-green foliage, topped with small soft lavender-blue pincushions. Somewhat similar to 'Butterfly Blue' Drought tolerant.
**HT/SP** 20–30 cm (8–12") / 20–30 cm (8–12")
**SOIL** Average to dry, well-drained soil.
**BLOOM** May–October
**USES** ❮⛰❤🦋❀ Edging, Rock garden

# SCROPHULARIA ☼◐
(Figwort)

**auriculata 'Variegata'** ZONE 5
[*S. aquatica* 'Variegata']
(Variegated Figwort)
A bold foliage perennial, valued for its handsome green and creamy-white variegated leaves. Plants remain evergreen in milder areas. This does best in rich, moist soils, especially at the waterside. Flowers are fairly insignificant and often trimmed off. Beautiful in mixed containers.
**HT/SP** 30–45 cm (12–18") / 30–60 cm (1–2')
**SOIL** Rich, moist to wet soil.
**BLOOM** June–July
**USES** ❤⚘ Borders, Waterside, Specimen

# SCUTELLARIA ☼
(Skullcap)

**alpina 'Arcobaleno'** ZONE 4
(Alpine Skullcap)
This is a little-known perennial that offers a pleasant splash of colour in the rock garden or at the edge of a sunny

border in early summer. Plants form a low mound of dark-green leaves, bearing chunky spikes of bicoloured flowers in many combinations of soft yellow, white, pink, rose or lavender-blue. This prefers a neutral to alkaline soil, or the addition of lime to acidic soils. Remove faded flowers to encourage more buds to form. Easily divided in spring or fall. Attractive to butterflies.
**HT/SP** 20–25 cm (8–10") / 25–30 cm (10–12")
**SOIL** Average to moist, well-drained soil.
**BLOOM** June–July
**USES** ⛰🦋 Edging, Rock garden

# SEDUM ☼◐
(Stonecrop)
Stonecrops are fleshy, succulent plants, suited to the sunny rock garden or border, although a number of types will also tolerate partial shade. These offer the gardener an extensive choice of foliage types with clusters of starry flowers in many shades. Low mat-forming varieties are good ground-covers for hot dry slopes and other difficult sites. Taller cultivars are superb in the late season border and the dried seed heads usually have good winter interest. Very attractive to butterflies.

**LOW-GROWING VARIETIES** ZONE 2
Most of these will form a thick mat, the stems rooting into the ground as they creep. Some types are evergreen, others die back to the ground in winter. Fast-spreading types (marked "vigorous and spreading") can easily smother out slow-growing alpines if planted side by side – on the other hand, they might be worth considering as a groundcover or lawn substitute over large areas. Choosing varieties carefully to match your landscaping requirements is key.

Most forms are easily propagated by breaking off non-flowering shoots about 5 cm (2") long and planting directly into the garden. Dividing in spring or early fall is also simple. Deciduous types (ones that drop their leaves in winter) will be more dense if the succulent stems are trimmed back in spring to about 3 cm (1") from the ground. This also removes the dead flower heads from the previous season. Extremely drought-tolerant.
**SOIL** Average to dry, well-drained soil.
**BLOOM** See individual descriptions.
**USES** ⛰Λ✿❤❀ Edging, Slopes, Walls

**acre 'Aureum'** (Golden Mossy Stonecrop) Forms a brilliant neon-yellow carpet in spring, later fading to soft green. Starry yellow clusters of flowers appear in June–July. Vigorous and spreading. Best to keep this out of the rock garden. Evergreen.
**HT/SP** 5–8 cm (2–3") / 30–60 cm (1–2')

**album 'Murale'** (Coral Carpet Stonecrop) A dense carpet of rounded green leaves, turning maroon in cold weather and bronze in the heat of summer. Light-pink flowers in June–July. Vigorous and spreading. Evergreen.
**HT/SP** 5–10 cm (2–4") / 30–60 cm (1–2')

**'Bertram Anderson'** An outstanding British selection. Low, slow-spreading clumps of deep burgundy-black leaves with bright purple-red flowers in July–August. Leaf colour is best in dry, sunny sites. The restrained habit makes it a good choice for the rock garden or in troughs. Deciduous.
**HT/SP** 10–15 cm (4–6") / 30–45 cm (12–18")

**cauticola 'Lidakense'** Forms a non-spreading clump of rounded blue-green leaves flushed with purple. Glistening pink star flowers appear August–October, clustered at the ends of each stem. Well-suited to growing in tubs or alpine trough gardens. A good candidate for any collection of fine alpine plants. Deciduous.
**HT/SP** 5–10 cm (2–4") / 20–30 cm (8–12")

**cyaneum** Rose Carpet [*S. ewersii* var. *homophyllum* 'Rosenteppich'] Makes a well-behaved clump of powdery blue-green leaves, with showy clusters of deep pink flowers in August–September. Deciduous.
**HT/SP** 10–15 cm (4–6") / 20–30 cm (8–12")

**ewersii** (Pink Stonecrop, Ewer's Stonecrop) Similar to Rose Carpet (listed above), forming a non-spreading mound of fleshy, rounded blue-green leaves. Bright rose-pink flowers in August–September. Superb for edging. Deciduous.
**HT/SP** 10–15 cm (4–6") / 15–30 cm (6–12")

*Scabiosa* 'Butterfly Blue'

*Scutellaria alpina* 'Arcobaleno'

*Sedum acre* 'Aureum'

*kamtschaticum* **(Russian Stonecrop)**
Low, spreading carpet of scalloped green leaves, bright-yellow starry flowers appear in June–July. One of the best for groundcover use or edging but not overly invasive. Tolerates both shade and moist soils. Deciduous.
HT/SP   10–15 cm (4–6″) / 30–60 cm (1–2′)

*kamtschaticum* **'Variegatum' (Variegated Russian Stonecrop)** This selection is more upright, forming a cushion or mound that is ideal for a border edging. The leaves are light green edged with creamy white, the flowers distinctive golden-orange in clusters on the ends of each stem. Non-invasive habit. Tolerates part shade. One of the best low selections for a wide variety of garden uses. Of all the variegated Stonecrops this is the one least inclined to revert back to green. Deciduous.
HT/SP   15–20 cm (6–8″) / 30–60 cm (1–2′)

*oreganum* **(Oregon Stonecrop)** The thick, shiny green leaves of this species have always reminded me of a tiny Jade plant, even turning the same red colour in full sun during the summer. Clusters of yellow flowers appear in June–July. Native to mountains along the Pacific coast, and well suited to summer-arid climates. Vigorous and spreading habit. Evergreen.
HT/SP   10–15 cm (4–6″) / 30–60 cm (1–2′)

*reflexum* [*S. rupestre*] **(Blue Spruce Stonecrop)** With a vigorous and spreading habit, this forms a thick mat with upright stems of bluish-green needle-shaped leaves. Showy clusters of yellow flowers appear June–August. Inclined to stay evergreen but benefits from a hard trim back in early spring. One of the best forms for groundcover use.

Sedum e. 'Rosenteppich'

Sedum k. 'Variegatum'

Sedum oreganum

Sedum sexangulare

Sedum 'Silver Moon'

Sedum spurium Red Form

HT/SP   15–20 cm (6–8″) / 30–60 cm (1–2′)

*sexangulare* **(Six-sided Stonecrop)** Tiny bright-green leaves spiral tightly on the stems. Clusters of yellow flowers are produced in summer. Good winter effect, developing a bronze tone. Vigorous and spreading. Evergreen.
HT/SP   8–10 cm (3–4″) / 30–60 cm (1–2′)

**'Silver Moon' (Silver Moon Stonecrop)** This hybrid forms a low, slow-spreading mat of powdery silver-blue leaves with clusters of bright-yellow starry flowers in June–July. The effect is similar to the Spoon-leaved Stonecrops listed below, and like them this also performs best in the Pacific Northwest. Wonderful in containers. Evergreen. Zone 5–9.
HT/SP   10–15 cm (4–6″) / 15–30 cm (6–12″)

*spathulifolium* **(Spoon-leaved Stonecrop)** The species itself is seldom seen, but two excellent selections are widely grown, especially so in the Pacific Northwest where these seem best adapted. They form slow-spreading rosettes of fleshy, rounded leaves, taking on bright red tones during hot, dry summer weather. Starry yellow flowers appear in July–August. Superb for edging, in the rock garden or well-drained containers and troughs. Excellent winter drainage is the key to success in colder regions. Evergreen. Zones 5–9. **'Cape Blanco'** ('Capa Blanca') has bright silvery-white leaves. **'Purpureum'** features unusual powdery purple-blue leaves. They look especially stunning together.
HT/SP   10–15 cm (4–6″) / 20–30 cm (8–12″)

*spurium* **(Dragon's Blood Stonecrop, Two-row Stonecrop)** One of the most popular low species, flowering in summer with very showy clusters of red, pink or white flowers. The foliage is thick and dense, in various shades from green to rich bronzy-red although usually fading during the summer heat. Tolerant of moisture and part shade. Deciduous in winter. **Red Form** has deep beet-red leaves in spring, clusters of ruby flowers. **'Roseum'** produces soft-pink blooms over a vigorous mat of green leaves. **'Summer Glory'** is similar, with flowers in a brighter pink shade. **'Tricolor'** has green leaves dappled with pink and creamy white, and soft-pink flowers. It has a tendency to revert to green, so be sure to remove any all-green stems.
HT/SP   10–15 cm (4–6″) / 30–60 cm (1–2′)

*ternatum* **'Larinem Park' ['Shale Barrens'] (Whorled Stonecrop)** An eastern US native with a distinct preference for shady areas with average to moist conditions. Plants make a low carpet of rounded light-green leaves, the

clusters of white flowers always appearing before any of the other Stonecrops, in May–June. A terrific groundcover for the bright woodland garden, even tolerating dry shade. Evergreen.
HT/SP   10–15 cm (4–6″) / 30–60 cm (1–2′)

**'Vera Jameson'** Extremely popular as an edging plant. Produces rich mahogany-purple foliage on lax stems that usually splay out to form a somewhat floppy mound, weighted down by the heads of dusky-pink flowers. Blooms July–September. I have killed 'Vera Jameson' in my own garden where she just didn't have the perfect winter drainage she demands. Best in a rock garden or raised bed. Plants may grow less floppy if the soil is on the lean and dry side. Deciduous.
HT/SP   15–20 cm (6–8″) / 30–45 cm (12–18″)

**TALLER VARIETIES**          ZONE 2
More upright in habit, these are all late-blooming perennials that provide outstanding fall colour with their large clusters of flowers. Suitable for mass planting, especially around shrubs or taller ornamental grasses. For the most part they prefer average moisture conditions but will tolerate periods of drought, perhaps growing shorter as a result.

Most are excellent for cutting, but if you can resist doing so the reward will be seed-heads that remain sturdy and attractive for most of the winter. In rich soils these sometimes have a tendency to flop over from the weight of the flowers – pinching the tips in June is a simple way to prevent flopping later in the fall. All the tall forms will die back to the ground in winter. Remove the dead tops in late winter or early spring before new growth begins. Attractive to butterflies.
**SOIL**   Average well-drained soil.
**BLOOM** August–October
**USES**   ✂🦋🐝❀ Borders, Massing

*alboroseum* **'Mediovariegatum'** [*S. spectabile* **'Mediovariegatum'**] **(Variegated Autumn Stonecrop)** Similar to 'Brilliant' in stature, the large powdery-green leaves have a creamy-yellow blotch in the centre. Flowers are greenish-white with a flush of pink but I think of this mainly as a foliage plant for the border edge. Best with afternoon shade. Any all-green shoots should be rogued out before they take over. Blooms August–September.
HT/SP   40–50 cm (16–20″) / 30–45 cm (12–18″)

**Autumn Joy ['Herbstfreude'] (Autumn Joy Stonecrop)** Broccoli-like buds open into massive heads of dusty-pink flowers, gradually ageing to bronzy-red seed heads. Long considered to be one of the top ten best perennials, thriving in a wide range of climates. Generally long-lived and trouble free.

HT/SP  30–60 cm (1–2') / 45–60 cm (18–24")

**'Danmark'** (Autumn Stonecrop) Waxy bright-green foliage is topped with clusters of deep-red flowers held on fairly tall stems. Especially good for cutting.

HT/SP  45–60 cm (18–24") / 45–60 cm (18–24")

**'Frosty Morn'** [*S. alboroseum* **'Frosty Morn'**] (Variegated Autumn Stonecrop) A variegated selection, brought back from Japan a number of years ago. The apple-green leaves are strongly edged in creamy white. Heads of soft-pink flowers are an added attraction. This is inclined to flop badly unless pinched in June. It sometimes reverts back to plain green, especially in hot summer areas.

HT/SP  60–70 cm (24–28") / 45–60 cm (18–24")

**'Green Expectations'** (Autumn Stonecrop) Heads of flowers are in an interesting greenish-yellow shade. Foliage is the usual waxy grey-green.

HT/SP  45–60 cm (18–24") / 45–60 cm (18–24")

**'Lynda Windsor'** (Purple Autumn Stonecrop) New British variety with deep purple-black foliage and clusters of ruby-red flowers that contrast magnificently. Sturdy and compact habit.

HT/SP  30–40 cm (12–16") / 30–45 cm (12–18")

**'Northgo'** (Autumn Stonecrop) Foliage is more greyish in tone, somewhat like 'Matrona', with tall stems of soft-pink flowers.

HT/SP  45–60 cm (18–24") / 45–60 cm (18–24")

**'Purple Emperor'** (Purple Autumn Stonecrop) A brand-new introduction that holds great promise. Foliage is rich dark purple-black, with contrasting heads of dusty-pink flowers. The habit is compact and branching – not floppy. I would choose this over 'Vera Jameson' any day!

HT/SP  30–40 cm (12–16") / 45–60 cm (18–24")

*spectabile* **'Brilliant'** (Showy Stonecrop) Fairly similar in appearance to 'Autumn Joy' but with flowers of a glowing deep mauve-pink, later turning to rusty red. Keep these two away from each other as they clash terribly!

HT/SP  45–60 cm (18–24") / 45–60 cm (18–24")

*spectabile* **'Neon'** (Showy Stonecrop) A sport of 'Brilliant' with even brighter rosy magenta-pink heads. It certainly glows.

HT/SP  45–60 cm (18–24") / 45–60 cm (18–24")

*spectabile* **'Stardust'** (White Showy Stonecrop) I always think this selection is a refreshing change from pink. Large, glistening flower heads begin snow-white, ageing to soft pink then finally brownish seed heads. Foliage is powdery green.

HT/SP  45–60 cm (18–24") / 45–60 cm (18–24")

*telephium* **'Matrona'** (Autumn Stonecrop) A fairly new introduction from Germany, with a compact and tidy habit. The leaves are frosty grey-green in colour, often with a hairline of pink along the edges. Branching beet-red stems bear mid-sized clusters of green buds, changing to soft-pink flowers. Superb in containers or near the front of the border. Much superior to the older but similar introduction 'Morchen'.

HT/SP  40–50 cm (16–20") / 45–60 cm (18–24")

*telephium* subsp. *ruprechtii* (Autumn Stonecrop) Large, fleshy blue-grey leaves are flushed with purple and edged with pink. Flowers range from creamy-yellow to soft pink. The habit is a bit lax, best put to advantage spilling out of containers or over a wall.

HT/SP  30–40 cm (12–16") / 45–60 cm (18–24")

# SEMPERVIVUM ☼◐
## (Hen-and-Chicks, Hens-and-Chickens)

Well-known succulents, with evergreen rosettes of leaves surrounded by smaller rosettes known as "chicks". These are useful for edging borders, in rock gardens, walls, or container gardens. Tolerant of a wide variety of soils, even pure sand, their main requirement is good drainage. Starry flowers rise up on short stems in summer. In Europe these are often seen growing in the gravel on rooftop gardens.

Propagation could not be easier – simply remove the chicks by tugging on them, and plant them wherever you want to start a new colony. The chicks will form their own roots in a few weeks. If you're only familiar with the old green form, it may come as a surprise to know that there are hundreds of named selections of *Sempervivum*. Collecting them can be fun, and a large number can be easily squeezed into the limited space of even a balcony or deck!

**Species and hybrids**  ZONE 1

Serious collectors of named varieties usually end up dealing with specialist mail-order nurseries, but by keeping your eyes open at garden centres a surprisingly large number of types may easily be gathered together. Rosettes vary a lot in size, ranging in colour from green to blue, red, grey, and purple, sometimes also delightfully multicoloured. Flowers can also vary from pink through to cream or red. Dark-leaved forms show their best colour in the colder months, often fading out to powdery green in the summer heat.

HT/SP  10–20 cm (4–8") / 15–30 cm (6–12")
SOIL  Average to dry, well-drained soil.
BLOOM June–August
USES  △ ⋀ ⋏ ▲ ♥ ▨ ⬚ Edging, Troughs, Walls

*arachnoideum* (Cobweb Hen-and-Chicks) Fine silvery hairs join together the leaf tips, delicate and intricate like a tiny spider's web. Flowers are usually pink. A terrific novelty plant for children's gardens!

HT  5–10 cm (2–4")

*tectorum* Big rosettes, the frosty green leaves sometimes tipped with red during winter and spring. Flowers are cherry pink. This is the old-fashioned form so often encountered.

**'More Honey'** Large rosettes of somewhat hairy apple-green leaves, tipped with orange-red in the colder months.

**'Oddity'** Each frosty-green leaf is curled into a tube, becoming tipped with bronze-red during winter. Totally bizarre – this always reminds me of a rolled tongue. Seems to be a slow grower. Fairly small rosettes.

**'Purple Beauty'** Medium-sized rosettes of rich purple-red turn green in summer.

**'Sanford's Hybrid'** Very large rosettes with gorgeous mahogany-red tones in winter and spring.

**'Silverine'** Frosty grey-green leaves are flushed with red towards the base. Deep pink flowers.

**'Thayne'** Rosettes of powdery blue-green leaves, tipped with maroon in spring.

# SENECIO ◐●
## (Groundsel)

*aureus*  ZONE 3
[*Packera aurea*]
(Golden Groundsel, Squaw-weed)
A wildflower native to eastern North America. Plants form a clump of fresh

Sedum 'Frosty Morn'

Sedum telephium 'Matrona'

Sedum spectabile 'Brilliant'

Sempervivum Hybrids

Sempervivum arachnoideum

green leaves, coming up first thing in spring. Purple buds appear fairly soon after, bursting into clusters of bright-yellow star flowers. This will form a nice ground cover in damp shady areas, combining well with Hostas or ferns. Not difficult to naturalize, especially in wet areas along streams or ponds where plants will self seed. This is fairly new to gardens but promises to be a useful perennial for adding spring colour to shady areas.

**HT/SP** 20–40 cm (8–16") / 30–45 cm (12–18")
**SOIL** Prefers a rich, moist woodland soil.
**BLOOM** April–May
**USES** ✂◿ Woodland, Edging

## SIDALCEA ☀☼
**(Prairie Mallow, Checker Mallow)**

**Hybrids** ZONE 4
These produce elegant long spikes of satiny pink flowers, like small single Hollyhocks. Clumps are upright and narrow, with long stems that are excellent for cutting. Cut back after blooming to encourage a second flush. Best in cool-summer regions. These dislike lime soils. There are several colour selections.

**SP** 30–45 cm (12–18")
**SOIL** Rich well-drained soil, preferably acidic.
**BLOOM** June–August
**USES** ✂♥🦋➤ Borders

**'Brilliant'** Spikes of glowing rose-pink flowers.

**HT** 60–75 cm (24–30")

**'Little Princess'** A new compact selection. Good repeat-blooming habit, with spikes of soft-pink flowers. Shows good promise as an edging plant or in containers.

**HT** 40–50 cm (16–20")

**'Party Girl'** A seed strain, ranging in shades from soft-pink to deep magenta. **'Stark's'** Hybrids are very similar.

**HT** 60–90 cm (2–3')

## SILENE ☼
**(Campion, Catchfly)**
These have flowers similar to *Lychnis*, but the perennial species in cultivation are mostly low plants for rock gardens, walls or edging.

*compacta* ZONE 4
**[*S. orientalis*]**
**(Oriental Campion, Pink Catchfly)**
A little-known biennial, featuring clusters of bright magenta-pink flowers held on upright stems through the summer months. Stems are nice for cutting, the flowers fragrant. Regular cutting or dead-heading will keep plants in bloom for much longer. Allow a few heads to set seed to produce future generations. Seedlings are easily moved in spring or early fall. Attractive to butterflies.

**HT/SP** 60–75 cm (24–30") / 30–40 cm (12–16")
**SOIL** Average to moist, well-drained soil.
**BLOOM** June–August
**USES** ✂🦋 Borders

*mexicana* **'Hot Stuff'** ZONE 6
**(Mexican Catchfly)**
A recent introduction to the perennial garden, best suited to sunny sites with well-drained soil. Plants form a bushy mound of glossy green foliage, bearing clusters of star-shaped flowers in a bright magenta-pink shade. Remove faded flower heads for continued blooming into the summer. Excellent for cutting. May act as a short-lived perennial but will likely self seed. Nice in containers.

**HT/SP** 45–55 cm (18–22") / 25–30 cm (10–12")
**SOIL** Average well-drained soil.
**BLOOM** June–July
**USES** ✂♥ Borders

*schafta* ZONE 3
**(Autumn Catchfly)**
Starry magenta-pink flowers look a bit like Moss Phlox, appearing over a low tuft or mound of bright-green leaves. Especially good for late-season colour in the rock garden, when little else is in bloom. Also nice for edging. Performs best when grown in a gritty, well-drained soil. Drought tolerant once established. Not long lived, but self-sown seedlings sometimes appear.

**HT/SP** 10–15 cm (4–6") / 20–30 cm (8–12")
**SOIL** Prefers a very well-drained soil with plenty of grit.
**BLOOM** July–September
**USES** ◿♥🪴 Edging, Rock garden

*uniflora* ZONE 4
**[*S. maritima*]**
**(Sea Campion, Rock Campion)**
The species itself can occasionally be found, forming a tough low mound of

powdery grey-green leaves with small white flowers that look a bit like *Dianthus*. It does well in average border conditions but looks especially good in a rock garden or growing over the top of a wall. Drought tolerant. The two selections below are among the easiest and showiest of summer-blooming rock garden plants.

**HT/SP** 10–15 cm (4–6") / 30–45 cm (12–18")
**SOIL** Tolerates a wide range of soil conditions.
**BLOOM** June–August
**USES** ◿♥🪴 Edging, Walls

**'Druett's Variegated'** The almost fleshy powdery-green leaves are smartly edged in creamy white. Curiously ballooned white flowers are a bonus in summer, but this plant is a star for the foliage alone. Contrast this with bold-leaved plants, like Bergenia, or let it cascade out of containers. Inclined to revert to green.

**HT** 5–10 cm (2–4")

**'Swan Lake'** ['Robin Whitebreast']
Fluffy double white flowers are so full of petals they look like tiny ballerina tutus. Unfortunately these usually lie right on top of the foliage unless clumps are grown spilling over a wall or pot. Dead-heading should keep plants in flower for weeks. I love this plant – it's worth trying to find just the perfect spot to feature it in. Appears to be hardy to Zone 2.

## SISYRINCHIUM ☼☼
**(Blue-eyed Grass)**
Dwarf relatives of the *Iris*, forming low tufts of grassy leaves with clusters of small starry flowers. Plants will self-seed if the location suits them. Especially nice in the rock garden but also valuable for tucking into odd places, like at the base of a wall or corner of a flagstone patio. These appear to be hardier than is generally believed. Clumps are easily divided in spring or early fall.

*angustifolium* **'Lucerne'** ZONE 4
Native to the eastern part of the continent, this selection was discovered at a nursery in Switzerland. Flowers are bright blue with a golden-yellow eye, produced above a low tuft of iris-like leaves. Perhaps more tolerant of hot, humid summers than some of the others. Could well turn out to be hardy in Zones 2–3.

**HT/SP** 15–20 cm (6–8") / 15–20 cm (6–8")
**SOIL** Average to moist, well-drained soil.
**BLOOM** May–July
**USES** ◿♥ Rock garden, Waterside

**Hybrids** ZONE 5
A number of excellent named forms have appeared, expanding the range of colours and most especially the flower size. These make delightful rock garden

Sempervivum 'Purple Beauty'

Sidalcea 'Party Girl'

Silene mexicana 'Hot Stuff'

Silene uniflora 'Swan Lake'

or edging plants. Plan to divide plants every 3–4 years.

| | |
|---|---|
| **SP** | 15–20 cm (6–8") |
| **SOIL** | Average to moist well-drained soil. |
| **BLOOM** | May–July |
| **USES** | ▲⛲ Edging, Rock gardens |

**'Californian Skies'** Especially large blooms in a rich bright-blue shade. Long blooming season.

**HT**  15–20 cm (6–8")

**'Marion'** Good-sized lavender-purple flowers with darker streaks and a cheery yellow eye.

**HT**  10–15 cm (4–6")

**'Quaint and Queer'** A British introduction featuring big flowers (for a *Sisyrinchium*) in a strange mixture of yellow, mauve and brown. Taller habit than other forms. Hardiness is not yet fully known.

**HT**  20–30 cm (8–12")

### *idahoense* var. *bellum*    ZONE 4
### [*S. bellum*]
Native to the western USA, this sturdy species produces short stems of delicate violet-blue flowers in late spring. Neat clumps of grassy leaves are useful for edging. Will grow at the waterside. Fairly adaptable to soil conditions.

| | |
|---|---|
| **HT/SP** | 10–15 cm (4–6") / 15–20 cm (6–8") |
| **SOIL** | Average to moist, well-drained soil. |
| **BLOOM** | May–June |
| **USES** | ▲⛲ Rock garden, Waterside |

## SOLIDAGO ☀◐
(Goldenrod)

European breeders have been working to produce superior large-flowered forms for the commercial cut flower trade, and nowadays these hybrids may be found year round at every retail florist. Most of the garden forms are better-behaved than the wild roadside types, with less of a tendency to spread by roots or seed. In gardens their branching clusters of golden flowers combine well with the soft blues and purples of Asters in the fall border. Goldenrod does not cause hay fever but always takes the blame – the real culprit is Ragweed. Attractive to butterflies.

### *flexicaulis* 'Variegata'    ZONE 4
(Variegated Zigzag Goldenrod)
Zigzag Goldenrod is native over most of the eastern part of the continent. This selection has fairly large, pointy green leaves streaked with chartreuse and gold, particularly in early summer. Golden-yellow flowers are held in small clusters rather than the usual big mop heads. Frankly, I am tempted to cut the plant back in midsummer to rejuvenate the beautiful foliage effect and sacrifice the blooms. Consider trying this at the border edge or in containers.

| | |
|---|---|
| **HT/SP** | 45–60 cm (18–24") / 45–60 cm (18–24") |
| **SOIL** | Prefers a rich, moist soil. |
| **BLOOM** | July–September |
| **USES** | ✂⛲❀ Borders, Edging |

### Hybrids    ZONE 2
The hybrids have been selected over the years by breeders in Europe, most notably in Germany and England. As a group these are very useful to the late summer and autumn border scheme, forming wide leafy clumps that are full of colour for several weeks. They don't always lack the invasive tendencies of our native species, so keep a watchful eye on the plants and don't be afraid to thin the clumps down in size every couple of years. Deadhead after flowering to prevent self seeding. Powdery mildew is sometimes a problem, usually a sign that plants are under drought stress. All are excellent for cutting. Many different selections exist.

| | |
|---|---|
| **SP** | 45–60 cm (18–24") |
| **SOIL** | Average to moist well-drained soil. |
| **BLOOM** | August–October |
| **USES** | ✂❀ Borders, Massing, Meadows |

**Golden Baby ['Goldkind']** Medium-tall in habit, with large mop-shaped heads of golden-yellow flowers.

**HT**  60–70 cm (24–28")

### *rugosa* 'Fireworks'    ZONE 4
A clumping variety selected in North Carolina, proving itself to be among the best of the bunch. The flowers are like exploding heads of golden yellow, clever enough to fool your friends into not even recognizing it as Goldenrod. Plants have good strong stems and an upright habit. The commercial area of my tiny village has a street planting featuring this variety surrounded by *Sedum* 'Autumn Joy' – each autumn, they make a truly magnificent show together.

| | |
|---|---|
| **HT/SP** | 90–120 cm (3–4') / 60–75 cm (24–30") |
| **SOIL** | Average to moist, well-drained soil. |
| **BLOOM** | August–October |
| **USES** | ✂❀⛲ Massing, Borders |

### *sphacelata* 'Golden Fleece'    ZONE 4
(Heart-leaf Goldenrod)
Unusual heart-shaped leaves form a low clump early in the season, later bearing branching wands of golden flowers. The effect is very different from the usual roadside mop-headed forms. Especially effective when massed as a groundcover around ornamental grasses. Introduced a number of years ago by the Mt. Cuba Center in Delaware.

| | |
|---|---|
| **HT/SP** | 45–60 cm (18–24") / 45–60 cm (18–24") |
| **SOIL** | Average to moist, well-drained soil. |
| **BLOOM** | August–October |
| **USES** | ✂∿❀⛲ Massing, Borders |

### *virgaurea* 'Praecox'    ZONE 2
(Early Goldenrod)
Selected from a European native, this is usually the first Goldenrod to flower in summer. Plants form a bushy green mound with tall, strong stems of golden-yellow blooms. Excellent for cutting.

| | |
|---|---|
| **HT/SP** | 75–90 cm (30–36") / 45–60 cm (18–24") |
| **SOIL** | Average to moist, well-drained soil. |
| **BLOOM** | July–September |
| **USES** | ✂❀ Massing, Borders |

## × SOLIDASTER ☀◐
(Solidaster)

Interesting hybrids between *Aster* and *Solidago*. Useful in the late summer border but most especially as cut flowers. The effect is like soft-yellow Baby's Breath.

### *luteus*    ZONE 4
(Yellow Solidaster)
Starry yellow and pale cream flowers are arranged in airy sprays. Popular with florists, and sold year-round for cutting. Nice filler in the late summer border. May require staking. Dislikes drying out, and inclined to get powdery mildew if it does.

| | |
|---|---|
| **HT/SP** | 60–75 cm (24–30") / 45–60 cm (18–24") |
| **SOIL** | Average to moist well-drained soil. |
| **BLOOM** | July–October |
| **USES** | ✂❀⛲ Borders, Meadows |

**'Lemore'** Wide-branching panicles of soft primrose-yellow flowers. Late.

**HT**  60–75 cm (24–30")

## STACHYS ☀◐
(Lamb's-ears)

### *byzantina*    ZONE 3
### [*S. olympica*]
(Common Lamb's-ears)
An extremely popular edging plant, valued for its low spreading mat of woolly silver-grey leaves. Spikes of

*Sisyrinchium* 'Californian Skies'

*Sisyrinchium idahoense* var. *bellum*

*Solidago* Golden Baby

*Solidago rugosa* 'Fireworks'

pinkish flowers appear in early summer but are often clipped off to keep plants short and tidy – in fact, it's best to cut the whole plant back hard to 8 cm (3″) when the flower spikes appear. Gardeners in humid summer regions sometimes have problems with rotting during the summer months. Lamb's-ears are easily divided in spring or early fall. Evergreen in mild-winter regions. Fairly drought-tolerant once established.

**HT/SP** 30–45 cm (12–18″) / 30–60 cm (1–2′)
**SOIL** Average to dry, well-drained soil.
**BLOOM** June
**USES** 🔺 M• ♈♠🎋 Edging, Borders

**'Big Ears' ['Helene von Stein'] (Giant Lamb's-ears)** Foliage is easily twice the size of a regular Lamb's-ears and a little bit more on the green side of grey. With a strongly clumping habit and tendency to seldom flower, this is the best selection for low-maintenance landscape plantings. Mine always looks terrible by spring, so I cut it back to 5 cm (2″) stubs and it quickly gets fresh leaves. A really great combination I once saw was 'Big Ears' planted in front of *Phlox paniculata* 'Orange Perfection' in Marion Jarvie's garden in Thornhill, Ontario.

**HT/SP** 30–45 cm (12–18″) / 60–75 cm (24–30″)

**'Primrose Heron'** Felty leaves appear chartreuse-yellow in the spring, becoming light green later in the season. Needs a hard trim back at flowering time.

*macrantha*　　　　　　ZONE 2
[*S. grandiflora*]
**(Big Betony)**
Betony lacks the familiar woolly leaves of Lamb's-ears, forming a low clump of slightly crinkled fresh-green leaves. Showy violet to pink flowers are held on upright spikes, appearing in early summer. Plants appreciate a moist site

and look perfect beside a pond or stream. Easily divided in early spring. Plants will produce fresh foliage if cut back hard after blooming.

**HT/SP** 30–60 cm (1–2′) / 30–60 cm (1–2′)
**SOIL** Prefers a rich moist, well-drained soil.
**BLOOM** June–August
**USES** ✂♠🎋 Borders, Waterside

**'Rosea'** Bright spikes of rose-pink blooms.

*monieri* **'Hummelo'**　　　ZONE 4
**(Alpine Betony)**
Quite new to North American gardens, this rugged plant produces showy spikes of bright-purple blooms overtop a low mound of crispy green leaves. Deadheading regularly will encourage it to continue flowering for most of the summer. Short enough for edging but really most effective when mass planted in front of things like Daylilies or ornamental grasses. Selected by renowned designer Piet Oudolf at his nursery in Holland. Promises to be an outstanding new introduction.

**HT/SP** 45–50 cm (18–20″) / 45–60 cm (18–24″)
**SOIL** Average to moist, well-drained soil.
**BLOOM** June–August
**USES** ✂♠🎋 Borders

## STATICE see GONIOLIMON, LIMONIUM

## STOKESIA ☼
**(Stokes' Aster)**

*laevis*　　　　　　ZONE 5
A native North American wildflower. Flowers are lavender-blue, something like a double Shasta Daisy, beginning in midsummer and valuable for a long-season display. Plants exhibit good heat tolerance so they are widely used by designers in the southern USA. Excellent for cutting. Evergreen in mild-winter regions. Resents winter wet, so choose a well-drained soil or grow in a raised bed. A winter mulch is recommended in Zones 4–5. Several good selections have been introduced in recent years. Attractive to butterflies.

**HT/SP** 30–60 cm (1–2′) / 30–45 cm (12–18″)
**SOIL** Average to moist well-drained soil.
**BLOOM** July–September
**USES** ✂♠🦋🔺♠ Borders

**'Blue Danube'** Very large soft lavender-blue flowers. An older selection, but still reliable.
**'Klaus Jelitto'** Huge flowers of soft blue. Medium habit.
**'Mary Gregory'** Compact habit. A bit of a departure from the rest, with blooms of soft creamy-yellow.

**HT** 30–45 cm (12–18″)

**'Purple Parasols'** Blooms open soft-blue, soon changing to bright violet-purple.

**HT** 45–50 cm (18–20″)

## SYMPHYTUM ☼•
**(Comfrey)**
Rugged, indestructible perennials with the same tough constitution as the common herb varieties. These are grown for their attractive bold, hairy leaves that quickly form a clump in early spring. The short spikes of bell-shaped flowers look similar in appearance to *Pulmonaria*. Best in a moist, rich soil where they will spread steadily. If you've had bad experiences with the herb Comfrey – it gets huge, flops in summer, has a reputation for spreading – please consider trying some of these better-behaved ornamental forms.
**CAUTION: All are harmful if eaten.**

**HT/SP** 20–30 cm (8–12″) / 45–60 cm (18–24″)
**SOIL** Tolerates a wide range of soil conditions.
**BLOOM** May–July
**USES** M• Borders, Massing

*ibericum*　　　　　　ZONE 4
[*S. grandiflorum*]
**(Yellow-flowered Comfrey)**
A low-growing species, with clusters of pale creamy-yellow flowers in late spring. Often recommended as a good groundcover for dry shady areas. Foliage will rejuvenate if cut back hard in midsummer. Those who know this plant appreciate its workhorse abilities.

**HT/SP** 20–30 cm (8–12″) / 45–60 cm (18–24″)
**SOIL** Tolerates a wide range of soil conditions.
**BLOOM** May–July
**USES** M•♠🎋 Woodland, Massing

**'Goldsmith'**　　　　　ZONE 4
**(Dwarf Variegated Comfrey)**
Grab this plant when you see it! It gives wonderful textural effect in moist, shady areas, forming a low spreading clump of coarse light-green leaves, strongly dappled in creamy-yellow. Red buds change into soft-blue dangling bells. English garden writer Beth Chatto did a wonderful combination of this plant mingling with *Lamium maculatum* 'White Nancy', colourful for the whole season long. I find 'Goldsmith' does not appreciate very dry shade.

**HT/SP** 15–20 cm (6–8″) / 30–45 cm (12–18″)
**SOIL** Prefers a rich, moist soil.
**BLOOM** May–July
**USES** 🔺M•♠ Woodland, Massing

**'Rubrum'**　　　　　　ZONE 3
[*S. × rubrum*]
**(Red-flowered Comfrey)**
Clumps of dark-green foliage, with fairly showy clusters of dark red bells appearing in late spring. Excellent for massing as a groundcover among shrubs. Said to tolerate dry shade. Spreads to form a patch.

**HT/SP** 30–40 cm (12–16″) / 45–60 cm (18–24″)
**SOIL** Tolerates a wide range of soil conditions.
**BLOOM** May–July
**USES** ✂M•♠🎋 Woodland, Massing

Stachys monieri 'Hummelo'

Stachys byzantina 'Big Ears'

Stachys b. 'Primrose Heron'

Symphytum 'Goldsmith'

Stokesia laevis 'Klaus Jelitto'

***uplandicum* 'Axminster Gold'** ZONE 4
**(Variegated Russian Comfrey)**
For the daring gardener this makes a
bold and spectacular clump of huge
dark-green leaves, strongly edged in
bright creamy yellow. Clusters of pale
pink and blue bell-flowers are identical
to the herbal comfrey. This must have a
rich, fertile soil with plenty of moisture.
Appreciates part shade or protection
from afternoon sun. If this monster gets
shabby in midsummer just cut it back
to the ground to force fresh new leaves.
Well suited to waterside plantings.
**HT/SP** 75–90 cm (30–36") / 75–90 cm (30–36")
**SOIL** Prefers a rich, moist soil.
**BLOOM** June–July
**USES** ✂☙ Specimen, Waterside

# TANACETUM ☼
**(Tansy)**
Some plants formerly included under
*Chrysanthemum* have now been
moved here. These are all sturdy
summer-blooming daisies, and very
hardy. Most are excellent for cutting. Attractive to butterflies.

***coccineum*** ZONE 2
**[*Chrysanthemum coccineum*]**
**(Painted Daisy)**
Old-fashioned cut flowers with large
red, pink or white daisies on wiry
stems, appearing in early summer.
Plants form a clump of ferny green
leaves. Deadhead regularly to encour-
age continued blooming. Short-lived
unless divided every couple of years.
Although named selections exist in
Europe, the forms grown here are
mostly seed strains, but still excellent.
These combine beautifully with Siberian
Iris, Catmints and anything else with
blue or violet flowers.
**HT/SP** 45–75 cm (18–30") / 30–45 cm (12–18")
**SOIL** Average well-drained soil.
**BLOOM** June–July
**USES** ✂☙🦋 Borders

**Double Mixture** This strain produces a
high percentage of double and semi-
double flowers in a mixture of colours.
**'James Kelway'** Deep vermilion-red
single flowers with a yellow eye.
**'Robinson's Pink'** Bright rose-pink
single petals surround a yellow centre.
**Robinson's Single Hybrids** Mixture of
colours, large single daisies.

***niveum* 'Jackpot'** ZONE 3
**(Snow Daisy)**
Quite new to North American gardens,
and getting rave reviews from all over.
Plants form a mound of finely-cut
silvery-grey foliage, loaded with small
white, yellow-eyed daisies for months
on end. Combines beautifully in the
border with nearly anything else, and is
especially useful in containers. Although not a long-lived perennial, this

will often self sow. Drought tolerant
once established.
**HT/SP** 30–45 cm (12–18") / 30–60 cm (1–2')
**SOIL** Average to dry, well-drained soil.
**BLOOM** June–October
**USES** △☙✂☙🦋 Borders

***parthenium*** ZONE 3
**[*Chrysanthemum parthenium*]**
**(Feverfew, Matricaria)**
Branching sprays of small daisies
appear for many weeks, almost like
little button mums. Flowers are excellent for cutting. Foliage is bushy and
aromatic. Plants will stay nice and
compact if pinched back by half in May
or June. These are short-lived perennials but readily self-seed and can then be
moved to where you want them while
the seedlings are small. Use a winter
mulch in Zones 3–5. There are several
selections. This is often included in the
herb garden, the leaves used to make
natural pharmaceuticals.
**SP** 25–30 cm (10–12")
**SOIL** Average to moist, well-drained soil.
**BLOOM** July–October
**USES** ✂☙🦋 Borders, Containers

**'Aureum' ['Golden Moss'] (Golden**
**Feverfew)** Beautiful chartreuse-yellow
foliage, setting off single white flowers
with a yellow eye. Gardeners who grow
this plant value it highly for filling in
gaps anywhere in the border, and most
especially for edging.
**HT** 30–45 cm (12–18")

**Double White** Pure white double
button flowers. A taller form, the best
for cutting.
**HT** 30–60 cm (1–2')

**'Golden Ball'** Golden-yellow double
button flowers. Compact habit.
**HT** 30–45 cm (12–18")

**'White Stars'** Dwarf, bushy habit. Loads
of yellow-eyed white daisies.
**HT** 20–30 cm (8–12")

# TEUCRIUM ☼◐
**(Germander)**
Interesting foliage plants, well-suited to
formal edging or mass planting. Their
short spikes of mint-like flowers have a
delicate effect.

***chamaedrys*** ZONE 4
**(Creeping Germander,**
**Wall Germander)**
An evergreen, mounding plant that is
often used for edging borders or herb
gardens. Shiny green leaves form a
bushy mound, spreading to form a
small patch. Short spikes of rosy-purple
flowers appear in late summer. Evergreen in mild-winter regions, although
plants stay bushier if pruned back to
10 cm (4") in the spring. A winter
mulch is recommended in Zones 4–5.

Reported to be attractive to cats.
Drought-tolerant once established.
**HT/SP** 25–30 cm (10–12") / 30–45 cm (12–18")
**SOIL** Tolerates a wide range of soil conditions.
**BLOOM** July–August
**USES** △◭⌒☙✂☙🦋 Edging, Rock garden

**'Nanum'** Nice compact habit, the
perfect size for edging purposes.
**HT** 15–20 cm (6–8")

**'Summer Sunshine' (Golden German-**
**der)** Discovered a few years ago by Jack
Broxholme of Cavendish Perennials in
Burlington, Ontario. This is a gorgeous
sport of 'Nanum', the leaves on each
stem tip are bright butter-yellow in
spring, later fading to chartreuse for the
rest of the season. This colour really
sets off the pink flower spikes in a
unique way. A versatile plant for sun or
part shade.
**HT** 15–20 cm (6–8")

# THALICTRUM ◐
**(Meadow-rue)**
Beautiful woodland perennials from
various parts of the world, all of these
have lacy foliage similar to a Columbine
or Maidenhair Fern. The loose cloud-
like sprays of flowers are useful for
cutting. Although these are usually tall,
their see-through appearance means
they can be moved up toward the front
of a border. All appreciate a cool woodland setting, although some will tolerate
full sun if they have plenty of moisture.
Plants may be increased by division in
the spring, although some forms have
rather woody roots that resent being
disturbed and will take a season to
settle back in place. The hardiness
zones below are fairly conservative, and
many should prove to winter fine in
Zones 2–3.

*Symphytum* 'Rubrum'

*Tanacetum coccineum* Single Mixture

*Tanacetum niveum* 'Jackpot'

*Tanacetum parthenium* 'Aureum'

***aquilegiifolium***     ZONE 3
**(Columbine Meadow-rue)**
Very delicate mauve flowers are held in
a large, open spray. Plants form an
upright clump of ferny heat-tolerant
foliage. Fairly compact, early blooming.
**HT/SP** 60–90 cm (2–3′) / 45–60 cm (18–24″)
**SOIL** Prefers a rich, moist soil.
**BLOOM** May–July
**USES** ✄◁✿ Borders, Woodland gardens

***delavayi* 'Hewitt's Double'**     ZONE 3
**(Double Meadow-rue)**
Large airy clouds of double mauve
flowers, similar to Baby's Breath.
Foliage is very lacy and fern-like. This
variety gets fairly tall and usually re-
quires staking. Plants increase slowly
and are often difficult to obtain. Excel-
lent for cutting, fresh or dried.
**HT/SP** 120–150 cm (4–5′) / 45–60 cm (18–24″)
**SOIL** Prefers a rich, moist soil.
**BLOOM** June–August
**USES** ✄ Borders, Woodland gardens

***filamentosum***
**'Heronswood Form'**     ZONE 5
**(White Meadow-rue)**
A new compact selection, featuring
sprays of pristine white flowers that con-
tinue to bloom for weeks on end. Foliage
is lacy and green. This promises to be a
plant of great versatility, for edging, con-
tainers or in the woodland garden.
**HT/SP** 25–30 cm (10–12″) / 30–45 cm (12–18″)
**SOIL** Prefers a rich, moist soil.
**BLOOM** June–August
**USES** ✄◁✿ Edging, Woodland gardens

***kiusianum***     ZONE 4
**(Dwarf Korean Meadow-rue)**
This is a delightful miniature type,
perfect for edging or sprinkling through
a moist woodland area. Sprays of lilac-
mauve flowers appear for weeks during
the summer. Seems to have a prefer-

ence for dappled shade. Also delightful
in trough gardens or mixed containers.
**HT/SP** 10–15 cm (4–6″) / 30–40 cm (12–16″)
**SOIL** Prefers a rich, moist soil.
**BLOOM** June–August
**USES** ◁✿ Edging, Woodland gardens

***lucidum***     ZONE 5
**(Shiny Meadow-rue)**
Exceptionally beautiful foliage, ferny in
texture with a glossy dark-green finish.
Clouds of ivory to creamy-yellow
flowers appear on tall stems in early
summer. Both the flowers and foliage
are superb for cutting.
**HT/SP** 90–150 cm (3–5′) / 45–60 cm (18–24″)
**SOIL** Prefers a rich, moist soil.
**BLOOM** June–July
**USES** ✄◁ Borders, Woodland gardens

***rochebruneanum***     ZONE 4
**(Lavender Mist Meadow-rue)**
Big sprays of lavender-mauve flowers
are held on tall dark-purple stems.
Foliage forms an elegant low mound.
Some claim this to be the best taller
species for average garden conditions,
with strong self-supporting stems.
**HT/SP** 150–180 cm (5–6′) / 45–60 cm (18–24″)
**SOIL** Prefers a rich, moist soil.
**BLOOM** July–August
**USES** ✄ Borders, Woodland gardens

# THYMUS ☼
**(Thyme)**
Bushy or mat-forming herbs with small
aromatic leaves and short spikes of
flowers. Upright forms are good for
massing or using as a low hedge. Creeping varieties make an attractive groundcover or lawn substitute for small areas,
even tolerating light traffic. All prefer a
sunny warm site with excellent drainage.
Bushy forms benefit from a light clipping after flowering, to maintain a
compact habit and encourage new
wood. All are drought-tolerant once established. The small flower heads are attractive to bees and butterflies.

Creeping or mat-forming types are
easily divided by ripping apart the patch
into small pieces, in spring or early fall.
This is the best way to get a lot of tiny
plants for establishing between flagstones or in the crevices of walls. Bushy
forms generally grow from a single stem
or two and therefore can't be divided.
Sometimes branches that lie along the
ground will layer themselves with new
roots, and can then be removed from
the mother plant. Commercial propagation is usually by cuttings taken in
spring before plants bloom.

Taxonomically, these continue to be
in a state of flux – ongoing DNA analysis
at Kew Gardens is gradually unveiling
the true species identities of selections
which have long been known and
grown with less-than-correct names.

Like most gardeners, my patience with
this kind of botanical correctness
reaches a limit at some stage. I care
more about whether a particular plant
is a *good one* for my garden, regardless
of its name!

**'Broad-leaf English'**     ZONE 5
Forms a low, mounding bush of dark
green leaves, with clusters of soft laven-
der-mauve flowers in summer. Excellent
flavour, one of the best for cooking.
Clip lightly after blooming to maintain
bushiness. Possibly a selection of
*T. vulgaris* or *T. pulegioides*.
**HT/SP** 15–20 cm (6–8″) / 20–30 cm (8–12″)
**SOIL** Average to dry, well-drained soil.
**BLOOM** June–July
**USES** ◁✿▲🦋✿ Edging, Rock garden

**× *citriodorus***     ZONE 4
**(Lemon Thyme)**
A complex group of hybrids, most
having extremely fragrant lemon-
scented leaves. The habit, foliage colour
and hardiness vary considerably
between the named cultivars. The
upright, bushy-growing varieties are
among the best cooking herbs but also
have terrific ornamental value.
**SOIL** Average to dry, well-drained soil.
**BLOOM** June–August
**USES** ◁⋀•▲🦋✿ Edging, Herb gardens,
Walls

**'Gold Edge' (Golden Lemon Thyme)** Delightful strong lemon fragrance. Green
and yellow variegated foliage on an
upright spreading bush. Soft-pink
flowers appear in summer. Widely
grown under this name in North
America, but it is likely invalid.
**HT/SP** 25–30 cm (10–12″) / 30–45 cm (12–18″)

**'Silver Queen' (Silver Thyme)** A bushy,
mounding variety. Leaves are light
green, variegated on the edges with
silvery white. An attractive ornamental,
and one of the best for cooking. Foliage
has an elusive lemon fragrance. Lilac-
pink flowers. More tender than 'Gold
Edge'. Zones 6–9.
**HT/SP** 25–30 cm (10–12″) / 30–45 cm (12–18″)

**'Doone Valley'**     ZONE 4
**(Hybrid Creeping Thyme)**
Fairly low creeping type, the dark-green
foliage is tipped with bright gold from
fall through spring, fading to all-green
in the summer. A good display of
magenta-pink flowers. Pleasant lemon
fragrance. A versatile plant with year-
round interest.
**HT/SP** 5–10 cm (2–4″) / 30–60 cm (1–2′)
**SOIL** Average to dry, well-drained soil.
**BLOOM** July–August
**USES** ◁⋀•▲🦋✿ Edging, Walls

*Thalictrum delavayi* 'Hewitt's Double'

*Thalictrum kiusianum*

*Thymus serpyllum*

**'Hartington Silver'** ZONE 4
**['Highland Cream']**
**(Variegated Creeping Thyme)**
Recently arrived from Britain, this is a very low, ground-hugging selection. The tiny green leaves are brightly splashed with creamy white. Has clusters of soft shell-pink flowers. Growth is slow and tight, making this a great choice for between flagstones or in alpine troughs.
HT/SP  2–5 cm (1–2") / 20–30 cm (8–12")
SOIL  Average to dry, well-drained soil.
BLOOM June–July
USES  △◯◟▲☀❦ Edging, Troughs

*leucotrichus* ZONE 4
**(Moonlight Thyme)**
A delightful variety, forming a semi-upright bushy mound of grey-green foliage, with masses of soft-pink flowers in early summer. Foliage taste and fragrance is sharp and spicy. For rock gardens or edging.
HT/SP  10–20 cm (4–8") / 30–45 cm (12–18")
SOIL  Average to dry, well-drained soil.
BLOOM June–July
USES  △▲☀❦ Edging, Rock garden

*praecox* ZONE 2
**[*T. serpyllum*]**
**(Creeping Thyme, Mother-of-Thyme)**
Very flat mats of tiny leaves, smothered with flowers in summer. Excellent between paving stones and in rock gardens. There are many selections, all of them forming a very dense, evergreen carpet. As a group these are extremely popular for groundcover purposes. Plants thrive in hot, sunny sites with good drainage.

British botanists are now leaning towards grouping most of these selections under *T. serpyllum*, which is what we all used to call them in the first place! I plan to see what happens over the next few years before hopping on that train. Don't say I didn't warn you.
HT/SP  2–5 cm (1–2") / 30–45 cm (12–18")
SOIL  Average to dry, well-drained soil.
BLOOM June–July
USES  △◯◟▲☀❦ Edging, Walls

**'Albiflorus' (White Moss Thyme)** A very flat mat of light-green leaves with clear white flowers. Slower to establish than the pink or purple forms but unforgettable when in bloom.
**'Coccineus' (Red Creeping Thyme)** Deep magenta-red flowers smother the carpet of tiny dark-green leaves.
**'Elfin'** An extremely compact selection best suited to the rock garden or alpine trough. Low buns of tiny grey-green leaves bear soft-pink flowers in summer. Not a fast spreader.
**Nutmeg-scented (Nutmeg Thyme)** Nutmeg-scented green leaves, smothered by mauve-pink flowers in summer.

A strong grower, ideal as a drought-tolerant lawn substitute.
**'Pink Chintz'** Fuzzy dark-green leaves looks a bit like Woolly Thyme. Flowers are in a unique shade of soft salmon-pink. Good vigorous habit.
**'Purple Carpet'** Similar habit to 'Coccineus' in size and habit, with flowers of bright mauve-purple. A chance seedling discovered and introduced by Heritage Perennials.

*pseudolanuginosus* ZONE 2
**(Woolly Thyme)**
Fuzzy olive to grey-green foliage, with sparse soft-pink flowers in summer. Perhaps the best form for groundcover use, with a dense and fast-spreading habit. That being said, gardeners in regions with hot, humid summers struggle to grow this, as the fuzzy leaves can hold moisture and easily rot. Avoid using overhead irrigation.
HT/SP  2–5 cm (1–2") / 30–60 cm (1–2')
SOIL  Average to dry, well-drained soil.
BLOOM June–July
USES  △◯◟▲☀❦ Groundcover, Edging

*pulegioides* ZONE 2
**[*T. serpyllum*]**
**(Mother-of-Thyme)**
For years this species has been grown from seed and commonly offered in North America as *T. serpyllum*. It is a vigorous grower, forming a mat of bright green leaves with showy clusters of rose-purple flowers. This is a rugged and hardy plant, most effective when mass planted as a lawn substitute, although just a wee bit tall to comfortably walk upon. I'm glad to have finally figured out this puzzle – it always bothered me that these plants looked so different from common selections like 'Coccineus'.
HT/SP  15–20 cm (6–8") / 30–60 cm (1–2')
SOIL  Average to dry, well-drained soil.
BLOOM June–July
USES  △◯◟▲☀❦ Massing, Edging

**'Bertram Anderson' ['E.B. Anderson']**
One of the best carpeting forms, light green in summer but showy during the cooler months when the foliage changes to bright gold with red tips. Mauve flowers are somewhat shy to appear. Mild lemon fragrance. Zones 4–9.
HT/SP  5–7 cm (2–3") / 20–30 cm (8–12")

**Creeping Lemon** The true name is still a mystery, but this is an excellent lemon-scented form of Mother-of-Thyme. Foliage is medium green, with mauve flowers.
HT/SP  10–15 cm (4–6") / 30–60 cm (1–2')

**'Spicy Orange'** ZONE 4
**(Orange-scented Thyme)**
This unique Thyme has needle-shaped green leaves with a strong spicy-orange fragrance, smothered by pale-pink flowers in summer. Very good as a low

groundcover, particularly for planting between flagstones. Evergreen.
HT/SP  4–8 cm (2–3") / 25–30 cm (10–12")
SOIL  Average to dry, well-drained soil.
BLOOM June–July
USES  △◯◟▲☀❦ Edging, Groundcover

*vulgaris* ZONE 5
**(Common Thyme)**
Also called English Thyme or Cooking Thyme. This is the type most often grown in herb gardens and used for flavouring a wide variety of savoury foods. Plants form a low, bushy mound of narrow grey-green leaves. Clusters of pink flowers appear in summer. Nice spicy fragrance and flavour. Useful for edging or in the rock garden as a low shrub.
HT/SP  15–20 cm (6–8") / 30–60 cm (1–2')
SOIL  Average to dry, well-drained soil.
BLOOM June–July
USES  △▲☀❦ Edging, Herb gardens

# TIARELLA ❀●
**(Foamflower)**
Closely related to Coral Bells. Forms similar low clumps of leaves with airy sprays of light pink or white flowers in late spring or early summer. The species are woodland plants mostly native to North America, but several hybrid selections have been developed in recent years and some of these are now widely available. There are both spreading and non-spreading forms.

*cordifolia* ZONE 3
**(Creeping Foamflower, Allegheny Foamflower)**
This is a spreading species, best suited for groundcover use in the shady border or woodland. Forms a low clump of hairy green leaves, sending ground-hugging runners out in all directions that will take root and form new plants. Airy spikes of white or pale-

Thymus 'Doone Valley'
Thymus praecox 'Coccineus'
Thymus serpyllum 'Pink Chintz'
Thymus pseudolanuginosus
Thymus praecox 'Purple Carpet'
Thymus praecox 'Elfin'

pink flowers appear in late spring. Excellent bronzy winter colour. Combines nicely with ferns and other woodland plants. Evergreen.

**HT/SP** 15–30 cm (6–12″) / 45–60 cm (18–24″)
**SOIL** Prefers a rich moist, well-drained soil.
**BLOOM** May–July
**USES** ⛰︎〰︎▲🪴 Edging, Woodland gardens

**'Oakleaf'** Foliage is attractively lobed, somewhat like an oak leaf. Deep red winter colour. Spikes of flowers are a pleasing pale-pink shade. A non-spreading clump form, excellent for edging and rock gardens.

**HT/SP** 20–30 cm (8–12″) / 25–30 cm (10–12″)

**'Running Tapestry'** Heart-shaped green leaves with contrasting red veins, the clumps sending out runners in all directions. Short spikes of airy white flowers. Good bronzy winter colour. An excellent selection for using as a small groundcover.

**HT/SP** 20–30 cm (8–12″) / 45–60 cm (18–24″)

### Hybrids      ZONE 4

Breeders have been at work lately making all kinds of new Foamflower selections, some of them rivaling the best of the newer Coral Bells in garden worthiness. New leaf shapes and colours as well as larger and darker flower shades are now available. As a group, these require light shade and evenly moist soils without the competition of vigorous tree roots. The forms listed below all have a clumping habit unless otherwise noted.

**SOIL** Prefers a rich moist, well-drained soil.
**BLOOM** May–July
**USES** ⛰︎▲🪴 Edging, Woodland gardens

**'Cygnet'** Deeply-cut or skeletonized dark-green leaves, with contrasting black veins. Fragrant soft-pink spikes appear on fairly tall stems.

**HT/SP** 30–45 cm (12–18″) / 30–40 cm (12–16″)

**'Dark Eyes'** Maple-shaped leaves, dark green with a maroon-black blotch in the centre. Pink buds open to airy white spikes. Good bronze winter colour. Sometimes repeat flowers. Semi-running habit.

**HT/SP** 20–40 cm (8–16″) / 25–40 cm (10–16″)

**'Inkblot'** Pale pink flowers contrasting against rounded green leaves with an inky-black blotch in the centre. Compact.

**HT/SP** 25–40 cm (10–16″) / 25–30 cm (10–12″)

**'Mint Chocolate'** Leaves are long and maple-shaped, dark green with a spidery black pattern in the middle. Pale pink flower spikes. Good bronze tones in the winter months.

**HT/SP** 20–40 cm (8–16″) / 25–30 cm (10–12″)

**'Ninja'** Deeply indented light-green leaves, shaped a bit like a Ninja star with a purple-brown star pattern in the centre. Near-white flower spikes. Good bronzy-black winter colour.

**HT/SP** 20–40 cm (8–16″) / 25–30 cm (10–12″)

**'Skeleton Key'** Deeply indented or skeletonized dark-green leaves have a delicate appearance. Spikes of white flowers. Bronzy-purple winter tones.

**HT/SP** 20–40 cm (8–16″) / 25–30 cm (10–12″)

**'Spanish Cross'** A compact selection, the leaves are deeply indented with a purple-black star-shaped central pattern. Airy shell-pink flowers. Bronze winter colour.

**HT/SP** 20–25 cm (8–10″) / 25–30 cm (10–12″)

**'Spring Symphony'** One of the most striking selections to be introduced, with an exceptionally showy display of fragrant soft-pink flower spikes. The foliage is deeply cut, with purple-black veining in the centre. Nice compact habit. Tolerates summer heat and humidity. Rich bronze-purple winter colour.

**HT/SP** 20–25 cm (8–10″) / 25–30 cm (10–12″)

**'Tiger Stripe'** Glossy dark green leaves are striped and mottled in bronzy-purple. Short spikes of pale-pink flowers. Compact habit.

**HT/SP** 20–35 cm (8–12″) / 25–30 cm (10–12″)

### *wherryi*      ZONE 4
#### (Wherry's Foamflower)

Almost identical to *T. cordifolia* in general appearance, this species lacks the spreading runners so may be a better choice for edging purposes. Leaves are more or less rounded in outline, with slight indentations. Flowers are very soft pink.

**HT/SP** 15–30 cm (6–12″) / 25–30 cm (10–12″)
**SOIL** Prefers a rich moist, well-drained soil.
**BLOOM** May–July
**USES** ⛰︎▲🪴 Edging, Woodland gardens

**'Heronswood Mist'** Found at the famous Heronswood Nursery in Washington State. The foliage is attractively

speckled all over with light green, white and creamy yellow. Takes on a pink cast during the colder months. Spikes of white flowers are an added bonus, but this is primarily a foliage plant to be featured along the border edge. I have found this form to be a slow grower, in need of excellent drainage.

**HT/SP** 15–30 cm (6–12″) / 25–30 cm (10–12″)

**TOVARA see PERSICARIA**

### TRADESCANTIA ☀︎◑
#### (Spiderwort)

**× *andersoniana* Hybrids**    ZONE 3

These form upright, grassy-looking clumps with showy triangular flowers that open in succession over several weeks. In regions with cool summer nights these will sometimes continue to flower all summer long if regularly deadheaded. Plants benefit from a hard shearing back after flowering to tidy them up and to encourage repeat blooming in early fall. Best in a moist location to keep the foliage from scorching. There are several named cultivars in various jewel-toned shades of soft and deep blue, purple, pink, magenta and white. Attractive to butterflies.

**HT/SP** 30–60 cm (1–2′) / 45–60 cm (18–24″)
**SOIL** Average to moist well-drained soil.
**BLOOM** June–September
**USES** 🦋🐛 Borders, Waterside

**'Bilberry Ice'** An excellent newer selection, the flowers are lavender-blue, flushed with white towards the edges.

**HT** 40–50 cm (16–20″)

**'Blue and Gold' ['Sweet Kate']** This recent introduction has unique chartreuse-yellow foliage, a gorgeous contrast to flowers of glowing violet-blue. May need protection from afternoon sun. Consider this as an accent for the border edge or in mixed containers. Beautiful at the waterside.

**HT** 45–55 cm (18–22″)

**'Caerulea Plena'** Ruffled double flowers, with deep violet-purple petals.

**HT** 40–50 cm (16–20″)

**'Concord Grape'** One of the best recent American selections. Frosted blue-green foliage, with masses of small electric-purple flowers. Fairly compact habit. Attractive both in and out of flower. Good repeat blooming habit. If I had to choose just one Spiderwort, this would be it.

**HT** 40–45 cm (16–18″)

**'Hawaiian Punch'** Small magenta-pink flowers over a clump of narrow grassy leaves.

**HT** 40–45 cm (16–18″)

*Tiarella cordifolia* 'Running Tapestry'

*Tiarella cordifolia*

*Tiarella wherryi* 'Heronswood Mist'

*Tradescantia* 'Blue and Gold'

**'In the Navy'** Small lavender-blue blossoms with a darker stripe on each petal. Narrow foliage, compact habit.

HT     30–40 cm (12–16")

**'Little Doll'** Small soft lavender-blue flowers, the petal edges flushed with white. A compact selection, useful for edging. Narrow foliage.

HT     30–45 cm (12–18")

**'Navajo Princess'** Pearly-white flowers are flushed with soft blue towards the centre.

HT     40–45 cm (16–18")

**'Osprey'** Large white flowers with contrasting violet-blue stamens.

HT     45–60 cm (18–24")

**'Purple Profusion'** Compact mound of narrow leaves, loads of small deep royal-purple flowers.

HT     30–45 cm (12–18")

**'Red Grape'** Small flowers in an unusual dusky wine-red shade, compact mound of narrow frosted grey-green leaves.

HT     30–45 cm (12–18")

**'True Blue'** Small electric-blue flowers, narrow compact foliage.

HT     40–50 cm (16–20")

## TRICYRTIS ☽•
### (Toad-lily)

These are strange plants, the starfish-shaped flowers often bizarrely spotted to such a degree they look like something from another planet. I love them because they are among the last perennials to flower, giving me something to look forward to in late fall when other gardeners have already called it quits for the season. Toad-lilies are shade lovers, and often form substantial clumps with relatively little attention needed. Planting them in a frontal position is wise, since the flowers are subtle and easily lost among other tall plants. Many of the newer selections also feature interesting foliage that looks attractive for months on end.

   Most types tolerate average soil, even dry shade, but will form an impressive mound if given rich, moist conditions. Gardeners in short-season areas often find the plants get cut down by frost before they have a chance to flower. Some of the earlier flowering forms might be more reliable in colder regions. Dividing clumps (in spring) every 3–4 years will keep the plants vigorous and showy.

HT/SP     60–90 cm (2–3') / 45–60 cm (18–24")
SOIL     Prefers a rich, moist soil.
BLOOM September–November
USES     ✂⊿△🏺 Woodland gardens, Borders

*formosana*     ZONE 4
[*T. stolonifera*]
(Formosa Toad-lily)

Quite similar in appearance to the Japanese Toad Lily, although the various selections often bloom a bit earlier and might be better choices for short-season regions. Plants are nice spreaders but not at all invasive. Botanists keep bouncing the various selections back and forth between this species and *T. hirta*, but many of them may in fact be hybrids. Whatever you call them, they enjoy the same moist woodland conditions and provide similar attractive star-shaped flowers, usually marked with purple or burgundy spots.

**'Dark Beauty'** A late-flowering selection. Soft-mauve petals are heavily spotted in bright purple, with a yellow eye. Mid-sized habit.

HT     70–80 cm (28–32")

**'Samurai'** A rather compact form from Japan, features green leaves neatly edged in golden yellow. Flowers are medium purple with darker spotting. An ideal size for edging or in the shady rock garden. Said to be a little less hardy. Zones 5–9.

HT     40–50 cm (16–20")

**'Seiryu'** ['Hatatogisa'] This made the rounds for years under the name 'Hatatogisa', which turned out to simply be the common name for Toad-lily in Japanese. Flowers are pale blue, nearly turquoise at the tips, with a white centre and violet spotting. Mid-sized.

HT     50–60 cm (20–24")

*hirta*     ZONE 4
(Japanese Toad-lily)

Arching stems produce a succession of white star-shaped flowers, usually heavily spotted with dark purple. Foliage is medium green and lush in appearance, the leaf base clasping around the stem. Plants gradually spread underground to form a broad clump, but new growth can make a late spring appearance. Several selections have become available in the last few years.

**'Albomarginata'** Flowers are white with purple spots. Foliage is dark-green, the leaves edged in creamy white. Not a vigorous grower, but plants will slowly form a nice sized mound. Protect from afternoon sun.

### Hybrids     ZONE 4

Many of the selected forms appear to be hybrids between various species. These vary a fair bit in flower and foliage colour and size as well as blooming season.

**'Lightning Strike'** My favourite variegated selection, the green leaves are heavily streaked all over with golden yellow, rather than just along the edges. In summer the gold fades to more of a chartreuse green. Flowers are very soft mauve with light purple spotting. Compact habit.

HT     50–60 cm (20–24")

**'Tojen'** ['Togen'] Spot-free lavender-purple edged flowers with a white centre. One of the earliest and showiest forms in bloom. Foliage is especially large.

HT     60–90 cm (2–3')

## TRIFOLIUM ☀☽
### (Clover)

Clover is most familiar as a hay crop or lawn weed, but there are a few ornamental types that are occasionally grown in gardens.

*repens*     ZONE 4
(Dutch Clover)

These are ornamental selections of the same clover that grows in the lawn. Although plants can spread beyond where intended, they make a handsome edging or groundcover in moist, sunny areas. White flowers appear in late spring, but the leaves are the real ornamental feature. A hard shearing back at blooming time will keep plants attractive the whole season. Grow these in pots or planters if you're afraid they might become invasive. Easily divided in spring or early fall. Evergreen in mild winter regions. Likely hardy to Zones 2–3.

HT/SP     10–12 cm (4–5") / 30–45 cm (12–18")
SOIL     Average to moist well-drained soil.
BLOOM June
USES     ⋏⊿▲🏺 Edging

**'Dragon's Blood'** Leaves are variegated with green and creamy-white, splashed with a bright blood-red marking. This is a recently introduced form with a very showy appearance.

*Tradescantia* 'Concord Grape'

*Tricyrtis hirta*

*Tricyrtis* 'Tojen'

**'Pentaphyllum'** (Black-leaved Clover)
Dark purple to near-black leaves, narrowly edged in green. A fair number of lucky 4-leaved clovers always seem to appear. This is a deep, rich colour that works especially well for edging around gold or yellow-leaved perennials.

# TRILLIUM ☼•
## (Trillium)
Trilliums need almost no introduction. They are among our most treasured native woodland wildflowers. As urban properties become more shady, gardeners often go on a quest for things like trilliums, imagining them to be an easy solution to the problems of dry shade. The truth is, however, that for every ten trilliums purchased, perhaps one actually lives more than a year or two and thrives in the inhospitable conditions provided in the average home garden – dry shade and unimproved heavy clay soil.

Of even more concern is the fact that, even today, a large number of the trilliums sold in garden centres and nurseries have been dug from native populations – ripped from the wild and stuck into pots, then sold quickly before the plants become dormant in summer. Needless to say, this whole process throws the plants into a state of shock, the main cause of high mortality in new plantings.

My advice is to be a smart consumer. Insist on knowing if the wildflowers you purchased were wild dug or not. The key phrase is **'nursery propagated'**, not just 'nursery grown.' If the retail store cannot guarantee plants to be nursery propagated, then please refrain from buying them. Re-

moving the pot is an easy way to get a sense of the history – a nursery propagated plant should have plenty of roots right out to the sides and bottom of the pot. If you see few roots, then beware.

Trilliums take from 3–5 years or more to reach flowering size from seed. If Trilliums are being offered for about the same price as other plants in similar sized containers, be suspicious. A few good specialty mail-order nurseries offer nursery-propagated Trilliums, including some of the more unusual Asian species.

### *grandiflorum*                    ZONE 2
### (Great White Trillium, Showy Trillium)
Native over a large area of eastern North America, and probably the most familiar species. This is the provincial flower of Ontario. Flowers are among the largest, with wide-open white petals and a set of three slightly smaller leaves just below. Foliage is green, usually disappearing entirely by mid summer and especially so if the soil becomes dry. Division is possible, best done in late summer or early fall when plants are completely dormant.

HT/SP  20–50 cm (8–20") / 30–45 cm (12–18")
SOIL   Prefers a rich moist, well-drained soil.
BLOOM March–May
USES   △ Woodland, Shady rock gardens

## TRITOMA see KNIPHOFIA

# TROLLIUS ☼ ◐
## (Globeflower)
Some people call these buttercups – a name better reserved for *Ranunculus*, but really rather fitting here as well. Flowers are rounded in shape, often with many rows of petals in shades of bright golden yellow to orange. Foliage is lush and green, forming a low clump at the base. These are easy plants for the early summer border. Clumps are easily divided in early fall or spring.

### *chinensis* 'Golden Queen'    ZONE 2
### (Chinese Globeflower)
Medium to tall in habit, with semi-double golden-yellow petals and a contrasting tuft of orange stamens. Blooms a bit later than the hybrid types.

HT/SP  75–90 cm (30–36") / 45–60 cm (18–24")
SOIL   Average to moist well-drained soil.
BLOOM May–June
USES   ✄ Borders, Meadow gardens

### × *cultorum* Hybrids           ZONE 2
Large round buttercup flowers rise above leafy clumps of deeply lobed foliage in late spring. The showy flowers are sometimes used for cutting, although they last only a few days. Many named selections exist, all are in shades of yellow to orange, including some gorgeous pale forms. Clumps can be

sheared back in summer if they get tired looking.

HT/SP  60–90 cm (2–3') / 45–60 cm (18–24")
SOIL   Average to moist well-drained soil.
BLOOM May–June
USES   ✄ Borders, Meadow gardens

**'Cheddar'** Semi-double flowers are in a lovely soft primrose-yellow shade, a colour that blends better in the border than some of the deeper-toned forms.
HT     65–70 cm (24–30")

**'Cressida'** Semi-double flowers, a slightly creamier shade than 'Cheddar'. A good substitute for the selection **'Alabaster'**, which is similar but difficult to obtain. 'Cressida' always makes me chuckle – it's a clever pun on the Shakespeare play *Troilus and Cressida*.
HT     65–70 cm (24–30")

**'Glory of Leiden'** A compact habit, with large chrome-yellow flowers.
HT     50–60 cm (20–24")

**'Lemon Queen'** Double flowers of bright lemon-peel yellow. Fairly compact habit.
HT     55–60 cm (22–24")

**'Orange Crest'** Soft orange petals with contrasting deep orange stamens in the middle. Compact habit.
HT     55–60 cm (22–24")

**'Orange Princess'** Tall stems of double flowers in a glowing golden-orange tone.
HT     75–90 cm (30–36")

### *pumilus*                        ZONE 3
### (Dwarf Globeflower)
A rock garden or edging species, forming a low mound of shiny green leaves. Flowers are small single buttercups of bright yellow. Said to repeat bloom in regions with cool summers.

HT/SP  20–30 cm (8–12") / 25–30 cm (10–12")
SOIL   Average to moist well-drained soil.
BLOOM May–June
USES   △▼ Rock gardens, Edging

### *yunnanensis*                    ZONE 4
### (Yunnan Globeflower)
Said to be the largest flowered *Trollius*. Has glistening yellow buttercups on branching stems, held well above the low foliage mound.

HT/SP  40–50 cm (16–20") / 25–30 cm (10–12")
SOIL   Average to moist well-drained soil.
BLOOM May–June
USES   ✄ Borders

## TUNICA see PETRORHAGIA

# VANCOUVERIA ☼•
## (Vancouveria)

### *hexandra*                       ZONE 4
### (American Barrenwort, Insideout Flower)
Closely related to the true Barrenwort (*Epimedium*) this is a species native from the Pacific Northwest down into

*Trifolium repens* 'Pentaphyllum'

*Trollius* × *cultorum* 'Alabaster'

*Trollius pumilus*

*Trollius yunnanensis*

California. Plants form a low mound of fine-textured evergreen leaves, bearing airy sprays of white flowers above in late spring. The habit is clumping at first, but these will slowly spread to form a small patch. Although often recommended for dry shade conditions, these truly are happiest in a rich, moist woodland soil on the acidic side. Occasionally mass planted as a groundcover, but being generally in short supply these are more often used for edging or in the shady rock garden.

**HT/SP** 20–25 cm (8–10") / 25–30 cm (10–12")
**SOIL** Prefers a rich moist, well-drained soil.
**BLOOM** May–June
**USES** 🔺〽🏺🌲 Woodland, Shady rock gardens

# VERBASCUM ☼
## (Mullein)

Related to the common roadside Mullein, the garden forms are interesting and showy plants for sunny borders. All have upright spikes of flowers and leaves arranged in a low flat rosette, with upright candelabra-like spikes of showy flowers. They are superb cut flowers for those with a daring sense of design. Plants are generally biennial or short-lived perennials. Gardeners who have tried these dramatic plants would never be without them.

### *bombyciferum*                    ZONE 3
### (Giant Silver Mullein)

Silvery-white felted leaves form a large rosette the first year, sending up tall stately spires of yellow flowers the following summer. A spectacular specimen plant, usually treated as a biennial. The dramatic effect is best shown by surrounding plants with very low neighbours, featuring them as a focal point towards the border front. Will self-seed – all over the place, to be quite honest. Remove any unwanted seedlings or move them while small. Very drought tolerant and able to grow well on poor, dry soil.

**HT/SP** 150–180 cm (5–6') / 45–60 cm (18–24")
**SOIL** Average to dry, well-drained soil.
**BLOOM** June–August
**USES** ✂❮🏺 Specimen, Borders, Tubs

**'Banana Custard'** A selected seed strain, probably belonging to this species or at any rate quite similar in habit. Foliage is more on the green side, with spires of soft-yellow flowers.

### Hybrids                    ZONE 5

A terrific group of showy, long-blooming varieties suited to the sunny border. Branching spikes of flowers continue to bloom all summer if dead-headed regularly, producing plenty of new side shoots from the main stem. These generally are short-lived (2–3 years) and propagated by root cuttings. Sometimes careful removal of small "pups" found at the base in spring can be successful.

Foliage forms a low green rosette. There are several wonderful selections now readily available. Some gardeners in Zones 3–4 have reported good success with these.

**HT/SP** 60–90 cm (2–3') / 30–45 cm (12–18")
**SOIL** Average to dry, well-drained soil.
**BLOOM** June–August
**USES** ✂❮🏺 Specimen, Borders, Tubs

**'Helen Johnson'** One of the best forms, the soft coppery-orange flowers are flushed with cream, with contrasting violet stamens. Foliage is grey-green in colour. A true "designer" plant, always in high demand.

**HT** 75–90 cm (30–36")

**'Jackie'** A very compact form, the flowers are soft apricot yellow with a contrasting butterscotch eye. An ideal size for containers.

**HT** 40–45 cm (16–18")

**'Pink Petticoats'** Leaf rosette is silvery-green with a delightful felty texture. Good strong stems hold solid-looking spikes of glowing apricot-pink to salmon flowers, with delicately ruffled petals. The flowers remind me a bit of a *Diascia*. Plants behave fairly well as a perennial if faded spikes are removed to prevent seeding. You'll want to do this anyway to encourage repeat blooming.

**HT** 70–90 cm (30–36")

**'Raspberry Ripple'** Introduced just a couple of years ago, with gorgeous soft-pink blooms streaked in deeper raspberry red.

**HT** 75–90 cm (30–36")

**'Southern Charm'** One of the first hybrid seed strains, producing a range of soft pastel colours, including apricot, pink, cream and lavender. The leaves have a crinkly appearance. Should perpetuate fairly well by self seeding.

**HT** 60–90 cm (2–3')

**'Summer Sorbet'** Magenta-purple spikes, each flower has a dark-purple eye.

**HT** 60–75 cm (24–30")

### *phoeniceum*                    ZONE 4
### (Purple Mullein)

Although the plain species is purple, the modern strains produce a range of shades from white through to pink, rose, purple and magenta. Spikes are fairly tall and nice for cutting. Generally acts as a self-seeding biennial, although small sideshoots or "pups" at the base may be carefully removed in spring to start new plants.

**HT/SP** 60–120 cm (2–4') / 30–45 cm (12–18")
**SOIL** Average to dry, well-drained soil.
**BLOOM** May–July
**USES** ✂❮🏺 Borders

# VERBENA ☼
## (Verbena)

Most of the perennial species of Verbena are generally on the tender side and are often grown as long-flowering annuals. Excellent drainage in winter is a big factor in their survival.

### *bonariensis*                    ZONE 7
### (Brazilian Verbena, Tall Verbena)

Stiff, upright branching stems hold clusters of magenta-purple flowers from early summer through late fall. A large grouping makes an unforgettable display. Despite the height this gives an open and airy appearance, lending itself well to creating a very dramatic effect towards the border front. These don't take up much elbow room and are easily tucked in between other plants. Very heat tolerant. In many regions this is grown as a self-seeding annual. Powdery mildew can be a problem.

**HT/SP** 90–120 cm (3–4') / 30–60 cm (1–2')
**SOIL** Average to dry, well-drained soil.
**BLOOM** June–October
**USES** ✂❮🐝🦋🏺 Massing, Borders

### **'Homestead Purple'**                    ZONE 7
### (Trailing Verbena)

Found growing in an old garden in Georgia, this has quickly become the most popular Verbena across the continent. Plants form a low, trailing mound of small green leaves, producing clusters of rich purple flowers throughout the summer and fall. To survive the winter this requires excellent drainage and even then gardeners might find that new plants are more vigorous. However, it still has a perennial "look" about it and a loyal following. Both drought and heat tolerant, this does well in the border or rock garden but is especially useful as a trailing plant cascading from

*Verbascum* 'Jackie'

*Verbascum* 'Raspberry Ripple'

*Verbascum* 'Pink Petticoats'

tubs, hanging baskets or window boxes. Resistance to powdery mildew is good. Remove faded blooms every couple of weeks, or pinch plants to make them especially bushy.

**HT/SP** 15–20 cm (6–8") / 45–60 cm (18–24")
**SOIL** Average to dry, well-drained soil.
**BLOOM** June–October
**USES** ⬛M⬥☀🦋🎍 Massing, Walls, Edging

### *rigida*      ZONE 7
### (Rigid Verbena)

Widely grown in southern gardens, this species is extremely tolerant of heat and humidity. The effect is like a shorter version of *V. bonariensis*, with clusters of bright-purple flowers held on the ends of wiry stems. A frontal position in the border works well, or use this as an underplanting to something tall and bold, like a Canna lily. Plants will often self-seed in colder regions. Superb in containers. 'Polaris' is a dwarf selection with flowers of soft silver blue.

**HT/SP** 30–60 cm (1–2') / 30–45 cm (12–18")
**SOIL** Average to dry, well-drained soil.
**BLOOM** June–October
**USES** ✂☀🦋🎍 Massing, Walls, Edging

## VERNONIA ☀
### (Ironweed)

### *noveboracensis*      ZONE 4
### (New York Ironweed)

In a sunny moist site this plant will form a bold and impressive clump of dark green leaves, with masses of magenta-purple flowers in late summer and fall. The flower heads are sort of shaggy looking, always reminding me a bit of *Liatris*, but in clusters rather than a spike arrangement. This little-known eastern native is especially useful towards the back of large borders. Those with a passion for the dramatic sometimes plunk it right up front and

centre – "it" being the operative word; with a big plant like this you usually only need one! The new soft yellow *Helianthus* 'Lemon Queen' would make a beautiful companion. By the way, Ironweed is not weedy in the least.

**HT/SP** 180–210 cm (6–7') / 90–100 cm (36–40")
**SOIL** Prefers a rich, moist soil.
**BLOOM** August–October
**USES** ✂🦋 Borders, Meadows

## VERONICA ☀◑
### (Speedwell)

These are showy garden perennials, some with upright spikes of flowers, others form low mounds suitable for edging or the rock garden. Some of the best true-blue shades are to be found among the Speedwells. Taller types produce excellent cut flowers. Clumps may be easily divided in spring or early fall, something best done every 3–4 years. Powdery mildew can be troublesome, particularly in warm and humid regions.

### *allionii*      ZONE 2
### (French Alpine Speedwell)

An outstanding plant for edging, producing a display of chubby bright-blue spikes in early summer, flowering for longer in cool summer regions. Inclined to remain evergreen in mild winter areas. Well suited to the rock garden.

**HT/SP** 10–15 cm (4–6") / 20–30 cm (8–12")
**SOIL** Average well-drained soil.
**BLOOM** June–August
**USES** ⬛☀▲ Edging, Rock gardens

### *austriaca*      ZONE 2
### [*V. teucrium*]
### (Hungarian Speedwell, Austrian Speedwell)

Several selections exist, and these are popular for a splash of blue at the border edge in early summer. Sometimes the plants have a tendency to flop out in all directions, making a hard trim back after blooming necessary. The foliage grows back quickly to form a low, fresh-green mound.

**HT/SP** 15–20 cm (6–8") / 30–40 cm (12–16")
**SOIL** Average well-drained soil.
**BLOOM** May–July
**USES** ⬛☀ Edging, Borders

'**Ionian Skies**' A beautiful soft china-blue shade, especially good for contrasting with gold or yellow companions.
'**Shirley Blue**' Brilliant sky-blue flowers. Exceptionally showy.

### *filifolia*      ZONE 4
### (Fern-leaved Speedwell)

Quite unlike any of the other species, this is a little gem for the rock garden. Forms a low carpet of ferny green foliage set with small sky blue flowers in late spring. Not to be confused with

the lawn weed *V. filiformis*. Evergreen in mild winter regions.

**HT/SP** 5–10 cm (2–4") / 30–45 cm (12–18")
**SOIL** Average to moist, well-drained soil.
**BLOOM** May–June
**USES** ⬛M⬥☀ Walls, Edging

### *gentianoides*      ZONE 2
### (Broad-leaved Speedwell, Gentian Speedwell)

The foliage looks completely different from all the spike-forming types, with broad light-green leaves that first form a low rosette. Upright spikes of light powder-blue flowers rise taller in late spring. Trim the dead spikes off and the plants make an effective coarse edging for the border front. Evergreen in mild winter regions.

**HT/SP** 30–40 cm (12–16") / 30–45 cm (12–18")
**SOIL** Average to moist, well-drained soil.
**BLOOM** May–June
**USES** ✂☀▲ Edging, Borders

'**Barbara Sherwood**' Spikes of soft powder-blue flowers, each streaked with darker violet veins.
'**Variegata**' Leaves are streaked and edged in creamy white, with the typical powder-blue flowers. Good for season-long interest.

### *liwanensis*      ZONE 3
### (Turkish Speedwell)

A tough drought-resistant evergreen groundcover, this forms a flat green mat studded with small bright blue flowers in late spring. Its dense habit makes this an ideal lawn substitute, tolerating occasional walking. Foliage turns bronzy in extreme heat and sun. Plants may be clipped or mowed after flowering to maintain a dense habit. Terrific when underplanted with spring-flowering bulbs. Requires good drainage.

**HT/SP** 3–5 cm (1–2") / 30–45 cm (12–18")
**SOIL** Average to dry, well-drained soil.
**BLOOM** April–June
**USES** ⬛M⬥☀🎍 Groundcover, Lawn substitute

### *longifolia*      ZONE 3
### (Tall Speedwell, Long-leaf Speedwell)

This species produces the best stems for cutting, with long, fat spikes that often droop gracefully at the tips. Foliage is bright green and fairly coarse in texture. Plants generally need to be staked and look most effective in the middle to back of a sunny border.

**HT/SP** 90–100 cm (36–40") / 60–70 cm (24–28")
**SOIL** Average to moist, well-drained soil.
**BLOOM** June–August
**USES** ✂🦋 Borders, Massing

**Blue Giant** ['**Blauriesin**'] Long spikes of rich violet blue. Exceptionally good for cutting.
**White Giant** ['**Schneeriesin**'] Pure white spikes, a good counterpart to the blue form.

*Verbena* 'Homestead Purple'

*Verbena rigida*

*Vernonia noveboracensis*

*Veronica austriaca* 'Ionian Skies'

*montana* '**Corinne Tremaine**' ZONE 3
(**Variegated Mountain Speedwell**)
Stems are trailing and held nearly flat to
the ground, the light-green leaves
brightly edged in creamy white to soft
yellow. Small soft lilac-blue flowers
appear in late spring, but this is mainly a
bright foliage groundcover. Hangs nicely
over the edges of containers or baskets.
HT/SP  8–10 cm (3–4") / 30–60 cm (1–2')
SOIL  Average to moist, well-drained soil.
BLOOM May–June
USES  ⚠ Rock gardens

*peduncularis* '**Georgia Blue**' ZONE 4
(**Russian Speedwell**)
Introduced a few years ago from central
Asia, this remains my personal favourite
of the low, creeping Speedwells. The
small green leaves form a low mat,
studded with small flowers of the most
incredible sapphire-blue. The evergreen leaves turn bronzy during the
colder months and usually retain this
tone at blooming time. Mow plants
back hard right after flowering to keep
the patch dense and weedproof.
HT/SP  10–15 cm (4–6") / 45–60 cm (18–24")
SOIL  Average to moist, well-drained soil.
BLOOM April–May
USES  ⚠ Walls, Edging

*prostrata*                    ZONE 4
(**Creeping Speedwell**)
Another low mound or mat-forming
species, the foliage is usually olive
green in colour. Bright sky-blue flowers
appear on short spikes during late
spring and early summer. Showy in the
rock garden but also large enough for
edging. Clip back hard after blooming.
Several good selections exist.
HT/SP  10–15 cm (4–6") / 30–45 cm (12–18")
SOIL  Average to dry, well-drained soil.
BLOOM May–June
USES  ⚠ Rock gardens, Edging

'**Aztec Gold**' ['**Buttercup**'] A new gold-
leaved selection with better sun tolerance than 'Trehane'. Foliage is bright
buttery-gold, the leaves on the stem tips
a contrasting chartreuse shade, becoming all chartreuse if grown in the shade.
Flowers are bright blue to lavender.

**Blue Mirror** ['**Blauspiegel**'] Nice
compact German selection with flowers
of bright, clear blue.

'**Trehane**' Bright chartreuse-yellow
foliage is a terrific contrast to the spikes
of rich blue flowers. May prefer afternoon shade in warm regions.

*repens*                    ZONE 2
(**Creeping Speedwell**)
After years of being confused I've finally
realized that a number of different
plants masquerade under this name.
The true species forms a completely flat
carpet of tiny green leaves, studded with
little white flowers in late spring. Although sometimes recommended as a

groundcover, it is much better suited to
growing between paving stones or in
the rock garden. In warm, humid
regions the mat is inclined to die out in
places during the summer, so regular
renewal will be necessary. Hold back
on the fertilizer or your flagstones will
disappear! Evergreen.
HT/SP  1–2 cm (½–1") / 15–30 cm (6–12")
SOIL  Average well-drained soil.
BLOOM May–June
USES  ⚠ Rock gardens, Between
      flagstones

'**Sunshine**' Bright buttery-yellow leaves
are the main feature here. This looks
amazing when grown between dark-
coloured rocks. Also nice in alpine
troughs. Could this finally be the perfect
contrast plant to the black-leaved
Mondo Grass (*Ophiopogon*)?

*spicata*                    ZONE 2
(**Spike Speedwell**)
The most commonly grown species,
these form bushy border plants with
upright spikes of violet-blue flowers for
many weeks. Excellent for cutting. Many
selections of this species exist, in a
variety of colours and heights. I find that
moist soils are helpful in keeping down
powdery mildew infections. If plants do
succumb, just trim them back hard as
soon as flowering is over. Plants respond
fairly well to regular deadheading.
SP  30–45 cm (12–18")
SOIL  Average to moist, well-drained soil.
BLOOM June–August
USES  ✂ Borders, Massing

'**Giles van Hees**' A good compact selection with clear rose-pink flowers. Long
blooming season.
HT  15–20 cm (6–8")

'**Icicle**' Clear white spikes. Late blooming.
HT  45–50 cm (18–20")

subsp. *incana* [*V. incana*] (**Woolly
Speedwell**) Unique and valuable for its
silver-grey, slightly woolly foliage.
Spikes of violet-blue flowers contrast
beautifully. An excellent foliage plant for
edging or massing. Cut back hard after
blooming to keep clumps low and
bushy. This form grows especially well
on the Prairies.
HT  30–60 cm (1–2')

**Red Fox** ['**Rotfuchs**'] Spikes of bright
rose-pink flowers, fairly compact habit.
HT  30–40 cm (12–16")

'**Royal Candles**' An exceptionally good
new form. Loads of bright-blue flower
spikes over a compact and bushy
mound. One of the best for edging.
HT  20–30 cm (8–12")

'**Sunny Border Blue**'         ZONE 3
This long-blooming hybrid features
short, branching spikes of deep violet-
blue flowers all summer long. The

bright green foliage is unusually crin-
kled and remains fresh-looking
throughout the season, showing excel-
lent mildew resistance. Useful for
massing or edging. Selected as the
*Perennial Plant of the Year* for 1993.
HT/SP  30–45 cm (12–18") / 30 cm (1')
SOIL  Average to moist, well-drained soil.
BLOOM July–September
USES  ✂ Borders

'**Waterperry Blue**'          ZONE 4
(**Creeping Speedwell**)
An exceptionally long-blooming low
creeper, producing small soft-blue
flowers with a white eye. The glossy
green foliage forms a low mat, well
suited to the rock garden or trailing
over the edges of containers. The new
flush of spring leaves is sometimes
tinged with bronzy purple. Also useful
between flagstones. Evergreen in mild
winter regions.
HT/SP  3–5 cm (1–2") / 25–30 cm (10–12")
SOIL  Average to moist, well-drained soil.
BLOOM May–September
USES  ⚠ Edging, Rock gardens

*whitleyi*                    ZONE 3
(**Whitley's Speedwell**)
Another of my favourite indestructible
plants, this makes an outstanding low
mat suitable for edging or in the rock
garden. The tiny filigreed leaves are grey-
green in colour, becoming smothered by
tiny sapphire-blue flowers in spring. In
cool summer regions blooming sometimes continues well into the summer.
Whitley's Speedwell is quite tolerant of
hot, sunny sites. It could be considered
for planting between flagstones, especially in lean, gravelly soil. Evergreen.
HT/SP  5–10 cm (2–4") / 30–60 cm (1–2')
SOIL  Average to dry, well-drained soil.
BLOOM May–June
USES  ⚠ Edging, Walls

*Veronica peduncularis* '**Georgia Blue**'

*Veronica prostrata* **Blue Mirror**

*Veronica spicata* '**Royal Candles**'

*Veronica gentianoides* '**Barbara Sherwood**'

# VERONICASTRUM ☼
## (Culver's-root)

Very closely related to *Veronica*, and sometimes included with them. These are native North American wildflowers of great garden value. They prefer a sunny location with a rich, moist soil.

### *virginicum*                    ZONE 3
### [*Veronica virginica*]

Forming impressive large clumps, these differ from *Veronica* in that the leaves are whorled, arranged on the stem like the spokes of an umbrella. Flowers are held in long wands that arch gracefully, appearing for several weeks during late summer and fall. Excellent for cutting. Lots of moisture is needed for these to do their best. Flowers of the plain species vary in colour from pale pink to soft powder blue. Plants are often sold by colour. Several good new Dutch selections are now making their way here ('Apollo', 'Fascination', 'Temptation'). Grab whatever types you find available — you can't go wrong with any of them.

**HT/SP**  120–180 cm (4–6') / 90–100 cm (36–40")
**SOIL**  Prefers a rich, moist soil.
**BLOOM** August–September
**USES**  ✂ 🦋 Borders, Meadows

**'Lila Karina' ['Lilac Carina']** I admit to some confusion around this one. The cultivar name is often listed as a *Veronica longifolia* selection, although the plant displays the tell-tale whorled leaves that should place it firmly here. Whatever it ends up being correctly called, this produces flowers of a soft lavender-mauve shade, on a slightly more compact bush than the species.

**HT**  90–100 cm (36–40")

# VINCA ☼•
## (Periwinkle, Vinca)

### *minor*                    ZONE 3
### (Common Periwinkle, Creeping Myrtle)

Extremely popular as a groundcover, valued for forming a thick mat of glossy evergreen leaves, studded with periwinkle-blue flowers during the spring. Very shade tolerant, and in cool-summer regions it also usually puts up with full sun conditions. Periwinkle forms a good, reliable cover for large and small areas, filling in quickly. Plants may be clipped back or even mowed in late summer to help thicken them out. The non-flowering stems run along the ground in every direction, rooting as they go. Rooted plantlets may be easily moved in spring or fall to start a new patch. Many selections exist, apart from the usual blue-flowered green-leaved form.

**HT/SP**  10–15 cm (4–6") / 60–90 cm (2–3')
**SOIL**  Tolerates a wide range of soil conditions.
**BLOOM** March–May
**USES**  〰〰▲♥🐛 Massing, Woodland gardens

**'Alba'** Rich green leaves are studded with loads of white flowers.
**'Atropurpurea'** Deep violet-purple to wine-coloured flowers. A welcome change from the usual blue form.
**'Emily Joy'** Deep green foliage with a nice display of large white flowers. A recent introduction.
**'Illumination'** A brand new and amazing selection, featuring bright golden-yellow leaves boldly edged in dark green. This virtually glows in the dark! Bright blue flowers in spring contrast well against the foliage. By far the most vigorous of the many variegated forms of Periwinkle.
**'Sterling Silver'** Leaves are green with a good silvery-white edge. Bright blue flowers.
**'Variegata'** Medium-green leaves are narrowly edged in creamy white. A slower growing selection, best used in smaller areas. Flowers are blue.

# VIOLA ☼
## (Violet, Pansy)

This group includes the violets of woodlands and meadows as well as the small hardy garden pansies known as violas. All are of easy culture, preferring a cool partly shady location.

### *cornuta* Hybrids                    ZONE 4
### (Perennial Pansy, Winter Pansy, Horned Violet)

Like smaller-flowered versions of the big flashy annual pansies, these are generally much hardier, being more tolerant of both summer heat and winter cold. They are popular for winter bedding, and tuck in perfectly all over the garden. Excellent for massing with tulips and other spring bulbs, in containers or under shrubs. Plants will tolerate full sun during the cooler months.

There are several good older seed strains in shades of apricot, yellow, blue, purple, bronzy-red, cream and white. Recent breeding has created modern small-flowered strains in an astounding range of shades and bicolours. In addition there are vegetatively-produced selections, usually grown from cuttings.

Whatever the variety, Perennial Pansies certainly perform their best in mild winter regions with cool summers. There they act as short-lived perennials, surviving for sometimes 2–3 years before getting old and tired. In cool regions they will perform fine in full sun. Those of us in hotter climates need to cut the plants back hard in early summer. This should force low vegetative growth that survives until fall, when they once again start to flower. Another approach is to plant them in the fall, enjoy until late May then remove them and replace with annuals. A loose winter mulch of evergreen boughs is recommended in Zones 4–5.

**HT/SP**  10–20 cm (4–8") / 15–20 cm (6–8")
**SOIL**  Average to moist well-drained soil.
**BLOOM** March–October
**USES**  ▲•♥▲ Massing, Edging, Borders

**'Baby Franjo'** Tiny clear-yellow flowers, like a Johnny Jump-up. Plants are compact.
**HT**  10–12 cm (4–5")

**'Baby Lucia'** A counterpart to 'Baby Franjo', featuring tiny flowers of soft sky blue.
**HT**  10–12 cm (4–5")

**'Babyface' Series** A new group of selections with a compact habit. The bicoloured flowers are small, with cute little whiskered faces. Shades include soft blue, yellow, gold, red and white.
**HT**  10–15 cm (4–6")

**'Black Magic'** One of the darkest flowers in existence, petals are close to jet black with a charming yellow eye. This came to North America originally from Australia. Nobody seems certain whether or not it's identical to the British selection 'Molly Sanderson', but they are extremely similar. Must be propagated vegetatively.
**'Arkwright's Ruby'** Still an excellent older strain, with big flowers. Blooms are deep brick-red with maroon-black blotching and a contrasting yellow eye. The occasional flower has a yellow spot on the lower petal, almost like a lip stained with mustard.
**'Blue Perfection'** A large-flowered strain offering a range of light to

Veronica spicata incana

Veronica whitleyi

Veronicastrum virginicum 'Lilac Karina'

Vinca minor 'Illumination'

medium blue shades with a contrasting yellow eye.

**'Boughton Blue'** Charming soft powder-blue flowers with a yellow eye. Propagated vegetatively.

**'Chantreyland'** An older strain, but still offering an otherwise rare shade of glowing apricot-orange. Large blooms.

**'Columbine'** A real stunning form, the white flowers are strongly edged in dark purple, with a contrasting yellow eye. Propagated vegetatively.

**'Etain'** Creamy-white petals are edged in lavender purple, with a blotch of bright yellow. Propagated vegetatively.

**'Penny' Series** Quite compact and loaded with flowers, these cover a wide range of shades including blue, yellow, orange, pink, mauve, purple and white. Plants flower well during the winter months in mild regions.

HT       10–15 cm (4–6″)

**'Purple Showers'** Showy bright purple flowers with a yellow eye. Stems hold the blooms well above the foliage. Propagated vegetatively.

**'Rebecca'** White petals are heavily marbled and streaked with mauve and deep violet purple. Contrasting yellow eye. Propagated vegetatively.

**'White Perfection'** Large blooms are snow-white with a yellow eye, occasionally stained or flushed with icy blue.

### 'Dancing Geisha'          ZONE 5
### (Fanleaf Violet)
Like the variety below, this Japanese selection is mainly grown for its attractive foliage. Leaves are deeply indented like a maple, streaked with green, pewter and silvery white. Flowers are small, ranging from pale blue to white. Well behaved, not a rampant self seeder.

HT/SP   15–20 cm (6–8″) / 15–20 cm (6–8″)
SOIL      Prefers a rich moist, well-drained soil.
BLOOM April–May
USES      ▲ 🏺 Woodland gardens, Edging

### *grypoceras* var. *exilis*     ZONE 4
### [*V. koreana* 'Syletta']
### (Silver Korean Violet)
I don't even care if this plant blooms, because the rounded leaves are so heavily patterned in silver they nearly resemble an exotic cyclamen. Short stems of mauve purple flowers appear in spring as an added bonus. Superb for edging or in the shady rock garden. It would be truly amazing if this thing self seeded all over the place, but it only does so in a modest way. Watch for slugs. Evergreen in mild winter regions.

HT/SP   5–10 cm (2–4″) / 15–20 cm (6–8″)
SOIL      Prefers a rich moist, well-drained soil.
BLOOM April–June
USES      ▲ 🏺 ▲ Woodland gardens, Edging

### *labradorica*          ZONE 3
### [*V. riviniana* Purpurea Group]
### (Purple Labrador Violet)
A charming little rock garden violet, the low tufts of purple-tinged leaves produce loads of tiny mauve wild-violet type flowers. Blooms in spring and usually again in the autumn – or all season long in regions with cool summers. Likes a cool, moist spot and protection from hot afternoon sun. Plants will self seed but usually in moderation.

HT/SP   5–10 cm (2–4″) / 15–20 cm (6–8″)
SOIL      Prefers a rich moist, well-drained soil.
BLOOM April–June
USES      ▲ 🏺 Woodland gardens, Borders

### *obliqua*          ZONE 3
### [*V. cucullata*]
### (Blue Marsh Violet)
Lush clumps of heart-shaped leaves are excellent for massing in the shade garden, though they tolerate sun, if given enough moisture. Large classic violet flowers are held just above the leaves. Flowers have a very slight fragrance. A native to eastern North America, and very often incorrectly sold as *V. odorata* (the true fragrant Sweet Violet of England, which is rarely available in North America). There are a few colour selections. Whatever you do, keep this out of the rock garden because it self-seeds prolifically. Deciduous in winter.

HT/SP   10–15 cm (4–6″) / 15–30 cm (6–12″)
SOIL      Average to moist, well-drained soil.
BLOOM March–June
USES      〰️🏺 Woodland gardens, Borders

**'Royal Robe'** The most common form, with vibrant violet-blue flowers.

**'White Czar'** Cute little white flowers with a yellow eye.

### *pedata*          ZONE 3
### (Bird's-foot Violet)
Another of our native forms, growing in meadows of eastern North America. This species seems to appreciate a fair bit of sun as well as good drainage. The leaves are deeply divided, like the foot of a bird. Small violet-blue flowers appear in late spring. Tame enough for the rock garden or border edge.

HT/SP   10–15 cm (4–6″) / 15–20 cm (6–8″)
SOIL      Average well-drained soil.
BLOOM April–June
USES      ▲🏺 Rock gardens, Edging

### 'Sorbet' Series          ZONE 4
### (Perennial Pansy, Winter Pansy)
Quite new on the scene, these vigorous hardy pansy hybrids have some of the most amazing shades ever developed, with new combinations still coming out each year. The flowers are small and very charming, often showing tiny little whiskered faces. Treat these the same as the various Cornuta hybrids listed above.

HT/SP   10–15 cm (4–6″) / 15–20 cm (6–8″)
SOIL      Average to moist, well-drained soil.
BLOOM March–October
USES      ▲🏺▲ Massing, Edging, Borders

**'Antique Shades'** A return to the cat-faced patterns of a century ago, in a range of rich shades and bicolours.

**'Beaconsfield'** A charming soft blue and deep-violet combination.

**'Black Delight'** Velvety purple-black flowers. Much smaller than 'Black Magic'.

**'Blackberry Cream'** Bicoloured blooms of purple and creamy yellow.

**'Blue Heaven'** Rich, deep blue.

**'Blueberry Cream'** Soft blue and creamy-yellow bicolour.

**'Coconut'** Pure white flowers.

**'Coconut Swirl'** One of the most attractive, the flowers are creamy white with a picotee blue edging and blue whiskers.

**'French Vanilla'** Ivory white to very soft creamy yellow.

**'Lavender Ice'** Clear lavender blue with a white face and whiskers.

**'Lemon Chiffon'** A range of soft and bright yellow shades and bicolours.

**'Lemon Swirl'** Another truly amazing breakthrough. Flowers are soft yellow with a rich lavender-blue picotee edging.

**'Plum Velvet'** Rich, deep purple.

**'Purple Duet'** Deep purple and violet-blue bicolour.

**'Red Wing'** Bicoloured flowers of bright yellow and maroon red with old-fashioned whiskering.

**'Yellow Delight'** Clear, bright lemon yellow.

**'Yellow Frost'** Bright yellow and blue bicolour.

Viola 'Purple Showers'

Viola cornuta 'Etain'

Viola 'Columbine'

Viola Sorbet 'Blueberry Cream'

Viola labradorica

**'Yesterday, Today and Tomorrow'**
Flowers begin white, ageing first to soft blue and finishing out a rich lavender-blue shade. All three colours occur on the plant simultaneously.

***soraria***    ZONE 3
**(Woolly Blue Violet)**
Another species native to eastern North America. Very similar in habit and flowering to *V. obliqua*, for spring flowering and a carpet of heart-shaped leaves all season long. Prolific self-seeder. The selections below are more commonly offered. If you grow more than one variety, try to keep them in different parts of the garden so they don't interbreed.
HT/SP  15–20 cm (6–8″) / 15–30 cm (6–12″)
SOIL    Average to moist soil.
BLOOM April–June
USES    Woodland gardens, Borders

**'Freckles'** (Freckled Violet) Pearly white flowers, heavily spotted and freckled with china-blue. I find the seedlings vary a fair bit in the amount of spotting. Rogue out any that you don't like in order to try and maintain a good form in the garden.
**'Rubra'** A compact form with especially nice wine-red flowers.
HT    10–15 cm (4–6″)

***tricolor***    ZONE 2
**(Johnny Jump-up, Heartsease)**
Although usually treated as a bedding annual, Jump-ups will often overwinter or at least re-establish themselves by self-seeding. Their tiny pansy flowers appear from early spring through late fall, especially when the nights are cool. Keep these out of the alpine garden to prevent seedlings from taking over. In the border they have an interesting way of weaving themselves through other plants, almost with an inclination to

climb. A good hard trim to about 8 cm (3″) in June will force new bushy growth to develop at the base and help plants to survive the heat of the summer.
HT/SP  10–15 cm (4–6″) / 15–20 cm (6–8″)
SOIL    Average to moist soil.
BLOOM March–November
USES    Massing, Borders, Edging

**'Blue Elf'** ['King Henry'] Probably my favourite form. The flowers are rich violet blue with a tiny yellow eye.
**'Helen Mount'** The traditional form, with flowers in a striking combination of violet, yellow and mauve.
**'Twilight'** ['Cuty'] Bicoloured flowers of deep blue and soft cream.

## WALDSTEINIA ☾•
**(Barren Strawberry)**

***ternata***    ZONE 3
**(Siberian Barren Strawberry)**
Recently, in a survey of the most widely-used groundcover plants in Germany and the Netherlands, I was astonished to see this plant right up near the top of the list. Oddly enough, few know this little gem in North America, and seldom do you see it in a large planting. I think it still languishes in obscurity and will soon find a rightful spot in our gardens. Barren Strawberry makes a low, dense mat of shiny semi-evergreen leaves that somewhat resemble those of a strawberry. The carpet is punctuated by little bright-yellow flowers in the spring. The plants are tough, spreading by short stolons – but not in a scary way, so this may be safely used in both small and large areas. Tolerates summer drought. I'm trying it in dry shade under a Mock Orange, underplanted with tulips. I'll let you know the results.
HT/SP  10–15 cm (4–6″) / 30–45 cm (12–18″)
SOIL    Tolerates a wide range of soil conditions.
BLOOM April–May
USES    Massing, Edging

## ZANTEDESCHIA ☼◑
**(Calla Lily)**

***aethiopica***    ZONE 8
**(White Calla)**
The hardiest type of Calla, overwintering outdoors in the Pacific Northwest. In colder regions these may be grown in containers and easily stored indoors for the winter – just cut the plant back to 5 cm (2″) and stick the pot in the basement until March, watering once in a while so the soil doesn't dry out. They form good-sized clumps of broad, leathery leaves. Funnel-shaped white flowers have a rude yellow spadix in the centre and are produced on and off for the whole season. Reported to tolerate summer heat and humidity well.
**CAUTION: Harmful if eaten/skin and eye irritant.** Wear gloves when handling.
HT/SP  60–90 cm (2–3′) / 30–60 cm (1–2′)
SOIL    Prefers a rich moist, well-drained soil.
BLOOM June–October
USES    Specimen

**'Crowborough'** The most common hardy selection, with white blooms.

*Viola sororia* 'Freckles'
*Viola* Sorbet 'Purple Duet'
*Viola* 'Yesterday, Today & Tomorrow'
*Zantedeschia aethiopica* 'Crowborough'
*Waldsteinia ternata*

**FACING PAGE**

Perennials can be used together in endless combinations to suit your personal taste in both colour and texture. On the page opposite, the plants in the top row all fit into the "cool" range of tones, with violet, blue, rose and pink predominating. Cool tones are usually easy to combine, one of the main reasons these colours are so popular.

The middle row shows gardens with a just a few different kinds of plants, chosen carefully and used together in large patches or drifts. This technique is ideal for lower maintenance gardens.

The bottom row shows some ways to achieve interest in shadier parts of the garden. Although flowers make up only a small and fleeting part of the design, the effect is still one of lush texture and foliage colour. Always remember – clever foliage texture is the best way to create excitement in shady corners.

Perhaps we can blame it on the fact that they don't produce big and flashy flowers – but, as a group, ferns are probably the most under-valued perennials. They provide forms and textures that are totally unlike other kinds of plants. Ferns are unique and generally easy-to-grow plants that are the perfect tool for adding some interest to an otherwise dark and shady part of the garden. In short, ferns are great workhorses.

# FERNS

Ferns are valuable garden plants of great dependability and beauty. Their leaves – known as fronds – may be lacy or leathery, plain green or variegated, and provide a long season of interest. Rarely suffering from pests and diseases, they offer the gardener trouble-free elegance.

Naturally inhabiting woodland areas, most ferns thrive in the shade and protection provided by trees. They perform best in a rich, well-drained soil that is high in organic matter and retains plenty of moisture through the hot summer months.

Ferns were tremendously popular in Victorian times, and many of the British well-to-do had ferneries — shady garden areas or whole greenhouses devoted to fern collections. As we become more aware of the value of foliage texture in modern landscaping, we are beginning to rediscover the refreshing diversity of hardy ferns. Fortunately, some of the best ferns have been introduced back into nursery production, so today's selection is much better than what was available just a few years ago.

There are numerous kinds of hardy ferns available in garden centres. While some species are deciduous, dying back to the ground for winter, others are evergreen, providing attractive winter foliage in the garden, especially in mild-winter areas. Ferns vary in texture and height as well, from low, spreading mounds to bold and upright clumps. Even the smallest garden can have a woodland feeling by planting a few ferns along with other shade loving perennials such as Hostas, Primulas and Astilbes.

Try to start with vigorous container-grown plants that have been grown from spores or divisions and have had a chance to develop a strong healthy root system. Even today a good many of the ferns (and other wildflowers) being sold have been collected and dug from the wild; buying such plants will only serve to encourage collectors to continue depleting our valuable, limited natural stands of native plants, some of them rare and endangered! When you buy any woodland wildflowers or ferns, be sure to find out whether or not they have been

nursery propagated (as opposed to dug from the wild and then nursery grown in pots). All of the ferns listed here can be commercially grown from spores or by tissue culture cloning, so there is no excuse for removing plants from the wild.

### Tips on Planting and Care

Dry shade conditions under evergreens or large-leaved maple trees will kill most ferns. Ferns require moist, humus-rich soil. To improve your soil, dig in 4–6″ of well-rotted compost, peat moss or other organic matter to increase its moisture holding ability.

Some ferns can grow well under trees, but tree roots tend to rob the soil of water and nutrients. Also, rain may not penetrate the canopy. You will have to provide regular watering to these types of areas if you want to grow ferns, especially while young plants are trying to get established. It is a good idea to mulch deeply around your ferns with compost or leaf litter once a year. This will improve the soil, keep roots cool and help to retain moisture.

If your ferns are forming large patches, or you wish to increase the size of your patch – perhaps even to trade with friends — you might want to tackle dividing your plants. This is very simple to do in early spring, and is exactly like dividing any other perennial that forms a clump or patch. One word of caution, however; don't try to divide a plant that has only one main crown with no smaller plants surrounding it. Wait a year or two and if you notice secondary shoots (called "offsets") developing beside the main crown, carefully sneak these away in the spring using a sharp knife and hand trowel.

Where winters are very cold, cover ferns with evergreen boughs or mulch with leaves in the fall to protect them. Any natural leaf-fall that accumulates should be left to decompose; the rich leaf-mould that results over many years is the best possible fertilizer for ferns and other woodland plants.

Evergreen ferns may look somewhat tattered by late winter. If so, trim off any unsightly foliage in early spring. Varieties marked EVERGREEN usually remain so in Zones 7–9, but may become deciduous in colder regions or exposed windy areas.

## ADIANTUM ❉•
(Maidenhair Fern)

### pedatum     ZONE 2
(Northern Maidenhair Fern)
One of the most popular species, with its very delicate, fan-shaped fronds. Stems are shiny and black, with light green lacy leaves, turning bright gold in fall. Slowly spreads to form a rounded medium-sized clump. This fern is a real gem, doing well with good moisture. Suited to the rock garden, woodland or among shrubs. Clumps may be carefully divided in spring, after 4–5 years. Native. DECIDUOUS.

HT/SP    30–60 cm (1–2′) / 30–60 cm (1–2′)
SOIL      Prefers a rich, moist, well-drained soil.
USES     △⅋❮❦ Woodland, Edging

## ARACHNIODES ❉•
(Holly Fern)

### simplicior var. variegata     ZONE 6
(Variegated Holly Fern)
This unusual fern in not encountered all that often. Fronds are triangular in shape, with a smooth, glossy finish. Each leaflet is dark green with a yellow band down the centre vein. Plants are late to emerge in spring, so mark the spot well to avoid disturbing the roots. Clumps are of medium size, with an arching habit, attractive well into late fall. Tolerates summer heat and humidity. Trim any unattractive leaves off in spring. SEMI-EVERGREEN.

HT/SP    30–40 cm (12–16″) / 60–75 cm (24–30″)
SOIL      Prefers a rich, moist, well-drained soil.
USES     △❦ Edging, Woodland

## ASPLENIUM ❉•
(Spleenwort)
Valued for their symmetrical clumps of glossy fronds. This group is moderately difficult to grow, best suited to a shady rock garden. They do especially well on steep rocky slopes and walls, benefiting from extra-good drainage at the crown of the plants.

### ebenoides     ZONE 5
[Asplenosorus ebenoides]
(Dragon's-tail Fern,
Scott's Spleenwort)
This is a little fern, with shiny green triangular fronds. It's a naturally-occurring hybrid native to eastern North America, although rare in nature. Best in a shaded rockery or trough garden where it can be seen. Also suited to growing in indoor terrariums. EVERGREEN.

HT/SP    15–20 cm (6–8″) / 20–30 cm (8–12″)
SOIL      Rich, moist alkaline to neutral soil.
USES     △▲❦ Rock gardens, Troughs

### scolopendrium     ZONE 4
[Phyllitis scolopendrium]
(Hart's-tongue Fern)
A lime-tolerant species, often a challenge to grow. The shiny green strap-shaped fronds are not at all divided. This looks like a hardy Bird's-nest fern. Although native (and rare) in parts of eastern North America, the forms being propagated in the trade are European strains, apparently much easier to succeed with in a garden setting. Even so, it demands excellent drainage. EVERGREEN.

HT/SP    30–40 cm (12–16″) / 30–45 cm (12–18″)
SOIL      Prefers a moist, well-drained alkaline soil.
USES     △❦▲ Rock gardens, Woodland

'Kaye's Lacerated' (Crispy Hart's-Tongue Fern) Frond edges are ruffled or crimped, with bizarre forked ends. Very unusual.

HT      15–20 cm (6–8″)

## ATHYRIUM ❉•
(Lady Fern)
Delicate and lacy-looking ferns, with their triangular fronds divided into many small leaflets. These are all good garden performers of easy culture, forming dense low to medium-sized mounds that clump nicely, with no tendency to get out of control. Excellent for massing or edging. Best in a slightly acidic, humus-rich soil that stays evenly moist.

### filix-femina     ZONE 3
(Lady Fern)
Lacy-looking fronds are bright green, forming a dense mound. An easy species for any shady corner, even adapting to sunny sites with plenty of moisture. Great for massing. Many fancy cultivated types were selected from the European forms of Lady Fern during Victorian times. DECIDUOUS.

HT/SP    30–60 cm (1–2′) / 60–70 cm (24–28″)
SOIL      Prefers a rich, moist, well-drained soil.
USES     △⋀•❦ Massing, Woodland

'Frizelliae' (Tatting Fern) Totally unique, with an open and airy appearance. Arching fronds bear little bunches of tiny leaves arranged in alternating half-moons along each side to the tips. Bright green colour. The dwarf habit makes this suited to the shady rock garden.

HT/SP    15–30 cm (6–12″) / 20–30 cm (8–12″)

'Vernoniae Cristatum' (Miss Vernon's Crested Lady Fern) Fronds have a crisped, tasseled appearance, the ends uniquely forked or crested.

HT      50–60 cm (20–24″)

### niponicum 'Pictum'     ZONE 4
(Japanese Painted Fern)
Gardeners from coast to coast have now discovered this delightful and easy-to-grow fern. It forms sturdy low clumps of arching fronds, olive-green in colour with a handsome metallic-grey sheen. The leaf stems are deep burgundy. No other hardy fern offers this sort of foliage colour, making this extremely useful anywhere with average to moist soil and some protection from hot afternoon sun. If I could have only one fern in my garden, Japanese Painted Fern would be my personal first choice. Clumps size up well, making division in spring possible after 3–4 years. Some gardeners in Zone 3 report good results growing this. DECIDUOUS.

HT/SP    30–60 cm (1–2′) / 30–45 cm (12–18″)
SOIL      Prefers a rich moist, well-drained soil.
USES     △⋀•❦ Massing, Edging

### otophorum     ZONE 4
(Eared Lady Fern, Auriculate
Lady Fern)
This Japanese species is a nice selection for edging in the woodland or shady rock garden. Plants form clumps of arching triangular leaves, at first pale green with maroon stems, then changing to grey-green. Well behaved and non-spreading. Adapts well to containers. DECIDUOUS.

HT/SP    30–45 cm (12–18″) / 30–45 cm (12–18″)
SOIL      Moist, humus-rich soil.
USES     △⋀•❦ Massing, Edging

## BLECHNUM ❉•
(Hard Fern)

### spicant     ZONE 5
(Deer Fern)
One of the best-known species native to the Pacific Northwest. Forms a medium-sized clump of leathery sterile leaves, with contrasting fertile fronds shooting straight up from the centre. This requires humus-rich acidic soils and shady conditions. Will handle full sun in wet situations. EVERGREEN.

HT/SP    45–60 cm (18–24″) / 45–60 cm (18–24″)
SOIL      Prefers a rich, moist acidic soil.
USES     △⋀•❦▲ Massing, Borders

Asplenium scolopendrium

Adiantum pedatum

Athyrium f-femina 'Frizelliae'

Athyrium otophorum

Athyrium 'Vernoniae Cristatum'

# CHEILANTHES ☼◐
## (Lip Fern)

An exception among shade-loving ferns, this is a group of species that prefer sunny locations, adapting well to drier situations. A sunny rock garden is the ideal spot, the plants placed so that the roots are in a cool rock crevice or between boulders. Use a loose gravelly soil with plenty of humus and sandy grit for good drainage.

SOIL  Prefers a well-drained, gritty limestone and humus mix.
USES  ▲▼🔰 Walls, Rock gardens

### argentea                          ZONE 5
### (Silvery Lip Fern)

A cute, low-mounding plant with interesting star-shaped fronds. Leaflets are green on top, the underside coated with a white wax that helps to conserve moisture. Prefers limestone rocks and slightly alkaline soil. Grows well in walls. DECIDUOUS.

HT/SP  10–15 cm (4–6") / 15–30 cm (6–12")

### lanosa                            ZONE 5
### (Hairy Lip Fern)

Low tufted clumps are made up of very finely divided dark green fronds, covered on both sides with soft rust-brown hairs. An easy grower in sunny to lightly shaded rock gardens with excellent drainage. Native to the South-western USA. DECIDUOUS.

HT/SP  15–30 cm (6–12") / 20–30 cm (8–12")

# CYRTOMIUM ☼●
## (Holly Fern)

### falcatum                          ZONE 7
### (Japanese Holly Fern)

Beautifully glossy, leathery leaflets make this species unique among hardy ferns. Tolerant of arid conditions, and much-used in the southern and south-western USA. This species seems to prefer lime soils, and grows especially well beside a sidewalk or house foundation. Although this loves moisture it needs very good drainage. In cold-winter regions this is sometime grown in containers and wintered indoors. EVERGREEN.

HT/SP  30–60 cm (1–2') / 45–60 cm (18–24")
SOIL  Prefers a rich, moist soil.
USES  ▲M▼▲ Edging, Massing

# DENNSTAEDTIA ☼◑●
## (Cup Fern)

### punctilobula                      ZONE 3
### (Hay-scented Fern)

Native to Eastern North America, this is a common fern in gardens and in the wild. Plants spread underground to form a large colony. The fronds are large and lacy, triangular in shape and with a distinctive light-green colour. Quite tolerant of summer heat and humidity, and also one of the most sun-

tolerant of hardy ferns. Give it plenty of room to spread. The fronds give off a pleasant hay-like scent when brushed against. Drought tolerant. DECIDUOUS.

HT/SP  45–70 cm (18–28") / 60–90 cm (2–3')
SOIL  Average to moist, well-drained soil.
USES  M▼🔰 Massing, Woodland

# DRYOPTERIS ☼●
## (Wood Fern, Shield Fern)

Medium sized ferns, good for massing or groundcover plantings. Their broad, triangular fronds have the classic fern appearance, arranged in a strong-growing clump. Mostly native to northern temperate regions, many excellent garden ferns are represented in this group.

### affinis 'The King'               ZONE 2
### ['Cristata']
### (Golden-scaled Male Fern)

Popular since Victorian times, this strongly clumping fern forms a medium to tall mound of large, arching fronds. The leaflets on each frond are forked or crested on the tips, giving a somewhat fluffy appearance. Of fairly easy care and not invasive. Old fronds should be trimmed back in the spring. SEMI-EVERGREEN.

HT/SP  60–120 cm (2–4') / 75–90 cm (30–36")
SOIL  Prefers a rich, moist, well-drained soil.
USES  ✂◄▼ Specimen, Woodland

### carthusiana                       ZONE 2
### [D. spinulosa]
### (Toothed Wood Fern)

A very easy garden fern, native all over the Northern Hemisphere. The tall, bright green fronds are widely used by florists for cut foliage. Good for naturalizing in woodland areas. Does especially well in wet soils. DECIDUOUS.

HT/SP  60–90 cm (2–3') / 30–45 cm (12–18")
SOIL  Prefers a rich, moist to wet soil.
USES  ✂◄M▼ Massing, Woodland

### celsa                             ZONE 4
### (Log Fern)

Log Fern is native to the Southeastern USA, growing naturally in moist woodlands and swamps. Plants form tall clumps of arching triangular green fronds with a glossy finish. Remains semi-evergreen in mild winter regions. Clumps are well-behaved and not at all invasive. Excellent as a specimen in the woodland garden. Prefers acidic soils. SEMI-EVERGREEN.

HT/SP  90–120 cm (3–4') / 60–75 cm (24–30")
SOIL  Prefers a rich, moist to wet acidic soil.
USES  ▼▲ Specimen, Massing

### × complexa 'Robusta'              ZONE 4
### [D. filix-mas 'Undulata Robusta']
### (Hybrid Robust Male Fern)

A hybrid fern of British garden origin, this selection can form a very tall specimen in a rich, moist setting. It forms a strong clump of large dark-green

fronds, which arch gracefully under their own weight. Bold enough to use as a specimen, but also combines well with large Hosta and other shade lovers. Semi-evergreen in mild winter regions, but the old fronds should be trimmed off in spring. SEMI-EVERGREEN.

HT/SP  90–120 cm (3–4') / 75–90 cm (30–36")
SOIL  Prefers a rich, moist, well-drained soil.
USES  ▼ Specimen, Borders

### cycadina                          ZONE 5
### [D. atrata]
### (Shaggy Shield Fern,
### Black Wood Fern)

A medium-sized Asian species, this forms a clump of light golden-green fronds, the stems covered in tiny black scales. The appearance is stiff and leathery, with an arching habit. Plants are not inclined to spread. Trim off any old fronds in spring if they look untidy. EVERGREEN.

HT/SP  30–75 cm (12–30") / 45–60 cm (18–24")
SOIL  Prefers a rich, moist, well-drained soil.
USES  ▲M▼▲ Massing, Borders

### dilitata                          ZONE 4
### [D. austriaca]
### (Broad Buckler Fern)

Graceful, wide-spreading dark green fronds. Tolerant of wet sites, but adapting well to average conditions. Plants form well-behaved non-running clumps. This is a European species with many named selections, all of easy culture. Any ugly leaves from the previous season should be trimmed off in early spring. SEMI-EVERGREEN.

HT/SP  60–90 cm (2–3') / 60–90 cm (2–3')
SOIL  Prefers a rich, moist, slightly acidic soil.
USES  ▲M▼▲ Massing, Borders

Blechnum spicant

Cyrtomium falcatum

Dryopteris × complexa 'Robusta'

Dryopteris celsa

Dryopteris d. 'Jimmy Dyce'

Cheilanthes argentea

**'Jimmy Dyce' (Jimmy's Upright Broad Buckler Fern)** A unique form, the fronds are stiffly upright in habit, with a blue-green colour. Highly regarded by fern experts.

**HT**　30–60 cm (1–2')

**'Lepidota Cristata' (Lacy Crested Broad Buckler Fern)** Very finely cut leaflets with lacy forked tips. Fronds are dark green with brownish scales along the stems. Compact habit.

**HT**　30–60 cm (1–2')

**'Recurved Form' (Recurved Broad Buckler Fern)** Large triangular fronds, quite lacy, each leaflet curling under in an unusual way – almost skeletal in effect. The overall form is tall, arching and open.

**HT**　90–120 cm (3–4')

### *erythrosora* ZONE 5
### (Autumn Fern)

Next to the Japanese Painted Fern, this species is one of the most colourful of hardy ferns. Plants form a dense mound, the new young fronds showing coppery-pink tones, contrasting well against the older glossy green fronds. Effective when massed as a ground-cover and short enough for edging a walkway. Easy and adaptable. Trim all the old fronds back in spring to make room for fresh-looking replacements. Tolerates a fair bit of sun, with plenty of moisture. EVERGREEN.

**HT/SP**　30–60 cm (1–2') / 45–60 cm (18–24")
**SOIL**　Prefers a rich, moist, well-drained soil.
**USES**　⛰🌱🏆▲ Borders, Edging

### *expansa* ZONE 5
### (Northwest Wood Fern)

Native to the woodlands of the Pacific Northwest, this fern in often seen growing wild in damp moss or on rotting logs. Plants form an upright clump of finely divided dark green fronds, well suited to massing in a woodland garden. This is a well-behaved non-invasive species. DECIDUOUS.

**HT/SP**　60–90 cm (2–3') / 45–60 cm (18–24")
**SOIL**　Prefers a rich, moist, well-drained acidic soil.
**USES**　🌱🏆 Woodland, Massing

### *filix-mas* ZONE 2
### (Male Fern)

One of the easiest and most common of the large woodland ferns. The species form has elegant triangular soft-looking green fronds, being particularly effective when mass planted. It tolerates a fair bit of sun if the site is wet. Native all across the Northern Hemisphere. Many fancy-leaved selections exist. DECIDUOUS.

**HT/SP**　75–120 cm (30–48") / 60–90 cm (2–3')
**SOIL**　Prefers a rich, moist to wet soil.
**USES**　🌱🏆 Massing, Borders

**'Barnesii' (Barnes' Narrow Male Fern)** Very slender upright habit with a slightly ruffled appearance. An excellent specimen fern that takes up very little space.

**HT/SP**　75–90 cm (30–36") / 30–45 cm (12–18")

**'Crispatissima' (Dwarf Crinkled Male Fern)** Nice compact habit, the triangular fronds are heavily crimped and ruffled. Good for edging.

**HT/SP**　30–60 cm (1–2') / 30–60 cm (1–2')

**'Linearis Polydactyla' (Slender Crested Male Fern)** Long and arching fronds, the individual leaflets are very small, giving an open and skeletal appearance. Contrasts well with bolder-leaved perennials, like Hosta. Zone 4.

**HT/SP**　75–120 cm (30–48") / 60–90 cm (2–3')

### *marginalis* ZONE 2
### (Leather Wood Fern, Marginal Wood Fern)

A fern native to woodland areas of north-eastern North America, this adapts well to gardens that offer similar moist, shady conditions. Plants form leathery green fronds, arranged in a single-crowned clump. Not invasive. Foliage remains evergreen in most regions, but may benefit from clipping back in late winter. Easy and reliable. EVERGREEN.

**HT/SP**　45–60 cm (18–24") / 60–75 cm (24–30")
**SOIL**　Prefers a moist, humus-rich soil.
**USES**　🏆▲ Specimen, Borders

### × *remota* ZONE 4
### (Scaly Buckler Fern)

A naturally-occurring European hybrid species, this fern is highly rated and performs well in a wide range of climates. Graceful, arching green fronds are lacy in appearance, forming a dense and bushy mound. One of the best selections for massed plantings, also suitable for containers. Evergreen in mild winter regions, but the fronds should be trimmed back in early spring. EVERGREEN.

**HT/SP**　60–90 cm (2–3') / 60–90 cm (2–3')
**SOIL**　Prefers a rich, moist, well-drained soil.
**USES**　⛰🌱🏆▲ Specimen, Massing

## GYMNOCARPIUM ⚘•
## (Oak Fern)

### *dryopteris* ZONE 2
### (Oak Fern)

Oak Fern is native all across the Northern Hemisphere. Plants perform best in regions with cool summers, forming a small patch of branching triangular bright-green fronds, with a tissue-thin texture. Slightly spreading in habit but not at all invasive. Beautiful for edging in the woodland or rock garden. DECIDUOUS.

**HT/SP**　15–30 cm (6–12") / 30–45 cm (12–18")
**SOIL**　Prefers a rich, moist, well-drained soil.
**USES**　▲⛰🌱🏆 Edging, Massing

## MATTEUCCIA ⚘•
## (Ostrich Fern, Fiddlehead Fern)

### *struthiopteris* ZONE 1
### [*M. pensylvanica*]
### (Common Ostrich Fern)

This is the main species of fern harvested for its edible fiddleheads. Plants will form a wide-spreading patch of upright triangular green fronds. Perhaps the most common fern grown in gardens, easy to the point it may become invasive. Makes a good but tall groundcover for steep slopes or damp areas. In warm-summer regions I find this fern often looks a little worse for wear by August. Native. DECIDUOUS.

**HT/SP**　90–120 cm (3–4') / 60–90 cm (2–3')
**SOIL**　Prefers a rich, moist to wet soil.
**USES**　🌱🏆 Waterside, Massing

## OSMUNDA ☀⚘•
## (Flowering Fern)

Several important native fern species are included here, all of them having leafy green sterile fronds and bizarre-looking fertile fronds or sections of the sterile frond that bear spores and no leaves. These are tolerant of full sun conditions as long as the soil remains evenly moist.

### *cinnamomea* ZONE 2
### (Cinnamon Fern)

Large triangular sterile fronds are similar to the Ostrich Fern. Fertile fronds are leafless, shooting up from the centre of the clump in late spring, in an attractive cinnamon-brown shade. Prefers a lime-free acidic soil and tons of moisture. This forms a large clump, sizeable enough to use as a specimen. Native. DECIDUOUS.

**HT/SP**　70–150 cm (28–60") / 60–90 cm (2–3')
**SOIL**　Prefers a rich, moist to wet acidic soil.
**USES**　🏆 Specimen, Waterside

Dryopteris filix-mas

Dryopteris erythrosora

Dryopteris × remota

Matteuccia struthiopteris

Osmunda claytoniana

### *claytoniana*  ZONE 2
### (Interrupted Fern)

Another fern native throughout much of eastern North America, thriving in woodland areas with rich, moist soil on the acidic side. It forms an upright clump of light-green sterile fronds, oddly interrupted by jet-black fertile fronds partway up the stem. Makes a nice addition to cut flower arrangements. Adapts well to garden conditions, even in direct sun with plenty of moisture. Medium to large in size. DECIDUOUS.

**HT/SP**  60–90 cm (2–3') / 75–90 cm (30–36")
**SOIL**  Prefers a rich, moist, well-drained soil.
**USES**  ✂❦ Specimen, Woodland

### *regalis*  ZONE 3
### (Royal Fern)

A truly unique and spectacular fern. It forms a large crown, sending out a ring of arching leathery green fronds. The fertile spore-bearing pinnae are clustered together at the ends of the fronds and mature to a rich golden-brown. Use this as a specimen plant, or for massing. Lime-tolerant, also sun-tolerant with plenty of moisture. Native. DECIDUOUS.

**HT/SP**  90–150 cm (3–5') / 60–90 cm (2–3')
**SOIL**  Prefers a rich, moist to wet acidic soil.
**USES**  ❦ Specimen, Borders

**'Purpurascens' (Purple-stemmed Royal Fern)** In this variation the stems are purplish in colour, otherwise the habit is identical to the species.

## POLYSTICHUM ☙●
### (Holly Fern, Sword Fern, Shield Fern)

Mostly upright-growing ferns, with leathery fronds that are arranged in a formal-looking clump. Some of our best native ferns are among these. None are invasive.

### *acrostichoides*  ZONE 3
### (Christmas Fern)

Leathery, dark green fronds were once used for decoration at Christmas. This is one of the most dependable evergreen ferns, particularly in eastern North America. It forms a medium-sized clump that is the perfect size for a shady rock garden or for edging. Prefers a lime-free soil, and protection from winter winds. Old fronds should be trimmed back in early spring. Native. EVERGREEN.

**HT/SP**  30–60 cm (1–2') / 30–60 cm (1–2')
**SOIL**  Prefers a rich, moist, well-drained soil.
**USES**  ▲〽❦▲ Massing, Borders

### *braunii*  ZONE 4
### (Braun's Holly Fern)

This features thick dark-green and leathery fronds, the stalks covered with contrasting golden-brown scales. Plants have a dense, upright and arching form, producing a single-crowned clump. Protect from late spring frosts with evergreen boughs or dry leaves. Native all across the Northern Hemisphere. Easy and reliable. EVERGREEN.

**HT/SP**  30–75 cm (12–30") / 30–60 cm (1–2')
**SOIL**  Prefers a rich, moist, well-drained soil.
**USES**  ▲〽❦▲ Massing, Borders

### *munitum*  ZONE 6
### (Western Sword Fern, Alaska Fern)

A vigorous grower, native along the West coast and very commonly seen in shady woodland areas. The leathery, dark green fronds form a bold clump that gets bigger each year. Although excellent for naturalizing in the Pacific Northwest, this is a poor performer in Eastern North America. The fronds are sometimes harvested as floral greens. EVERGREEN.

**HT/SP**  90–120 cm (3–4') / 60–120 cm (2–4')
**SOIL**  Prefers a rich, moist, well-drained acidic soil.
**USES**  〽❦▲ Specimen, Massing

### *polyblepharum*  ZONE 5
### (Japanese Tassel Fern)

Wide-spreading, glossy dark green fronds with a tassel-like appearance as they emerge. Sensitive to late spring frosts. Medium sized. Appreciates even moisture and partial shade. EVERGREEN.

**HT/SP**  30–60 cm (1–2') / 45–60 cm (18–24")
**SOIL**  Prefers a rich, moist, well-drained soil.
**USES**  ▲▲ Edging, Rock Garden

### *setiferum*  ZONE 5
### (Soft Shield Fern)

One of the most common garden ferns in Europe, with hundreds of forms selected during Victorian times, most of these no longer available. Plants form a graceful arching clump of grass-green fronds that have a feathery and soft texture. Prefers high humidity and evenly moist soil. Trim off the old fronds in early spring. SEMI-EVERGREEN.

**HT/SP**  60–70 cm (24–28") / 60–70 cm (24–28")
**SOIL**  Prefers a rich, moist, well-drained acidic soil.
**USES**  〽❦▲ Massing, Borders

**'Divisilobum' (Feathery Shield Fern)** Extremely divided leaflets have an especially feathery appearance. Grows a bit shorter than the species.

**HT/SP**  30–70 cm (12–28") / 45–60 cm (18–24")

### *tsussimense*  ZONE 6
### (Korean Rock Fern)

A versatile and well-behaved little evergreen species. The small, triangular green fronds have contrasting black stems. New leaves have a purplish cast. Heat tolerant. Sometimes grown as an indoor fern. Good choice for the rock garden. EVERGREEN.

**HT/SP**  15–30 cm (6–12") / 30–40 cm (12–16")
**SOIL**  Prefers a rich, moist, well-drained soil.
**USES**  ▲〽❦▲ Edging, Rock gardens

## THELYPTERIS ☙●
### (Beech Fern)

### *decursive-pinnata*  ZONE 4
### [*Phegopteris decursive-pinnata*]
### (Japanese Beech Fern)

A handsome, medium-sized fern with narrow, triangular fronds that remain bright green all season long. It will tolerate sunny spots with plenty of moisture, the foliage colour then becoming more of a lemon-lime shade. Slowly spreads to form a small patch, without becoming invasive. Easy and vigorous. DECIDUOUS.

**HT/SP**  30–60 cm (1–2') / 45–60 cm (18–24")
**SOIL**  Prefers a rich, moist, acidic soil.
**USES**  ▲〽❦ Edging, Woodland gardens

*Polystichum acrostichoides*

*Polystichum polyblepharum*

*Polystichum munitum*

*Thelypteris decursive-pinnata*

*Polystichum setiferum*

Finally it seems that Ornamental Grasses are enjoying their heyday in gardens. Now widely grown and appreciated in both public and private gardens, the grasses appear to have moved well beyond the "fad" stage to become an important and valuable group of plants for garden designers in all kinds of climates.

# ASSES

For many people it seems one of the biggest garden obstacles to overcome is an unfounded fear of grasses. I blame this on the ubiquitous Ribbon Grass, so often passed over the garden fence from neighbour to neighbour. Its wide-spreading character is well known and seldom appreciated, yet even this grass can be put to good use with careful placement.

Grasses can be used in so many ways for landscape design; from bold specimen subjects to large massed plantings waving in the breeze; as a low groundcover or edging, in the border, or growing in containers and tubs.

Some grasses are grown for their colourful foliage in green, gold, red, cream or white; often attractively striped or banded. Others may be valued more for their showy flower plumes, spikes or seed heads. Several kinds provide dramatic and lasting interest throughout the winter months. A few varieties can do all of these things!

Ornamental Grasses combine well with almost any kind of plant. Although they can be used in a special border devoted exclusively to grasses, the effect is usually more like a collection rather than a border, and is probably best suited to botanical or demonstration gardens. The most successful way to use grasses – in the smaller residential gardens that most of us have – is to integrate them in a mixed planting along with perennials, annuals, bulbs, deciduous shrubs and evergreens.

## Grasses for every garden

The selection of grasses has never been better than it is today, with an astounding range of height, spread, colour and flowering times available. There should be room in every garden for a least one variety of ornamental grass, as they can fill such a wide variety of functions.

Tall, upright-growing types create linear (up-and-down) interest visually, especially when used towards the back of a border. Their bold lines break up space over a long season, some remaining attractive into the winter.

Medium-sized grasses may be effectively massed together, particularly in

gardens with a low-maintenance emphasis. Spring flowering bulbs combine well with these for early season interest. They are often just the perfect size to integrate into a perennial or mixed border design without becoming the centre of attention.

Low-growing grasses are ideal for edging around shrubs or combining with spreading evergreens. When mass-planted, they can often form an attractive low-maintenance groundcover.

There are recommended varieties for nearly every climate zone in North America, so gardeners in most regions can make use of ornamental grasses. Without question, milder climate zones have a larger palette of hardy grasses available, but some of the best grasses are fortunately very hardy and will withstand extremes of cold, some even down to chilly Zone 2!

Grasses can be divided into two basic groups, based on their growth cycles. Getting to know their growth pattern helps a lot with understanding the best timing for dividing or pruning grasses.

**Cool season grasses** – These begin their foliage growth in early spring, reaching their full size before the summer heat hits. They are usually low to medium-sized plants, often tending to brown out in hot summer weather. Clipping or mowing in June or July usually encourages lush regrowth for fall interest. Divide these in late summer or early spring. Several types remain evergreen in mild winter areas. Blue Fescue (*Festuca*) is probably the most familiar cool-season type.

**Warm season grasses** – Among these are the stars of the late summer and fall border. Some form tall clumps, often with showy spikes or plumes of flowers. These grasses usually like plenty of light and hot summer weather, showing few signs of new foliage growth until spring has truly arrived. They should be pruned back in late winter before new growth begins. Warm-season grasses should generally be divided while dormant, in early spring only.

## Grasses for Special Uses
**Showy seed-heads in late summer/fall** – Andropogon, Bouteloua, Briza, Calamagrostis, Carex pendula, Chasmanthium, Cortaderia, Deschampsia, Miscanthus, Molinia, Panicum, Pennisetum, Saccharum, Stipa, Typha.

**Grasses native to North America** – Andropogon, Bouteloua, Carex grayii, Carex muskingumensis, Chasmanthium latifolium, Hierochloe,

Panicum virgatum, Spartina, Stipa tenuissima.

**Grasses that spread invasively by underground rhizomes –** Arundo donax, Glyceria, Hierochloe, Leymus arenarius, Miscanthus sacchariflorus, Phalaris, Spartina, Typha.

**Grasses that may self seed prolifically** (note: removing seed heads before they fully develop will prevent self seeding.) Alopecurus, Andropogon, Bouteloua, Briza, Carex (non-variegated types), Chasmanthium, Deschampsia, Festuca, Milium, *Miscanthus sinensis, Panicum, *Pennisetum, Stipa tenuissima. (* seldom sets seed north of New York City)

**Grasses with good winter interest –** Acorus (evergreen types), Andropogon, Arundo, Calamagrostis, Carex (evergreen types), Chasmanthium, Cortaderia, Festuca,

Helictotrichon, Juncus, Luzula, Miscanthus, Panicum, Pennisetum, Saccharum, Spartina, Uncinia.

**Drought-tolerant grasses** (once established) – Andropogon, Bouteloua, Calamagrostis, Cortaderia, Elymus magellanicus, Festuca, Helictotrichon, Leymus, Panicum, Saccharum, Sesleria, Stipa.

**Grasses for damp or moist soils –** Acorus, Alopecurus, Arrhenatherum, Arundo, Briza, Calamagrostis, Carex, Chasmanthium, Cortaderia, Deschampsia, Glyceria, Hakonechloa, Hierochloe, Leymus, Luzula, Milium, Miscanthus, Molinia, Panicum, Pennisetum, Phalaris, Saccharum, Sesleria, Spartina, Typha, Uncinia.

**Grasses for wet soils** (waterside) – Acorus, Carex (some), Chasmanthium, Deschampsia, Glyceria, Juncus, Miscanthus, Molinia, Phalaris, Sesleria, Spartina, Typha, Uncinia.

**Shade-tolerant grasses –** Carex (many), Chasmanthium, Deschampsia, Hakonechloa, Luzula, Milium, Sesleria.

## ACORUS ☀◑
### (Sweet Flag)

Not true grasses actually, these are in the Arum or Philodendron family but their clumps of grassy, sword-shaped leaves give them a grass-like appearance and function in the garden. The fragrant roots of certain species have been used for centuries in perfume manufacturing. These are happiest growing in wet or boggy sites, especially beside water.

### *calamus* 'Argenteostriatus'    ZONE 4
### ['Variegatus']
### (Variegated Tall Sweet Flag)

This is a herbaceous species, dying back to the ground each winter. Plants spread slowly to form a sizable clump, looking for all the world like a variegated Iris, with lengthwise stripes of green and creamy yellow. Greenish flowers are insignificant. Effective beside a pond, this will even grow directly in shallow water. Reported to tolerate some shade. Despite being a water lover, this delightful plant seems to put up with average border conditions. I once saw a stunning combination of this growing up through a mound of Artemisia 'Powis Castle', with a backdrop of fall flowering Sedum.

**HT/SP**  60–90 cm (2–3') / 45–60 cm (18–24")
**SOIL**    Rich, moist to wet soil.
**BLOOM** June–July
**USES**   ☙ Waterside, Specimen

### *gramineus*    ZONE 5
### (Japanese Sweet Flag)

An evergreen species, forming handsome low clumps of narrow grassy leaves. Frequently seen in Japanese-style gardens alongside moist areas or mass planted as a groundcover. As these are slow to establish, space closely at planting time to encourage a fast fill. Foliage is fragrant when bruised. Like the species above, the greenish flowers hold little interest. A winter mulch is recommended in Zones 5–6 to help prevent windburn. The selections below are more frequently seen than the plain green species itself.

**SP**    25–30 cm (10–12")
**SOIL**  Prefers a rich, moist to wet soil.
**BLOOM** June–July
**USES**   ▲△ᴧᴀ☙ Edging, Waterside

### 'Licorice' (Licorice Sweet Flag)
Apparently a Chinese selection, recently introduced to the herbal trade but quite interesting as an ornamental. The narrow green leaves smell strongly of licorice when bruised. Possibly a bit hardier than the variegated forms.

**HT**    20–30 cm (8–12")

### 'Minimus Aureus' [*var. pusillus*]
### (Miniature Golden Sweet Flag)
A real cute little dwarf form. Foliage is solid golden-yellow and absolutely glows in massed plantings. Useful in a damp rock garden or for edging along a small pool. Slow growing.

**HT/SP** 5–10 cm (2–4") / 15–30 cm (6–12")

### 'Variegatus' ['Argenteostriatus']
### (Variegated Sweet Flag)
Leaves are brightly striped along their length with green and creamy white. Best in part shade. Fine for massing. In mild winter regions it makes a beautiful container plant.

**HT**    20–30 cm (8–12")

## ALOPECURUS ☀◑
### (Foxtail Grass)

### *pratensis* 'Aureovariegatus'    ZONE 3
### (Variegated Meadow Foxtail)

The narrow leaves are striped lengthwise with golden-yellow and green, especially bright and showy in the cool spring months. Clumps spread steadily and can be used as a groundcover over a small area. I have seen this used well as a foil below late tulips, the grass foliage serving to disguise the dying tulip leaves in summer. Short tan-coloured spikes appear in late spring but they're nothing special – remove seed heads to prevent self-sowing. In warm summer regions this may need to be cut back hard in midsummer to rejuvenate. Easily divided in spring or early fall. Cool-season.

**HT/SP** 45–60 cm (18–24") / 30–60 cm (1–2')
**SOIL**  Average to moist, well-drained soil.
**BLOOM** May–June
**USES**   ᴧᴀ☙ Borders, Edging

## ANDROPOGON ☀
### (Bluestem)

Native North American grasses, these were once an important component of the native tall-grass prairie communities, which have now all but disappeared. Valuable grasses for late-season interest, developing rich foliage colours in the fall, as well as having beautiful seed-heads. Warm-season.

### *scoparius* 'The Blues'    ZONE 3
### [*Schizachyrium scoparium* 'The Blues']
### (Little Bluestem)

A selected form of Little Bluestem with especially good blue-green foliage and contrasting coppery-pink plumes. This grass has a good clumping habit that makes it well suited for use in the border, although it can flop a bit in really rich soils. Also effective for mass plantings or naturalizing. The ripening plumes develop a dark coppery-brown colour, an excellent contrast to the foliage as it turns from green to bronzy-orange in the fall. One of the best grasses for winter interest, standing up well to snow and ice. Drought tolerant.

**HT/SP** 60–90 cm (2–3') / 45–60 cm (18–24")
**SOIL**  Tolerates a wide range of soil conditions.
**BLOOM** August–September
**USES**   ✂❮☙ Borders, Meadows

## ARRHENATHERUM ☀◑
### (Oat Grass)

### *elatius subsp.*
### *bulbosum* 'Variegatum'    ZONE 2
### (Variegated Bulbous Oat Grass)

One of the showiest grasses for cold winter regions. Plants form a cascading low clump of cream and green striped leaves. Tan-coloured spikes may appear in early summer but are not significant. Combines nicely with bulbs in the spring garden or as a bright border edging. In warm summer regions or dry areas the plants usually brown out in July and should then be clipped back to force another flush of growth towards late summer. Drought tolerant once established. Easily divided in spring or early fall. Cool-season.

**HT/SP** 30–45 cm (12–18") / 30–60 cm (1–2')
**SOIL**  Tolerates a wide range of soil conditions.
**BLOOM** June
**USES**   ☙ Edging, Borders

## ARUNDO ☀
### (Giant Reed)

### *donax*    ZONE 6

Even in the first season these become truly imposing and enormous plants, something about their appearance always hinting at bamboo. Where hardy, clumps will spread underground from woody rhizomes to form a broad patch of tall, hollow canes. Leaves are blue-green, arching gracefully out in a layered manner. In colder climates these are most often used as a foliage focal point in annual bedding schemes, then potted up to winter indoors. These make an effective and fast-growing

*Acorus calamus* 'Argenteostriatus'

*Acorus gramineus* 'Minimus Aureus'

*Arrhenatherum elatius* 'Variegatum'

screen or windbreak. Large pinkish spikes appear in very late fall, but only if the summer has been hot. Heat tolerant. Warm-season.

**'Versicolor' ['Variegata'] (Variegated Giant Reed)** Leaves of this form are strongly striped with creamy-yellow and green. A popular specimen plant in large parks, often mistaken for some strange giant corn. Granted, this can get huge, but if you have a bold sense of design it makes a great centre-piece for large tubs.

| | |
|---|---|
| **HT/SP** | 180–350 cm (6–12') / 90–150 cm (3–5') |
| **SOIL** | Average to moist, well-drained soil. |
| **BLOOM** | October–November |
| **USES** | ♉ Specimen, Waterside, Screen |

## AVENA see Helictotrichon

# BOUTELOUA ☼
## (Grama Grass)

*gracilis*                    ZONE 3
### (Mosquito Grass, Blue Grama)
Another important native North American grass, this was a common component of the short-grass prairie plant community on the western plains. Mosquito Grass makes a low tuft of olive green leaves, with medium-tall stems producing unusual spikes of bristly flowers that are held at an odd angle, somewhat resembling a flying insect. Well-behaved in the sunny border or rock garden. Clumping in habit, although it may self sow. Reasonable winter interest. Drought-tolerant. Warm-season.

| | |
|---|---|
| **HT/SP** | 30–60 cm (1–2') / 25–30 cm (10–12") |
| **SOIL** | Average to dry, well-drained soil. |
| **BLOOM** | June–September |
| **USES** | △⅌✂♉⅘ Rock gardens, Borders |

# BRIZA ☼
## (Quaking Grass)

*media*                    ZONE 4
Loose clusters of delicate heart-shaped flowers are used for fresh or dried arranging. Plants form a low tuft of narrow green leaves. Effective when combined with heaths and heathers in a moor planting. I like this also as a border edging in any sunny spot with reasonable soil. Clumps are easily divided in spring or early fall. Evergreen in milder areas. Cool-season.

| | |
|---|---|
| **HT/SP** | 30–60 cm (1–2') / 25–30 cm (10–12") |
| **SOIL** | Tolerates a wide range of soil conditions. |
| **BLOOM** | May–July |
| **USES** | △⅌✂▲♉⅘ Borders, Rock gardens |

# CALAMAGROSTIS ☼☽
## (Reed Grass)

These are favourite grasses of landscape designers, who value the stiff, upright linear effect they create. Plants are often massed in great numbers, their wands of flowers waving in the breeze. They are equally effective used within a border in smaller groupings, remaining attractive well into the winter. Clumps are very easily divided in early spring. Cool-season, but heat-tolerant.

| | |
|---|---|
| **SP** | 60–70 cm (24–28") |
| **SOIL** | Tolerates a wide range of soil conditions. |
| **BLOOM** | June–October |
| **USES** | ✂◄♉⅘ Accent, Massing, Borders |

× *acutiflora* **'Karl Foerster'**    ZONE 3
**['Stricta']**
**(Foerster's Feather Reed Grass)**
Proving to be one of the sturdiest and most versatile landscape plants, and probably the best taller grass for cold climate regions. With its stiffly upright habit this can be one of the most effective vertical elements in the summer and fall border. Narrow clumps of green foliage bear spikes of soft greenish flowers early in the summer, first fading to rose then changing into stiff tan seedheads that stand up well to the rigours of winter. Can be used as a specimen but also extremely effective when planted in groups. Prairie gardeners, take note – this does just fine in your climate. Selected as the *Perennial Plant of the Year* for 2001.

| | |
|---|---|
| **HT** | 120–150 cm (4–5') |

**'Overdam' (Variegated Feather Reed Grass)** A smaller-growing selection, the narrow leaves are neatly striped in white and green, giving a silvery effect from any distance away. Spikes of tan seed heads are a nice contrast, although sometimes I'm tempted to cut off the flowers and grow this right at the border edge. Effective in the spring garden, later sort of fading into the background. A nice size for tubs and other containers of mixed perennials. Does not appear to be quite as hardy as 'Karl Foerster'. Zone 5 or possibly 4 with good winter snowcover.

| | |
|---|---|
| **HT** | 90–120 cm (3–4') |

# CAREX ☽•
## (Sedge)
Although not true grasses, the Sedges are similar in appearance and function. These mostly form low to medium-sized tufts of handsome leaves, usually with insignificant flowers. They are frequently used for groundcover plantings, performing especially well in moist or wet areas. The evergreen forms sometimes benefit from a light clipping in spring using sharp scissors to trim off any dead tips. Clumps may be divided, the best time usually being mid to late spring.

*berggrenii*                    ZONE 6
**(Dwarf Bronze Creeping Sedge)**
A relative newcomer to North American gardens, this forms a very short, tufted clump of coppery-brown leaves. Well suited to growing around a small pool.

In moist to wet soils this will handle full sun and develop especially rich colour. Flowers are insignificant. Clumps can be easily ripped apart in early spring. Evergreen.

| | |
|---|---|
| **HT/SP** | 5–10 cm (2–4") / 15–20 cm (6–8") |
| **SOIL** | Prefers a rich, moist to wet soil. |
| **BLOOM** | June–July |
| **USES** | △▲♉ Edging, Waterside |

*buchananii*                    ZONE 6
**(Leatherleaf Sedge)**
Creates an arching, tufted clump of cinnamon-brown, hairlike foliage. Tiny flowers appear in early summer but are insignificant. Excellent for contrasting with dwarf conifers or other evergreens, especially in the winter garden. Also nice beside water. Like most of the brown-leaved New Zealand Sedges, this has a tendency to seed around. Everbrown.

| | |
|---|---|
| **HT/SP** | 30–60 cm (1–2') / 30–45 cm (12–18") |
| **SOIL** | Average to moist, well-drained soil. |
| **BLOOM** | June–July |
| **USES** | △▲♉ Borders |

*caryophyllea* **'The Beatles'**    ZONE 5
**(Spring Sedge, Mop-headed Sedge)**
The perfect name for this low, mop-headed selection, the clumps of narrow dark-green leaves impersonating a 60's hairdo! Used as an edging to shady pathways, tolerating full sun with plenty of moisture. Especially good interplanted with the smaller spring-flowering bulbs. Evergreen in mild winter regions. Quite possibly hardy to Zones 3–4.

| | |
|---|---|
| **HT/SP** | 10–15 cm (4–6") / 20–30 cm (8–12") |
| **SOIL** | Prefers a rich, moist soil. |
| **BLOOM** | May–June |
| **USES** | △Ⓦ▲♉ Rock gardens, Edging |

*conica* **'Snowline'**                    ZONE 5
**(Variegated Japanese Sedge)**
An evergreen type, forming a low mound of narrow green leaves edged

*Bouteloua gracilis*

*Arundo donax* 'Versicolor'

*Calamagrostis* × 'Karl Foerster'

*Carex berggrenii*

*Carex buchananii*

in white, with a silvery appearance from any distance. Like 'Evergold' and most other evergreen forms, this is best suited to a moist, shady site. Excellent for edging. In cold winter regions the leaf tips may need to be trimmed in mid spring.

**HT/SP** 20–30 cm (8–12") / 30–60 cm (1–2')
**SOIL** Prefers a rich, moist soil.
**BLOOM** May–June
**USES** Edging, Woodland garden

### comans 'Frosted Curls'          ZONE 6
[C. albula 'Frosty Curls']
(Frosted Curls Sedge)

Unusual olive-green foliage that arches to form a mop-headed clump, the leaf-tips fading to near white. The texture is fine and soft, like a head of flowing hair. Especially effective in containers or massed along the border edge. Clumps may be divided in spring. Evergreen.

**HT/SP** 20–30 cm (8–12") / 30–45 cm (12–18")
**SOIL** Tolerates a wide range of soil conditions.
**BLOOM** June–July
**USES** Edging

### dolichostachya Gold Fountains
ZONE 5
[C. d. 'Kaga-nishiki']
(Gold Fountains Sedge)

Recently arrived from Japan, this handsome selection produces a mound of slender green leaves brightly edged in gold. Plants remain evergreen in mild winter regions. Although not yet fully tested for extreme cold hardiness, this seems to be the best striped evergreen form in Zones 5–6. Best in part shade but tolerant of full sun in cool-summer regions.

**HT/SP** 20–40 cm (8–16") / 30–60 cm (1–2')
**SOIL** Prefers a rich, moist soil.
**USES** Rock gardens, Edging

### flacca          ZONE 4
[C. glauca]
(Blue Creeping Sedge, Carnation Grass)

One of those under-appreciated plants, I always think, this is a low, creeping species with bright steel-blue leaves that fairly quickly forms a thick mat. It's an adaptable sedge, growing fine in most garden situations, including dry shade. Although evergreen, this often looks better with a hard clipping back in early spring. Flowers are insignificant. Easily divided by ripping the plants apart in spring.

**HT/SP** 10–20 cm (4–8") / 25–40 cm (10–16")
**SOIL** Tolerates a wide range of soil conditions.
**BLOOM** May–June
**USES** Edging, Massing

### grayi          ZONE 3
(Morning Star Sedge, Mace Sedge)

A native North American species, most at home in a wet spot beside a stream or pond. The fresh green leaves are narrow and leathery, forming an upright clump. Not grown as much for the foliage as for the interesting star-shaped seedpods that develop during the summer. These make bizarre cut flowers. Flowers are greenish and insignificant. Deciduous.

**HT/SP** 60–90 cm (2–3') / 45–60 cm (18–24")
**SOIL** Prefers a rich, moist to wet soil.
**BLOOM** May–June
**USES** Waterside

### 'Ice Dance'          ZONE 5
(Creeping Japanese Sedge)

Just recently introduced from Japan, this is a creeping evergreen selection, quite possibly the best one for mass planting as a groundcover. The foliage is narrow and green, strongly edged in creamy white. Plants slowly creep underground to make a patch, knitting together rather than clumping like most other forms, yet not at all invasive. Perfect for underplanting with early spring bulbs of all kinds. Easily divided in early spring.

**HT/SP** 20–30 cm (8–12") / 30–45 cm (12–18")
**SOIL** Prefers a rich, moist soil.
**BLOOM** May–June
**USES** Massing, Woodland garden

### muskingumensis          ZONE 4
(Palm Sedge)

Another native waterside species, this has an exotic and tropical appearance. Plants form graceful clumps of divided leaves similar in effect to papyrus. Equally at home beside water or in a moist border. It will also tolerate growing in pots set directly into a shallow pond. Full sun to part shade.

**HT/SP** 40–60 cm (16–24") / 45–60 cm (18–24")
**SOIL** Prefers a rich, moist to wet soil.
**BLOOM** May–June
**USES** Waterside, Massing

### morrowii 'Fisher's Form'          ZONE 5
(Variegated Japanese Sedge)

Slender green leaves are brightly edged in creamy white, forming a sturdy evergreen clump with a slightly more upright habit than older selections like 'Evergold'. Superb in the moist woodland garden with Hostas or ferns, and for edging pathways. Clumps may be divided in spring, but the pieces should be rather large for best success. Insignificant greenish flowers.

**HT/SP** 30–40 cm (12–16") / 45–60 cm (18–24")
**SOIL** Prefers a rich, moist soil.
**BLOOM** May–June
**USES** Edging, Woodland garden

### nigra          ZONE 4
(Black-flowered Sedge)

A deciduous, creeping species useful for mass planting beside a pond or stream. Plants are similar to C. flacca, usually blue-green in colour and quite narrow and grassy looking. Flowers are black, appearing in late spring. Will tolerate standing water fairly well.

**HT/SP** 15–25 cm (6–10") / 45–60 cm (18–24")
**SOIL** Prefers a rich, moist to wet soil.
**BLOOM** May–June
**USES** Edging, Waterside

**'Variegata' ['On-line'] (Variegated Black Sedge)** Narrow light-green leaves are edged in soft yellow. Much more ornamental than the plain green species.

### oshimensis 'Evergold'          ZONE 5
[C. hachijoensis 'Evergold']
(Variegated Japanese Sedge)

A real beauty for the shade garden, making a low, cascading mound of narrow creamy-yellow leaves, edged along the margins with green. Fairly successful in dry shade once established, although susceptible to wind burn during winter in colder regions. It truly shines in container plantings. Some gardeners actually bring these indoors for the winter. I once underplanted this with deep purple crocus, and it was a gorgeous spring effect. Evergreen.

**HT/SP** 15–20 cm (6–8") / 20–30 cm (8–12")
**SOIL** Tolerates a wide range of soil conditions.
**BLOOM** May–June
**USES** Edging, Woodland garden

### pendula          ZONE 7
(Great Drooping Sedge, Weeping Sedge)

Evergreen in mild winter areas, this species forms a broad clump of wide leaves with interesting arching spikes of flowers held on tall stems far above the mound. Useful for floral arranging, and a nice waterside feature in the garden. Often grown in containers as a specimen plant. May be wintered indoors in cold regions. Shade tolerant.

Carex flacca

Carex muskingumensis

Carex oshimensis 'Evergold'

**HT/SP** 90–120 cm (3–4') / 45–60 cm (18–24")
**SOIL** Average to moist or wet soil.
**BLOOM** May–July
**USES** ✂❧▼▲ Specimen, Waterside

### *siderosticha* ZONE 4
### (Broad-leaved Sedge)
On first glance the various forms of this species are easily mistaken for dwarf Hosta. The broad, sword-shaped leaves are bright green, spreading underground to form a fairly dense clump or patch. I find these to be an excellent choice as a groundcover among taller woodland plants, and especially good beside pathways. Foliage is deciduous, the fresh spring growth sometimes tinged with bright pink. Sharp scissors are needed in early spring to clip off the dead leaves from the previous season right down at ground level. Easily divided in spring or early fall. These all seem quite tolerant of dry shade, once established. The green-leaved species is seldom encountered, but several good variegated selections are readily available. Some gardeners in Zone 3 find these are reliably hardy.

**HT/SP** 15–20 cm (6–8") / 30–60 cm (1–2')
**SOIL** Prefers a rich, moist soil.
**BLOOM** May–June
**USES** ▲⋀⋗▼ Edging, Woodland gardens

**Island Brocade ['Shima-nishiki']** An absolutely stunning selection, the wide leaves have edges and stripes of rich golden-yellow in spring, later ageing to creamy yellow.
**'Variegata'** Wide, light-green leaves are edged in clean white, with the occasional streak or double stripe.

### *testacea* ZONE 6
### (Copper Hair Sedge)
Another of the strange but lovable species from New Zealand, forming a wiglike mound of very fine copper-orange to cinnamon-tan leaves. These can become visually lost in the garden without clever planning. Surrounding the clumps with a low silvery or golden-yellow groundcover is a sneaky trick that nearly always works. Evergreen where hardy.

**HT/SP** 30–40 cm (12–16") / 30–45 cm (12–18")
**SOIL** Average to moist, well-drained soil.
**BLOOM** June–July
**USES** ▲▼▲ Borders

## CHASMANTHIUM ☼◑●
## (Sea Oats)

### *latifolium* ZONE 5
### (Northern Sea Oats)
One of the best grasses for shady sites but adapting well to sunny areas with rich, moist soil. Upright clumps resemble a dwarf green bamboo at first, producing graceful, arching stems in late summer that hold dangling flower spikes. These move in the slightest

breeze, almost looking like swimming schools of little fishes. In autumn the whole plant develops warm bronzy tones, including the flowers, then settles down to more of a tan colour for winter effect. Great for cutting. May self-seed prolifically, although in my experience it has done so in a gentle way. Clumps may be easily divided in spring, but seldom actually require it. Native wildflower. Warm-season.

**HT/SP** 80–100 cm (32–40") / 45–60 cm (18–24")
**SOIL** Tolerates a wide range of soil conditions.
**BLOOM** July–September
**USES** ✂❧▼⅗ Borders, Woodland gardens

## CORTADERIA ☼
## (Pampas Grass)

### *selloana* ZONE 8
Visitors to the Pacific Northwest often come home with an urge to grow these spectacular specimen grasses. Typically the clumps are plunked into the middle of a front lawn. They bear their huge, fluffy ostrich-feather plumes on ten-foot tall stems in late summer, lasting throughout the winter months. The evergreen foliage is long and strap-shaped and extremely sharp along the edges – leather gloves are recommended when handling. Popular as a cut flower, either fresh or dried. Seeds will produce both male and female plants, the male ones being much less voluptuous in effect. Several variegated selections exist and all have superb striped foliage. Drought tolerant once established.

Those of us in colder regions who crave Pampas Grass in our gardens will generally have to settle for *Saccharum ravennae*, the so-called Northern Pampas Grass, or Ravennae Grass. Don't be tempted to transplant a piece of the grass commonly seen along roadsides in the Eastern part of the continent; Reed Grass (*Phragmites australis*) – often mistakenly called Pampas Grass – is a notorious thug when released into the garden, spreading to form a huge patch in no time. Leave it in the ditch!

**HT/SP** 240–350 cm (8–12') / 120–150 cm (4–5')
**SOIL** Average to moist, well-drained soil.
**BLOOM** August–November
**USES** ✂❧▼▲⅗ Specimen

**'Pumila' (Dwarf Pampas Grass)** A much hardier form, often seem in gardens along the Eastern seaboard. Plants produce smaller white plumes, although still large and showy. Leaves are narrower and grey-green in colour. Actually, this is a much better-sized plant for most landscaping situations. Hardy in Zone 7 and in sheltered parts of Zone 6.

**HT** 150–180 cm (5–6')

## DESCHAMPSIA ☼◑
## (Hair Grass)

### *cespitosa* ZONE 3
### (Tufted Hair Grass)
Widely grown in European gardens, these are slowly becoming better appreciated here in North America. They are clump-forming evergreen grasses, forming sturdy tufts of rich green leaves quite early in the season. Airy sprays of delicate green flowers appear in midsummer, maturing to bright gold or tan shades towards autumn. Flowers are sometimes in such great numbers that the leaves become totally hidden below. Most effective when massed or allowed to drape over more substantial plants. Clip back hard in early spring. Fairly shade tolerant. Cool-season.

**HT/SP** 85–100 cm (34–40") / 45–60 cm (18–24")
**SOIL** Average to moist, well-drained soil.
**BLOOM** July–October
**USES** ✂❧▼▲ Massing, Borders

**Bronze Veil ['Bronzeschleier']** Fine-textured sprays of bronzy-green flowers, maturing to beige. Early blooming.
**Gold Dust ['Goldstaub']** Airy heads of bright golden-yellow flowers. Late blooming.
**'Northern Lights'** A recent arrival, this is a non-blooming selection grown for its handsome foliage. Leaves are striped lengthwise with creamy-white and green, blushed with pink in the spring. May prefer part shade in warm summer regions. Zone 4.

**HT/SP** 20–30 cm (8–12") / 30–60 cm (1–2')

### *flexuosa* 'Tatra Gold' ZONE 4
### ['Aurea']
### (Golden Hair Grass)
This delightful grass forms a well-behaved clump of very fine leaves, like golden yellow hair, especially bright

*Carex siderosticha* 'Island Brocade'

*Chasmanthium latifolium*

*Cortaderia selloana* 'Pumila'

*Deschampsia flexuosa* 'Tartra Gold'

through the spring months. Upright stems in midsummer bear clouds of tiny, airy flowers in a bronzy-purple shade, maturing to beige. Light and billowing in effect, a wonderful contrast to bold-leaved plants. Seedlings that appear usually come true, and can be moved to a new location while small. Drought tolerant once established. Evergreen in mild winter regions. Cool-season.

**HT/SP** 40–50 cm (16–20″) / 45–60 cm (18–24″)
**SOIL** Tolerates a wide range of soil conditions.
**BLOOM** July–August
**USES** ✂🗡▲🌿 Massing, Borders

## ELYMUS ☼◐
(Wheatgrass)

*arenarius* see Leymus arenarius

*magellanicus*     ZONE 5
[*Agropyron magellanicum*]
(Blue Clumping Wheatgrass, Magellan Wheatgrass)
Although not yet widely available, this gorgeous blue-leaved grass is certainly one to add to the shopping list. Plants form a non-invasive clump of metallic silver-blue leaves, bearing taller stems of narrow blue flowers in early summer. It seems best suited to a well-drained rock garden, resenting both winter-wet soils and hot, humid summers. Semi-evergreen. Drought tolerant once established. Cool-season.

**HT/SP** 60–90 cm (2–3′) / 45–60 cm (18–24″)
**SOIL** Requires a well-drained soil.
**BLOOM** May–June
**USES** ▲🌿 Rock gardens

## ERIANTHUS see Saccharum

## FESTUCA ☼◐
(Fescue)
Fescues form low tufted clumps of fine-textured foliage, ranging from silver-blue to green. These are widely used for edging, or massed to create a low, hummocky groundcover. All are cool-season grasses, at their best in spring and early summer. Most remain evergreen in all but the coldest regions. Removing the faded flower heads will prevent self seeding. Fescue plants are easily divided in early spring.

*glauca*     ZONE 3
[*F. ovina glauca*]
(Blue Fescue)
Valued for their low tufts of steely-blue foliage. On most selections tan-coloured spikes rise above on short stems in late spring or early summer. Some people like these, others prefer to clip the flowers or seed-heads off by mid-summer to tidy the plants up. Nice in containers. Best in full sun and with superior drainage. I seldom recommend large massed plantings of Blue Fescue because after four or five years the odd plant here and there dies out, leaving awkward gaps that need to be replanted. Plants also never seem to grow together, looking more like a hedgehog colony rather than what I think of as an effective groundcover. Cool-season.

**HT/SP** 20–30 cm (8–12″) / 25–30 cm (10–12″)
**SOIL** Average to dry, well-drained soil.
**BLOOM** May–June
**USES** ▲🗡▲🌿 Rock gardens, Edging

**Blue Glow ['Blauglut']** A German selection. The stems of tan flowers are fairly tall, held above a clump of rich silver-blue leaves.

**HT** 30–45 cm (12–18″)

**'Elijah Blue'** The standard form now in North America, with a compact habit and rich blue colour that is retained well throughout the season.

**HT** 20–25 cm (8–10″)

**'Golden Toupee'** Unique for its hummock of golden-green leaves, with spikes of tan flowers. Possibly less hardy than other forms. Zone 4.

**HT** 15–20 cm (6–8″)

**'Jana's Blue'** Blue-green foliage with an exceptional and early display of tan-coloured spikes.

**HT** 20–25 cm (8–10″)

**Sea Urchin ['Seeigel']** An older selection, forming compact mounds of metallic blue-grey.

**HT** 15–25 cm (6–10″)

**'Select'** Produced from seed, this strain is somewhat variable but most plants should have good blue to silver-grey foliage.

**HT** 20–25 cm (8–10″)

**'Skinner's Blue'** A very hardy variety, selected at Skinner's Nursery in Mani-

toba. The colour leans towards turquoise-green, not as blue as other forms but the most reliable selection for the Canadian prairies. Zones 2–9.

**HT** 25–30 cm (10–12″)

## GLYCERIA ☼
(Manna Grass)

*maxima* 'Variegata'     ZONE 4
(Variegated Manna Grass)
Similar in appearance to Ribbon Grass, the leaves are striped lengthwise with green and creamy yellow. This is a vigorous, spreading grass best planted at the waterside, or contained carefully in the border by growing inside a sunken tub. Plants rarely produce flowers. Easily divided in spring or fall. Plants will tolerate growing in standing water. Cool-season.

**HT/SP** 50–90 cm (20–36″) / 60–90 cm (2–3′)
**SOIL** Prefers a rich, moist to wet soil.
**BLOOM** June–July
**USES** 〰🌾 Waterside

## HAKONECHLOA ◐•
(Hakone Grass)

*macra*     ZONE 5
(Japanese Woodland Grass)
A small group of shade-loving grasses that are slow to establish but well worth the wait. These Japanese woodlanders form arching mounds of leaves, cascading like a waterfall and always somehow managing to point in the proper direction – that is, towards the path or border edge. Small sprays of flowers appear towards late summer, nearly hidden by the foliage. Fall colour is often a good golden yellow or buff.

These make fine specimens, particularly the variegated selections listed below. The plain green species form is also good, although not nearly so easy to find. In mild regions they are superb in tubs or pots. Shade and good moisture are the main requirements for success, although full sun is tolerated in cool-summer regions. Division in spring is certainly possible, although I find that plants just sit there and take a couple of years to recover from the experience. Warm-season.

**HT/SP** 45–75 cm (18–30″) / 60–75 cm (24–30″)
**SOIL** Prefers a rich moist, well-drained soil.
**BLOOM** August–September
**USES** ▲🌾 Woodland gardens, Edging

**'Albostriata' ['Albovariegata']** (White-striped Hakone Grass) Leaves are striped lengthwise with green and creamy-white. This form is not as common as the gold-striped 'Aureola'. Plants are compact.

**HT** 30–45 cm (12–18″)

**'Aureola'** (Golden-variegated Hakone Grass) The most common form, leaves

*Hakonechloa macra* 'Aureola'

*Helictotrichon sempervirens*

*Festuca ovina glauca* 'Elijah Blue'

brightly striped in golden-yellow and green. Will tolerate morning sun. Absolutely magnificent when mature and well grown.

HT    30–65 cm (12–26")

## HELICTOTRICHON ☼
(Oat Grass)

***sempervirens***                    ZONE 3
(Blue Oat Grass)
Incredibly popular for its perfect, dome-shaped clumps of intensely blue leaves. This non-spreader is still the best blue grass for general purpose landscaping. Tan spikes appear above on graceful arching stems, although in some regions they mysteriously fail to appear. Technically evergreen, but often in need of serious trimming with scissors in the spring. Clumps may be divided in early spring. Reliable on the Prairies. Cool-season.

HT/SP  60–90 cm (2–3') / 60–70 cm (24–28")
SOIL   Average to dry, well-drained soil.
BLOOM  May–July
USES   ▲▼✂ Border

**Sapphire Fountain ['Saphirsprudel']**
Although this is said to have richer blue foliage, I fail to see much difference between it and the species. That being said, this was mainly selected for improved resistance to rust infections in warm, humid summer regions.

## HIEROCHLOE ☼
(Vanilla Grass)

***odorata***                          ZONE 3
(Sweet Grass)
Sweet Grass was extremely important to First Nations people and is still widely used for burning in various traditional ceremonies. Plants form a fast-spreading patch of narrow green leaves with short brown spikes of flowers appearing in early summer. Not particularly ornamental in effect but sometimes grown for the dried leaves, which smell strongly of fresh hay or vanilla. These can be used to make woven baskets, sachets and other crafts. May be grown as a vigorous groundcover in any moist, sunny area. A North American native wild flower. Easily divided in early spring. Cool-season.

HT/SP  25–50 cm (10–20") / 45–60 cm (18–24")
SOIL   Prefers a rich, moist soil.
BLOOM  May–July
USES   ⋀▼ Meadow, Herb gardens

## IMPERATA ☼☼
(Japanese Blood Grass)

***cylindrica*** 'Red Baron'          ZONE 5
['Rubra']
An unusual and dramatic grass that slowly forms a medium-sized clump. Leaves are green at the base and the most vibrant blood-red at the top. Excellent for massing, and particularly effective with some clever backlighting. This can be slow to establish, and may not always appreciate the site you have in mind; it seems to regard both hot, dry soils and heavy, wet soils with equal disdain. If unimproved clay soil is what your garden has to offer then Blood Grass may not be a wise choice. This selection of Imperata very rarely produces flowers. Warm-season.

HT/SP  45–50 cm (18–20") / 30–45 cm (12–18")
SOIL   Average to moist soil, needs excellent drainage.
USES   ▲⋀▼ Massing, Borders

## JUNCUS ☼☼
(Rush)

***effusus spiralis***               ZONE 4
(Spiral Rush, Corkscrew Rush)
The ornamental Rushes are waterside plants. Not true grasses, these have hollow cylindrical leaves, forming a neat clump and remaining evergreen in mild winter regions. The most common form grown is the Spiral Rush, the long leaves having a distinctive corkscrew or spiralled effect, looking like they just got home from the beauty parlor. The green flowers appear in early summer but are fairly insignificant. Sometimes grown commercially as a florist green. All of the forms do well in pots, which can be submerged into a water feature for the summer. In late fall it's best to bury the pot up to the rim in a sheltered corner of the garden, or winter it in a bright window indoors if you prefer. They are hardy in the garden, so long as a rich, moist to wet spot is provided. Any brown leaves should be trimmed back to the base in spring. Clumps may be divided in early spring.

HT/SP  45–60 cm (18–24") / 30–45 cm (12–18")
SOIL   Prefers a rich, moist to wet soil.
BLOOM  June–July
USES   ✂▼▲ Waterside, Specimen

**'Lemon Twist'** A brand new sport of 'Unicorn' that we discovered on our nursery. Plants are identical in habit and form but with a bright lemon-yellow streak running lengthwise along the spiralled leaves. A unique specimen plant, especially in containers.

HT    60–90 cm (2–3')

**'Unicorn'** (Unicorn Rush) Selected by the University of British Columbia Botanical Garden, this is like an exaggerated version of *spiralis*. The leaves are extremely curled, thicker and longer, making this even better as a unique specimen plant. Plants appreciate the same conditions, with moist to wet soil.

HT    60–90 cm (2–3')

## LEYMUS ☼☼
(Lyme Grass)
The various garden forms of Lyme Grass are almost all grown for their exceptionally beautiful steel-blue foliage. Most of them are invasive in the extreme, so some extra consideration in placing them is advised. Control the spread by planting inside a safe barrier, like a large plastic pot or bottomless bucket sunk two feet down in the ground. Or simply let it spread to help stabilize steep slopes or other problem areas. Large tubs or pots of Lyme Grass are very decorative.

***arenarius***                       ZONE 3
[Elymus arenarius]
(Blue Lyme Grass)
Despite its wandering nature this grass certainly has outstanding blue colour. The foliage is beautiful in the garden and can also be used for flower arranging. Plants quickly form a large patch. Spikes of tan flowers appear in summer. Easily divided in early spring. Tolerant of salt spray and also extremely drought resistant. Warm-season.

HT/SP  60–90 cm (2–3') / 60–90 cm (2–3')
SOIL   Tolerates a wide range of soil conditions.
BLOOM  July–August
USES   ✂⋀▼✂ Massing

## LIRIOPE see under Perennials

## LUZULA ☼●
(Wood Rush)
Grasslike plants, native to moist woodland sites but generally tolerant of dry shade. They spread slowly to form a low, dense groundcover of flat, softly hairy leaves. Although evergreen, they usually need a light trim in early spring with sharp scissors. Widely grown in European gardens, these

*Hierochloe odorata*

*Imperata cylindrica* 'Red Baron'

*Juncus effusus spiralis* 'Unicorn'

*Leymus arenarius*

deserve better appreciation here for their indestructible nature.

### *nivea*          ZONE 4
### (Snowy Wood Rush)

Upright, arching clumps of fuzzy grey-green leaves. Clusters of white flowers are showy in summer, good for cutting. Nice accent plant for the shade, particularly when mass planted.

**HT/SP** 30–60 cm (1–2') / 30–45 cm (12–18")
**SOIL** Average to moist soil, preferably acidic.
**BLOOM** May–June
**USES** ✄⊼⧍Mᵥ☗ Borders, Massing

### 'Ruby Stiletto'          ZONE 5
### (Ruby Wood Rush)

Originally discovered growing wild in British Columbia, this new form takes on beautiful bronzy-red shades during the colder months. Leaves become dark green during summer, looking similar in appearance to *L. sylvatica*. Greenish flowers are insignificant. Good for massing, particularly in winter garden designs. Evergreen.

**HT/SP** 25–30 cm (10–12") / 25–30 cm (10–12")
**SOIL** Tolerates a wide range of soil conditions.
**BLOOM** May–June
**USES** ⊼Mᵥ⧍☗☼ Borders, Massing

### *sylvatica*          ZONE 4
### (Greater Wood Rush)

This makes a dense clump of shiny, leathery green leaves, spreading moderately to form a thick groundcover, but not in an invasive way. Small clusters of brownish flowers are fairly insignificant. Grows well beneath trees and shrubs, even tolerating dry shade. Evergreen in mild winter regions. A few selections exist.

**HT/SP** 30–60 cm (1–2') / 30–60 cm (1–2')
**SOIL** Tolerates a wide range of soil conditions.
**BLOOM** May–June
**USES** ⊼Mᵥ⧍☗☼ Edging, Massing

'Aurea' (Golden Wood Rush) Foliage is chartreuse yellow, especially nice planted in front of blue Hostas.
'Marginata' (Variegated Wood Rush) Leaves have a narrow creamy-white edge. Plants seem to be less vigorous, perhaps better suited to small gardens.

## MILIUM ☼
## (Millet)

### *effusum* 'Aureum'          ZONE 5
### (Golden Wood Millet)

A colourful little grass to lighten up a shady corner with its bright golden-yellow new growth in spring. Plants form a low clump of foliage mingled with delicate sprays of flowers. Most effective in groups of three or more, planted in a cool moist location with other plants that like the same conditions. Can be short-lived but will usually self seed and come true. Cool-season.

**HT/SP** 30–40 cm (12–16") / 20–30 cm (8–12")
**SOIL** Prefers a rich, moist soil.
**BLOOM** May–June
**USES** ⧍☗ Edging, Woodland

## MISCANTHUS ☼☀☼
## (Miscanthus, Japanese Silver Grass, Maiden Grass)

The most widely-planted of the bold fall-flowering grasses, with dozens of selections to choose from; these offer a wide range of heights, flower colours and foliage effects. Most Miscanthus are well-suited to massed plantings in a low-maintenance garden, yet they also have what it takes to stand alone as specimen plants in the perennial or mixed border.

These are all warm-season grasses, tolerating heat and humidity very well, but beginning their growth late in the spring. Flowers are in fan-shaped panicles, showy in the fall border, and sometimes used for cutting. All have excellent winter interest. Cut back the dead stems in late winter or early spring, before new growth starts to shoot from the base. A hedge trimmer makes quick work of this job in large plantings. Division is best done in mid spring. With older clumps this takes substantial muscle power and perhaps an axe or saw.

Lately there has been some bad press about *Miscanthus sinensis*. In long-season regions with warm summers (like the Mid Atlantic states) certain of the early-flowering selections may produce viable seed which could become airborne, land outside of garden areas then germinate and produce new plants – in other words, there is some potential for invasiveness. In these regions the general recommendation is to plant either sterile cultivars or ones that flower very late and fail to

produce viable seed. For those of us in cool-summer areas (or north of New York City) it is less likely that any of the cultivars on the market will set viable seed. In cooler regions the invasive potential is very low-risk to nonexistent.

### 'Giganteus'          ZONE 4
### [*M. floridulus*]
### (Giant Silver Grass)

This hybrid grass is often incorrectly listed as *M. floridulus*, which is a different and smaller species seldom encountered true-to-form in North America. Giant Silver Grass is the granddaddy of this tribe, forming a very tall and wide clump of green leaves, the tips arching gracefully in layers. Sometimes used to create a living screen or fence. The corn-like stalks remain upright through the winter months. In regions with long and warm summers, reddish-pink flower spikes are produced in late fall, turning to silvery plumes as they mature. This tolerates part shade and poor soils. Usually the lower leaves turn brown and dry in late summer, giving the plant a "bare knees" look that can be avoided by planting something sizable in front. The roots are not invasive like *M. sacchariflorus* but the clumps do become rather wide in time. Plants will not usually self sow.

**HT/SP** 250–300 cm (8–10') / 90–120 cm (3–4')
**SOIL** Average to moist, well-drained soil.
**BLOOM** September–November
**USES** ✄ Specimen, Screen

### 'Purpurascens'          ZONE 3
### [*M. sinensis purpurascens*]
### (Orange Flame Grass)

This is a hybrid form, selected in Germany in the 1960's. In recent years it has proven to be hardy and useful over a very wide area, including Minnesota and the Canadian Prairies. Foliage is green through the summer months, developing rich tones of flame-orange and rust in autumn, although this seems to vary with climate and weather conditions. Flowers appear fairly early, the spikes slightly pink when they open, fairly quickly becoming silver. The mid-sized habit lends itself well to smaller gardens. Sturdy and fairly carefree. Considered to be sterile.

**HT/SP** 120–150 cm (4–5') / 75–90 cm (30–36")
**SOIL** Average to moist, well-drained soil.
**BLOOM** August–October
**USES** ✄☗ Borders, Specimen

### *sacchariflorus*          ZONE 3
### [*M. sacchariflorus* 'Robustus']
### (Silver Banner Grass)

A spreading species, quickly forming a broad patch of tall, stout corn-like stems, clothed by gracefully arching foliage with a bamboo-like, tropical ap-

*Miscanthus* 'Purpurascens'          *Millium effusum* 'Aureum'

*Luzula sylvatica* 'Marginata'

pearance. Silvery plumes turn reddish as they mature, and the foliage turns yellow in autumn. This plant will need to be contained to keep it in bounds as the roots have a terrible tendency to run. Recent trials in Minnesota have shown good hardiness in Zone 3. Plants may self-sow in long-summer regions.

**HT/SP** 180–240 cm (6–8') / 90–120 cm (3–4')
**SOIL** Average to moist or wet soil.
**BLOOM** August–October
**USES** ✂ Specimen, Screen

### *sinensis* ZONE 5
### (Miscanthus, Japanese Silver Grass, Eulalia)

A superb group of grasses, versatile both as specimens or in massed plantings. All bloom in the fall and hold their shape well into the winter, fading to shades of tan or cream and contrasting nicely with evergreens. Selections vary widely in leaf and flower colour, height, form and hardiness.

**SP** 90–120 cm (3–4')
**SOIL** Average to moist, well-drained soil.
**BLOOM** August–November
**USES** ✂ Specimen, Borders

**'Adagio'** (Dwarf Maiden Grass) Probably the best of the dwarf forms for smaller gardens. Leaves are narrow and silver in appearance, with pinkish spikes that are held well above, appearing in late summer. Foliage develops good yellow tones in the fall. Zone 6.

**HT** 90–120 cm (3–4')

**'Arabesque'** A reliable late-summer bloomer, with a display of soft silvery-pink plumes. Leaves are green and narrow. Mid-sized habit. Zone 6.

**HT** 120–150 cm (4–5')

**'Autumn Light'** Tall stems of silvery-white plumes appear in early fall, over a clump of narrow dark-green leaves. Zone 5.

**HT** 180–240 cm (6–8')

**'Cabaret'** (Variegated Miscanthus) Exceptionally wide leaves are creamy-white in the centre with marginal stripes of dark green. By far the boldest of the many variegated selections. Silvery-pink plumes only make an appearance in warm-summer regions. This has been proven to not self seed. Zone 6.

**HT** 180–270 cm (6–9')

**'Cosmopolitan'** (Variegated Miscanthus) Rather wide green leaves, boldly edged lengthwise with creamy white. Effective display of coppery-pink plumes. Occasionally sections will revert to green and these should be removed. This is one of the flashiest forms, but only reliably hardy to Zone 6.

**HT** 180–300 cm (6–10')

**'Gracillimus'** (Maiden Grass) Very narrow green leaves with an arching

habit, forming a large symmetrical clump. One of the best for formal plantings. Coppery-pink plumes may appear very late in warm regions, or not at all in cooler zones. Widely grown. Zone 5.

**HT** 150–210 cm (5–7')

**'Grosse Fontaine'** [Large Fountain] An early-blooming selection with silvery plumes in great numbers. Foliage is green and of average width, cascading gracefully. Zone 5.

**HT** 210–240 cm (7–8')

**'Malepartus'** Soft-pink plumes in September quickly turn white and fluffy. Green foliage turns golden in the autumn, often flushed with orange and bronze. Zone 5.

**HT** 180–210 cm (6–7')

**'Morning Light'** (Variegated Maiden Grass) Tightly rolled leaves are similar to 'Gracillimus', but with a narrow band of white on the margin. The effect from several feet away is silvery and shimmering. Very late to flower, with coppery-pink plumes. Originally from Japan, this introduction has quickly become popular. Does not self seed. Zone 5.

**HT** 120–180 cm (4–6')

**purpurascens** see Miscanthus 'Purpurascens'

**Red-silver** ['Rotsilber'] A compact German selection with outstanding large deep-red plumes in early fall. Green foliage develops good flame-red autumn colour as well. Zone 5.

**HT** 120–150 cm (4–5')

**'Sarabande'** (Maiden Grass) Very narrow and fine-textured silvery leaves. An early bloomer, with golden plumes. Zone 5.

**HT** 150–180 cm (5–6')

**Silver Feather** ['Silberfeder'] An older selection, a refined version of the species, with shimmering silvery-white plumes appearing in late August, held up high above the foliage. A reliable bloomer in cool summer regions. Zone 4.

**HT** 150–210 cm (5–7')

**Silver Arrow** ['Silberpfeil'] Similar in appearance to 'Variegatus', with brighter green and white variegation and a more upright habit. Plumes are very soft pink. Zone 6.

**HT** 180–240 cm (6–8')

**'Strictus'** (Porcupine Grass) Bright green leaves with showy golden horizontal banding. Stiff, upright clumps don't require staking, unlike the more floppy 'Zebrinus'. Plumes open soft pink, becoming silver. A unique specimen plant, especially when viewed up close. Zone 5.

**HT** 180–240 cm (6–8')

**'Undine'** (Maiden Grass) Large silvery plumes are held high above the mid-sized clump of narrow dark-green leaves. Among the showiest in flower. Zone 5.

**HT** 180–210 cm (6–7')

**'Variegatus'** (Variegated Silver Grass) Distinctive green and white striped leaves, forming an arching clump. Plumes are reddish-pink at first, becoming silver. An older selection, but still very bright and showy. Mature clumps may need staking. Zone 5.

**HT** 150–210 cm (5–7')

**'Yaku-jima'** (Dwarf Maiden Grass) Very compact selection from Japan. Leaves are rather narrow, with silvery plumes appearing towards late summer but often hidden among the leaves. A good selection for smaller gardens. Zone 6.

**HT** 90–120 cm (3–4')

**'Zebrinus'** (Zebra Grass) Exceedingly popular, the green leaves are banded horizontally with golden yellow. Plumes are coppery pink at first. The overall look is very similar to 'Strictus' but with a less upright habit. Often requires staking. Zone 5.

**HT** 180–240 cm (6–8')

# MOLINIA ☼ ◑
## (Moor Grass)

The Moor grasses have much to offer the garden designer. All are clumping in habit, with no inclination to seed about or spread in unwanted ways. Typically they form a low clump of foliage with taller wands of delicate flowers waving above in mid to late summer. Fall colour is usually a bright and glowing gold. In Europe these are often included as accents in large Heather plantings. Cool-season.

*Miscanthus sinensis* 'Strictus'

*Miscanthus sinensis* 'Sarabande'

*Miscanthus sinensis* Silver Arrow

### caerulea subsp. arundinacea 'Skyracer'          ZONE 4
### (Tall Moor Grass)

A tall-growing selection which has been well-described as a "kinetic sculpture". Open spikes of flowers are in constant motion from the slightest breeze, held far above the foliage on graceful, arching stems. Outstanding in front of a dark backdrop, especially when used as a specimen or focal point. It disappears if used at the back of the border. The entire plant turns the most amazing golden colour in autumn. Unfortunately, the winter effect is short, the stems usually getting bashed down by Christmas.

**HT/SP**  180–240 cm (6–8') / 75–90 cm (30–36")
**SOIL**  Average to moist, well-drained soil.
**BLOOM** July–October
**USES**  ✄◀☙ Specimen

### caerulea subsp. caerulea          ZONE 3
### (Dwarf Moor Grass)

A variable species that has produced a small number of excellent cultivars. Native to moist, acid moors in northern Europe but readily adapts to garden conditions. Plants form a low to medium-sized mound that looks good used either as a small specimen or when mass planted in the border. Good fall foliage colour. These take a couple of years to become established. One of the best grasses for northern regions, including the Prairies.

**HT/SP**  60–75 cm (24–30") / 30–60 cm (1–2')
**SOIL**  Average to moist, well-drained soil.
**BLOOM** July–October
**USES**  ✄◀☙ Borders, Massing

**Swamp Witch ['Moorhexe']** Flower spikes are bronzy-purple, held on poker-straight stems above a low mound of green foliage. The narrow,

upright habit is best seen with a low groundcover surrounding the plants.

**HT**  45–75 cm (18–30")

**'Variegata' (Variegated Moor Grass)** Forms a low mound of narrow leaves striped lengthwise with green and creamy yellow. Arching golden stems hold loose wands of purplish flowers. An absolutely shimmering grass for cool-summer regions.

**HT**  60–75 cm (24–30")

## OPHIOPOGON see under Perennials

## PANICUM ☼◔
### (Panic Grass)

Switch grass has made great strides in recent years. Some of the newer selections have become valuable additions to perennial and mixed borders all over the world. Native to North America, these were an important component of the original tallgrass prairie. Warm-season.

### virgatum          ZONE 3
### (Switch Grass)

One of the best grasses for multi-season interest, particularly for autumn display. Plants form a wide clump of narrow green leaves, with airy clouds of flowers in July giving way to reddish seed heads by late summer. These can have outstanding yellow and red fall foliage colour, although it seems to depend a lot on the kind of fall weather experienced. Foliage softens to tan for the winter but sometimes gets bashed down by snow and ice. Some gardeners experience loads of self-sown seedlings, although having growing 'Heavy Metal' for years in my own garden, it has never become a problem for me. Clumps are easily divided in early spring. Drought and salt tolerant.

**HT/SP**  120–180 cm (4–6') / 75–90 cm (30–36")
**SOIL**  Tolerates a wide range of soil conditions.
**BLOOM** August–October
**USES**  ✄◀☙✄ Borders, Massing

**'Haense Herms' (Red Switch Grass)** Green foliage develops reddish tips by late summer, then becomes all-burgundy in the autumn. Mid-sized in height, with an arching or cascading habit.

**HT**  90–120 cm (3–4')

**'Heavy Metal' (Blue Switch Grass)** Bright metallic-blue foliage is effective all season, developing yellow and red fall highlights. Good narrow and upright habit.

**HT**  120–150 cm (4–5')

**'Northwind'** Just recently introduced, this has a very narrow and tall habit, with olive-green foliage. Reliable golden fall colour. Shows much promise in the hands of clever designers.

**HT**  120–150 cm (4–5')

**'Prairie Sky' (Blue Switch Grass)** An even richer shade of blue than 'Heavy Metal'. Habit is somewhat more open and loose. Butter-gold autumn colour.

**HT**  90–120 cm (3–4')

**'Shenandoah' (Red Switch Grass)** The best of the bunch for gorgeous wine-burgundy colour in the fall. Leaf tips already show hints of red by midsummer. Recently introduced from Germany by Hans Simone.

**HT**  90–120 cm (3–4')

**'Strictum'** Very tall habit, with slightly blue foliage and a good display of reddish seedheads.

**HT**  120–180 cm (4–6')

**'Warrior' (Red Switch Grass)** A taller selection with reddish fall colour. Bushy habit.

**HT**  120–150 cm (4–5')

## PENNISETUM ☼
### (Fountain Grass)

A well-named grass, since the hundreds of soft bottlebrush flower spikes that arch out and move in the breeze do indeed resemble the spray of a fountain. The different species and selections now available vary greatly in hardiness, but most are quite effective even when treated as annuals in colder regions, especially in container plantings. Warm season.

### alopecuroides          ZONE 5
### (Perennial Fountain Grass)

The species itself forms medium-sized clumps of cascading green leaves. Flowers are buff to soft rose-coloured feathery spikes, held just above the leaves, followed by fuzzy bottlebrush seed-heads. Excellent fall and early winter effect, the foliage turns bright almond and lasts well until bashed down by ice storms. Flowering is best when given a hot and sunny location. The species itself varies somewhat in height, flower colour and hardiness. These are considered to have moderate drought tolerance but are happiest when supplied with regular moisture. Clumps are easily divided in spring. Several good selections exist.

Like Miscanthus, there is some need for concern regarding self seeding, particularly in regions with long, warm summers. Wide-leaved selections like 'Moudry' are the worst cultivars for setting copious amounts of viable seed, and dead-heading these before late fall is a good idea. In northern regions the more common selections like 'Hameln' will probably not have time to develop ripe seed.

Panicum virgatum 'Prairie Sky'

Panicum v. 'Shenandoah'

Panicum virgatum 'Warrior'

Pennisetum alop. 'Hameln'

Molinia caerulea 'Variegata'

Pennisetum alop. 'Moudry'

**HT/SP** 90–120 cm (3–4') / 60–90 cm (2–3')
**SOIL** Tolerates a wide range of soil conditions.
**BLOOM** August–October
**USES** ✂✿⚘ Borders, Massing

**'Hameln'** Probably the best selection for general landscape use, this forms slightly shorter clumps than the species and is said to flower a bit earlier and to be more reliably hardy. When grouping a large number of these together it's good to have a clonal selection like this one so that the patch looks even in habit, flower colour and blooming time. Spikes are silvery-white and held in view above the leaves.
**HT** 75–90 cm (30–36")

**'Little Bunny'** (Dwarf Fountain Grass) Quite dwarf in habit, making it ideal for edging, rock gardens or containers. The creamy plumes are small but produced in great numbers. Deadhead in late fall to prevent seedlings. Slightly less hardy. Zone 6.
**HT/SP** 30–45 cm (12–18") / 30–45 cm (12–18")

**'Moudry'** (Black-flowered Fountain Grass) Quite unique in the garden, with soft bottlebrush spikes of deep black-purple. This is one of the wide-leaved selections that can self-seed all over the place in warm summer regions. Deadheading in late fall is recommended. Late to flower. Zone 6.
**HT** 75–90 cm (30–36")

***glaucum*** **'Purple Majesty'** ANNUAL
(Purple Ornamental Millet)
Brand new for 2003. All America Gold Medal winner. This grass is an annual but in no time perennial gardeners will be using it in borders, containers and anywhere else that a dramatic colour effect is required. The leaves start out green in spring then turn a shimmering dark mahogany purple during the summer heat, creating a substantial clump. Long bottlebrush spikes of tan to gold flowers become shiny purple seed heads in the fall – these are terrific for cutting. Said to be highly drought tolerant. Wait until the spring weather warms before planting outdoors.
**HT/SP** 90–150 cm (3–5') / 75–90 cm (30–36")
**SOIL** Tolerates a wide range of soil conditions.
**BLOOM** July–October
**USES** ✂✿⚘ Containers, Specimen, Borders

***orientale*** ZONE 6
(Oriental Fountain Grass)
This species produces fluffy-looking spikes in a pearly-white shade, hinting at soft pink. Blooms are attractive for several months, beginning in late summer. Leaves are narrow and arching, and the overall look is truly like a fountain. Hardiness is better than first suspected, particularly with good drainage through the winter months. Plants are reported to dislike being

divided, seed being the best method for propagation. Sometimes grown as an annual for bedding or in containers. Fairly drought tolerant.
**HT/SP** 60–75 cm (24–30") / 60–75 cm (24–30")
**SOIL** Tolerates a wide range of soil conditions.
**BLOOM** July–October
**USES** ✂✿⚘ Rock gardens, Edging

***setaceum*** ZONE 9
(Tender Fountain Grass)
Widely used in public gardens and civic plantings as a centre-piece to flowering annual beds. Plants make a large cascading mound of green leaves with showy rosy-pink plumes in late summer and fall. Although not hardy in most areas, this remains a favourite tender grass for its dependable flower display, particularly the purple-leaved selection listed below. Not likely to self-seed outside of the extreme southern states.
**HT/SP** 90–120 cm (3–4') / 60–90 cm (2–3')
**SOIL** Average to moist, well-drained soil.
**BLOOM** August–October
**USES** ✂✿⚘ Containers, Specimen

**'Rubrum'** (Purple Fountain Grass) Beautiful burgundy or wine-red foliage contrasts well against the pink bottle-brush plumes. Always welcome in the perennial border, this looks especially exotic in container or tub plantings. True red-leaved forms can only be propagated by division. Plants must be wintered in a warm greenhouse or simply purchased new each season – no amount of mulch will bring this semi-tropical plant through even a Zone 7 winter.

# PHALARIS ☀◐
(Canary Grass)

***arundinacea*** ZONE 2
(Ribbon Grass)
These form a fast-spreading patch of leaves, brightly striped in various colours, depending on the selection. The plain green forms are not grown in gardens. Flowers are tan-coloured spikes and not particularly showy. Useful as a groundcover, especially in wet areas, but usually spreading too quickly for the border unless contained inside a large sunken pot. Nice in mixed containers or tubs. In warm summer regions Ribbon Grass can get very shabby-looking by late summer. Clipping plants back hard in early July will rejuvenate the foliage so it remains attractive until late fall. Cool-season.
**HT/SP** 60–90 cm (2–3') / 90–120 cm (3–4')
**SOIL** Average to moist or wet soil.
**BLOOM** June–July
**USES** ✂✿⚘ Massing, Waterside

**'Feesey'** ['Strawberries and Cream'] (Tricolor Ribbon Grass) Foliage of this form is very brightly striped lengthwise with mint-green and white. During the cooler months of spring and fall the

leaves take on tinges of bright pink. Slightly more compact than 'Picta', but otherwise similar in habit and use. Benefits from a midsummer clip in warm regions.
**HT** 45–70 cm (18–28")

**'Picta'** (Gardener's Garters, Ribbon Grass) When the term "ornamental grass" strikes fear in the minds of gardeners, inevitably they have had a previous encounter with this selection – so commonly passed from neighbour to neighbour. Despite its wandering nature and pushy reputation, there is no arguing that the green and white striped leaves are handsome in all but the hottest months of the year. Perhaps it's best to grow this in containers where the spreading roots will be kept in check. This historical variety has probably been grown in North American gardens longer than any other grass. Clip back hard in midsummer.
**HT** 60–90 cm (2–3')

## PHORMIUM see under Perennials

# SACCHARUM ☀
(Plume Grass)
This group of plants includes the Sugarcane, a tropical grass of great economic importance. The most important hardy form used to be known as *Erianthus*. Warm-season.

***ravennae*** ZONE 6
[*Erianthus ravennae*]
(Ravenna Grass, Northern Pampas Grass)
Those of us in colder regions will find this grass to be the best possible substitute for the much-coveted true Pampas Grass of mild-winter climates

*Pennisetum orientale*
*Pennisetum setaceum 'Rubrum'*
*Phalaris a. 'Picta'*
*Spartina p. 'Aureo-marginata'*
*Saccharum ravennae*

(Cortaderia). It forms stout clumps of grey-green leaves fairly low to the ground, with tall stems of big silvery plumes rising dramatically above in the autumn, lasting well through winter. Featuring this as a specimen surrounded by a low groundcover is far more effective than hiding it at the back of the border. Plants take three to four years to reach a mature size and become spectacular. Good drought tolerance. Some gardeners in Zone 5 are reporting success with this.

HT/SP   240–360 cm (8–12') / 80–90 cm (32–36")
SOIL    Tolerates a wide range of soil conditions.
BLOOM September–November
USES    ✂🌾 Specimen, Cut flower

## SESLERIA ☀◐
(Moor Grass)

### caerulea    ZONE 4
(Blue Moor Grass)
A tough little clump-forming grass with metallic blue-grey foliage and short spikes of purplish flowers that appear in early spring. Most effective when mass planted as a groundcover or low edging. Tolerates nearly any site in sun or part shade. Clumps are easily divided in spring or early fall. Evergreen in mild-winter regions. Cool-season.

HT/SP   15–20 cm (6–8") / 25–30 cm (10–12")
SOIL    Tolerates a wide range of soil conditions.
BLOOM April–May
USES    ⏶〰▲🌾 Edging, Massing

## SPARTINA ☀◐
(Cord Grass)

### pectinata 'Aureo-marginata' ZONE 4
(Variegated Cord Grass)
An upright grass, spreading quickly to form a patch or open clump. Stems are tall with strongly arching foliage of bright green with a narrow yellow margin. Most effective for massing, especially beside a pond or stream. Also nice at the back of the border. Good foliage for flower arranging. Drought-resistant once established. This could make a gorgeous centre-piece in a large tub. The species itself is native over much of North America but seldom grown in gardens. Warm-season.

HT/SP   150–210 cm (5–7') / 90–120 cm (3–4')
SOIL    Average to moist or wet soil.
BLOOM August–September
USES    ✂🌾 Waterside, Massing

## STIPA ☀
(Needle Grass)
Quite unique among grasses, *Stipa* are valued for their whiskered panicles or flower-heads. These are usually airy open sprays of tiny individual flowers held well above the leaves on the ends of graceful arching stems. Some types are especially valuable in hot, dry climates as they readily withstand drought. Cool-season.

### gigantea    ZONE 6
(Giant Feather Grass)
A spectacular plant for the sunny garden, preferring regions with cool summers and mild winters like the Pacific Northwest. Plants form a clump of grey-green foliage at the base, bearing very tall, arching stems of tan flower spikes through the summer months, which last well into winter. Best used as a specimen plant, surrounded by a low groundcover but also suitable for containers. Clumps should be pruned back hard in early spring before new growth resumes. Easily divided in early spring if desired. Plants dislike wet winters, so a well-drained soil is best. Evergreen in mild regions. Cool-season.

HT/SP   210–240 cm (7–8') / 90–120 cm (3–4')
SOIL    Average to dry, well-drained soil.
BLOOM June–August
USES    ✂🌾▲🌾 Specimen

### tenuissima    ZONE 6
[Nassella tenuissima]
(Mexican Feather Grass)
A beautiful compact species, the fine hair-like bright green leaves forming a low arching clump. Spikes of bearded green flowers begin to appear in mid-summer, soon changing into handsome, golden-blond plumes. Even just a few plants will constantly be in motion from the slightest breeze. A unique flower for cutting, either fresh or dried. This may prove to be far hardier than first thought as long as plants have excellent drainage, or they may act as a self-seeding annual. Terrific in mixed containers. Extremely drought tolerant. Cool-season.

HT/SP   45–60 cm (18–24") / 30–45 cm (12–18")
SOIL    Average to dry, well-drained soil.
BLOOM June–September
USES    ✂⏶🌾🌾 Borders, Rock gardens

## TYPHA ☀
(Cat-tail)

### latifolia 'Variegata'    ZONE 3
(Variegated Cat-tail)
A variegated version of our native Common Cat-tail, the leaves are striped lengthwise with mint-green and creamy white. Greenish flowers in early summer give way to the familiar cigar-shaped seed heads of rich chocolate brown. This is a vigorous spreader requiring a fair amount of space and a moist to wet site. Easily grown in tubs or pots set into smaller water features, the wandering nature then being easily controlled. Divide clumps in early spring.

HT/SP   90–120 cm (3–4') / 75–90 cm (30–36")
SOIL    Prefers a rich, moist to wet soil. Tolerates standing water.
BLOOM June–July
USES    ✂🌾 Waterside

### minima    ZONE 4
(Miniature Cat-tail)
This is like a miniature version of our native Cat-tail, on a scale better suited to the smaller garden. Narrow grassy leaves form a clump or small patch. Short and chubby dark-brown cat-tails appear in early summer. Prefers a wet to moist site, and is best at the waterside. Also worth trying in tubs or as a patio plant.

HT/SP   40–70 cm (16–28") / 30–60 cm (1–2')
SOIL    Prefers a rich, moist to wet soil. Tolerates standing water.
BLOOM June–July
USES    ✂🌾 Waterside

## UNCINIA ☀◐
(Hook Sedge)

### uncinata    ZONE 8
(Red Hook Sedge)
Native to New Zealand, this low-growing Sedge forms an arching mound of fine hairlike leaves in a beautiful shade of burnished bronzy-red. Evergreen in the milder winter areas where it is hardy. A beautiful contrast plant for the rock garden, moist border, or in containers and tubs. Flowers are insignificant. Trim tips lightly in spring with scissors, to tidy up. Clumps may be divided in early spring, and will probably self seed as well. In colder regions this may be grown in pots and wintered indoors.

HT/SP   30–45 cm (12–18") / 20–30 cm (8–12")
SOIL    Prefers a moist to wet soil.
BLOOM June
USES    ⏶🌾▲ Edging, Waterside

Stipa tenuissima

Stipa gigantea

Typha minima

# Pest & Disease Problems

Nothing gets the new perennial gardener in a state of panic more quickly than the appearance of a mysterious pest or disease during the course of the growing season. Before you run to the shed for a bottle of pesticide, it's wise to do a bit of research to try and figure out exactly what the problem is. Proper diagnosis is important because then you can put your efforts towards an effective solution before the problem spreads all over the garden.

## Prevention
Strong, healthy plants that are growing in fertile soil with regular watering are best able to cope with disease and insect infestations. Stressed or unhealthy plants seem to give off visual signals that attract a wide range of insect predators in particular, but sickly plants are also more susceptible to foliage diseases such as powdery mildew.

## Siting and spacing
Proper siting alone will meet the basic needs of many plants. Ensure plants are planted in an appropriate site for moisture, sunlight etc. Get a soil analysis to ensure nutrients are adequate in the soil and space plants far enough apart to ensure good air circulation and growth.

## Maintenance
Regular fertilizing, watering, deadheading, cutting back and division of perennials, particularly in a closely-spaced border setting, will help them to stay healthy.

## Good hygiene
General garden hygiene is a major factor in helping to prevent insect, fungal and bacterial disease problems. During the growing season, remove and dispose of dead or diseased plant material promptly by putting it in the garbage; don't put it in the compost heap or the problem may eventually spread all over the garden. Clean up the dead tops of perennials in late fall or early spring and put them on the compost. This activity does for the perennial garden what flossing does for your teeth: it removes the opportunity for insects and diseases to hide and possibly spread to other plants.

## Monitoring
Throughout the season, keep an eye out for plants that don't look quite right and deal with problems promptly before a major infestation happens. Usually the worst problems develop just as the cool spring weather warms up, especially in humid regions.

## Get help with identification
When in doubt, harvest a sample of the damaged portion of the plant, along with any insect pests if these are present. Place these in a sealed Ziploc bag and go in search of an expert to help you — maybe the pest expert at your favourite garden centre, the local Master Gardener's plant clinic, or a horticulturist at your local botanical garden or university extension department. Pest problems are extremely difficult to diagnose sight unseen, so a live sample is the best route to go whenever possible.

# Diseases

Because their spores are tiny and move in the air, fungal diseases seem to suddenly appear from nowhere. They are a sometimes a problem on certain perennials in some years yet not in others. Watering plants in the morning is helpful for disease control because sunlight will dry the foliage quickly and reduce the chances of disease spores germinating on moist leaf surfaces. Some of the more common diseases of perennial plants are listed here:

**Botrytis**: Buds or flowers develop brown or beige spots and do not develop normally. Tissue is soft and brown, sometimes with greyish fuzzy mould. Can also turn leaves or stems black; sometimes causes wilting. Usually worse during wet weather. *Damage*: Unsightly. Can lead to stem rot and in some cases root rot which kills the plant, especially tulips. *Recommended controls*: For susceptible plants, remove faded flowers and damaged stems or leaves promptly. Use a preventative fungicide. *Plant hosts*: Iris, Lilies, Peonies, Rudbeckia, Salvia, Tulips as well as annuals like Begonia, Dahlia, Gladiolus, Pelargonium, Petunia.

**Downy Mildew**: Not as well known as Powdery Mildew, and without the white spots. Leaves develop pale yellow or green spots on the upper surface with fuzzy white or grey spore bodies on the underside. Severely infected leaves shrivel up and turn brown quickly. *Damage*: Severe infections can kill or seriously weaken plants. *Recommended controls*: Spray with a preventative fungicide. Prune out and destroy infected areas of the plant. Remove badly infected plants and destroy. *Plant hosts*: Artemisia, Aster, Geum, Phlox subulata and other rock garden types, Potentilla.

**Leaf Spot**: Brown or black spots on leaves. Leaves usually don't drop off. Worst during wet, humid weather. *Damage*: Unsightly. Bad infestations may weaken plant. *Recommended controls*: Sanitation; remove infected leaves as noticed, clean up around plants in fall. Usually worse in warm humid weather but sometimes in cool, wet weather also. Avoid watering in the evening. Use a recommended spray or dust (check the label) when the spots begin to appear. Repeat every two weeks as necessary. *Plant hosts*: Wide range of perennials and other plants. Aster, Chrysanthemum, Coreopsis, Delphinium, Dianthus, Digitalis, English Ivy, Hemerocallis, Heuchera, Hosta, Iris, Paeonia, Phlox, Rudbeckia, Veronica.

**Powdery Mildew**: White powdery-looking spots or coating on the upper surface of leaves and stems. Most obvious by late summer or fall but the problem usually begins in early summer. Really gets going when humidity levels fluctuate widely; hot days and cooler nights. Powdery Mildew is usually quite host-specific – the fungus that infects Phlox will generally not spread to other types of plants.
*Damage*: Unsightly. Leaves may drop off. Severe, recurrent infestations can weaken plants.
*Recommended controls*: Many plants succumb to powdery mildew when they experience drought stress. Keep plants evenly moist. Avoid watering in the evening. Increase air circulation by growing susceptible plants away from walls or fences. Grow susceptible plants in full sun. Sanitation: clean up all infested dead tops and fallen leaves in autumn and destroy. Use a preventative fungicidal spray on susceptible plants every 5–10 days, starting in early summer – organic products containing sulphur are a good choice. Some gardeners report good success using horticultural oil as a spray. Select a mildew-resistant variety.
*Plant hosts*: Wide range of perennials, especially Aster, Chrysanthemum, Coreopsis, Delphinium, Lupinus, Monarda, Phlox paniculata, Rudbeckia, Solidago, Veronica.

**Root Rot**: Affecting a wide range of perennial plants, various fungal infections can cause root rot. Most often related to poor drainage conditions. Plants may suddenly start to wilt and not respond to extra water. Bases of stems may show cankers or soft, rotting lesions.
*Damage*: Leaves wilt, stems may collapse. Iris often will fall over at blooming time.
*Recommended controls*: Remove dying plants, including roots. Remedy bad drainage problems by installing drainage tile or building raised beds. Move unhappy plants to another area in the garden with better drainage. Reduce irrigation cycles on automatic systems, if necessary. Fungicidal drenches may help to save infected plants if applied early on.
*Plant hosts*: Wide range of perennials. Many alpine plants will get root rot when grown in soil that is too heavy. Especially susceptible: Dianthus, Lavender, Poppy, Rosemary. Bearded

Iris sometimes develop root rot but often this is a result of Iris Borer holes in the roots becoming infected by soil pathogens.

**Rust**: Orange, reddish or brown spots, usually on the undersides of leaves or on stems. Raised masses of spores may appear by midsummer. Rust diseases are caused by a fungal infection and are specific to certain plants or plant families.
*Damage*: Unsightly. Plants may be weakened.
*Recommended controls*: Sanitation; remove infected leaves regularly and destroy. Destroy dead tops in the autumn and clean up well beneath plants. Use a fungicide recommended for the specific rust/plant association.
*Plant hosts*: Wide range of perennials, especially the Hollyhock family (Alcea, Lavatera, Malva, Sidalcea), Aconitum, Coreopsis, Delphinium, Iris, Heuchera, Monarda, Phlox, Potentilla, some Ornamental Grasses. Daylily Rust is of great concern lately, since these plants are extremely popular.

**Viruses**: More difficult to diagnose, viruses can infect a wide range of perennial plants. Of most concern are yellowing, stunted plants that fail to grow in a healthy manner. Be suspicious of plants with oddly mottled leaves or leaves that appear distorted – crinkled and misshapen but not from insect damage.
*Damage*: Once symptoms become apparent the virus is usually throughout the entire plant system. Causes severe lack of vigour and can lead to death. No cure.
*Recommended controls*: Destroy and discard all infected plants before the problem spreads. Virus infections cannot be controlled with pesticides or home remedies. Many viruses are spread by insect pests, particularly aphids, leafhoppers, thrips and whitefly. Viruses can also spread by vegetative propagation, including dividing infected plants or taking cuttings. Control insect infestations and eliminate weeds that may be virus hosts.
*Plant hosts*: Wide range of perennials, especially: Chrysanthemum, Delphinium, Lilium, Paeonia, Primula.

**Wilts**: Arching or withered shoots, often with drooping, yellowing leaves. Sudden collapse of infected plants or stems, not due to lack of water.

Mysterious symptoms, similar to root rot.
*Damage*: Certain stems or entire plant dies.
*Recommended controls*: May be caused by a fungal or bacterial wilt infection within the plant stem tissue. Destroy and discard infected plants. Wilts are soil-borne so avoid putting another plant of the same kind in the vicinity. Pesticides will not have any effect.
*Plant hosts*: Wide range of perennials: Aster, Chrysanthemum, Dianthus, Peony, Phlox.

## Insects

The list of creepy-crawly things that most commonly affect perennials is not a long one. Hopefully the descriptions of insects and damage symptoms below will help to identify most of the insect pests you are likely to encounter. If you are unsure of the identity of a pest it's wise to try and get a diagnosis from a local expert, since pests vary quite a bit from region to region. An expert can also recommend the most effective control and proper timing to carry this out. Because the list of registered insecticides varies from region to region (also because new ones are constantly developed and older ones phased out) we do not list specific product names here in most cases. Always check the product labels at your local garden center or hardware store.

**Aphids**: Small green, red, brown or black soft-bodied insects that suck plant sap. Seen in clusters on stems, buds or the undersides of leaves. They usually secrete a sticky substance.
*Damage*: Deformed leaves (usually cupped), shoots or flowers. Black sooty mould may grow on the sticky secretions. Aphids can spread viral diseases.
*Recommended controls*: Hose aphids off with a blast of water. Spray with insecticidal soap. Remove affected shoots. Sprinkle with diatomaceous earth. Release ladybugs as natural predators. Use a recommended insecticide.
*Plant hosts*: Wide range of perennials and other garden plants. Especially: Chrysanthemum, Delphinium, Heuchera, Lupinus, Oriental Poppies.

**Caterpillars**: Crawling and worm-like, with many tiny legs. Smooth, spiny or hairy. Often green or brown but can be many colours. The adults are butterflies and moths.
*Damage*: Chew holes in leaves, sometimes stripping stems completely.
*Recommended controls*: Hand-picking. Spraying with B.T. (an organic bacterial spray that only affects caterpillars). Use a recommended insecticide if damage is severe. Bear in mind that most plants can spare a few leaves, a fair tradeoff for the beautiful butterflies you might enjoy later in the season. Butterflies can be beneficial, acting as pollinators.
*Plant hosts*: Silver-leaved plants such as Artemisia, Antennaria but many others also, including: Alcea, Asclepias, Aster, Foeniculum (Fennel), Helianthus, Parsley, Viola.

**Iris Borer**: Starts out as small worm-like larvae inside the leaf, working their way down to the rhizome and becoming large worm-like larvae.
*Damage*: The tunnels created often become a home to bacterial soft rot, causing the rhizome to turn to stinking mush and the leaf fans to fall over. A serious pest of Iris that can destroy the plants. Generally only of concern east of the Rocky Mountains.
*Recommended controls*: Sanitation; remove all dead or discolored leaves in summer and fall. Lift affected clumps; divide and soak affected rhizomes in a solution of 1 part bleach to 10 parts water; kill root borers by poking with a piece of wire; kill larvae within the leaves by squeezing between your thumb and forefinger. Replant in a new location. Some systemic insecticides are registered in certain regions for Iris Borer control.
*Plant hosts*: Iris, especially Bearded Iris, occasionally other types.

**Japanese Beetle**: Large, hard-shelled iridescent green beetles with coppery wings, usually seen from June to September. Not a problem west of the Rockies, on the prairies or in the Maritime provinces.
*Damage*: Beetles feed on flowers and leaves. Feeding may be severe where populations are high. Leaves are usually skeletonized. Larvae are grubs that feed on the roots of turfgrass and other plants.
*Recommended controls*: Hand picking or shaking beetles into a bucket of

water. Trap beetles with a hanging Japanese Beetle trap where infestations are severe. Use a recommended insecticidal spray or dust. Various biological controls may be locally available – check at your garden center.
*Plant hosts*: Wide range of plants, including the foliage of many trees, flowers of roses, fruit of cultivated and wild grapes. Perennial favourites include Hollyhock (Alcea) and Hibiscus but the beetles may nibble on a variety of others.

**Leafminers**: Tiny little worm-like larvae that tunnel and feed inside leaves.
*Damage*: White, yellow or brown blotches on leaves, tunnels or trails can be easily seen.
*Recommended controls*: Sanitation; remove and discard affected leaves. Mulching with gravel under the plants may help. Cut back foliage to force attractive fresh leaves (especially with Columbines). Leafminer damage can be prevented by using systemic insecticides but it's really more of a cosmetic problem and hardly worth the bother for most perennials.
*Plant hosts*: A few perennials especially Aquilegia (Columbine), Chrysanthemum, Delphinium, Eupatorium. A whole host of trees and shrubs are also susceptible.

**Lily Beetle, Lily Leaf Beetle**: A problem now in parts of eastern Canada and the Northeastern USA. Lily Beetles were introduced from Europe and are slowly gaining more territory. Adults are 6 mm (¼″) long beetles with a red body and black head, antennae and legs. The larvae look a bit like slugs and are covered in their own excrement.
*Damage*: Adults and larvae both feed on the leaves, stems and flowers of Lilies. They can defoliate plants very quickly.
*Recommended controls*: Hand picking and drowning adults and larvae. Search for rows of yellowish eggs on the undersides of leaves in spring, and squish. This pest is not likely to appear on the labels of most wide-spectrum garden insecticides. Where infestations are severe, gardeners may be forced to stop growing Lilies for a few years.
*Plant hosts*: True Lilies (Lilium) but not Daylilies. In England this pest is also known to attack Polygonatum and other members of the Lily family.

**Nematodes**: Tiny microscopic worms, usually living in the soil and feeding on plant roots.
*Damage*: Stunted growth, not caused by lack of water or fertilizer. Galls may be present on roots. Certain types of leaf nematode cause strange puckering or angular blotching on the foliage.
*Recommended controls*: Destroy infected plants. Avoid planting the same species in that spot for several years. Chemical controls are costly and impractical for home gardeners. French marigolds are said to kill nematodes by trapping them in their roots.
*Plant hosts*: Wide range of perennials but most especially: Aconitum, Chrysanthemum, Delphinium, Peony, Poppy. The problem is more widespread than most people realize, especially in regions with mild winters.

**Slugs & Snails**: Soft-bodied, slimy rounded or long mollusks, big or small. Not a true insect. Snails have a hard spiral-shaped shell.
*Damage*: General feeding on leaves, rasping holes.
*Recommended controls*: Sanitation; clean up garden debris where they like to hide; remove mulch in spring to allow sun at the soil to destroy adults and eggs. Pick off by hand on overcast days or in early morning. Trap beneath boards or burlap or try the old trick of saucers filled with stale beer. Use a recommended pesticide – several new slug/snail controls have recently hit the market. Hosta experts recommend mulching with pine needles or crushed eggshells.
*Plant hosts*: Wide range of perennials, but especially Hosta, Hellebore, Primula, Delphinium, Hollyhock, Viola. Slugs love shady places and many of the plants that grow in them.

**Spider Mites, Mites**: Tiny spider-like bugs, usually red, yellow or brown, found on the underside of leaves. Fine webs may be visible to the naked eye on close inspection. They suck plant sap and are usually present in large numbers.
*Damage*: Pale yellow-looking leaves, distorted growth, silver or white spots on leaves.
*Recommended controls*: First, reduce populations with a sharp blast of water to the underside of the leaves. Use a spray of insecticidal soap

or a recommended insecticide but both will need to be repeated every 5–7 days for a few weeks.

*Plant hosts*: Wide range of perennials, especially Daylily (Hemerocallis), also Buddleja, Heuchera, Potentilla.

**Spittlebug**:  This insect surrounds itself with foamy, frothy white stuff that looks like spit; this covers and protects the little greenish-brown insects while they're young.

*Damage*: Mainly the spittle looks unsightly. Insects suck on plant juices and can cause distorted leaves or new growth in late spring and early summer.

*Recommended controls*: Blast the spittle masses away with water. If infestations are severe, use a recommended insecticide.

*Plant hosts*: Wide range of perennials, especially: Aster, Solidago.

**Thrips**:  Very small, narrow winged insect, a bit like a miniscule mosquito.

*Damage*: Sucks plant juices, causing brown or silver streaks or spots on flowers or leaves. Known to spread viruses.

*Recommended controls*: Destroy affected flowers. Use a recommended insecticide.

*Plant hosts*: Gladiola in particular, also a wide range of perennials; Daylilies, Lilies, Iris.

**Weevils**:  Strawberry Root Weevil in particular is becoming a problem with certain types of perennials. There are two stages: larvae or grubs live in the soil as white C-shaped bodies with brown heads, about 1 cm (½″) in length. Adults are dark brown beetle-like insects about 6 mm (¼″) in length with rows of pits along the back and a snout-shaped mouth. These feed at night on leaves.

*Damage*: Grubs eat plant roots and tunnel in the crowns, causing stunted growth and serious wilting. Adults chew leaves, often notching the edges of thick leaves like Rhododendrons.

*Recommended controls*: Grubs are difficult to control. Aim efforts at trapping and killing adults (underneath boards or burlap) to prevent them laying eggs. Use a registered insecticide to spray lower branches and soil beneath shrubs where adults are hiding. Where infestations are bad, avoid growing susceptible plants for two to three years.

*Plant hosts*: Grubs feed on roots of strawberries (Fragaria), Bergenia, Heuchera and possibly Heucherella and Tiarella. Adults feed on a wide range of woody ornamentals, especially eastern white cedar, spruce, juniper and Rhododendron.

**Whitefly**:  Tiny triangular soft-bodied flies, powdery white in colour. Will fly up in a mass when disturbed.

*Damage*: These suck plant juices. Leaves turn yellowish, new growth sometimes appears stunted or distorted. Blackish sooty mould may grow on their secretions.

*Recommended controls*: Insecticidal soap as a spray every 5–7 days, or as a dip for potted plants. Many other recommended insecticides are available.

*Plant hosts*: Wide range of perennials. Particularly troublesome on plants that need to be wintered indoors such as Fuchsia, Brugmansia, Hibiscus. Spray plants several times in late fall before bringing indoors.

# Index